Leadership and Followership in an Organizational Change Context

Sajjad Nawaz Khan
Iqra University, Pakistan

A volume in the Advances in Business Strategy and Competitive Advantage (ABSCA) Book Series

IGI Global
PUBLISHER of TIMELY KNOWLEDGE

Published in the United States of America by
IGI Global
Business Science Reference (an imprint of IGI Global)
701 E. Chocolate Avenue
Hershey PA, USA 17033
Tel: 717-533-8845
Fax: 717-533-8661
E-mail: cust@igi-global.com
Web site: http://www.igi-global.com

Library of Congress Cataloging-in-Publication Data

Names: Khan, Sajjad Nawaz, DATE- editor.
Title: Leadership and followership in an organizational change context / Sajjad Nawaz Khan, editor.
Description: Hershey, PA : Business Science Reference, [2022] | Includes bibliographical references and index. | Description based on print version record and CIP data provided by publisher; resource not viewed.
Identifiers: LCCN 2019043597 (print) | LCCN 2019043598 (ebook) | ISBN 9781799828099 (ebook) | ISBN 9781799828075 (hardcover) | ISBN 9781799828082 (paperback) | ISBN 9781799828075¬q(hardcover) | ISBN 9781799828082¬q(paperback) | ISBN 9781799828099¬q(ebook)
Subjects: LCSH: Leadership. | Followership. | Organizational change.
Classification: LCC HD57.7 (ebook) | LCC HD57.7 .L43137 2020 (print) | DDC 658.4/092--dc23
LC record available at https://lccn.loc.gov/2019043597

This book is published in the IGI Global book series Advances in Business Strategy and Competitive Advantage (ABSCA) (ISSN: 2327-3429; eISSN: 2327-3437)

British Cataloguing in Publication Data
A Cataloguing in Publication record for this book is available from the British Library.

Advances in Business Strategy and Competitive Advantage (ABSCA) Book Series

ISSN:2327-3429
EISSN:2327-3437

Editor-in-Chief: Patricia Ordóñez de Pablos, Universidad de Oviedo, Spain

MISSION

Business entities are constantly seeking new ways through which to gain advantage over their competitors and strengthen their position within the business environment. With competition at an all-time high due to technological advancements allowing for competition on a global scale, firms continue to seek new ways through which to improve and strengthen their business processes, procedures, and profitability.

The **Advances in Business Strategy and Competitive Advantage (ABSCA) Book Series** is a timely series responding to the high demand for state-of-the-art research on how business strategies are created, implemented and re-designed to meet the demands of globalized competitive markets. With a focus on local and global challenges, business opportunities and the needs of society, the **ABSCA** encourages scientific discourse on doing business and managing information technologies for the creation of sustainable competitive advantage.

COVERAGE

- Strategic Alliances
- Cost Leadership Strategy
- Resource-Based Competition
- Differentiation Strategy
- Tacit Knowledge
- Customer-Orientation Strategy
- Outsourcing
- International Business Strategy
- Adaptive Enterprise
- Strategic Management

IGI Global is currently accepting manuscripts for publication within this series. To submit a proposal for a volume in this series, please contact our Acquisition Editors at Acquisitions@igi-global.com or visit: http://www.igi-global.com/publish/.

The Advances in Business Strategy and Competitive Advantage (ABSCA) Book Series (ISSN 2327-3429) is published by IGI Global, 701 E. Chocolate Avenue, Hershey, PA 17033-1240, USA, www.igi-global.com. This series is composed of titles available for purchase individually; each title is edited to be contextually exclusive from any other title within the series. For pricing and ordering information please visit http://www.igi-global.com/book-series/advances-business-strategy-competitive-advantage/73672. Postmaster: Send all address changes to above address.

Titles in this Series

For a list of additional titles in this series, please visit:
http://www.igi-global.com/book-series/advances-business-strategy-competitive-advantage/73672

Emerging Ecosystem-Centric Business Models for Sustainable Value Creation
Xenia Ziouvelou (National Centre for Scientific Research "Demokritos", Greece & University of Southampton, UK) and Frank McGroarty (University of Southampton, UK)
Business Science Reference • © 2022 • 237pp • H/C (ISBN: 9781799848431) • US $195.00

ICT as Innovator Between Tourism and Culture
Célia M. Q. Ramos (University of Algarve, Portugal) Silvia Quinteiro (University of Algarve, Portugal) and Alexandra R. Gonçalves (University of Algarve, Portugal)
Business Science Reference • © 2022 • 330pp • H/C (ISBN: 9781799881650) • US $215.00

Impact of Disruptive Technologies on the Sharing Economy
Ford Lumban Gaol (Bina Nusantara University, Jakarta, Indonesia) Natalia Filimonova (Vladimir State University, Russia) and Chandan Acharya (College of Staten Island, City University of New York, USA)
Business Science Reference • © 2021 • 269pp • H/C (ISBN: 9781799803614) • US $245.00

Global Corporate Social Responsibility Initiatives for Reluctant Businesses
Syed Abdul Rehman Khan (School of Management and Engineering, Xuzhou University of Technology, Xuzhou, China & Department of Business Administration, ILMA University, Karachi, Pakistan & Beijing Key Laboratory of Urban Spatial Engineering, Beijing, China) Zhang Yu (Chang'an University, China) Mirela Panait (Petroleum-Gas University of Ploiesti, Romania & Institute of National Economy, Bucharest, Romania) Laeeq Razzak Janjua (Poznan University of Economics and Business, Poland) and Adeel Shah (Institute of Business Management, Pakistan)
Business Science Reference • © 2021 • 280pp • H/C (ISBN: 9781799839880) • US $195.00

Impacts and Implications for the Sports Industry in the Post-COVID-19 Era
Armand Faganel (University of Primorska, Slovenia) Igor Rižnar (University of Primorska, Slovenia) and Arne Baruca (Texas A&M University, USA)
Business Science Reference • © 2021 • 304pp • H/C (ISBN: 9781799867807) • US $215.00

For an entire list of titles in this series, please visit:
http://www.igi-global.com/book-series/advances-business-strategy-competitive-advantage/73672

IGI Global
PUBLISHER of TIMELY KNOWLEDGE

701 East Chocolate Avenue, Hershey, PA 17033, USA
Tel: 717-533-8845 x100 • Fax: 717-533-8661
E-Mail: cust@igi-global.com • www.igi-global.com

Table of Contents

Detailed Table of Contents

Leadership is the backbone of organizational success, and it is evident from the fact that leadership has been researched for more than 50 years. In literature, leadership has been discussed based on different schools of thoughts. This chapter articulates different leadership approaches in order to provide a clear understanding of leadership development with the passage of time. It describes trait approach, behavioral approach, and contingency approach to leadership. Furthermore, it also explains full range leadership model and some emerging leadership styles in the organizational context.

This chapter elucidates Keith Grint's model of leadership as a viable dynamic option in our complex world. By locating the model within a social constructionist frame, this chapter demonstrates how far we have come in the evolving stream of leadership research. Seven main characteristics of the Grint's model of leadership are discussed to demonstrate how the model can help us to understand wicked problems, such as the COVID-19 pandemic in Malaysia. The author also identifies two weaknesses of Grint's model: (1) organisational culture and (2) followership. Lastly, to address the two weaknesses, the author proposes an integrated model of leadership that combines the understanding of an adhocracy culture based on the competing value framework and Kelly's effective followership model. In conclusion, the integrative framework of leadership offers leadership researchers a model with more explanatory power in understanding the leadership phenomenon within the social constructionist supposition.

The main aim of the chapter is to identify the leadership style that promotes succession planning through the existence of leadership development practices within organizations. The middle and top leaders are very important to identify and develop new leaders within the organization. The authors reach three main conclusions: 1) The laissez-faire leadership style is related to the succession planning. Succession planning is positively influenced by leaders that adopt a passive leadership style. 2) There are some practices of leadership development that are related to the existence of succession planning in organizations. 3) The 360º feedback and coaching/executive coaching are related to the succession planning. These practices promote the human capital development, so it is assumed that succession planning may be related to the leader development. Theoretically they concluded that organizations should have a leadership pipeline in order to prepare leaders to assume leadership positions.

Higher education today consists of a complex myriad of varying levels with individuals tasked to perform multiple roles and responsibilities. Faculty and staff find themselves tasked with multiple responsibilities and fewer resources. Many who embark on the journey of becoming academic administrators and leaders in higher education often do so based on their technical expertise and successes as a faculty member within the institution. Few organizations prepare faculty to step into leadership roles with the appropriate training. One area which often lacks training is in the area of individual leadership capabilities and connecting with others within the organization to accomplish a common goal. This chapter will provide insight into five critical domains necessary for individuals to focus on developing before entering into a leadership role within a higher education institution. Within each domain are central and core competencies which help to determine effectiveness in higher education leadership.

Ratan Tata is an Indian industrialist and philanthropist. He is a visionary leader and managing change is second nature to him. His leadership exudes confidence in others and has inspired many to become leaders in his own company, and through his service-oriented nature, influenced several others outside of his organizational space. Tata's leadership commands respect throughout the world, which is highlighted by the numerous prestigious awards bestowed upon him. This chapter aims to present and explain his leadership practices through case scenarios. These lessons on leadership are transferable and may guide future leaders of tomorrow to lead our world with wisdom, dignity, humility, and authenticity.

Trade union leadership and followership are complimentary and symbiotic. Pragmatic followership serves to engender effective trade union leadership. Union leaders are expected to work with and stand by their members in order to attain union mandates. Union ethos demands that leaders must place the interest and welfare of workers as their most paramount goal and work assiduously towards satisfying them. Union members must consider the antecedents and pedigree of aspirants and ensure that only unionists with track records of tenaciously and selflessly championing the union's cause should be elected as leaders. Through leadership by example, trust, integrity, and candor, union leaders can bring about positive changes to both workers and their union. Finally, the authors called on union leaders to be alive to their responsibilities and demonstrate ethical and servant forms of leadership in order to cope with the challenges of giving vent to the aspirations of their members.

Organizations are increasingly investing in human resource development. The positive psychology approach warns of the importance of strengthening the forces. Leveraging the strengths is a way to achieve better results and even minimize the weaknesses of the leader. It is this assumption that positive psychology adds to the human resource development, which includes the leadership development. This chapter aims to propose a theoretical model about positive leader development supported by the positive psychology approach. This model comes from the literature to the evolution of leadership and organizational theories and the positive psychology. Positive leader development model seeks to enhance leadership development within an organization with a positive psychology approach. The literature shows the advantages of strengthening forces in the organizational context. So, it is necessary to systematize a theoretical model that facilitates the positive leader development in organizations. The proposed model is based on the study by Malinga, Stander, and Nell.

Nearly no organizational phenomenon has garnered as much attention as organizational change. It appears as one of the fascinating and nearly eroticizing inducements for business organizations, and it has been highly acknowledging as a response. Highlighting the importance this phenomenon holds in the current environment, there is a huge and still growing body of research concentrating on organizational change. This chapter briefly explains the overview of the three major organizational change approaches (teleological approaches and evolutionary approaches and psychological approaches), which highlight organizational change through different models and theories.

Innovation is one of the most likely factors to boost effectiveness, efficiency, and sustainability of an organization, regardless of its sector of activity, as for instance, the armed forces. The absence of innovation can affect the organizations in different ways, from suboptimal operational effectiveness and improvement of organization processes (administrative, operational, or logistics), bringing with it negative impacts on human resources motivation – the main keepers of knowledge, institutional culture, and organizational values. Innovative organizations also generate a stronger sense of belonging across their ranks and structures and fosters effectiveness in fulfilling organizations' missions. Hence, fostering innovation across any typology of organization is crucial and requires a proper approach to promote the desirable involvement of the entire workforce. This text, based on a review of some relevant literature, exposes critical enabling factors. Based on a cause-and-effect analysis, it proposes some recommendations for the practitioner as well as the academic.

Followers are underrepresented in the organizational change literature despite their considerable influence on change success. Politics, culture, motivation, communication, and readiness have a large impact on change success, and these influences are examined in the change context. Each of these are influenced by leaders and followers. The role of authentic followers in enabling positive change through their organizational engagement is explored in depth. This chapter demonstrates that while the influential role of leaders in change is established, the authentic follower represents a large body of potential change agents with the capacity to positively influence the success of change. Many behaviors of the authentic follower make them an ideal candidate for this role, including moral potency, high levels of engagement in organizational structure, and flexibility. Further research highlighting the value of the authentic follower is warranted.

Preface

After more than five decades of research and theories on the qualities and behaviours of an effective leader it has since been acknowledged that leadership and followership are two intricately intertwined concepts in effective leadership and organizational success (Collinson, 2009). Additionally, most of the previous leadership research was leader-centric, that highlighted followers as recipients of leadership outcomes (Uhl-Bien et al., 2014). Currently, followership is an emerging field of study explaining the behavioural (Kelley, 2008), relational (Meindl, 1995), cognitive (Sy, 2010) and constructionist (DeRue & Ashford, 2010) perspectives of followers. On the other hand, nearly no organizational phenomenon has altered as much attention as organizational change. It appears as one of the fascinating and nearly eroticizing inducements for business organizations, and it has been highly acknowledging as a response. Highlighting the importance, this phenomenon holds in the current environment, there is a huge and still growing body of research concentrating on organizational change (Schwarz, 2012; Wetzel & Van Gorp, 2014). Change is a basic, notable and recurring part of life. As a result, it has become one of the big comforts in organization theory (Wetzel & Van Gorp, 2014).

It has been said that without leadership there is no change and improvement (Atkinson & Mackenzie, 1999). Supported by Senior and Fleming (2006) a leader is a change agent who takes initiative and brings successful change for organizations. From organizational change perspectives, there have been numerous practitioner-oriented debates focusing on the leadership role and followers' resistance but on the other hand, the number of empirical studies that examine the relationship between leader behaviour and employees' reactions towards change is very limited (Herold et al., 2008; Holten & Brenner 2015; Oreg & Berson, 2011). Past research has indicated that if leadership is change-oriented, participative, informative and fair, it produces positive reactions towards change (Holten & Brenner 2015; Oreg et al., 2011). During organizational change, leaders perform an important role both as a role model and driver of change, and their behaviour influence the interests of followers (Skakon et al., 2010).

ORGANIZATION OF THE BOOK

The book is organized into 11 chapters. A brief description of each of the chapters follows:

Chapter 1 is dedicated to the review of leadership literature explaining that leadership is the backbone of organizational success, and it is evident from the fact that leadership is being researched for more than fifty years. The relevant literature suggests that leadership has been discussed based on different schools of thought. This chapter is devoted to articulating different leadership approaches to understand leadership development with time clearly. It describes the trait approach, behavioral approach, and contingency approach to leadership. Furthermore, it also explains the full range of leadership models and some emerging leadership styles in an organizational context.

Chapter 2 elucidates Keith Grint's model of leadership as a viable dynamic option in our complex world. By locating the model within a social constructionist frame, this chapter demonstrates how far we have come in the evolving stream of leadership research. Seven main characteristics of the Grint's model of leadership are discussed to demonstrate how the model can help us to understand wicked problems, such as the COVID-19 pandemic in Malaysia. The author also identifies two weaknesses of the Grint's model: (1) organizational culture, and (2) followership. Lastly, to address the two weaknesses, the author proposes an integrated model of leadership that combines the understanding of an adhocracy culture based on the competing value framework and Kelly's effective followership model. In conclusion, the integrative framework of leadership offers leadership researchers a model with more explanatory power in understanding the leadership phenomenon within the social constructionist supposition.

Chapter 3 highlights the leadership style that promotes succession planning through the existence of leadership development practices within organizations. The middle and top leaders are very important to identify and develop new leaders within the organization. We reach three main conclusions: 1) The laissez-faire leadership style is related to the succession planning. Succession planning is positively influenced by leaders that adopt a passive leadership style; 2) There are some practices of leadership development that are related to the existence of succession planning in organizations; 3) The 360º Feedback and Coaching/Executive Coaching are related to the Succession planning. These practices promote the human capital development, so it is assumed that succession planning may be related to the leader development. Theoretically we concluded that organizations should have a leadership pipeline in order to prepare leaders to assume leadership positions.

Chapter 4 highlights that higher education today consists of a complex myriad of varying levels with individuals tasked to perform multiple roles and responsibilities.

Faculty and staff no longer perform a single set of responsibilities; instead, they find themselves tasked with multiple responsibilities and fewer resources (Morris & Laipple, 2015). Many who embark on the journey of becoming academic administrators and leaders in higher education often do so based on their technical expertise and successes as a faculty member within the institution. Few organizations prepare faculty to step into leadership roles with the appropriate training. One such area, which often lacks training, is in the area of individual leadership capabilities and connecting with individuals to accomplish a common goal.

Chapter 5 discusses about Ratan Tata, an Indian industrialist and philanthropist. He is a visionary leader and managing change is second nature to him. His leadership exudes confidence in others and has inspired many to become leaders in his own company, and through his service oriented nature, influenced several others outside of his organizational space. Tata's leadership commands respect throughout the world, which is highlighted by the numerous prestigious awards bestowed upon him. This book chapter aims to present and explain his leadership practices through case scenarios. These lessons on leadership are transferable and may guide future leaders of tomorrow to lead our world with wisdom, dignity, humility and authenticity.

Chapter 6 discusses how trade union leadership and followership are complimentary and symbiotic. Pragmatic followership serves to engender effective trade union leadership. Union leaders are expected to work with and stand by their members in order to attain union mandates. Union ethos demands that leaders must place the interest and welfare of workers as their most paramount goal and work assiduously towards satisfying them. Union members must consider the antecedents and pedigree of aspirants and ensure that only unionists with track records of tenaciously and selflessly championing the union's cause should be elected as leaders. Through leadership by example, trust, integrity and candor, union leaders can bring about positive changes to both workers and their union. Finally, the authors called on union leaders to be alive to their responsibilities and demonstrate ethical and servant forms of leadership in order to cope with the challenges of giving vent to the aspirations of their members

Chapter 7 highlighted the theoretical Model of positive leadership. Organizations are increasingly investing in human resource development. The positive psychology approach warns to the importance of strengthening the forces. Leveraging the strengths is a way to achieve better results and even minimize the weaknesses of the leader. It is this assumption that positive psychology adds to the human resource development, which includes the leadership development. This research aims to propose a theoretical model about positive leader development supported by the positive psychology approach. This model comes from the literature to the evolution of leadership and organizational theories and the positive psychology. Positive Leader Development Model seeks to enhance leadership development within an organization with a positive psychology approach. The literature shows the advantages of strengthening forces in the organizational context. So, it is necessary to systematize a theoretical model that facilitates the positive leader development in organizations. The proposed model is based on the study by Malinga, Stander, and Nell (2019).

Chapter 8 highlights the review of the literature on organizational change and emphasized that nearly no organizational phenomenon has altered as much attention as organizational change. It appears as one of the fascinating and nearly eroticizing inducements for business organizations, and it has been highly acknowledging as a response. Highlighting the importance, this phenomenon holds in the current environment, there is a huge and still growing body of research concentrating on organizational change This chapter briefly explains the overview of the three major organizational change approaches (teleological approaches and evolutionary approaches and psychological approaches), which highlight organizational change through different models and theories.

Chapter 9 shows how innovation is one of the most likely factors to boost effectiveness, efficiency and sustainability of an organization, regardless of its sector of activity, as for instance, the armed forces. The absence of innovation can affect the organizations in different ways, from suboptimal operational effectiveness and improvement of organization processes (administrative, operational, or logistics), bringing with it negative impacts on human resources motivation - the main keepers of knowledge, institutional culture, and organizational values. Innovative organizations also generate a stronger sense of belonging across their ranks and structures and fosters effectiveness in fulfilling organizations' missions. Hence, fostering innovation across any typology of organization is crucial, and requires a proper approach to promote the desirable involvement of the entire workforce. This text, based on a review of some relevant literature, exposes critical enabling factors. Based on a cause-and-effect analysis it proposes some recommendations for the practitioner as well as the academic.

Chapter 10 highlights the role of followers in an organizational change culture. Followers are underrepresented in the organizational change literature despite their considerable influence on change success. Politics, culture, motivation, communication, and readiness have a large impact on change success, and these influences are examined in the change context. Each of these, influenced by leaders and followers. The role of authentic followers in enabling positive change through their organizational engagement is explored in depth. This Chapter demonstrates that while the influential role of leaders in change is established, the authentic follower represents a large body of potential change agents with the capacity to positively influence the success of change. Many behaviors of the authentic follower make them an ideal candidate for this role, including moral potency, high levels of engagement in organizational structure, and flexibility. Further research highlighting the value of the authentic follower is warranted.

Chapter 11 discusses about the organizational culture, emphasizing that culture of fear, control, and meaninglessness can effectively kill the entrepreneurial spirit within an organization. This chapter will explore why such a culture typically takes root and how it is deadly for the organization's entrepreneurial orientation. The paper is based on an interdisciplinary reflective analysis done by exploring disciplines including depth psychology, neuroscience, positive psychology, and organizational behavior. The chapter argues from the perspectives of these disciplines that it is perhaps the factor of safety, risk-taking, collaboration, and meaningfulness if present in organizational culture, will eventually cultivate the spirit of entrepreneurship in an organization. While discussing these factors, the chapter also explains how seemingly irrational forces of the unconscious mind keep the leadership from adopting a behavior which is fundamentally important in fostering a culture where entrepreneurial behavior takes root. The paper also explains how these psychic forces can be turned around to cultivate an entrepreneurial culture in an organization.

REFERENCES

Atkinson, P., & Mackenzie, R. (1999). Without leadership there is no change. *Management Services*, *43*(8), 8–11.

Collinson, D. L. (2009). Rethinking Leadership and Followership. In S. R. C. C. L. Cooper (Ed.), *Sage Handbook of Organizational Behaviour*. Sage. doi:10.4135/9781849200455.n16

Herold, D. M., Fedor, D. B., Caldwell, S., & Liu, Y. (2008). The effects of transformational and change leadership on employees' commitment to a change: A multilevel study. *The Journal of Applied Psychology*, *93*(2), 346–357. doi:10.1037/0021-9010.93.2.346 PMID:18361637

Holten, A. L., & Brenner, S. O. (2015). Leadership style and the process of organizational change. *Leadership and Organization Development Journal*, *36*(1), 2–16. doi:10.1108/LODJ-11-2012-0155

Kelley, R. E. (2008). Rethinking followership. In The Art of Followership: How Great Followers Create Great Leaders and Organizations (pp. 5-16). Wiley.

Malinga, K. S., Stander, M., & Nell, W. (2019). Positive leadership: Moving towards an integrated definition and interventions. *Theoretical Approaches to Multi-Cultural Positive Psychological Interventions*, 201-228.

Meindl, J. R. (1995). The romance of leadership as a follower-centric theory: A social constructionist approach. *The Leadership Quarterly*, *6*(3), 329–341. doi:10.1016/1048-9843(95)90012-8

Morris, T. L., & Laipple, J. S. (2015). Leadership challenges: Perceptions of effectiveness of deans and chairs. *Journal of Higher Education Management*, *30*(1), 110–118.

Oreg, S., & Berson, Y. (2011). Leadership and Employees' reactions to Change: The Role of Leaders' personal Attributes and Transformational Leadership Style. *Personnel Psychology*, *64*(3), 627–659. doi:10.1111/j.1744-6570.2011.01221.x

Oreg, S., Vakola, M., & Armenakis, A. (2011). Change recipients' reactions to organizational change A 60-year review of quantitative studies. *The Journal of Applied Behavioral Science*, *47*(4), 461–524. doi:10.1177/0021886310396550

Schwarz, G. M. (2012). Shaking fruit out of the tree: Temporal effects and life cycle in organizational change research. *The Journal of Applied Behavioral Science*, *48*(3), 342–379. doi:10.1177/0021886312439098

Senior, B., & Fleming, J. (2006). *Organizational Change*. Pearson Education.

Skakon, J., Nielsen, K., Borg, V., & Guzman, J. (2010). Are leaders' well-being, behaviours and style associated with the affective well-being of their employees? A systematic review of three decades of research. *Work and Stress*, *24*(2), 107–139. doi:10.1080/02678373.2010.495262

Sy, T. (2010). What do you think of followers? Examining the content, structure, and consequences of implicit followership theories. *Organizational Behavior and Human Decision Processes*, *113*(2), 73–84. doi:10.1016/j.obhdp.2010.06.001

Uhl-Bien, M., Riggio, R. E., Lowe, K. B., & Carsten, M. K. (2014). Followership theory: A review and research agenda. *The Leadership Quarterly*, *25*(1), 83–104. doi:10.1016/j.leaqua.2013.11.007

Wetzel, R., & Van Gorp, L. (2014). Eighteen shades of grey? An explorative literature review into the theoretical flavours of organizational change research. *Journal of Organizational Change Management*, *27*(1), 115–146. doi:10.1108/JOCM-01-2013-0007

Chapter 1
Overview of Leadership Approaches

Sajjad Nawaz Khan
https://orcid.org/0000-0003-1366-9080
Iqra University, Pakistan

Hafiz Mudassir Rehman
https://orcid.org/0000-0001-9114-0989
Universiti Tunku Abdul Rahman, Malaysia

Mudaser Javaid
Iqra University, Pakistan

ABSTRACT

Leadership is the backbone of organizational success, and it is evident from the fact that leadership has been researched for more than 50 years. In literature, leadership has been discussed based on different schools of thoughts. This chapter articulates different leadership approaches in order to provide a clear understanding of leadership development with the passage of time. It describes trait approach, behavioral approach, and contingency approach to leadership. Furthermore, it also explains full range leadership model and some emerging leadership styles in the organizational context.

DOI: 10.4018/978-1-7998-2807-5.ch001

INTRODUCTION

According to Northouse (2010), there are many ways to complete the sentence, "leadership is…" Similarly, Stogdill (1974, p.259) claimed that "[There are] almost as many definitions of leadership as there are persons who have attempted to define the concept." According to Burns (1978: p. 2), "Leadership is one of the most observed and least understood phenomena on earth. In spite of the number of ways which conceptualized leadership, the following five components can be identified as critical to the phenomenon: a) leadership requires influence, b) leadership requires common goals, c) leadership is a process, and d) leadership occurs in groups (Northouse, 2010). Based on these components, Northouse (2010, p.3) defined leadership as "a process whereby an individual influences a group of individuals to achieve a common goal." In this definition, leadership as a process means that it is not the characteristics or trait that makes a leader but implies that it is the interactive event between a leader and his/her followers. Leadership involves influence; without influence, there is no leadership. Leadership exhibits in groups; the group ranges from a small task group to individuals encompassing a whole organization. Finally, leadership works towards a common goal. The word common means that leaders and their followers pursue a common purpose to achieve any desired goals (Northouse, 2010).

BACKGROUND

Is leadership necessary for organizational change? In answering this question, Burke (2008, pp. 227-228) noted that "what has not been clear from the literature is the impact of leadership on organizational change, and there is little evidence that scientifically demonstrates the leader's impact" (Ford et al., 2008). Many leadership theories have been developed, and each theory explains leadership with a different point of view, like early theories focusing on the trait or inner qualities of a leader. Other approaches are concerned with the skills and abilities, followed by the leader in a particular situation. Later, contemporary theories include the full range leadership model, including the debate about followers and the leader-followers' relation (Sloan, 2009). This chapter discusses leadership development by explaining three main approaches (trait approach, behavioral approach, and contingency approach). Furthermore, it also highlights the emerging perspective of leadership.

Trait Approach

The trait approach is the earliest and the most popular leadership approach in research, which tries to classify a set of common traits in leaders. These theories [approaches] explain "what" an effective leader is, not "how" to effectively lead, so these are also called content theories. The trait approach undertakes that specific social, physical, and personal attributes are inherent in leaders (Allen, 1998). Traits are comparatively stable and enduring characteristics of an individual that may consist of psychological and physical factors (Penney et al., 2015). According to Northouse (2015), among all the traits that different researchers have identified, some traits are central and commonly found in all identified traits, like intelligence, self-confidence, integrity, determination, and sociability.

Intellectual ability or intelligence is positively related to leadership. Zaccaro et al. (2004) found that leaders have higher intelligence than followers. For a leader to acquire problem-solving and social judgment skills, intelligence played a significant role in developing such skills (Northouse, 2015). According to Penney et al. (2015), intelligence seems reasonable as leadership is challenging and performs complex tasks like problem-solving, managing change, and monitoring others. However, leaders who portray above-average intelligence against non-leaders would be disadvantaged if the leader exhibits more intelligence than followers (Bass, 1981; Kirkpatrick & Locke, 1991).

Self-confidence is another common leadership trait that explains the ability to be aware of one's skills and competencies. It is considered a general term that encircles similar constructs like self-esteem and self-efficacy (Northouse, 2013; Yukl, 2013). In his reviews, Stogdill (1948; 1974, as cited in Penney et al., 2015) confirmed that approximately all studies examined in the reviews reported a positive relationship between leadership and self-confidence and showed that leaders exhibit higher self-esteem and self-confidence than followers. Leadership has been proven in influencing others, and self-confident, which allows the leaders to control others to avoid inappropriately and steer them in the right direction (Northouse, 2015).

Integrity is the third common trait found in all reviews, which explains the quality of trustworthiness and honesty. Individuals who possess a robust set of principles and assume responsibility for their actions are referred to have integrity (Northouse, 2015). Academicians have identified that integrity is essential in stimulating follower's favorable attitudes towards their leader and towards their work (such as trust, commitment, work engagement, job satisfaction), and in encouraging follower performances (in-role and extra-role) (Northouse, 2010; Simons et al., 2015).

Determination is the fourth trait of leadership that the researchers commonly find. Determinations refer to characteristics such as persistence, dominance, initiation, and drive. Individuals with determination are proactive and can accept obstacles as a challenge. Determination shows power in times of crises and change where followers need guidance and support (Northouse, 2015). A meta-analysis conducted by Judge et al. (2002) confirmed a strong association between determination and leadership (both effectiveness and emergence).

The final trait of leadership is sociability. It explains the leader's inclination to find pleasant social situations and relationships (Northouse, 2013; Penney et al., 2015). Stogdill's reviews of many studies found that 49 studies demonstrated a positive relationship between sociability and leadership (Penney et al., 2015). Therefore, people high in sociability seem to be more friendly, outgoing, tactful, and concerned for others' well-being and may be perceived as more effective leaders than people with lower sociability (Penney et al., 2015).

In the context of organizational change, leadership traits play a critical role in implementing successful change programs. Researchers identified many leadership traits in shaping employees' reactions towards organizational change; like self-efficacy (Paglis & Green, 2002), emotional intelligence (George, 2000; Nordin, 2011), integrity (Veríssimo & Lacerda, 2015), motivation (Bass, 1998) and vision (Warrick, 2011). Likewise, Nordin (2011) identified that emotional intelligence contributes to explaining organizational change readiness.

According to Bass (2008) and Warrick (2011), motivation and vision articulation have contributed to shaping employees' attitudes towards organizational change. Therefore, leaders' traits contributed mainly to differentiate leaders from non-leaders in the organizational change context. Managers possessing above mentioned traits would be considered influential leaders in a rapidly changing business environment.

The list of these five traits is not all-inclusive, while other traits shown in Table 2.1 are also related to effective leadership. Studies found mixed results regarding the relationship between leadership and characteristics. Some researchers claimed a few universal traits of the administration and differentiated leaders from non-leaders (Mann, 1959; Stogdill, 1974). Conversely, others have proved that there are consistencies among features linked to leadership effectiveness or emergence (Judge et al., 2002; Zaccaro et al., 2004). Table (2.1) combined different traits identified by other researchers. The most common features identified by various researchers are highlighted in bold in the table (2.1).

The trait approach is not free from criticism; the major criticism from scholars is that trait research has ignored the situational and environmental factors that play an essential role in leader effectiveness (Horner, 1997; Northouse, 2015). Individuals with certain traits that make them leaders in one situation may not be a leader in a changed situation. It is challenging to work with specific characteristics as a leader in isolation because situational factors affect the leader's characteristics. Another criticism is related to the failure of a definitive list of leadership traits. Many studies have been conducted in the last 100 years, and many of the studies produced the list of traits that have appeared endless. The reason is that the trait approach is based on the subjective determination of the essential characteristics (Northouse, 2015, 2013).

Table 1.

Stogdill (1948)	Maan (1959)	Stogdill (1974)	Lord, Devader, and Alliger (1986)	Krikpatrick and Lock (1991)	Zaccaro Kemp, and Bader (2004)
Intelligence Alertness Insight Responsibility Initiative Persistence Self-confidence **Sociability**	**Intelligence** Masculinity Adjustment **Dominance** Extraversion Conservatism	Achievement Persistence Insight Initiative Self-confidence Responsibility Cooperativeness Tolerance Influence **Sociability**	Intelligence Masculinity **Dominance**	Drive Motivation **Integrity** Confidence Cognitive ability Task knowledge	Cognitive ability Extraversion Consciousness Emotional stability Openness Agreeableness Motivation Social intelligence Self-monitoring Emotional intelligence Problem solving

Behavioral Approach

The behavioral approach is distinguished from the trait approach as the trait approach focused on the physical and psychological characteristics that differentiate leaders from non-leaders. In contrast, the behavioral approach emphasized how leaders act and what they do. The behavioral approach diverts the researchers' attention towards the action leaders take in different situations (Northouse, 2015). The behavioral approach deals with leaders' actions in their position and how they relate to leadership effectiveness. The predisposition of the theory and the majority of the research of behavioral approach identified two main aspects of leaders' behavior: leaders must accomplish the task, and they know how to get work done by others (Gibson et al., 2003). Behavioral theorists believed that leaders could be trained, while the trait approach believed that leaders are born (Gibson et al., 2003; Northouse, 2013; Robbins, 2001). Many modern behavioral theories are the two theories developed from the early 1950s until the late 1960s, the Ohio State studies (1942) and the Michigan studies (1950).

Yukl (2002) suggests that from the last 40 years' leadership behavioral approaches have been deeply influenced by the famous Ohio State and University of Michigan research. Ohio State research program suggested that leader behavior was based on the two critical latent dimensions: consideration and initiating structure. Consideration consists of behaviors representing mutual trust, respect, and particular affinity between a group and a supervisor. Consideration appeared to highlight a more profound concern for the needs of members of the group and add behaviors like allowing participation in decision making and encourage followers for more two-way communication (Northouse, 2015; Robbins, 2006). Initiating structure includes the supervisor's behavior to organize and explain group activities and his relation to the group. Thus, the leader assigns tasks, formulate ways of doing things, plans for the future, and pushes members for production. This dimension emphasizes blatant attempts to achieve organizational goals (Northouse, 2010; Robbins, 2001). A majority of research confirmed that consideration is commonly contemplated to be correlated with lower turnover and job satisfaction while initiating structure linked with effectiveness and efficiency in task performance (Robbins, 2001). According to Northouse (2010, 2015), these two behaviors are independent and distinct; they were thought of as not two points on one continuum but as two separate continua. The leader may exhibit both behaviors differently, like a leader can be high in consideration and high or low in initiating structure.

In the meantime, another study developed by the University of Michigan concentrated on the identification of leaders' behavior in the direction of small groups and measures of performance of the groups which recommend two forms of leadership: employee-oriented (employee needs and interpersonal relations), production-oriented (technical and production feature of a job) (Cartwright & Zaner, 1960; Katz & kahn, 1951, as cited in Northouse, 2015). Employee-oriented leadership behavior was more supportive, thoughtful, and appreciative followers for contribution and idea generation that look pretty similar to the many behaviors recognized as a consideration in Ohio State studies (Northouse, 2013). On the other hand, the production-oriented behavior described leader behavior mainly concern with planning and coordinating followers' goals, and "did not occur at the expense of concern for human relations" (Yukl, 2002: p. 53). Workers are considered a means for getting work done; production-oriented behavior looks similar to the initiating structure cluster of Ohio State studies.

To summarize, behavioral theories identified that leadership is comprised of two general types of behavior: relationship behaviour and task behavior. The main concern of the behaviour approach is to explain how these two types of behaviors help leaders influence others to accomplish a goal (Northouse, 2013). But research reviews have underlined several shortcomings compared to the trait theories. The first is that behavioral approaches failed to find generally accepted behaviors that work in all situations (Northouse 2013; Yukl, 2002). According to Hersey, Blanchard, and Johnson (2001: pp. 94-95), "no dominant style appears. Instead, various combinations are evident" prolonged research practices to locate best leadership attitude, behavior, or style proved to be inclusive (Chemers, 1995; Hersey et al., 2001; Northouse, 2010). The second latent limitation of broadly defined behavior categories like initiating structure and consideration is that they can mask subtle differences in leaders' behaviors essential for leaders' effectiveness. Without sufficiently exploring the variance specified by particular leader behaviors, it is not easy to precisely pinpoint which behaviors explain variance in leadership effectiveness in a specific scenario like organizational change (Bryman, 1992; Northouse, 2015).

Contingency Approach

According to Chemers (1995), to distinguish leadership research, the third historical period is called the contingency approach. During the 1960s to the early 1980s, this approach was developed as the most effective leadership approach. Situational favourability to define leader effectiveness is one example of the contingency approach that considers two variables: first is the degree to which leaders' situation is encouraging to influence, and second is leadership style (Fiedler, 1971). The concept of Fiedler situational favourability, or the ease of influence on followers, was explained as the combination of task structure, position power, and leader-member relations. Contingency suggests that a leader's effectiveness depends on how well the leader's style fits the context or situation. To understand leader effectiveness, it is necessary to understand the situation in which a leader operates (Northouse, 2015).

Task structure is the situational variable that explains the leader's ability to demonstrate task requirements to followers because clear and complete tasks give full control to the leader. At the same time, vague and unclear missions hinder the leader's ability to control and influence (Northouse, 2015). The second situational variable is position power which highlighted the amount of authority a leader exhibits in reward and punishment. Strong position power enables leaders to make things right and take corrective actions against followers if any misconduct or deviation from the standards (Northouse, 2013, 2010). Leader-member relation, which is the third situational variable, described the degree of loyalty, trust, and confidence that followers feel in the group for their leader. Therefore, if the group atmosphere is positive and obtained followers' faith, like and confident with their leader, the leader-member relations are defined as positive and good (Northouse, 2015).

The basic assumption of the behavioral approach is that the leadership style and effectiveness are highly dependent on situational or contingency variables (Gibson et al., 2003; Robbins, 2006). In conclusion contingency approach has provided new ways of considering the impact of the situation on leaders. It does not need people to be effective in all situations. Organizations should try to put leaders in optimal positions, in positions that are ideal for their style of leadership (Northouse, 2013).

Despite its popularity among researchers, the behavioral approach has also been a subject of considerable criticism due to lack of clarity and inconsistency validation (Northouse, 2010; Robbins, 2006; Yukl & Van Fleet, 1992). Another criticism is that there is no good way to explain what an organization should do in case of a mismatch between the working environment and the leadership style because contingency theory fails to explain how leaders should adopt different types to different situational contingencies to improve leadership effectiveness. Conversely, it focuses on changing the situation to fit the leader's styles (Northouse, 2013; Yulk, 2012).

Full Range Leadership Model

The full range leadership model (FRLM) is part of the "New Leadership" paradigm (Bryman, 1992). Bass (1985) full-range leadership theory diverts the focus of leadership researches from trait, behavioral and contingency approaches to the more inspirational and emotional effects of leaders on followers (Antonakis & House, 2013). The full range leadership model (FRLM) contains nine factors that comprise three significant categories of leaders' behavior (styles), ranging from transformational to transactional to completely inactive (laissez-faire) behavior (Barbuto, 2005; Bass & Avolio, 1995, 1997). The following section explained each of these styles in detail (Figure 2.2).

Transformational Leadership Style

Transformational leaders are proactive and act as change agents by stimulating and transforming followers' motives, beliefs, and attitudes from a lower to a higher level of arousal. By transcending collective interest, transformational leaders raise followers' awareness that helps them to achieve extraordinary goals. Transformational leaders transfer vision, strengthen emotional association with followers and make them aware of and believe in attaining high-order goals (Antonakis & House, 2013; Antonakis et al., 2003). Transformational leadership comprises of the following five factors.

Idealized Influence

Antonakis et al. (2003) have explained idealized influence as an attribute and as behavior. Idealized influence as an attribute refers to that a leader influences followers by social charisma, and followers perceive a leader as a role model and assertive, confident, and ethics-focused. Idealized influence attribute is the emotional component of transformational leadership, which theoretically shifts the self-interests of followers towards the combined interest of the greater good (Antonakis & House, 2013). Idealized influence as a behavior pointed out the charismatic proactive actions of the leader based on the sense of mission, beliefs, and values. Simply idealized influence concern with the leaders' standards, principles, and power. The leader helps followers to build their vision and inspire them to align their values with the interests of group purposes (Antonakis & House, 2013; Northouse, 2015). In examining leadership styles, Trottier et al. (2008) claimed that idealized influence is the strongest predictor of satisfaction among other components. In essence, idealized influence or charisma described exceptional individuals who make followers follow the vision put forward by them (Northouse, 2013).

Inspirational Motivation

Inspirational motivation explained the leader's characteristics to inspire and motivate subordinates to fulfill goals and objectives that may have previously appeared unattainable. Leaders, through emotional motivation, arouse followers' expectations to achieve tasks and combine them with higher performance, thus creating a self-fulfilling prophecy (Antonakis & House, 2013; Humphreys & Einstein, 2003). The core of inspirational motivation is a vision, follower encouragement, autonomy, and working with followers. Practically, leaders use emotional appeals and symbols to focus on group efforts to enhance team spirit to achieve more than they may succeed with their self-interest (Bass et al., 2003; Diaz-Saenz, 2011; Northouse, 2015). The combination of idealized influence and inspirational motivation is called charismatic-inspirational leadership (Bass, 1998).

Intellectual Stimulation

According to Diaz-Saenz (2011), leaders with intellectual stimulation encourage followers to be creative and innovative in dealing with old problems in new ways. A leader with intellectual stimulation does not criticize followers publically, but creativity is encouraged to motivate and encourage followers for better performance. Intellectual stimulation is characterized by encouraging creativity, problem-solving, decision-making capability, support, and follower participation (Avolio & Bass, 2002). Intellectual stimulation further involves challenging frameworks, basic assumptions, and followers' ideas to get them to think in new different ways and find various alternatives (Dumdum et al., 2013). In summary, intellectual stimulation means encouraging followers to think out of the box and give them opportunities to make their own decisions in difficult situations.

Individualize Consideration

Leader exhibit individualizes consideration to deal with each follower as an individual and consider their individual needs, aspirations, and abilities. Leaders with individualized consideration will help followers develop their strengths and spend time guiding and coaching followers (Diaz-Saenz, 2011). Leaders, who demonstrate individualized consideration, provide followers with a learning environment for developing and furnishing skills and confidence with recognition and diversified values (Bass & Riggio, 2006)—individualized consideration deals as a basic transformational leadership approach to providing socio-emotional support and viewing and accepting followers as essential contributors to the organizational success (Antonakis & House, 2013; Sarros & Santora, 2001). The core characteristics of the individualized consideration are adapting and responding to the follower's individual needs in a supportive and helpful manner (Avolio & Bass, 2002; Dumdum et al., 2013).

Transactional Leadership Style

Transactional leadership is based on the exchange of reward against the achievement of goals, and necessary actions will be taken for inadequate performance. It mainly concerns the objective setting, monitoring, and controlling outcomes (Antonakis et al., 2003, 2013; Avolio & Bass, 2002). Burns (1978, p.9) summarized transactional leadership as:

"Transactional leadership occurs "when one person takes the initiative in making contact with others for an exchange of valued things. The exchange could be economic or political, or psychological. Each person recognizes the other as a person....." Following are the components of transactional leadership based on Burns (1978) and Bass (1985, 1998).

Contingent Reward

Contingent reward refers to emotional and economic exchanges by clarifying role requirements and praising and rewarding needed outcomes. The contingent reward is relatively effective in motivating followers because it is considered a constructive transaction (Antonakis & House, 2013). In this approach, leaders view their relationship with followers based on exchange and expect to guide followers to the directions of goals achievement (Bass, 2008; Sarros & Santora, 2001). In this approach, it is the leader's responsibility to clarify roles and responsibilities for achieving targets. Ryan and Tipu (2013) examined FRLM and identified a two-factor structure of FRM, which was active leadership and passive-avoidant leadership. Operational leadership comprises transformational leadership, contingent reward, and active management by exception. At the same time, passive-avoidant administration contained management by exception passive and laissez- fair elements.

Management by Exception

Management by exception refers to the behavior by which leaders continually monitor their followers' performance and take corrective actions when needed (Bass, 2008;

Dumdum et al., 2013; Howell & Avolio, 1993). Management by exception can be active or passive. Passive management by exception, leaders actively monitor follower performance, notice errors, and take action before error causes serious problems. Active management by exception is a proactive approach adopted by the transactional leader. In contrast, passive management by exception approach is reactive. The leader only takes action after the problem had been identified or deviation occurs before intervening (Antonakis & House 2013; Avolio & Bass, 2002); the leader does not monitor followers actively and waits until the results.

Laissez-Fair Leadership Style

Finally, laissez fair leadership approach is referred to as non-leadership or the most passive and ineffective leadership approach. Within this approach, the leader is not interested in any cooperation or participation and stays away from followers hence; it shows the leader's inability to do so. In this approach, leaders are considered "inactive rather than reactive or proactive" (Bass, 1990 p. 550). Bass (1990, p. 545) differentiated laissez fair leadership from other types of leadership as:

"Laissez-faire leadership should not be confused with democratic, relations oriented, participative, or considerate leadership behavior. Nor should it be confused with delegation or management by exception."

Criticism of Full Range Leadership Model (FRLM)

Despite its importance in leadership research, FRLM also gets criticism in the research community. One of the weaknesses most commonly highlighted is the propensity among researchers to idealize transformational leadership up to the extent that too much credit is assigned to the leader. In contrast, other constructs that lead to organizational, group, or individual development are ignored (Diaz-Saenz, 2011). Ryan and Tipu (2013) analyzed FRLM and identified that contingent reward and management by exception active were correlated with transformational leadership factors. It showed that FRLM constructs are not unique to each leadership style (Tejada et al., 2001). FRLM is considered the leader-centric approach, which focuses on one person being the most crucial part of the leadership process, and followers are the passive participants inspired and motivated by leaders (Northouse, 2010; Uhl-bien et al., 2014).

Emerging Leadership Styles

Servant Leadership

Servant Leadership is a school of thought based on the idea that a servant leader's main priority is to cater to the employee first to induce a high-performing and developed workforce. The founder of this philosophy, Robert K. Greenleaf, described Servant Leadership as an opportunity for the Leader and the employee to grow simultaneously. The increased personal growth of both parties would eventually result in the betterment of the organization. Servant Leadership sets their priorities accordingly; Employees first, organization second, themselves last. (Eva, Robin, Sendjaya, Dierendonck, & Liden, 2019).

Servant Leadership can most probably invite an organizational change since the Leadership is based on serving the employees first; if the Leader can create a connection between the followers and the organization, it will allow the employees to own the organization and, most importantly, be more accepting of an organizational change.

Servant leaders are developing people, sharing Leadership, displaying authenticity, valuing people, providing Leadership, and building community (Laub 1999). Similarly, Wong and Page (2003) mentioned that SL is visionary Leadership, servanthood, responsible Leadership, Courageous Leadership, and emphasizing honesty, authenticity, power, and pride (vulnerability and humidity) and developing and empowering others. To lead a team effectively, SL provides accountability, gives support, emphasizes accurate self-evaluation, fosters collaboration, provides clear information, and values the people (Irving and Longbotham 2007). Furthermore, Greenleaf placed "going beyond one's self-interest" as a core characteristic of servant Leadership. Although mentioned in other leadership theories, it has never been given the central position it has in servant leadership theory. The servant-leader is governed by creating opportunities to help followers grow (Luthans & Avolio, 2003). Compared to other leadership styles where the goal is the organization's well-being, a servant leader is genuinely concerned with serving followers (Greenleaf, 1977), as is also indicated by Stone, Russell, and Patterson (2004). This person-oriented attitude makes way for safe and strong relationships within the organization. Furthermore, as Greenleaf (1998) puts it, servants chosen to be leaders are greatly supported by their employees because they have committed themselves and are reliable. In this way, an atmosphere is created that encourages followers to become the very best they can.

Authentic Leadership

As the name suggests, Authentic Leadership is a theory that focuses on the authenticity of a leader, which is built through a direct relationship between the follower and the leader. This leadership philosophy is based on moral grounds, and the leader can improve the quality of the performance through trust and support. The positive encouragement from the leader evolves into the growth of the employees hence resulting in better performance. Authentic leadership's transparency can also help revive an organization or even bring about organizational change by showing the employees how the organization is declining or how their good performance has benefited it; this will give a well-understood nudge. When considering the qualities of an authentic leader, we observe four main components of authentic leadership: self-awareness, relation transparency between the leader and the follower, balanced approach, and a moral perspective. (Banks, Mccauley, Gardner, & Guler, 2016).

Authentic leadership refers to the leader personally treating each employee and affecting each employee with authenticity to engage in the organization. Authentic leadership is understood as a pattern of behavior role to reflect the effects on working employees (Fu & Deshpande 2012). The original administration maintains the relation between their followers based on sincerity and positive behaviors (Norman, Avolio & Luthans, 2010). An authentic leader is to be passionately smart to develop behavior (Avolio & Gardner, 2005). Authentic leadership has a positive influence on their employees when they share knowledge between them for organization productivity. Leader behavior involves communicative actions that are observable and understandable words (Walumbwa et al., 2008). Authentic leader's mission is to serve collective interests (Caldwell & Hayes, 2010); they will foster and shape their collaborators' behaviors, such as knowledge-sharing behaviors that help the organization for productivity. According to Caldwell and Hayes (2010), the willingness of leaders to share knowledge is a critical factor in building positive behavior among employees. An authentic leader's behavior can influence other employees to create such positive behavior as a standard accepted by the people (De Vries, Bakker-Pieper & Oostenveld 2010). The authentic leader could also impact employee's behavior, such as knowledge sharing behavior.

Distribute Leadership

Distribute Leadership is a type of Leadership shared amongst a group of people working in an organization, primarily used in educational institutions. It has also made its way to corporate organizations and the tourism industry. This brings immediate attention to the leadership activity rather than individual Leadership and its features. It allows the distribution of Leadership throughout the employees, empowering them and promoting growth amongst them. Distribute Leadership is more procedural rather than relying upon individual action. However, the emergence of Distributed Leadership can be seen through mutual trust, which will inevitably result in a 'shared role space.' (Harris & Deflaminis, 2016).

Distribute Leadership, and its unique nature opens many opportunities in terms of growth and improvement as it involves a border horizon of perspectives from different mindsets during the improvement process to better understand the sources of critical challenges, to involve more people in planning strategies for overcoming these challenges and this attention to distributed leadership principles will increase the chances of meaningful and sustainable change. (Hurwitz, 2017) This unconventional way of Leadership can influence organizational change through its involvement of a group of people; when each person feels equally involved, they will most probably work better, move forward, and adapt to the changes.

Distributed Leadership has emerged as a leadership approach that produces successful performance in challenging contexts (Harris, 2002). As organization faces the challenge of reformation, distributed Leadership might provide a valuable focus for developing effective Leadership in organizations. Distributed Leadership is where responsibility and leadership action is shared amongst several personnel. It requires interaction among leaders, followers, and situations (Spillane, 2006) and focuses on the interrelations of people and their situations by considering individual's expertise, knowledge, and skills. The aim of distributed Leadership in organizations is to enhance productivity and innovation by building employee's capacity to lead learning. Duignan (2006) posits that distributed Leadership has a clear purpose of whole organizations improvement by improving quality of work and education. Organization leaders try to build a culture that engages every manager and employee in the workplace in learning to make their organization successful.

Change Leadership

This type of leadership is based upon having the ability to promote change within the organization. According to Higgs and Rowland, Change Leadership is defined as a leader who can influence followers and motivate them through personal advocacy, vision, and drive (By, Hughes, & Ford, 2016). Similarly, we see that Change leadership's primary focus is to bring about large-scale change in an organization and the need for empowered employees to participate in that change actively. What drives the change leaders is their motivation, enthusiasm, and vision that allows them to see beyond, and through these traits, they transform their visions into reality.

While the terms are often used interchangeably, many researchers, including Kotter (2008), consider change management and change leadership quite different concepts. Change management is "a set of basic tools or structures intended to keep any change effort under control" (Kotter, 2008). Kotter argues that the goal of change management is to minimize the distractions and impacts of the change: to get the project completed on time, on-target, and on budget. There is no space for unanticipated outcomes in this type of approach: what is needed is control and restriction. Meyer et al. (2007) assert that change initiatives often have a time-bound urgency component. Furthermore, they acknowledge that leadership behaviors that minimize follower resistance to change, such as building trust and regular communication, are challenging when leaders perceive that there is insufficient time to dedicate to these strategies that require a more extended period to be impactful. Many leaders perceive time to be a luxury they do not have in planning change.

FUTURE RESEARCH DIRECTIONS

Future research could expand beyond the leadership styles to include other factors which make leaders visionaries and innovative. Most of the study was focused on leader centric perspective and ignored other factors such as traits of leaders and followers. Five decades, Personality is the part of leadership success, and it has gained the attention of industries to explore more visionaries, the unexplored side of leadership. Further research explores the differential characteristics of a leadership development program's content and structural attributes for those with low initial levels of leader's self-efficacy compared to one for those with high initial levels of leader's self-efficacy. The research would extend the current study and the applicability of a leadership development program beyond emerging leaders. In today's rapidly changing environment, organizational structures are flatter, and the concepts of leadership are also changing like shared leadership, distributed leadership, and team leadership. Given that different levels of LSE respond differently to challenges, further enhancing the understanding as to what constitutes an appropriate level of challenge and how this can be effectively managed for different levels of LSE would provide helpful information for those implementing development programs.

CONCLUSION

This chapter reviewed and discussed the leadership literature. The intent was to understand what work or job content and structural elements affected the development of Leaders and why other attributes were important. While initial levels of leaders predicted the gains, active engagement of employees with job content with repeated opportunities to practice leadership skills at appropriate levels of the challenge was a definitive factor in leaders' development. Part of the rationale for the study was to provide some evidence that leadership development programs are a worthwhile undertaking, particularly when they enhance leadership styles. While the research has contributed to our overall understanding of trait approach, behavioral approach, contingency approach, and leadership styles such as transformational, transactional, authentic, servant, distributive, and change, only additional research will address the myriad of new questions the study.

ACKNOWLEDGMENT

This research received no specific grant from any funding agency in the public, commercial, or not-for-profit sectors.

REFERENCES

Allen, D. W. (1998). How nurses become leaders: Perceptions and beliefs about leadership development. *The Journal of Nursing Administration*, *28*(9), 15–20. doi:10.1097/00005110-199809000-00005 PMID:9745657

Antonakis, J., Avolio, B. J., & Sivasubramaniam, N. (2003). Context and leadership: An examination of the nine-factor full-range leadership theory using the Multifactor Leadership Questionnaire. *The Leadership Quarterly*, *14*(3), 261–295. doi:10.1016/S1048-9843(03)00030-4

Antonakis, J., & House, R. J. (2013). The full-range leadership theory: The way forward. In Transformational and Charismatic Leadership: The Road Ahead 10th Anniversary Edition. Emerald Group Publishing Limited.

Avolio, B., & Bass, B. (2002). *Manual for the multifactor leadership questionnaire (Form 5X)*. Mindgarden.

Avolio, B. J., & Gardner, W. L. (2005). Authentic leadership development: Getting to the root of positive forms of leadership. *The Leadership Quarterly*, *16*(3), 315–338. doi:10.1016/j.leaqua.2005.03.001

Banks, G. C., Mccauley, K. D., Gardner, W. L., & Guler, C. E. (2016). A meta-analytic review of authentic and transformational leadership: A test for redundancy. *The Leadership Quarterly*, *27*(4), 634–652. doi:10.1016/j.leaqua.2016.02.006

Barbuto, J. E. Jr. (2005). Motivation and transactional, charismatic, and transformational leadership: A test of antecedents. *Journal of Leadership & Organizational Studies*, *11*(4), 26–40. doi:10.1177/107179190501100403

Bass, B., & Avolio, B. (1995). *MLQ Multifactor Leadership Questionnaire*. Mind Garden.

Bass, B. M. (1981). *Stogdill's Handbook of Leadership*. Free Press.

Bass, B. M. (1985). *Leadership and Performance Beyond Expectations: Free Press*. Collier Macmillan.

Bass, B. M. (1998). *Transformational Leadership: Industry, Military and Educational Impact. Majah*. Lawrence Erlbaum.

Bass, B. M., & Avolio, B. J. (1997). *Full Range Leadership Development: Manual for the Multifactor Leadership Questionnaire*. Mind Garden.

Bass, B. M., Avolio, B. J., Jung, D. I., & Berson, Y. (2003). Predicting unit performance by assessing transformational and transactional leadership. *The Journal of Applied Psychology, 88*(2), 207–218. doi:10.1037/0021-9010.88.2.207 PMID:12731705

Bass, B. M., & Riggio, R. E. (2006). *Transformational Leadership*. Lawrence Erlbaum Associates. doi:10.4324/9781410617095

Bryman, A. (1992). *Charisma and Leadership in Organizations*. Sage Publications.

Burke, W. W. (2008). Organization Change: Theory and Practice (2nd ed.). Los Angeles, CA: sage.

Burns, J. M. (1978). Leadership; Harper and Row Publishers; New York, NY. *Business Review (Federal Reserve Bank of Philadelphia), 57*(2), 106–114.

By, R. T., Hughes, M., & Ford, J. (2016). Change Leadership: Oxymoron and Myths. *Journal of Change Management, 16*(1), 8–17. doi:10.1080/14697017.2016.1137425

Caldwell, C., Hayes, L. A., & Long, D. T. (2010). Leadership, trustworthiness, and ethical stewardship. *Journal of Business Ethics, 96*(4), 497–512. doi:10.100710551-010-0489-y

Chemers, M. M. (1995). Contemporary leadership theory. In J. T. Wren (Ed.), *The Leader's Companion: Insights On Leadership Through the Ages* (pp. 83–99). Free Press.

De Vries, R. E., Bakker-Pieper, A., & Oostenveld, W. (2010). Leadership= communication? The relations of leaders' communication styles with leadership styles, knowledge sharing and leadership outcomes. *Journal of Business and Psychology, 25*(3), 367–380. doi:10.100710869-009-9140-2 PMID:20700375

Diaz-Saenz, H. R. (2011). Transformational leadership. In D. C. A. Bryman, K. Grint, B. Jackson, & M. Uhl-Bien (Eds.), The Sage Handbook of Leadership (pp. 299-310). Sage.

Duignan, P. (2006). *Educational leadership: key challenges and ethical tensions.* Cambridge University Press.

Dumdum, U. R., Lowe, K. B., & Avolio, B. J. (2013). A meta-analysis of transformational and transactional leadership correlates of effectiveness and satisfaction: An update and extension. In Transformational and Charismatic Leadership: The Road Ahead 10th Anniversary Edition (pp. 39-70). Emerald Group Publishing Limited.

Eva, N., Robin, M., Sendjaya, S., Dierendonck, D. V., & Liden, R. C. (2019). Servant Leadership: A systematic review and call for future research. *The Leadership Quarterly, 30*(1), 111–132. doi:10.1016/j.leaqua.2018.07.004

Fiedler, F. E. (1971). Validation and extension of the contingency model of leadership effectiveness: A review of empirical findings. *Psychological Bulletin, 76*(2), 128–148. doi:10.1037/h0031454 PMID:4942584

Ford, J. D., Ford, L. W., & D'Amelio, A. (2008). Resistance to change: The rest of the story. *Academy of Management Review, 33*(2), 362–377. doi:10.5465/amr.2008.31193235

Fu, W., & Deshpande, S. P. (2012). Factors impacting ethical behavior in a Chinese state-owned steel company. *Journal of Business Ethics, 105*(2), 231–237. doi:10.100710551-011-0962-2

George, J. M. (2000). Emotions and leadership: The role of emotional intelligence. *Human Relations, 53*(8), 1027–1055. doi:10.1177/0018726700538001

Gibson, J. L., Ivancevich, J. M., Donnelly, J. H., & Konopaske, R. (2003). *Organizations: Behaviour, structure, processes.* McGraw-Hill.

Greenleaf, R. K. (1977). *Servant leadership: A journey into the nature of legitimate power and greatness.* Paulist Press.

Greenleaf, R. K. (1998). *The power of servant-leadership.* Berrett-Koehler.

Harris, A. (2002). Effective leadership in schools facing challenging contexts. *School Leadership & Management, 22*(1), 15–26. doi:10.1080/13632430220143024a

Harris, A., & Deflaminis, J. (2016). Distributed leadership in practice. *Management in Education, 30*(4), 141–146. doi:10.1177/0892020616656734

Hersey, P., Blanchard, K. H., & Johnson, D. E. (2001). *Management of Organisational Behaviour* (8th ed.). Prentice-Hall.

Horner, M. (1997). Leadership theory: Past, present and future. *Team Performance Management*, *3*(4), 270–287. doi:10.1108/13527599710195402

Howell, J. M., & Avolio, B. J. (1993). Transformational leadership, transactional leadership, locus of control, and support for innovation: Key predictors of consolidated-business-unit performance. *The Journal of Applied Psychology*, *78*(6), 891–902. doi:10.1037/0021-9010.78.6.891

Humphreys, J. H., & Einstein, W. O. (2003). Nothing new under the sun: Transformational leadership from a historical perspective. *Management Decision*, *41*(1), 85–95. doi:10.1108/00251740310452934

Hurwitz, M. (2017). *Exploring Distributed Leadership: A Leader–Follower Collaborative Lens*. Distributed Leadership.

Irving, J. A., & Longbotham, G. J. (2007). Team effectiveness and six essential servant leadership themes: A regression model based on items in the organizational leadership assessment. *International Journal of Leadership Studies*, *2*(2), 98–113.

Kotter, J. P., & Schlesinger, L. A. (2008). *Choosing strategies for change*. Harvard.

Laub, J. A. (1999). *Assessing the servant organization: Development of the servant organizational leadership (SOLA) instrument*. Florida Atlantic University.

Luthans, F., & Avolio, B. (2003). Authentic leadership development. In K. S. Cameron & J. E. Dutton (Eds.), *Positive organizational scholarship*. Berrett-Koehler.

Mann, R. D. (1959). A review of the relationships between personality and performance in small groups. *Psychological Bulletin*, *56*(4), 241–270. doi:10.1037/h0044587

Meyer, J. P., Srinivas, E. S., Lal, J. B., & Topolnytsky, L. (2007). Employee commitment and support for an organizational change: Test of the three-component model in two cultures. *Journal of Occupational and Organizational Psychology*, *80*(2), 185–211. doi:10.1348/096317906X118685

Nordin, N. (2011). The influence of emotional intelligence, leadership behaviour and organizational commitment on organizational readiness for change in higher learning institution. *Procedia: Social and Behavioral Sciences*, *29*(3), 129–138. doi:10.1016/j.sbspro.2011.11.217

Norman, S. M., Avolio, B. J., & Luthans, F. (2010). The impact of positivity and transparency on trust in leaders and their perceived effectiveness. *The Leadership Quarterly*, *21*(3), 350–364. doi:10.1016/j.leaqua.2010.03.002

Northouse, P. (2010). *Leadership, Theory and Practice*. Sage.

Northouse, P. (2013). *Leadership, Theory and Practice*. Sage.

Northouse, P. (2015). *Leadership, Theory and Practice*. Sage.

Paglis, L. L., & Green, S. G. (2002). Leadership self-efficacy and managers' motivation for leading change. *Journal of Organizational Behavior: The International Journal of Industrial, Occupational and Organizational Psychology and Behavior*, *23*(2), 215–235. doi:10.1002/job.137

Penney, S. A., Kelloway, E. K., & O'Keefe, D. (Eds.). (2015). *Trait Theories of Leadership*. Routledge.

Robbins, S. P. (2001). *Organisational Behaviour: Global and Southern African Perspectives*. Pearson.

Ryan, J. C., & Tipu, S. A. (2013). Leadership effects on innovation propensity: A two-factor full range leadership model. *Journal of Business Research*, *66*(10), 2116–2129. doi:10.1016/j.jbusres.2013.02.038

Simons, T., Leroy, H., Collewaert, V., & Masschelein, S. (2015). How leader alignment of words and deeds affects followers: A meta-analysis of behavioural integrity research. *Journal of Business Ethics*, *132*(4), 831–844. doi:10.100710551-014-2332-3

Spillane, J. P. (2006). *Distributed leadership*. Jossey-Bass.

Stogdill, R. M. (1974). *Handbook of Leadership: A Survey of Theory and Research*. New York Free Press.

Trottier, T., Van Wart, M., & Wang, X. (2008). Examining the nature and significance of leadership in government organizations. *Public Administration Review*, *68*(2), 319–333. doi:10.1111/j.1540-6210.2007.00865.x

Veríssimo, J. M., & Lacerda, T. M. (2015). Does integrity matter for CSR practice in organizations? The mediating role of transformational leadership. *Business Ethics (Oxford, England)*, *24*(1), 34–51. doi:10.1111/beer.12065

Walumbwa, F. O., Avolio, B. J., Gardner, W. L., Wernsing, T. S., & Peterson, S. J. (2008). Authentic leadership: Development and validation of a theory-based measure. *Journal of Management*, *34*(1), 89–126. doi:10.1177/0149206307308913

Warrick, D. (2011). The urgent need for skilled transformational leaders: Integrating transformational leadership and organization development. *Journal of Leadership, Accountability and Ethics*, *8*(5), 11–26.

Wong, P. T., & Page, D. (2003). Servant leadership: An opponent-process model and the revised servant leadership profile. *Proceedings of the Servant Leadership Research Roundtable*.

Yukl, G. (2012). *Leadership in Organizations* (8th ed.). Prentice Hall.

Yukl, G., & Van Fleet, D. (1992). *Theory and Research on Leadership in Organizations*. Consulting Psychologists Press Inc.

Yukl, G. A. (2002). *Leadership in Organizations*. Prentice Hall.

Yukl, G. A. (2013). *Leadership in Organizations*. Pearson Education.

Zaccaro, S. J., Kemp, C., & Bader, P. (2004). Leader traits and attributes. In D. V. D. John Antonakis (Ed.), The Nature of Leadership (pp. 101–124). Academic Press.

KEY TERMS AND DEFINITIONS

Constructionist Approaches: These views explain followership as a relational interaction between individuals to co-construct leadership and followership.

Followership: Followership is the study of the follower roles and the following behavior during leadership.

Implicit Followership Theories: Implicit followership theories (IFTs) argued what leaders think about their followers (i.e., how followers' behaviors and characteristics shaped leader-follower relationships).

Implicit Leadership Theories: Implicit leadership theories (ILTs) explain what followers think about their leaders (i.e., how followers' cognitive categories or schema affect followers' perceptions about their leaders).

Role-Based Approaches: These approaches explain followership as a role played by the individual under a structured organizational hierarchy.

Chapter 2
(Re)constructing Leadership: Complexity and Flexibility

Seong-Yuen Toh
Sunway University, Malaysia

ABSTRACT

This chapter elucidates Keith Grint's model of leadership as a viable dynamic option in our complex world. By locating the model within a social constructionist frame, this chapter demonstrates how far we have come in the evolving stream of leadership research. Seven main characteristics of the Grint's model of leadership are discussed to demonstrate how the model can help us to understand wicked problems, such as the COVID-19 pandemic in Malaysia. The author also identifies two weaknesses of Grint's model: (1) organisational culture and (2) followership. Lastly, to address the two weaknesses, the author proposes an integrated model of leadership that combines the understanding of an adhocracy culture based on the competing value framework and Kelly's effective followership model. In conclusion, the integrative framework of leadership offers leadership researchers a model with more explanatory power in understanding the leadership phenomenon within the social constructionist supposition.

INTRODUCTION

When it comes to leadership, if things go badly, people tend to judge that leader's behaviours and other factors in very negative ways, regardless of what the leader has achieved in the past. In other words, leaders are blamed for the negative results, whether causes can be traced back to the leader or whether it was caused by an external factor outside the leader's influence. This means the outcomes "make" the

DOI: 10.4018/978-1-7998-2807-5.ch002

leader. In fact, we attribute leadership as accounting for up to 40% of the changes in performance of an organization (Day, 2014). This considerable effect indicates that a better understanding of the concept of leadership can be an effective lever to move the organization (to borrow a phrase from Archimedes). The ancient Chinese literature understands the value of naming correctly to facilitate successful outcomes.

Tzu-lu said, "If the Lord of Wei left the administration of his state to you, what would you put first?"

Confucius said, "If something has to be put first, it is, perhaps, the rectification of names."

Tzu-lu said, "Is that so? What a roundabout way you take! Why bring rectification in at all?"

Confucius said, "When names are not correct, what is said will not sound reasonable; when what is said does not sound reasonable, affairs will not culminate in success..." (Adair, 2013, p. 9-10)

When a crisis arises, the good leader must be decisive, demonstrating an intense desire to concentrate on the challenge while ignoring detractors. This hinges on correctly identifying (naming) the problem as a crisis. However, the correct naming of a problem is not a matter of just the correct identification of the nature of the problem. Indeed, Grint (2005) suggests that whether or not naming a problem as a crisis is in actuality the right response seems to rely less on whether the situation supposedly "is" a crisis, rather than on how best the situation should be better addressed. This is not to neglect that there is an "is" to the problem, but to recognise that there is manoeuvre room for those in leadership roles when it comes to persuading others as to the advantage of naming a problem a crisis or as something else. This chapter aims to provide a robust model of leadership (i.e., Keith Grint's model) that acknowledges this factor in understanding leadership.

To build up to that stage, first, the author reviewed the evolution of leadership research to gain an appreciation and understanding as to how we arrived at where we are situated now in the stream of leadership research. A broad survey will provide a bird's eye view on the state-of-the art trends in leadership research. About a century of leadership science has resulted in many paradigm changes and a great deal of ambiguity. Scholars in leadership have been disappointed by the vast number of false starts, modest scientific developments, and inconsistent results, on many occasions. Nevertheless, it was a three-steps-forward-two-steps-back situation, a slow, uneven progress. Second, we moved on then to develop a better understanding of leadership building from a conceptual differentiation of leadership and management referring to two models, and then turned to a more complex model developed by Keith Grint (2005, 2007, 2008, 2010, 2020). The details of the unique features of the model are discussed, concluding with a case study based on the nature of leadership related to the COVID-19 pandemic in Malaysia. Finally, an integrated model of leadership is proposed to strengthen the Grint's model by integrating it with the competing-value framework of organisational culture (Quinn & Rohrbaugh, 1983) and the followership model (Kelly, 1988). This integrative model is more robust in offering leadership flexibility in coping with the complexity of the organisational context by addressing the two weaknesses identified in the Grint's model, namely, organisational culture and followership.

AN OVERVIEW OF RESEARCH IN LEADERSHIP

This section offers a broad survey of the leadership research[1]. The "great man" viewpoint, which observed history as a result of the influence of extraordinary personalities, ushered in the systematic enquiry into the concept of leadership at the beginning of the twentieth century (Bass, 1990). Specific dispositional features (i.e., stable characteristics or *traits*) were thought to distinguish leaders from non-leaders, according to the "great man" school of thought. The theory proposes that some people have a unique hereditary that distinguishes them as leaders, and that these characteristics or inborn traits or attributes are what separates the leaders from the non-leaders. Trait research, however, was effectively shut down as a result of scholars' critical assessments of the limits of the findings, which caused researchers to shift their focus to leaders' behaviours. Nevertheless, in recent years, there has been a revival of research based on the trait approach to leadership[2].

The behavioural theories of leadership centred on the attitudes that leaders enacted in their *behaviour* towards followers, and how they viewed their followers, analogous to Lewin and Lippitt's (1938) research on democratic versus autocratic leaders. The behavioural strategy is primarily concerned about the actions and behaviours of leaders. The behavioural approach expanded the study of leadership to encompass the activities of leaders with followers in different ways by refocusing the study of leadership specifically to leaders' behaviours. Famous examples among others of this approach are the Michigan and Ohio studies that identify two broad behaviours of leaders (consideration/employee-orientation, and initiating structure/production-orientation). However, conflicting results propelled this leadership research project into disarray once more. It became clear that the success of an adopted leadership style was conditional on the situation. The ultimate objective was the discovery of a common set of leadership practises that reliably resulted in positive results. This objective, however, was never achieved due to contradictions in the study results.

The focus then shifted to the leadership *situation* as the contingency factor confounding the findings from the behavioural approach. The contingency approach, as its name suggests, places the emphasis on leadership in different circumstances. The theory's assumption is that unique circumstances necessitate different types of leadership behaviours. Based on this viewpoint, becoming a successful leader necessitates a person's ability to adapt his or her leadership style to the requirements of various circumstances. Two main figures of the contingency approach are House (1971) and Fiedler (1981). House (1971) developed a well-known contingency strategy, focusing on the role of the leader in clarifying the pathways that will lead to effective leadership. Fiedler claimed that leader-member relationship, the structure of tasks, and the leader's power position were linked to the effectiveness of leaders' behaviours. Fiedler claimed that leader-member interactions, mission structure, and the leader's power would decide the efficacy of the style of leadership practised; Fiedler is credited with the contingency theory movement of leadership.

House focused research efforts on the role of the leader in clarifying the pathways leading to followers' goals. Clearly, different situations do pose different demand on leadership, but because situations are diverse, complex, and distinct, the contingency approach failed to provide sufficient generic guideline for leaders on how to use the approach. The inability to usefully generalise the findings renders the model less effective in practise. Furthermore, contingency models tend to be very complicated to be useful. More recent development of the contingency approach to leadership focuses on a person-situation fit perspective (Ayman & Lauritsen, 2018). This condition of "fit" is analogous to Csikszentmihalyi's (2000) principle of "flow," which refers to when an individual's ability and experience perfectly match the needs of the situation. Leaders are at the peak of their ability in this state, voicing hope and feeling successful.

At about the same time, another approach shifted the focus to the *relationships* between leaders and followers. In essence, the relationships between leaders and their followers are represented by the leader-member exchange (LMX) theory (Graen & Uhl-Bien, 1995). Prior to the LMX theory, researchers thought of leadership as something that leaders did to their followers. This presumption meant that leaders viewed their followers together, as a whole, and with a common leadership style. The LMX theory questioned this premise and drew attention to possible differences between how the leader treated each follower. High-quality relationships between a leader and his or her followers are founded on loyalty and mutual respect (i.e., in relation to the in-group followers), while low-quality relationships are built on the enforcement of contractual commitments (i.e., in relation to the out-group followers). The out-group seems to be discriminated against, since the LMX theory divides the work unit into two groups, each of which receives different preferential treatments (Dansereau, 1995). For another weakness of the theory, researchers haven't looked at the effect of other factors on LMX dyads as the hypothesis is mostly tested in isolation. Workplace expectations and other corporate culture factors, for example, are likely to affect leader-member interaction (Schyns & Day, 2010).

Finally, the shift to a stronger emphasis on the followers in the leadership research began as a result of doubts about the methodology of using questionnaires in leadership studies. The legitimacy of leadership questionnaires has been criticized due to the implicit leadership theories of followers doing the questionnaire ratings. Researchers argued that scores could be corrupted by the implicit leadership theories of those doing the scoring in surveys, which has disputed the validity of questionnaire ratings (For example, Rush et al., 1977). Consequently, scepticism grew due to the recognition that followers' attribution plays a key role in leader evaluation. This viewpoint implies that what leaders do is primarily due to performance consequences, as attributed by their followers, influenced by the followers' implicit leadership theories. As a result, what leaders do could be entirely insignificant, given that positive outcomes influence how leaders are rated by their followers; and vice versa.

Meindl et al.'s (1985) notion of the romance of leadership backed up a paradigm based on followers' attribution wherein leadership. The romance of leadership is regarded as a descriptive phenomenon that makes followers perceive institutions as causal systems where leaders tend to be viewed as the most important factors for the performance of the organizations (Meindl et al., 1985). A recent shift in leadership towards a more follower-centric approach advocates that leadership effectiveness and follower commitment to a leader is dependent upon the attributes and perception of the followers. This shift in focus sees followers as co-constructors of leadership rather than as passive recipients of leadership. The follower-centric approach falls into the broad category of critical leadership theory labelled as the social construction of leadership. The increasing cynicism with many mainstream leadership theories has prompted scholars to seek new approaches to explain, interpret, and understand the dynamic processes and behaviours in leadership studies (Fairhurst & Grant, 2010).

Two interrelated features are typical in the social constructionist leadership approach. First, the theories reject a leader-centric approach in which the leader's attitude, style, or behaviours are seen as the main influencing forces on the thoughts and behaviours of followers. Many constructionist leadership methods, on the other hand, put an emphasis on followers' abilities to make sense of their workplace experiences (Meindl, 1995). Second, leadership is emphasised as a co-constructed fact, specifically the mechanisms and outcomes of engagement between and within leaders, followers, and other constituencies. As a result, there is a reluctance to accept approaches that construe leadership as contained in a leader's personal traits (e.g., personality theories), situational characteristics, or both. Social constructionists are most inclined to support an attributional, subjective interpretation of leadership (Meindl, 1993, 1995). In the following sections, the constructionist approach to leadership by Keith Grint is considered as a model that emerged from the consideration of two competing models of leadership (the bidimensional model and overlapping model).

UNDERSTANDING LEADERSHIP

In this section, two approaches are explored to understand the phenomenon of leadership. One way to understand leadership is to distinguish it from that which constitutes management. In many ways, leadership and management are related processes. Leadership, like management, entails power, which can be defined as the capacity to influence others. Acting "with" people is a requirement in both leadership and management. Management and leadership are also concerned with achieving effective goals. However, management and leadership are not the same thing. Although the study of leadership can be traced back to the Greek tradition, or even further back to ancient Chinese literature, management originated with the dawn of modern civilization at the turn of the twentieth century, especially during the industrialisation age (Wren & Bedeian, 2020). Management was developed as a discipline or a practise to make organisations (factories) run more smoothly and effectively by reducing complexity.

According to the famed Harvard professor, John Kotter (2001), complexity is something that management needs to contend with, whereas grappling with change is more related to the leadership role. Leadership has become more relevant as the corporate environment has become more competitive and volatile in recent years. More leaders are needed, in this sense, according to Kotter, because organisations are already over-managed and under led. Leaders help followers, key stakeholders, and others navigate the highly competitive and ever-changing business environment. According to this view, management's primary role is to add structure and maintain consistency within organisations, while leadership's primary function is to generate transformation and harness movement towards a grand vision. This understanding of the concepts of leadership and management seems to suggest that they are divergent concepts. Moderate doses of such a view perceive leadership and management as distinct, but complementary processes (For example, Northouse, 2021). This relationship can be considered bidimensional in the sense illustrated by Figure 1. Taken to the extreme, this view may suggest that leaders and managers are different types of individuals. For example, according to Zaleznik (1977), leaders are similar to artists who use imagination to work through confusion, whereas managers are problem-solvers who depend on rationality and control to set things in order. In essence, leaders and managers are different types of people. In a sense, it is very difficult to ask an artist do a manager's job properly. Managers, according to Zaleznik (1997), are reactive and like to work with others to solve challenges, but they do so without passion. The task of a manager is to limit options or choices for organisation members. Leaders, on the other hand, are said to be socially engaged and involved, according to Zaleznik. They try to mould solutions rather than react to them, and they act to broaden the range of choices available to address long-standing problems. The task of the leader is to expand and try new options. These are two different types of people.

Figure 1. Bidimensional model

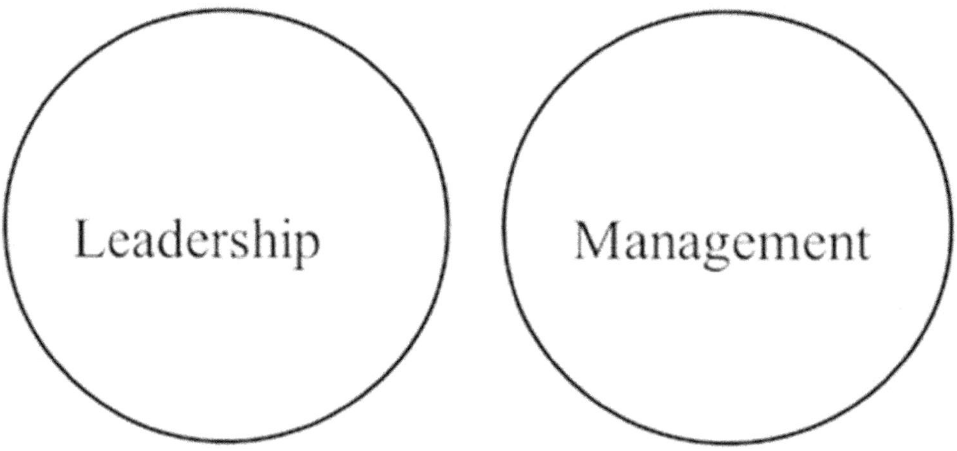

Recent research suggests that there is another way to conceptualise leadership and management. Simonet and Tett (2013) used 43 experts to describe the overlaps and gaps between leadership and management in relation to 63 distinct competencies. They observed that unique competencies associated with management included rule orientation, short-term planning, motivating extrinsically, orderliness, safety concern, and timeliness, whereas unique competency descriptors associated with leadership included motivating intrinsically, creative thinking, strategic planning, tolerance of ambiguity, and people reading. However, they further discovered that there was considerable overlapping where competencies are common to both leaders and managers, such as productivity, customer focus, professionalism, goal setting, financial concern, urgency, and so on. Figure 2 illustrates this relationship in an overlapping model. The model suggests that one cannot talk about leadership without also talking about management, and vice versa. This is an improved approach to understanding the concepts of leadership and management. The degree to which a manager exercises leadership over management depends on the level of the manager in their respective organisational hierarchy. For instance, a manager who holds a position higher up in the corporate hierarchy will need to exhibit a higher degree of competencies associated with leadership (For example, creative and strategic thinking). Conversely, a frontline manager at the lower end of the corporate hierarchy may need to be proficient in those competencies related to managing, such as orderliness and timeliness (For example, scheduling work for staff reporting to him or her). While management and leadership have their distinct characteristics, the two concepts are intertwined. Managers are interested in influencing others to achieve objectives. On the other hand, leaders are interested in administration, as they are involved in arranging, coordinating activities and tasks, staffing, and managing processes and systems. Recent research has sought to establish a generalizable model of leadership competency that brings together important competencies in various leadership domains (For examples, Çitaku and Ramadani (2020) and Seemiller and Whitney (2020)).

Figure 2. Competency model of leadership and management

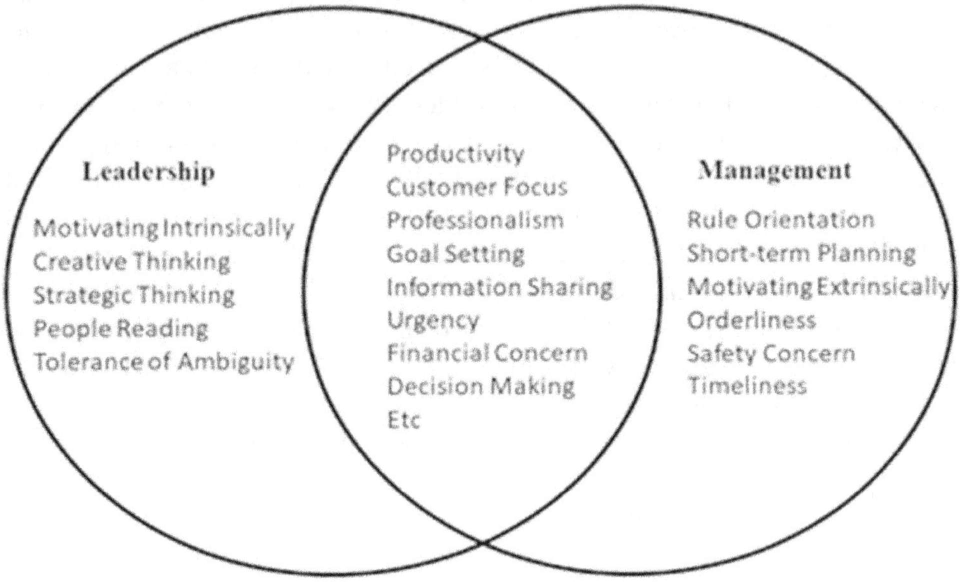

A BETTER WAY TO UNDERSTAND LEADERSHIP

In this section the author expounds on the Grint's model of leadership as a better way to understand the leadership phenomenon. This approach takes into consideration the situational context upon which leadership is exercised from a constructionist perspective. What counts as a "situation" and what counts as the best way to lead in that situation are subjective and debatable issues, not an objective "given" that it can be determined by some objective standards (Grint, 2005). This is a dynamic approach based on the original framework developed by Rittel and Webber (1973) and revitalised by Keith Grint (2005, 2007, 2008, 2010, 2020) to investigate how decision-makers persuade their followers that a specific course of action is required by construing the types of problem confronting them. This lesser-known model adopts a constructionist approach in problem identification, which offers uniquely robust explanatory power in making sense of how leadership works. It offers a view of leadership that is flexible and adaptable to complex challenges in the work context. Past situational theories presupposed the situational context as an objective given fact. For example, Fiedler's (1981) contingency theory of leadership indicates that leadership effectiveness depends on the right fit between the leader's preferred leadership style and a *given* situational context. The situation is a given, fixed, undisputed fact. However, a social constructionist approach observes the variability and inconsistencies of decision makers' accounts of the situations, examines the circumstances of how those accounts are developed, and attempts to comprehend how contradictory statements regarding leadership emerge and coexist. As such, Grint (2005, 2007, 2008, 2010, 2020) suggests that the situation is not a fixed entity, but is socially constructed by the leader and followers. Basically, Grint's model of leadership integrates Rittel and Webber's (1973) framework of tame, critical, and wicked problems with Etzioni's (1964) typology of compliance to understand how problems are socially constructed.

Rittel and Webber's (1973) framework structures problems as tame, wicked, and critical. A *tame problem* can be challenging and complicated but are not unique or novel. It is likely to have arisen before, and solutions to a tame problem exist, as there is a point at which the tamed problem is resolved. Therefore, a specific course of actions is known (from past experience) and the way to resolve a tame problem is by applying a specific course of action or setting up a process to ensure that the necessary steps are taken. Tame problems are associated with *management* whereby the role of the manager is to put into place appropriate processes to resolve the problems. An example of a tame problem is to build a nuclear power plant. While building a nuclear plant can be complicated, it has been done before, successfully. There are standards and guidelines available, people experienced in building nuclear plants can help, and there is an endpoint to such a problem. Building a nuclear plant as such is not unique, it is a tame problem.

A *wicked problem* is more than just a complicated problem. It is complex and often intractable, such that a course of action does not provide sufficient solution to resolve it. Wicked problems are novel and there is no "stopping" point, because every obvious "solution" often produces new (often unanticipated) problems. Furthermore, there is no "right" or "wrong" approach, but only better or worse alternatives to resolve a wicked problem. In another words, every solution involves trade-offs and compromises. Wicked problems are associated with *leadership*, because it requires harnessing capabilities of diverse stakeholders to take responsibility in a collaborative effort to address an intractable issue. An example of a wicked problem is the national transportation system. This is owing to the uniqueness of each case, the complicated and intractable nature of the problem, and its unresolved status (Noto & Bianchi, 2015).

A *critical problem* refers to a crisis case where the course of action is self-evident, but constrained by limited time for decision-making and action. A critical problem is associated with *command*, because of the need for authoritative, decisive decision-making. An example of a critical problem is a fire outbreak in an apartment building. The effective response to a fire outbreak is to instruct everyone to get out of the building immediately. Those aware of the fire will feel compelled to shout instructions and warnings to those unaware and to demand an immediate response.

Figure 3. A typology of problems, power, and authority

For the sake of clarity, visualise the relationships of the various factors in this model that two axes in a diagram. The two axes are the degree of uncertainty of solution to a problem and the degree of collaboration required for problem resolution. Figure 3 illustrates where the three authorities of leadership, management, and command are located.

Figure 3 illustrates that when the decision-maker successfully persuades followers that the problem they are confronted with is a wicked, tame, or a critical problem, the effective authority to be exercised that fits the situation is respectively leadership, management, or command authority. Accordingly, the role of the decision maker is to ask questions when he or she applies leadership authority, to organise processes when applying management authority, or to provide answers when applying command authority. Following Etzioni's (1964) typology of compliance (the horizontal axis), Grint suggests that the exercise of command authority when confronting critical problems involves the application of *coercion compliance,* which usually exists in totalitarian institutions, such as a prison or army camp. Similarly, *calculation compliance* is found in rational institutions such as business organisations where transactional exchange normally takes place. Finally, leadership authority inspires *normative compliance* in institutions where shared values thrive, such as in clubs and institutions.

This model, which is founded on a social construction of leadership, has a few advantages over the competency model of Simonet and Tett (2013). First, the competency model (Figure 2) assumes the situation is fixed. Second, the competency model assumes the followers perceive the leaders along the same dimensions of competencies. However, in this new model, whether the decision maker is a manager or leader depends on the situation. Furthermore, the situation is not an objective given fact, or a fixed element, as assumed in the competency model. The Grint's (2005, 2007, 2008, 2010, 2020) model considers the co-construction of the problem between the leader and the followers. In addition, the Grint's model considers other contextual factors, such as national culture, organisational culture, the media, and so on. In the next few sections, seven unique features of the model are discussed to bring out the model's strengths and weaknesses.

1. Decision Maker

This model accepts the active role of the decision-maker in shaping the followers' understanding of the situation they confront. According to Grint (2005), whether or not calling an issue a crisis is the appropriate solution depends less on whether the situation supposedly "is" a crisis and more on how the decision maker can best handle the situation. As suggested earlier, this is not to deny that the problem exists, but to acknowledge that those in positions of authority have room to manoeuvre in considering the benefits of persuading others with regard to referring to a problem as a crisis or something else. The decision maker matters in influencing others about the nature of the problem in a social constructionist view. Although the social construction of a problem can be disputed and challenged by the followers, depending on the power position of the decision marker, the view of the decision maker usually prevails. This was observed in the 2003 invasion of Iraq. The justification provided by the then president of the United States of America, George W. Bush, was that Iraq posed a critical problem because the president of Iraq, Saddam Hussein, was developing weapons of mass destruction (WMD), which posed an existential threat to the world. When evidence surfaced that there were no WMD, the narrative shifted to a concern for Saddam's poor human rights record instead. However, because America was the dominant superpower of the world, Bush's portrayal of the threat of Iraq as a *critical* problem convinced leaders from 40 countries, including the then prime minister of United Kingdom, Tony Blair, to support the invasion. Blair later regretted this decision (Mason et al., 2016).

2. Individual Differences of Decision Makers

Second, although Grint's (2005, 2007, 2008, 2010, 2020) model moves beyond the Zaleznikian view of management and leadership, it does not deny that such individual differences may influence the actions of decision makers. That is to say that *individual differences* can play a role in constituting the situation such that individuals *tend to favour* one approach over others. For instance, a decision maker can by nature favourably inclined towards orderly planning and organising of activities more attuned towards what a manager would do. As such, the decision maker would tend to be inclined to perceive most problems as *tame* and consequently set in place policies and procedures to solve the problems. Similarly, a decision maker who likes to give command and make unilateral decisions tends to see problems as *critical* and react accordingly. For example, in the author's experience, there was a CEO of a firm who normally remained out of sight (an absentee CEO), allowing his second in charge assume responsibilities for daily operations, but emerged not infrequently to handle "crisis" situations. Naturally, the CEO was inclined to perceive issues he confronted as critical, thus requiring decisive action. He addressed problems by giving instructions, and problems not personally addressed by the CEO were typically not labelled as critical. The CEO wore "crisis glasses." This suggests that decision makers are influenced by their preferences in how they legitimize their actions.

This claim is supported in the empirical leadership research. Intelligence (Antonakis et al., 2012) and personality (De Vries, 2012) are considered stable aspects of individual differences, and they are associated with different types of leadership styles. Chan and Drasgow's (2001) theory of individual differences and leadership demonstrates how both cognitive and non-cognitive differences affect leadership capabilities. People in authority have style preferences in handling problems. A full discussion on the relationships between individual differences and leadership styles goes beyond the scope of this work. It is sufficient to conclude that in the context of this study, this suggests that individual differences do make a difference in dispositional preference for the mode of problem solving, whether command, management, or leadership.

3. The Followers

Third, this model does not neglect the role of the *followers* in attributing leadership and in the construction of the problem. Certainly, Grint (2010) insists that power-hungry commanders are not the only ones addicted to command; anxiety-prone and responsibility-averse followers are also affected (Grint, 2010). Here Grint was concerned about why we, in general, are addicted to crisis and command and how our proclivity for crisis and command hinders our efforts to properly solve wicked problems. This thesis of anxiety-prone followers can be extended further with Popper's (2012) argument based on the psychoanalytical perspective that followers have a dominant need for security. Especially in time of uncertainties, the dormant construct of security in normal times becomes awakened in the followers. In weak psychological situations, according to Popper (2012), the followers search for a parental figure that acts like a protector. Collective regression occurs erasing differences among followers (For example, personality, education, social standing, etc.) and resulting in a quest for a primal father who can protect them. Popper suggested the generalizable principle that "unconscious collective attachment to leaders tends to occur in weak psychological situations when the reaction to the basic need for security is sharp, pervasive, and reaches large groups" (Popper, 2012, p. 37). Drawing from Walter Mischel, an Austrian-born American psychologist who specialized in personality theory and social psychology, Popper described a weak psychological situation (Cortina et al., 2020), wherein there is significant insecurity and uncertainty. Popper argued that people unconsciously desire autocratic leaders (i.e., commanders). This unconscious process is a Freudian psychoanalytical mechanism of projection and transference. Projection is the unconscious attribution of our ideals, wishes, desires, and fantasies to another person (E.g., We see our faults in others.). Carl Jung extended individual projection to the group-level (Weisstub & Galili-Weisstub, 2004), suggesting a level of collective unconscious attraction to a father figure; a commander, in Grint's term. Similarly, transference is represented in a person's response to another person as if that other person were a parent or other significant figure from his or her early childhood (a father figure). In Popper's nomenclature, common descriptions of leaders express close similarity with parental descriptions, for example, "my spiritual father," and "founding father." Popper explained that the common description of the Hitler phenomenon is that the German people were yearning for a strong man who provided protection, a safeguard, and a sense of security; it was basically a longing for a primal father. Such is the psychoanalytical perspective on the unconscious attraction of anxiety-prone followers to the commanding fatherly figure to offer a sense of security. This helps explain why we have an addiction to crisis and command.

Followers comprehend the universe through the lens of autocratic leadership because it achieves an overriding goal, such as reducing undesirable emotional states. Beyond a psychoanalytical perspective, the idea of follower attribution of leadership is grounded in empirical research (Junker & Van Dick, 2014). However, followers may not just act as a passive factor to be used by leaders; they can take charge of their own destiny in self-direction. Although it is true that followers often choose to be passive observers, neither engaging in nor objecting to their leaders' decisions and orders, it is also true that they may be strong supporters who are intensely loyal to or even hostile to their leaders and their causes. Followers can be constructive sense-makers, and their perceptions of leadership are crucial to our comprehension of leadership. This suggests that a reciprocal influencing process is the construction of the problem, the legitimizing of leadership. Nonetheless, the evidence seems to suggest that leaders and followers both tend to favour authoritarianism (Harms et al., 2018), thus supporting Grint's view of an addiction to command (Grint, 2010).

4. The Problem Itself

Fourth, this model recognises the *problem itself* as a contributing factor to its effective resolution. How the problem is construed is limited by various factors. In a social constructionist approach, a decision maker who is in a powerful position has greater influence on others regarding how a problem is defined. However, this does not mean that a problem can be construed in a haphazard or careless manner. All things being equal, a problem such as the construction of a building is clearly a tame problem and to construe it otherwise will depend on relevant contingency factors to convince the various constituencies of the decision maker. For example, during war time, building a nuclear bunker as shelter may be recognised as a critical problem due to the time constrain. The point is, what is convincing cannot be easily defined beforehand. A frontline manager may decide to close the bank earlier than normal because of an escalating riot outbreak two blocks down the road, by representing this as a *critical* problem in view of the safety of the staff and customers inside the bank. Such a unilateral decision (without consultation with higher authorities in the corporate hierarchy as a normal process in solving a *tame* problem) can later be defended as appropriate due to the nature of the problem that required immediate compliance to instructions. This example demonstrates how the skills of the frontline manager in discerning the action from the details of the problem that would persuade other constituents as to its appropriateness. By constituting the problem as critical, the frontline manager, who normally does not have the authority to pull the shuttle down on the bank earlier than the expected closing time, would convince others (even his/her superior) that such an action is warranted. These examples demonstrate that the problem in its context constrains how the problem can be best construed and, consequently, the efficacy of its resolution.

5. National Culture

Fifth, this model considers the *national culture* in influencing the depiction of problem types. In Malaysia's case, where power distance is one of the highest, if not the highest, in the world, followers respect leaders who exhibit symbolic prominence associated with a high-power status. Power distance is conceptualised (Hofstede, 2001; House et al., 2004) as the degree to which less powerful individuals in institutions and organisations within a country anticipate and recognise unequal power sharing. It concerns whether the followers as well as the leaders accept a society's injustice or discrimination of power. Malaysians are familiar with various power symbols, such as the King bestowing awards on individuals with prestigious titles such as "Tan Sri," and luxury cars as status symbols. Offices of very important people are usually on higher floors of a building and elaborate displays of pomp and music are often expect during the entrance of very important people during official functions.

Followers in such high-power-distance country tend to prefer autocratic leaders to provide instructions and commands. In societies with a high-power distance, the lower ranked individual will invariably yield to the higher ranked person, which they will accept as the normal social order. The higher-level individual acknowledges this fact as well and often imposes penalties for non-compliance. In contrast, in low-power-distance societies all want their views to be heard, regardless of rank or context. They will oppose or disagree with leaders they consider to be autocratic or patronising. What makes power distance unique in Asian context is that it is embedded in firmly ingrained beliefs in the broader society, making it far more difficult to change. This suggests an inclination for the leader in a high-power-distance society to construe problems as critical, which, in turn, followers willingly comply with execution directives. In such cases, subordinates in high-power-distance countries are more hesitant to criticise their bosses than workers in low-power-distance countries.

Although Malaysia is an extreme example in the region, it is far from alone. A brief look at other countries in the region's power distance index shows similarly high levels: The Philippines (Rodriguez, 2008), Indonesia (Irawanto, 2009), and Japan (Chew & Putti, 1995) are also high-power-distance societies. Similarly, autocratic decision-making in these societies is likely to be embraced and expected. Decision makers in high-power-distance countries use more rules and restrictions and depend less on subordinates' expertise in coping with daily activities than do decision makers in more egalitarian countries (Smith et al., 2002). This indicates that in a society with a high-power distance, such as Malaysia, the propensity to conceptualise issues as critical is amplified by the national culture.

6. Organisational Culture

Sixth, beside the national culture, the *organisational culture* also plays a role in influencing how problems are conceptualised. The claim here is that organisational cultures tend to shun or disincline decision makers to construe wicked problems. The way to understand the relationship between the new leadership model and organisational culture is to follow Keith Grint's application of Mary Douglas' conceptualisation of culture on two dimensions. Mary Douglas (2003) concluded that most organisational cultures could be captured using only two distinct criteria: grid and group. The concept of grid describes how important responsibilities and policies are in organisational culture; others are very strict, such as in a government bureaucracy, while some are very lax or liberal, such as in a casual club. The concept of *group* refers to how important a group is in a culture; certain societies

Figure 4. Four cultural types

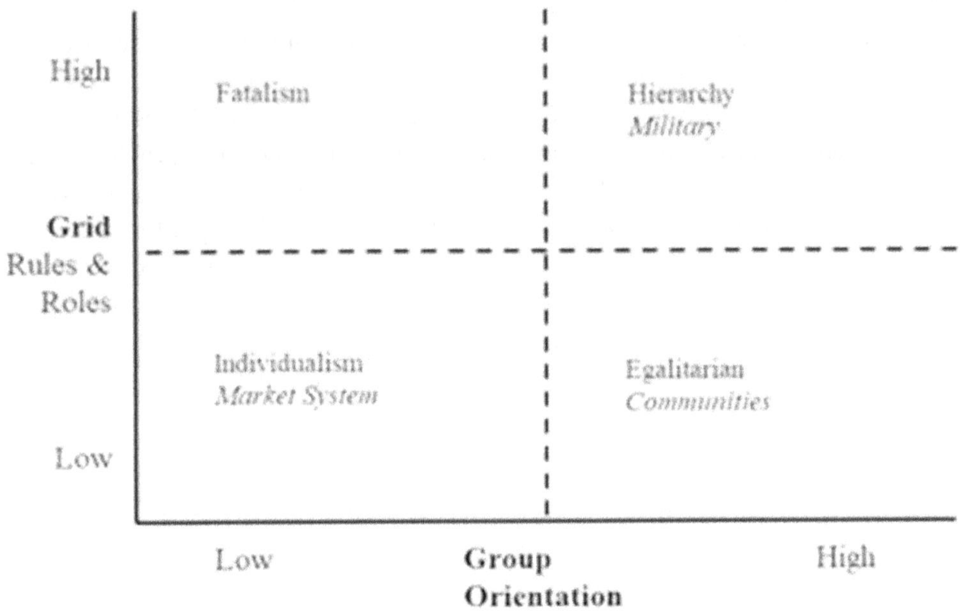

are entirely centred on the group, such as an online gaming team, while others are more independently focused, such as a meeting of individual academicians. This can be illustrated in a matrix using the two dimensions as shown in Figure 4.

As shown in Figure 4, the military is a type of organisation that embodies both a High Grid and a High Group *hierarchy* cultural configuration. In the military context, obedience to commands is expected. *Hierarchists* see the universe through a clear chain of command, and conflicts are seen as examples of a lack of proper order or their implementation of strictures. Therefore, for organisations with this type of culture, problems tend to be of the critical type, because critical problems required quick decision actions. An *egalitarian* culture exists in an ethos that has a high group focused, but deficiencies with respect to rules, regulations, and control, as reflect in the low grid. This is exemplified by such organisations where the group meeting is important and the quest for unity and harmony is crucial. Egalitarians are excellent at starting dialogues and meetings, but not very good at making decisions, and such decisions are often susceptible to herd instinct and groupthink. However, for the *individualist* culture, where the grid-score is low, and this is balanced by an equivalent low group orientation, individual ideas and freedom of expression have free reign. Rules and regulations are perceived as unnecessary constrains to such autonomy as free expression of ideas and opinions is preferred in this culture. Finally, the *fatalist* culture is where group orientation is absent, but the individuals consist of alienated individuals who feel that the forces at work are undermining them. Grint (2008) asserts that the fatalists have given up hope and remain subjugated to their fate. They tend to follow the leading of others and be subservient to their influence by being passive.

According to Grint (2008), although individualism and hierarchy cultures are suitable for addressing tame and critical problems, *none* of the four cultural types are suitable for addressing wicked problems. The reason is obvious for the individualism culture because, for example, when confronted with a tame or critical problem where the solutions to the problem are known, because the same problem has occurred and been resolved in a previous time. A manager, then, needs only to put the necessary processes and procedures in place to rationally resolve the problems; or a commander needs only to issue a firm directive for a critical problem. Similarly, in a hierarchy culture, for example, a critical problem needs only more rules and directives from a commander to sufficiently address it; or a tame problem needs the right process or standard operating procedures.

However, for wicked problems, none of the four cultural types are appropriate to offer a sufficient fit. The answers cannot come from the fatalism culture because decision makers do not see themselves capable of overcoming the constraints of their limitations. Whether imaginary or otherwise, cynicism of the fatalistic decision maker paralyses the organisation. Furthermore, the solutions for wicked problems cannot come from the egalitarian culture, because as Grint (2008) suggests, the egalitarian culture does not offer diversified enough solutions to resolve wicked problems due to its susceptibility to group conformance. Where group orientation is high, decision makers are unwilling to challenge group norms or offer contrarian perspectives. Novel and intractable problems also cannot be resolved by directives in a hierarchy culture. The novelty of the wicked problem denies the commander of the confidence to persuasively make a firm decision to convince constituents. Furthermore, the individualists cannot solve wicked problems alone. Therefore, the organisational culture types will tend to favour either a tame or critical problem construction, but not wicked problem construction. Similar to the disinclination towards wicked problems in our discussion of national culture, the influence of organisational cultures on the construction of problem also disinclines the depiction of problems away from wicked problems towards critical problem construction as depicted in Figure 5.

Figure 5. Influence of organisational culture

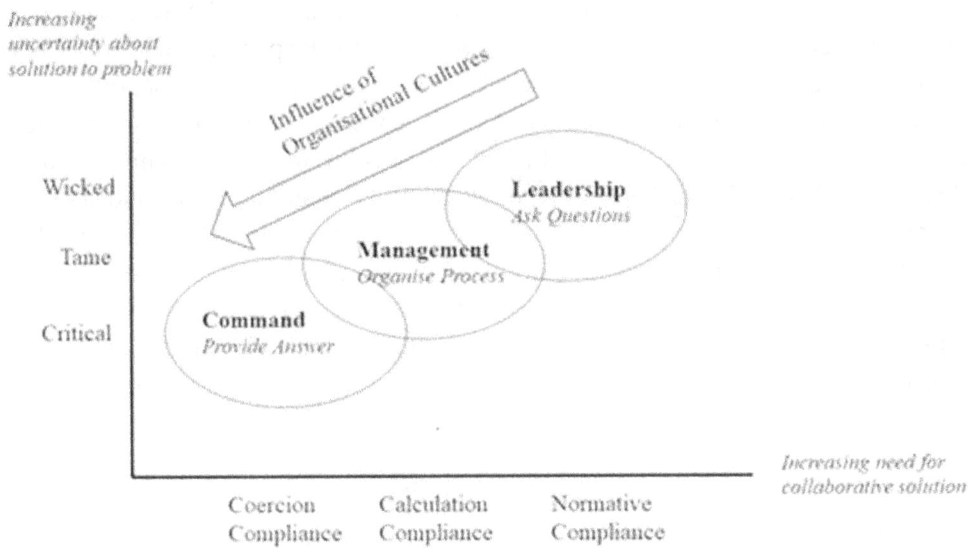

7. Media Influence

Lastly, the *media* plays a role in further disinclining wicked problem depiction. It is always in the media's best interests to portray issues as disasters in order to sell more copy and thereby increase advertising prices. For example, the H1N1 flu virus was depicted by the news media in a manner, which sounded an alarm of an emergency.

Research indicates that the media closely scrutinised any development connected with the H1N1 flu virus and emphasized the dangers over precautionary steps that could be taken to mitigate threats (Klemm et al., 2016). The sheer quantity of coverage, and a biased focused on the existential threat of H1N1, unwittingly misrepresented to the public a heightened risk perception. For instance, at one point, the *Daily Express* predicted (exaggeratedly) that the British National Health Service would be brought to a halt by the flu, overwhelming health service providers (Grint, 2010). Despite the fact that less people seemed to have died from the H1N1 flu than the other types of seasonal flu (which did not receive any media coverage), the paper predicted widespread infection and death, which did not happen. Details on the nature of and vulnerability to H1N1, such as references to the risk of hospitalisation or death, the transmission of the flu virus, and death statistics, were to great extent the most common themes of H1N1 news reports across countries and studies. Klemm et al.'s (2016) findings are consistent with previous studies that showed that a disproportionate volume of media coverage along such themes contributed to risk overestimation and public anxiety.

A similar phenomenon can be observed in the media's depiction of climate change (Mazur & Lee, 1993). The point is, such doomsday tales boost media sales and inadvertently promote a widespread expectation by the population to search for a leader as a saviour to resolve the depicted crisis (as was explained about followers' unconscious attraction for autocratic leaders). The media, to sell more, predisposed people to the construction of critical problems thus reinforcing the same trend as illustrated in Figure 5. Furthermore, there is a link between the media and society; what sells in the media is precisely due to what society demands. This means that people in the society are drawn to, consumed by, and demand crises (Grint, 2010), and media capitalises on this. This brings us back full circle to the unconscious attraction of followers (people in society) to a protective father figure (a commander) to resolve crises.

A CASE STUDY: COVID-19 AS A WICKED PROBLEM IN MALAYSIA

This case study focuses on the recent global Coronavirus of the 2019 (COVID-19) pandemic and how the government of Malaysia approached the problem. The purpose of this case study is to demonstrate how the social construction of the problem of COVID-19 in Malaysia influenced how the problem was tackled. By situating the pandemic within the Grint's (2020) model of leadership, a better perspective is gained on leadership. This is to demonstrate the applicability of the model to a specific current issue in the author's own home country. The purpose is not so much to establish generalisability of the Grint's model (although it contributes toward this) since the social construction of wicked problem has been generalised to different fields and contexts. For instances, it has recently been applied in the analysis of problems related to corporate social responsibility (Reinecke & Ansari, 2016), sweatshops conditions (Khan & Teicher, 2020), agriculture and pollution (Lintern et al., 2020), and sustainability (Teicher & Khan, 2020).

The pandemic first emerged in China during December 2019, which was confirmed by the World Health Organisation (WHO) a month later. The pandemic challenges not just both countries and their governments, but also leadership theory. In a world turned upside down, where many conventions have been abandoned, business as usual is unlikely to be restored anytime soon. The abrupt outbreak of the virus in 213 countries (Shah et al., 2020) devastated the global economy. This virus caused a wide array of respiratory and non-respiratory symptoms (Rothan & Byrareddy, 2020). Infection symptoms, such as fever, exhaustion, dry cough, myalgia, and dyspnoea are the most frequent symptoms observed within the first 2–14 days of being infected (Wang et al., 2020). Around 80% of patients experience and recover from mild infections. The remaining patients have extreme dyspnoea and low blood oxygen saturation infections, or they may be in a critical state of cardiac or multiple organ failures (Shah et al., 2020). Its severe global proliferation rate prompted the WHO to announce an urgent call for public health emergencies (Wu & McGoogan, 2020).

In Malaysia, the COVID-19 pandemic (Elengoe, 2020) began with two confirmed cases daily and accelerated rapidly to new record of more than 5,700 confirmed cases on January 29, 2021, which brought the cumulative number of cases since the pandemic hit the country to more than 203,000 cases and 733 deaths (Zainul, 2021). (The number of confirmed cases peaked at 9,020 on May 29, 2021 at the time of this publication.) After two rounds of restrictive movement control orders (MCOs) nationwide, the resurgence of the virus has prompted actions by the Malaysian government to enforce a third round of movement control order (MCO3.0) (Zack, 2021). Between the first and the third MCO, a cacophonic range of restrictions, standard operating procedures (SOP), and strategies were planned and announced to the public, amidst much confusion and complaints from the public (Wong, 2020). However, by reconsidering how governments and their representatives react to the outbreak of the epidemic, it is possible to achieve a greater understanding of how the pandemic can be handled, using the Grint's (2020) model.

The government's initial response was to consider the COVID-19 pandemic as a *critical* problem. Critical problems are emergencies that need a commander to coerce followers into line to avert an impending disaster—thus forcing schools and businesses to close for the near future, and banning travel are examples of such decision-making (Hassan, 2020). Ordering businesses to close without considering the greater economic impact exhibits decisiveness of the command type. Being decisive can also mean being decisively mistaken, because professional advice was not sought on the consequences of such actions. Given the novelty of the issue, even professional advice is not sufficient or offer limited help. However, over time, attempts to curtail the spread of the virus has resulted in new problems such as economic devastation, especially among those in small and medium enterprises (Foo et al, 2020), psychological distresses among the population (Sundarasen et al., 2020; Wong & Alias 2021) panic buying, and fluctuations in food prices (Arafat et al., 2020; Yau et al., 2020), and political turmoil (Case, 2021).

Consequentially, a shift in government focus is observed where competing factors and contributions from various stakeholders were considered in the decision-making. This suggests that in the later reactions to the pandemic, the government considered the pandemic as a *wicked* problem. Wicked problems are novel and complicated, may not be resolved easily, but may be ameliorated by a multi-stakeholder concerted approach. The role of those in leadership is to unite the people (followers), mostly to discuss challenges they would rather not confront, and make difficult trade-offs. As a collective effort, this could be seen in the attempts to persuade groups to stay at home, follow SOP, and to self-isolate (The Straits Times, 2020), as well as the "relaxed" nature of SOP to consider "livelihood" of the citizens (Tan, 2021). The roles of the authorities as leaders is to bring diverse groups on board to support one another whenever possible, and to allow them to confront the restrictions, take responsibilities for actions such as social distancing and self-quarantining, while ensuring that these choices are made equitably and without blaming others. The reality may be that Malaysians will have to live with the pandemic for the long term, and Malaysians will have to face this reality collectively finding trade-offs in collective decision-making and in responsibility-taking. This form of distributed leadership will serve the people better in tackling the COVID-19 pandemic.

The arrival of COVID-19 has no doubt turned the world upside down. Until the situation stabilises, the way in which problems are solved will not be the same. The pandemic has shown the drawbacks of how humanity tends to address problems as *critical* when what confronts us are, in fact, *wicked* problems. And it seems that in times of chaos, followers tend to seek out charismatic leaders or authoritarian leaders who, supposedly, will defuse the crisis either by being optimistic or simply denying the facts, regardless of how perplexing the problem might be. However, the author has indicated in preceding sections that the tendency is disproportionately predisposed towards construing the problem as a critical one, no doubt contributed by our media depiction of the issue and our national culture that favours an autocratic response.

In the next section, two weaknesses of the Grint's (2020) model are addressed, which includes a lack of supporting organisational culture for solving wicked problems, and the need for followers as co-constructors in leadership in solving wicked problems. By having an organisational culture and followers who are attuned towards solving wicked problems, it is the hope that the trend toward critical problem can at least be attenuated.

AN INTEGRATIVE FRAMEWORK OF LEADERSHIP

In the preceding sections, it was demonstrated how Grint (2007) revitalised the original framework established by Rittel and Webber in 1973 that locates and defines problems as *wicked, tame*, or *critical,* and the three modes of decision-making as *leadership, management,* and *command*, respectively. It has also been demonstrated that there is no good fit between the model of *organisational culture* and wicked problems. Furthermore, it is demonstrated that there is a tendency in society and among *followers* to prefer critical problem depictions. In this section, an integrated framework of leadership is proposed to address that these two weaknesses. First, two models are introduced as viable options for integration into Grint's (2007) model, and then the integration of the two models with the Grint's (2007) model is presented.

Firstly, the author proposes that the model of organisational culture that best addresses the goodness of fit with the Rittel and Webber (1973) framework is the competing values framework. Robert Quinn and John Rohrbaugh (1983) developed the competing values framework (CVF) in 1983. It examines leadership behaviour and how those behaviour leads to competences, as well as how such competencies contribute to organisational performance. Quinn and Rohrbaugh discovered that successful businesses could balance two competing factors: *focus* and *stability*. Some companies were successful when they concentrated on internal operations, while others were successful when they retained a favourable external positioning. Some organisations were successful because of their versatility and adaptability, while others were successful because of their continuity and stability. Along these two factors, four cultural types can be discerned.

The *market* culture shows organisations attempting to respond to emerging market demands. Adapting to the market mechanisms is one way to create successful organisations. Externally based, these organisations search for ways to compete, influence, and achieve a strategic edge over competitors. Market cultures are always aggressive, have an external focus, and are motivated by performance. In market cultures, leaders are always hard-driving rivals who are constantly looking for ideas and innovation to capture more market share.

Hierarchy culture is internally focused and guided by authority and order. It has a regimented and formalised work environment. The organization's leadership has a long-term view of the organisation as a predictable, cohesive system with clear guidelines and structured policies. As in Max Weber's original view of bureaucracy (Waters & Waters, 2015), the hierarchy culture has an approach to order and regulation of the organisation that flows from a strict chain of command. Position and authority are respected in hierarchies. Policies, methods, and protocols are often well defined.

Clans, in comparison to hierarchies, often have flatter organisations, with individuals and teams acting more independently. This is a people-oriented culture where workers are encouraged to share about themselves, executives are often viewed as peers, and professional growth and fulfilment are prioritised. Risk taking is rarer; the lack of stability and adaptability of this form of organisation is a disadvantage. They have an inner outlook and a sense of family, and members work well together, motivated by a deep sense of commitment to one another and a common goal. Rules exist, even though they are often unwritten, and they are often shared and instilled socially. Leaders in clan culture serve as facilitators and supporters, and they can even adopt a parental role.

Finally, *adhocracy* culture thrives in wicked problems. According to Grint, Douglas's (2003) cultural framework does not offer a good fit for handling wicked problems. In contrast, the adhocracy culture based on CVF offers the right fit. Adhocracy is externally orientated, intensely creative, and adaptable. Firms with this kind of culture enjoy taking risk-taking. The firm's growth is fuelled by innovative thinking and diversity. This form of organisational culture is adaptable; it has the internal resources to rebuild itself in times of instability. Adhocracy culture has much more autonomy and versatility than clan culture, which is important in today's fast-paced market environment. Whereas commercial growth favours those who can adapt quickly, an adhocracy will quickly shape teams to meet new obstacles. Visionary, creative capitalists who take reasonable risks to make major gains are the leaders of an adhocracy. These businesses are connected by their need to innovate, develop, and create quickly. As a result, they are impulsive, entrepreneurial, and driven to come up with fresh ideas and find new ways to succeed. While these organisations will grow quickly, they will have little control of their activities and will face more volatile situations than organisations with other cultural forms. Figure 6 provides a representation of the CVF model.

Secondly, the model of *followership* that avoids the dispositional tendency favouring a command mode of decision-making is Kelly's (1988) effective follower model. Many leaders, at various stages in their careers and often at all hours of the working day, play both leadership and follower roles, but not equally well. Leadership role is glamorous and draws a lot of interest. However, most of us are more often followers than leaders. As a result, followership is very much a part of our lives in organisations, but does not figure large in our thoughts. Consequently, our overemphasis on leadership prevents us from understanding the essence and significance of the roles of the follower. Kelly (1988) offers a useful guide to understand followership. Kelly's model has two dimensions. One dimension assesses autonomous, critical, and logical thinking as practised by followers. The other

Figure 6. Competing value framework

dimension is based on how passive or aggressive they are. Five types of followership are identified in the resulting model by Kelly, shown in Figure 7.

The *sheep* followers lack initiative and sense of duty and are passive and uncritical. According to Kelly, sheep complete the tasks assigned to them and then stop. *Yes people* followers are livelier, but they are also less enterprising. They can be fiercely deferential, even servile, when they are reliant on a leader for motivation. Leaders with poor judgement and self-confidence like *yes people* and tend to form partnerships with them, which can suffocate the organisation. *Alienated* followers are logical and independent thinkers who are passive in their task execution. Everything shuts them off at some point. They are often pessimistic and eventually fall into disgruntled acquiescence, and they seldom directly criticise a leader's initiatives. *Survivors* are in the middle. They are still sampling the wind and living by the motto "better safe than sorry." They have a knack for adapting to change. Like the Chinese bamboo, they bend with the wind, and resist taking risks and being too critical or active.

Finally, there are the *effective* followers, shown in the upper right-hand corner of the model in Figure 7, who think for themselves and carry out their roles and responsibilities with enthusiasm and confidence. Grint (2007, 2008) concludes that followers are addicted to and have proclivity for crisis and command, which hinders efforts to properly solve wicked problems. However, the *effective* followers in Kelly's model avoid such addictive tendencies because they are risk takers, self-starters, and independent problem solvers. Effective followers are independent, critical thinkers who temper their allegiances towards leaders and the firm to meet the demands of the organisation—or they find new ones. Effective followers understand how to harness the energy of deep engagement in ways that meet both organisational goals and the personal desires of their leaders. Effective followers address wicked problems well.

Figure 7. Model of effective follower

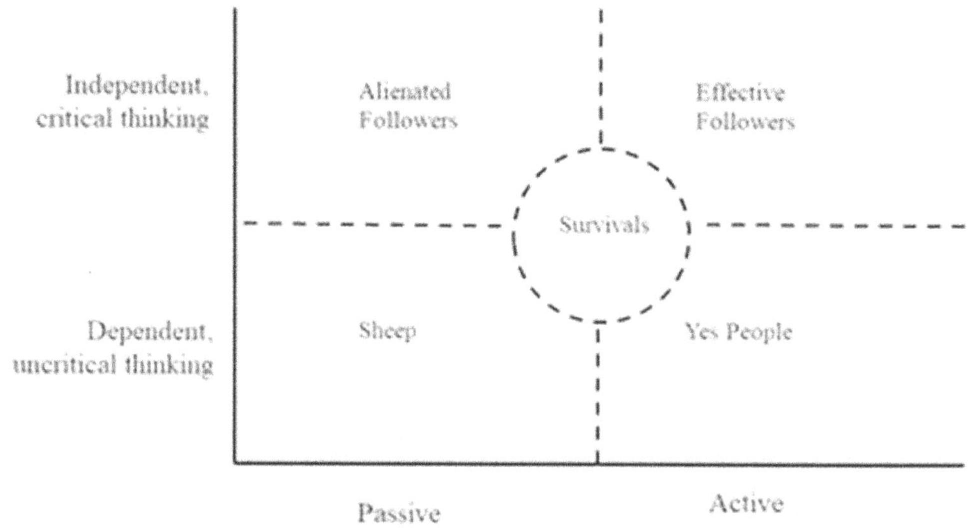

The CVF model and *effective follower* model can be integrated into the Rittel and Webber (1973) paradigm to offer a robust combination. In terms of CVF, the hierarchy culture is obviously a natural match for critical problems and the command approach to problem solving. The market and clan tradition are well suited to dealing with tamed challenges and management decision-making. In the market culture, managing the needs and demands of consumers provide a clear focus for what the managers must do. Similarly, in a clan culture, the needs of the organisational members are the main motivation of the managers. While the previous cultural paradigm by Mary Douglas (2003) does not gel well with the leadership mode in solving wicked problems, the *adhocracy culture* does. Adhocracy culture has the capacity to untangle uncertainty and is comfortable handling insecurity. Since adaptability and versatility are its core strengths, it has better capacity to make sense of uncertainty and volatility. Success in an adhocracy culture is defined by the ability to invent and adapt to extraordinary circumstances. This fits well with solving wicked problems that require concerted collaborative efforts from diverse stakeholders.

To address the second weakness, Kelly's (1988) model is adopted. Followers need to move beyond a passive acceptance of leadership influence or what Popper (2012) suggests, an "unconscious attraction" for autocratic leaders. In contrast, the *effective followers* as described by Kelly (1988) are trustworthy, truthful, and courageous, and do not blindly submit to authority. They develop themselves as critical thinkers who can be trusted with their experience and judgement. They offer credit where credit is due, acknowledging their errors and celebrating their own and their leader's successes. They shape their own opinions and ethical values, and are willing to stand up for what they believe in. This depiction of the followers again fits well with Grint's (2007, 2008) constructionist approach that distinguishes the followers as co-constructors of leadership, rather than passive receivers. The integrated model proposed here demonstrates how leadership, effective followers, and the adhocracy culture in which their relationship thrives, will come into mutual interaction to offer greater flexibility in addressing wicked problems both within the organisations and in society in general. As the problems confront the organisations and the world become more complex, there will be more problems that lend themselves more towards the wicked type. This implies a need for a more comprehensive model of leadership that integrates the aspect of followership, organisational culture, and leadership for solving wicked problems. This is what the author has attempted in this chapter. A representation of the integrated framework is shown in Figure 8.

Figure 8. Integrative framework of leadership

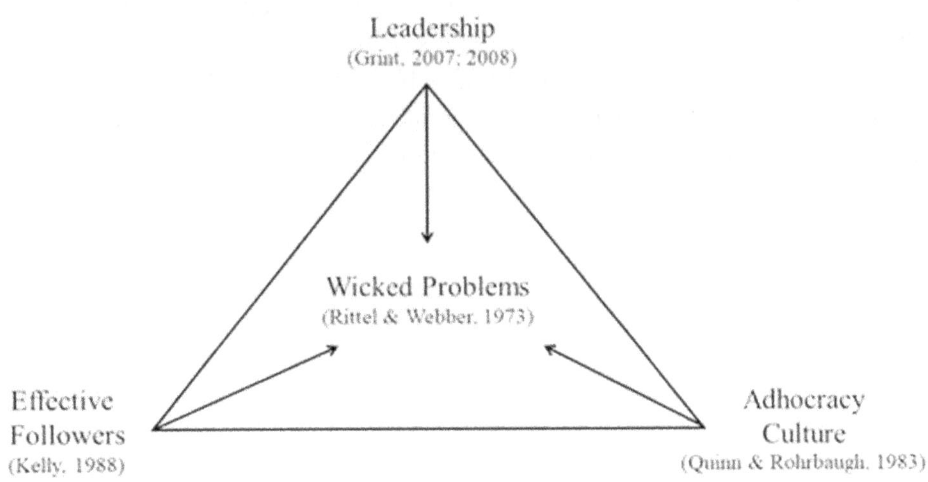

FUTURE RESARCH DIRECTIONS

The integrative framework addresses two areas of weaknesses in relation to Grint's model. Future studies should apply appropriate case study research in theory building and theory testing while considering boundary conditions of the framework. For theory building, case study research is appropriate to address the what and how questions. For examples: How exactly do effective followers aid leaders in handling wicked problems within an adhocracy organizational culture? What are the boundary conditions? For theory testing, case study research is appropriate to address the predictive bearing of the theory. Antecedences of the integrative framework such as psychological states and behaviors of leaders, followers, and other constituents, and events can be considered in forecasting short-term and long-term casual relationships.

CONCLUSION

In this chapter the author has elucidated Grint's (2007, 2008) model of leadership as a viable option in this complex world. By locating the model within a social constructionist frame, the author demonstrated how far humanity has come in the evolving stream of leadership research. Seven main characteristics of Grint's model of leadership were fleshed out to demonstrate how the model helps humanity to understand wicked problems like the COVID-19 pandemic in Malaysia. Along the way, two weaknesses of Grint's model were identified: (1) organisational culture, and (2) followership. To address the two weaknesses, the author proposed an integrated model of leadership that combined the understanding of an adhocracy culture based on the competing value framework and Kelly's (1988) effective followership model. In conclusion, this research into the integrative framework of leadership offers future leadership researchers a model with more explanatory power in understanding the leadership phenomenon as a social construction.

REFERENCES

Adair, J. (2013). *Confucius on Leadership*. Pan Macmillan.

Antonakis, J., & Day, D. V. (2018). Leadership: Past, present, and future. In The nature of leadership (pp. 3-26). Sage Publication.

Antonakis, J., Day, D. V., & Schyns, B. (2012). Leadership and individual differences: At the cusp of a renaissance. *The Leadership Quarterly*, *4*(23), 643–650. doi:10.1016/j.leaqua.2012.05.002

Arafat, S. Y., Kar, S. K., Menon, V., Kaliamoorthy, C., Mukherjee, S., Alradie-Mohamed, A., Sharma, P., Marthoenis, M., & Kabir, R. (2020). Panic buying: An insight from the content analysis of media reports during COVID-19 pandemic. *Neurology, Psychiatry & Brain Research, 37*, 100–103. doi:10.1016/j.npbr.2020.07.002 PMID:32834528

Ayman, R., & Lauritsen, M. (2018). Contingencies, context, situation, and leadership. In J. Antonakis & D. V. Day (Eds.), *The nature of leadership* (pp. 138–166). Sage Publications. doi:10.4135/9781506395029.n6

Bass, B. M. (1990). From transactional to transformational leadership: Learning to share the vision. *Organizational Dynamics, 18*(3), 19–31. doi:10.1016/0090-2616(90)90061-S

Case, W. (2021, January 31). *Pulling apart Malaysia's pandemic politics.* East Asia Forum. https://www.eastasiaforum.org/2021/01/31/pulling-apart-malaysias-pandemic-politics/

Chan, K. Y., & Drasgow, F. (2001). Toward a theory of individual differences and leadership: Understanding the motivation to lead. *The Journal of Applied Psychology, 86*(3), 481–498. doi:10.1037/0021-9010.86.3.481 PMID:11419808

Chew, I. K. H., & Putti, J. (1995). Relationship on work-related values of Singaporean and Japanese managers in Singapore. *Human Relations, 48*(10), 1149–1170. doi:10.1177/001872679504801003

Çitaku, F., & Ramadani, H. (2020). Leadership Competency Model-Drenica: Generalizability of Leadership Competencies. *International Journal of Organizational Leadership, 9*(3), 152–162.

Cortina, J. M., Köhler, T., Keeler, K. R., & Pugh, S. D. (2020). Situation strength as a basis for interactions in psychological models. *Psychological Methods.* https://doi-org.ezproxy.sunway.edu.my/10.1037/met0000372

Csikszentmihalyi, M. (2000). *Flow: The psychology of optimal experience.* Harper & Row.

Dansereau, F. (1995). A dyadic approach to leadership: Creating and nurturing this approach under fire. *The Leadership Quarterly, 6*(4), 479–490. doi:10.1016/1048-9843(95)90022-5

Day, D. V. (2014). Introduction: Leadership and organizations. In D. V. David (Ed.), *The Oxford handbook of leadership and organizations* (pp. 3–12). Oxford University Press.

De Vries, R. E. (2012). Personality predictors of leadership styles and the self–other agreement problem. *The Leadership Quarterly, 23*(5), 809–821. doi:10.1016/j.leaqua.2012.03.002

Douglas, M. (2003). *Natural symbols*. Routledge. (Original work published 1970)

Elengoe, A. (2020). COVID-19 outbreak in Malaysia. *Osong Public Health and Research Perspectives, 11*(3), 93–100. doi:10.24171/j.phrp.2020.11.3.08 PMID:32494567

Etzioni. (1964). *Modern organizations*. Prentice Hall.

Fairhurst, G. T., & Grant, D. (2010). The social construction of leadership: A sailing guide. *Management Communication Quarterly, 24*(2), 171–210. doi:10.1177/0893318909359697

Fiedler, F. E. (1981). Leadership effectiveness. *The American Behavioral Scientist, 24*(5), 619–632. doi:10.1177/000276428102400503

Foo, L. P., Chin, M. Y., Tan, K. L., & Phuah, K. T. (2020). The impact of COVID-19 on tourism industry in Malaysia. *Current Issues in Tourism*, 1–5. doi:10.1080/13683500.2020.1777951

Graen, G. B., & Uhl-Bien, M. (1995). Relationship-based approach to leadership: Development of leader-member exchange (LMX) theory of leadership over 25 years: Applying a multi-level multi-domain perspective. *The Leadership Quarterly, 6*(2), 219–247. doi:10.1016/1048-9843(95)90036-5

Grint, K. (2005). Problems, problems, problems: The social construction of 'leadership'. *Human Relations, 58*(11), 1467–1494. doi:10.1177/0018726705061314

Grint, K. (2007). *Leadership, management, and command: Rethinking D-Day*. Springer.

Grint, K. (2008). Wicked problems and clumsy solutions: The role of leadership. *Clinical Leader, 1*(2), 11–25.

Grint, K. (2010). The cuckoo clock syndrome: Addicted to command, allergic to leadership. *European Management Journal, 28*(4), 306–313. doi:10.1016/j.emj.2010.05.002

Grint, K. (2020). Leadership, management and command in the time of the Coronavirus. *Leadership, 16*(3), 314–319. doi:10.1177/1742715020922445

Harms, P. D., Wood, D., Landay, K., Lester, P. B., & Lester, G. V. (2018). Autocratic leaders and authoritarian followers revisited: A review and agenda for the future. *The Leadership Quarterly*, *29*(1), 105–122. doi:10.1016/j.leaqua.2017.12.007

Hassan, H. (2020, March 17). *Malaysia bans travel abroad, shuts schools and businesses over coronavirus spread; lockdown till March 31*. The Straits Times. https://www.straitstimes.com/asia/se-asia/malaysia-to-impose-lockdown-from-wednesday-to-march-31

Hofstede, G. (2001). *Culture's consequences: Comparing values, behaviors, institutions and organizations across nations*. Sage publications.

House, R. J. (1971). A path goal theory of leader effectiveness. *Administrative Science Quarterly*, *16*(3), 321–339. doi:10.2307/2391905

House, R. J., Hanges, P. J., Javidan, M., Dorfman, P. W., & Gupta, V. (Eds.). (2004). *Culture, leadership, and organizations: The GLOBE study of 62 societies*. Sage Publications.

Irawanto, D. W. (2009). An analysis of national culture and leadership practices in Indonesia. *Journal of Diversity Management*, *4*(2), 41–48. doi:10.19030/jdm.v4i2.4957

Junker, N. M., & Van Dick, R. (2014). Implicit theories in organizational settings: A systematic review and research agenda of implicit leadership and followership theories. *The Leadership Quarterly*, *25*(6), 1154–1173. doi:10.1016/j.leaqua.2014.09.002

Kelly, R. E. (1988). In praise of followers, in Managing People and Organizations. *Harvard Business Review*.

Klemm, C., Das, E., & Hartmann, T. (2016). Swine flu and hype: A systematic review of media dramatization of the H1N1 influenza pandemic. *Journal of Risk Research*, *19*(1), 1–20. doi:10.1080/13669877.2014.923029

Kotter, J. P. (2001). What leaders really do. *Harvard Business Review*, *79*(11). PMID:10104518

Lewin, K., & Lippitt, R. (1938). An experimental approach to the study of autocracy and democracy: A preliminary note. *Sociometry*, *1*(3/4), 292–300. doi:10.2307/2785585

Lintern, A., McPhillips, L., Winfrey, B., Duncan, J., & Grady, C. (2020). Best Management Practices for Diffuse Nutrient Pollution: Wicked Problems Across Urban and Agricultural Watersheds. *Environmental Science & Technology*, *54*(15), 9159–9174. doi:10.1021/acs.est.9b07511 PMID:32644784

Lönngren, J., & Van Poeck, K. (2020). Wicked problems: A mapping review of the literature. *International Journal of Sustainable Development and World Ecology*, 1–22.

Lord, R. G., Day, D. V., Zaccaro, S. J., Avolio, B. J., & Eagly, A. H. (2017). Leadership in applied psychology: Three waves of theory and research. *The Journal of Applied Psychology*, *102*(3), 434–451. doi:10.1037/apl0000089 PMID:28125257

Mason, R., Asthana, A., & Stewart, H. (2016, July 6). Tony Blair: 'I express more sorrow, regret and apology than you can ever believe'. *The Guardian*. https://www.theguardian.com/uk-news/2016/jul/06/tony-blair-deliberately-exaggerated-threat-from-iraq-chilcot-report-war-inquiry

Mazur, A., & Lee, J. (1993). Sounding the global alarm: Environmental issues in the US national news. *Social Studies of Science*, *23*(4), 681–720. doi:10.1177/030631293023004003

Meindl, J. R. (1993). Reinventing leadership: A radical, social psychological approach. In J. K. Munighan (Ed.), *Social psychology in organizations: Advances in theory and research* (pp. 89–118). Prentice Hall.

Meindl, J. R. (1995). The romance of leadership as a follower-centric theory: A social constructionist approach. *The Leadership Quarterly*, *6*(3), 329–341. doi:10.1016/1048-9843(95)90012-8

Meindl, J. R., Ehrlich, S. B., & Dukerich, J. M. (1985). The romance of leadership. *Administrative Science Quarterly*, *30*(1), 78–102. doi:10.2307/2392813

Northouse, P. G. (2021). *Leadership: Theory and practice*. Sage Publications.

Noto, G., & Bianchi, C. (2015). Dealing with multi-level governance and wicked problems in urban transportation systems: The case of Palermo municipality. *Systems*, *3*(3), 62–80. doi:10.3390ystems3030062

Popper, M. (2012). *Fact and fantasy about leadership*. Edward Elgar Publishing. doi:10.4337/9780857936158

Quinn, R. E., & Rohrbaugh, J. (1983). A spatial model of effectiveness criteria: Towards a competing values approach to organizational analysis. *Management Science*, *29*(3), 363–377. doi:10.1287/mnsc.29.3.363

Reinecke, J., & Ansari, S. (2016). Taming wicked problems: The role of framing in the construction of corporate social responsibility. *Journal of Management Studies*, *53*(3), 299–329. doi:10.1111/joms.12137

Rittel, H. W., & Webber, M. M. (1973). Dilemmas in a general theory of planning. *Policy Sciences*, *4*(2), 155–169. doi:10.1007/BF01405730

Rodriguez, K. P. (2008). Apparel brand endorsers and their effects on purchase intentions: A study of Philippine consumers. *Philippine Management Review*, *15*(1), 83–99.

Rothan, H. A., & Byrareddy, S. N. (2020). The epidemiology and pathogenesis of coronavirus disease (COVID-19) outbreak. *Journal of Autoimmunity*, *109*, 102433–102438. doi:10.1016/j.jaut.2020.102433 PMID:32113704

Rush, M. C., Thomas, J. C., & Lord, R. G. (1977). Implicit leadership theory: A potential threat to the internal validity of leader behavior questionnaires. *Organizational Behavior and Human Performance*, *20*(1), 93–110. doi:10.1016/0030-5073(77)90046-0

Schyns, B., & Day, D. (2010). Critique and review of leader–member exchange theory: Issues of agreement, consensus, and excellence. *European Journal of Work and Organizational Psychology*, *19*(1), 1–29. doi:10.1080/13594320903024922

Seemiller, C., & Whitney, R. (2020). Creating a taxonomy of leadership competency development. *Journal of Leadership Education*, *19*(1).

Shah, A. U. M., Safri, S. N. A., Thevadas, R., Noordin, N. K., Abd Rahman, A., Sekawi, Z., Ideris, A., & Sultan, M. T. H. (2020). COVID-19 Outbreak in Malaysia: Actions Taken by the Malaysian Government. *International Journal of Infectious Diseases*, *97*, 108–116. doi:10.1016/j.ijid.2020.05.093 PMID:32497808

Simonet, D. V., & Tett, R. P. (2013). Five perspectives on the leadership–management relationship: A competency-based evaluation and integration. *Journal of Leadership & Organizational Studies*, *20*(2), 199–213. doi:10.1177/1548051812467205

Smith, P. B., Peterson, M. F., & Schwartz, S. H. (2002). Cultural values, sources of guidance, and their relevance to managerial behavior: A 47-nation study. *Journal of Cross-Cultural Psychology*, *33*(2), 188–208. doi:10.1177/0022022102033002005

Sundarasen, S., Chinna, K., Kamaludin, K., Nurunnabi, M., Baloch, G. M., Khoshaim, H. B., Hossain, S. F. A., & Sukayt, A. (2020). Psychological impact of COVID-19 and lockdown among university students in Malaysia: Implications and policy recommendations. *International Journal of Environmental Research and Public Health*, *17*(17), 6206. doi:10.3390/ijerph17176206 PMID:32867024

Tan, V. (2021, May 11). *MCO 3.0 not as strict as first lockdown, key is to balance health and livelihoods: Ismail Sabri.* The Channel News Asia. https://www.channelnewsasia. com/ news/asia/malaysia-covid-19-mco-3-0-not-strict-balance-health-livelihoods-14786172

Teicher, J., & Khan, S. I. (2020). Working in 'sweatshops': Outsourcing to developing nations. In P. Holland & C. Brewster (Eds.), *Contemporary Work and the Future of Employment in Developed Countries*. Routledge.

The Straits Times. (2020, December 29). *Malaysia advises asymptomatic patients to self-isolate at home.* https://www.straitstimes. com/asia/se-asia/malaysia-advises-asymptomatic-patients-to-self-isolate-at-home#:~:text=KUALA%20LUMPUR%20 %E2%80%A2%20Malaysia%20is,involving%20foreign%20workers%20are%20 surging

Wang, D., Hu, B., Hu, C., Zhu, F., Liu, X., Zhang, J., Wang, B., Xiang, H., Cheng, Z., Xiong, Y., Zhao, Y., Li, Y., Wang, X., & Peng, Z. (2020). Clinical characteristics of 138 hospitalized patients with 2019 novel coronavirus–infected pneumonia in Wuhan, China. *Journal of the American Medical Association, 323*(11), 1061–1069. doi:10.1001/jama.2020.1585 PMID:32031570

Waters, T., & Waters, D. (Eds.). (2015). *Weber's Rationalism and Modern Society*. Palgrave MacMillan.

Weisstub, E., & Galili-Weisstub, E. (2004). Collective trauma and cultural complexes. In The cultural complex: Contemporary Jungian perspectives on psyche and society. Bruner-Routledge.

Wong, C. W. (2020, October 22). *Malaysia govt's U-turns, confusion and double standards in Covid-19 fight.* The Straits Times. https://www.straitstimes.com/asia/se-asia/malaysia-govts-u-turns-confusion-and-double-standards-in-covid-19-fight

Wong, L. P., & Alias, H. (2021). Temporal changes in psychobehavioural responses during the early phase of the COVID-19 pandemic in Malaysia. *Journal of Behavioral Medicine, 44*(1), 18–28. doi:10.100710865-020-00172-z PMID:32757088

Wren, D. A., & Bedeian, A. G. (2020). *The evolution of management thought*. John Wiley & Sons.

Wu, Z., & McGoogan, J. M. (2020). Characteristics of and important lessons from the coronavirus disease 2019 (COVID-19) outbreak in China: Summary of a report of 72 314 cases from the Chinese Center for Disease Control and Prevention. *Journal of the American Medical Association, 323*(13), 1239–1242. doi:10.1001/jama.2020.2648 PMID:32091533

Yau, E. K. B., Ping, N. P. T., Shoesmith, W. D., James, S., Hadi, N. M. N., & Loo, J. L. (2020). The behaviour changes in response to COVID-19 pandemic within Malaysia. *The Malaysian Journal of Medical Sciences: MJMS, 27*(2), 45–50. doi:10.21315/mjms2020.27.2.5 PMID:32788840

Zack, J. (2021, May 10). *PM: Whole country under MCO from May 12-June 7.* The Star. https://www.thestar.com.my/news/nation/2021/05/10/pm-whole-country-under-mco-from-may-12-june-7

Zainul, E. (2021, Jan 29). *Malaysia's daily new cases hit new record.* The Edge. https://www.theedgemarkets.com/article/malaysias-daily-new-cases-hit-new-record-5725-cumulative-cases-surpass-200000mark

Zaleznik, A. (1977). Managers and leaders: Are they different. *Harvard Business Review*, 67–78. PMID:14723179

KEY TERMS AND DEFINITIONS

Adhocracy Culture: Adhocracy culture is an externally orientated, intensely creative, and high adaptable type of organizational culture.

Competing-Value Framework: This is an organisational culture framework which consists of a 2x2 matrix with two axes: High-low stability and Internal-external focus.

Critical Problem: A critical problem is a time-constrained problem that requires self-evident decisions or actions.

Effective Follower: An effective follower is an independent critical thinker who is actively engaged at work.

Social Construction of Leadership: This is the view that leadership is a social process of sense-making to solve problems where the leaders and followers are co-creators of meanings in a context.

Tame Problem: A tame problem is a non-unique problem with existing solutions.

Wicked Problem: A wicked problem is a novel problem which is often intractable. There is no obvious solutions or end point to the problem. The COVID-19 pandemic is an example of a wicked problem.

ENDNOTES

1 For good overviews of the trends in leadership research, see Antonakis et al. (2018), Day (2014), and Lord et al. (2017).

2 For a good overview of this resurgence of interests, see a dedicated issue on individual differences in leadership research, *The Leadership Quarterly*, Volume 24, Issue 1, February 2013.

Chapter 3
Leadership Style and Succession Planning

Paula Cristina Nunes Figueiredo
https://orcid.org/0000-0002-5267-546X
Universidade Lusófona de Humanidades e Tecnologias, Portugal

ABSTRACT

The main aim of the chapter is to identify the leadership style that promotes succession planning through the existence of leadership development practices within organizations. The middle and top leaders are very important to identify and develop new leaders within the organization. The authors reach three main conclusions: 1) The laissez-faire leadership style is related to the succession planning. Succession planning is positively influenced by leaders that adopt a passive leadership style. 2) There are some practices of leadership development that are related to the existence of succession planning in organizations. 3) The 360º feedback and coaching/executive coaching are related to the succession planning. These practices promote the human capital development, so it is assumed that succession planning may be related to the leader development. Theoretically they concluded that organizations should have a leadership pipeline in order to prepare leaders to assume leadership positions.

INTRODUCTION

Succession planning has been the focus of research since the 70s of the last century. This theme falls into two areas of knowledge - Human resources management and, increasingly, the business strategy. Succession planning promotes the human capital development and ensures continuity of the organization's strategy. Succession planning arises from the concern of several authors in finding ways to address the

DOI: 10.4018/978-1-7998-2807-5.ch003

shortage of leaders and the quality of leadership because that could jeopardize the organization's future (Erickson, 2010; Henderson & Provo, 2006; Ingraham, 2006; Manderscheid, 2008; Intagliata, Ulrich, & Smallwood, 2000). Succession planning is assumed as the identification of potential to assume greater responsibility in the organization, providing critical development experiences (Kowalewski, Moretti, & McGee, 2011). It is essential that leaders become involved in supporting the development of other leaders with high potential. Organizations need to create a database that can be used to make better staffing decisions for key jobs. At first sight, succession planning is associated with the selection of leaders, career development, talent management and leadership development. We intend to make an approach between the succession planning with leadership styles and leadership development. We believe that there are some styles that are concerned to promote succession planning within the organization by implementing leadership development practices. Therefore, the research question is: Is there any relationship between the leadership styles and succession planning within the organization?

Whereas the leadership development requires the implementation of some practices in the organization, it is also important to check whether there is a relationship between these practices and succession planning. Thus, the paper's aims are to identify the leadership style that promotes the succession planning and which practices of leadership development are used in a group of Portuguese companies in the service industry. The paper is structured into 6 parts and they are: i) Background; ii) Methodology; iii) Analysis and discussion of results; iv) Conclusions and Limitations; v) Implications; and, vi) Recommendations and Future researches.

BACKGROUND

Organizations have increasingly complex and demanding environments. Gareth Morgan, in his book *Images of organization*, seeks to better understand this environment, using metaphors. These reflect the daily life of organizations. This paper has underlying the metaphor of organizations as brains, where "*organizations are information-processing systems capable of learning to learn*" (Morgan, 1986, 80). In 1991, Peter Senge emerges with the approach of Learning Organizations. This gave rise to the proliferation of scientific studies, contributing to greater prominence of human resource development (HRD) in economic terms and organizational (Tomé, 2011). In organizational context, the HRD function is very important for the leadership development because it allows connection between corporate and business-unit strategies. Without this connection, high potentials can leave the organization for lack of opportunities. On the other hand, it is essential integrate the human resource systems with leadership development, as shown in *Figure 1*. There

Figure 1. Integrated Leadership Development Systems

is no development without strategic planning, succession planning, recruitment, and selection according to the organization's needs, a process of performance assessment, a plan for training and development of customized career.

The leader's role and leadership in organizations have been topics of several scientific studies. According to the leadership theories, several approaches have been made throughout time. Some researchers focused on the leader's role, seeking to answer the question: "*How can I be in effective leader?*" (Day, 2001, 605). The focus is on the leader's role in organizations and how it can make it more effective. Other researchers have a relational approach that is centered in the leadership process, seeking to answer the question: "*How can I participate productively in the leadership process?*" (Day, 2001, 605). The author did a literature review about leadership development, identifying differences between leadership development and leader development. For him, both approaches are incomplete (Day, 2001, 605).

Over recent years, the leadership development has proliferated in organizations, because several authors have been concerned with the impact of the reform and the departure of the leaders from the baby boomer generation, not only in North America but in Europe too. According to Ludwick, "*the impact on organization is going to be dramatic and leadership is going to increasingly important role in the success or failure of organizations of all types*" (Ludwick, 2007, 23). Corroborating the same ideas, Field states that "*a major demographic change is on the horizon, and if portends a leadership crisis for many organizations*" (Field, 2007, 3). According to the author, 50% of executives in the U.S. are being reformed in the next 5years. Therefore, the author is concerned with training and development of new leaders. According to many surveys, the CEO (Chief Executive Officer) succession is a matter of business continuity to Top20 Companies because "*95% have a CEO succession plan*" (Brant, Dooley, & Iman, 2008) and, "*59% of companies did not have succession planning processes sufficient to prepare internal candidates for critical appointments*" (Brant, Dooley, & Iman, 2008, 18). The importance of succession is not proportionate to the preparation of succession because "*48% say that they haven´t seen a copy of the succession plan within the last year*" (Pellet, 2008, 62). In this regard, there are two pressing issues. One is the leaders' succession, because organizations are still very connected to the leaders of the previous generation, in some cases, the founders themselves (O'Leary, 2009, 4). There are few organizations that have bothered to prepare the succession process. The other issue relates to the need to develop leadership within organizations, not only by the succession process, but also due to the emerging competitive environment. It is necessary to prepare leaders, developing their leadership skills so that they are better able to meet future challenges. Succession planning refers not only CEO' succession, but it must cover the team of leaders too - top and middle leaders. Throughout the evolution of this issue, there has been a shift in focus - from CEO to Team Leadership. In order to clarify the issue of succession planning, in the theoretical part is made an investigation and analysis of the concepts found in the literature.

Succession Planning

During the 70s to mid-90s of last century, the growth of globalization led to an increased focus by the top teams on differentiation strategy and the need for sustainable core competencies (Ready, 2002, 63). The development of new leaders was not a priority because it was a task of HR professionals and, in some organizations, it was the responsibility of specialized organizations. This approach was clearly inadequate and resulted in severe lack of effective leadership. Drotter says that is necessary to improve the leadership pipeline (Drotter, 2010, 11).

Throughout the evolution of succession planning, there has been a concentration "*on upper level management and today, companies are utilizing this planning for all levels of their organization*" (Kowalewski, Moretti, & McGee, 2011, 99). Further important issue that is found in the literature, it is the origin of the leaders. Goldsmith tells us that it depends on the organizations and the context. If the leader from the outside presents a high risk, then one should whenever possible develop the leader/successor internally (Goldsmith, 2009, 5). Through interviews with some CEOs of major global companies, it seems that most of them prefer an internal successor due to the importance of knowledge, history, and culture of the organization. They also emphasize that the development of leaders is an obligation of the CEO (Behan, Kirschner, & Snyder, 2009, 32). According to Brant *et al.* (2008, 17), leadership is the most critical factor in the success of any organization. In the several studies cited by the authors (Hewitt, 2005; Ritter, 2003, 2005; Rothwell, 2005) more than 50% of participating companies (some of them in the Top 20 USA Companies), state that: - succession planning is important for success and, companies prefer to train internally leaders, although not always have enough candidates. Another finding is that only 1% of HR executives considered "excellent" the succession process and 66% consider it "bad". More than 50% of HR executives believe that succession planning is important, but in practice, they identify some difficulties in the process. By them, CEOs and senior executives do not take responsibility for the succession process. They have to identify and prepare successors, aligning business strategy and succession planning (Brant *et al.*, 2008, 17).

Within the field of research, it is possible to find many papers on succession planning because there are several authors who care about this issue. Garman and Glawe claim that there is no solid study on succession planning case, there is a set of individual opinions based on experience. Regarding the state of art, it appears that the first literature review was published in 1994 and developed by Kesner and Sebora. The paper explores three stages of investigation: i) 1950s to 1960s - the emergence of the field; ii) 1970s - the development of theory and empirical investigation; and, iii) 1980s to 1994 - Explosive growth (Kesner & Sebora, 1994, 327). Thus, the paper reflects the foundations of succession literature, using the expressions *'Executive Succession'* and *'CEO transition/succession'*. The CEO succession planning is important; however, organizations have other leaders who need to be trained and prepared for the future. This is one of the criticisms of the early approaches about this theme. The latest streams of thought show that the capacity of the leadership is in the team (David Day, Gronn, & Salas, 2004), then the leadership must be focused on the team (Morgeson, DeRue, & Karam, 2010), because leadership influences the team performance (Zaccaro, Rittman, & Marks, 2001). Therefore, the team dynamics contribute to the concept of team leadership. For House and Aditya, team leadership refers to a distributed leadership - delegated leadership, co-leadership and peer leadership (House & Aditya, 1997, 440). Within the field of training and leadership development, the focus remains in team effectiveness (Santos, Caetano, & Tavares, 2015).

Giambatista, Rowe and Riaz made a critical review of the leader succession from 1994 to 2005 and they consider "*the use of existing organizational theory as well as the development of new unique theory to succession*" (Giambatista, Rowe, & Riaz, 2005, 980). According to them, the state of the art is fragmented and variable. Research has grown in the several areas of knowledge such as organizational theory, strategy, organizational behavior, and finance. This fragmentation leads to the need to read the documents of the several theories and researchers can get more comprehensive theoretical explanations (Giambatista, Rowe, & Riaz, 2005, 981).

Overall, the concept of succession planning has been used to describe "*a wide variety of activities involving the planning for key transitions in leadership within organizations*" (Garman & Glawe, 2004, 119). Recently, succession planning has been practiced routinely and systematically in several larger organizations and not just the top leaders. Succession planning is done on the levels below. Succession planning is not just finding a successor but having someone to develop skills and be available to rise to the level of top management. Organizations need to develop a superior leadership training; "*when succession planning is treated as a regular and structured process that's part of the board's agenda, it becomes a strategic process that's intimately related to performance and encompasses all mission-critical positions*" (Ludwick, 2007, 25). In *Table 1*, we show several concepts.

Table 1. Definitions of Succession Planning

Succession Planning is "*the use of a deliberate process to ensure that staff are developed who are able to replace senior management as required*" (Ludwick, 2007, 25).
Succession Planning is "*an ongoing dynamic process that assists a business or organization in aligning its goals and its human capital needs*" (Butler & Roche-Tarry, 2002 cited by Kowalewski *et al.*, 2011, 99).
Succession Planning "*involves the identification and development of potential successor in an organization*" (Kowalewski *et al.*, 2011, 99).
Succession Planning include "*identification of critical management positions within the organization, identification of future vacancies in those positions and identification of managers who would potentially fit into these vacancies*" (Orellano & Miller, 1997 cited by Kowalewski *et al.*, 2011, 100).
Succession Planning is a "*structured process involving the identification and preparation of a potential successor to assume a new role. By 'structured' we refer to a process having some reliable structure and/or custom, thereby excluding from the definition the more ad hoc or 'just in time' identification of successors*" (Garman & Glawe, 2004, 120).

The succession should be planned. The best practices of an organization not always result in good results in other organizations. The organization's context influences the succession process. Succession is an easier way to attract and retain talent and to enable the implementation of the strategy and the discovery of the weaknesses of the organization (Dutra & Griesedieck, 2010, 14). According to Goldsmith, there are ways to make more efficient succession. Succession Planning should be called Succession Development because the plan does not develop anyone and the focus should be on development and, the results should be measured instead of the process. This should have simple and realistic procedures (Goldsmith, 2009, 15). Succession planning has evolved in order to integrate talent management in many organizations (Garman & Glawe, 2004, 126). Similarly, Groves presents a paper that seeks to integrate the best practices in leadership development and succession planning (Groves, 2007, 241). The author establishes a model that shows how an integrated leadership development and succession planning process requires active participation manager. This model is based on the leadership development practices found in the literature review about leadership development, conducted by Day (2001).

Leadership Styles

In the past 50 years, researchers have focused on identifying the leadership styles, the characteristics or personality traits of great leaders (George, Sims, McLean, & Mayer, 2007, 1). Other authors have focused on the idea that it is possible to make a leader, through the development of competences (Goleman, 1998, 82). The concepts of leadership and leader have evolved over time with the emergence of new research and theories. Research is aimed at contributing to development of effective leadership. To better understand the generations' perceptions of what makes a leader effective Deal concluded that perceptions are very similar over time. All generations want their leaders to be considerate of others. "*All generations said effective leaders are participative, team-oriented, charismatic and humane oriented, and they are less sure that being hierarchical and autonomous makes a leader effective* (Deal, 2014, 66).

The researchers began by looking for the most effective leadership style to the stable environment of organizations. With the complexity and the constant need for change, the researchers begin to identify several leadership styles. Leaders begin to adapt their leadership style to situations and contexts. This perspective comes up with the situational theories and it is enhanced with the emotional element introduced by Boyatzis and Goleman (2000). Bass and Avolio include previous theories on components of Transactional Leadership while the charisma, social awareness and concern for others are part of the Transformational Leadership style (Avolio, Bass, & Jung, 1999; Bass, 1990, 1997; Bass & Avolio, 1993). The paradigm of transactional and transformational leadership is considered by Bass as universal because the same conception of the phenomenon can be observed in several organizations and cultures. In line with the Bass' theory, transformational and transactional leadership are distinct and complementary processes that can be used simultaneously in different situations by leader. Transformational leadership is mostly used at the beginning of the organization's activity and change's times and transactional leadership is used during times of slow evolution and stable environments (Cunha *et al.* 2006, 372). The model has evolved over time specifying in more detail the dimensions of leadership from transformational leadership to the laissez-faire or passive. The model defines the components that characterize each dimension and which items allow assessing the leadership style.

Transformational leadership refers to the process where leaders promote the commitment of followers and encourage them to overcome their personal interests on behalf of the organization's goals, thus producing great changes and high performance (Cunha *et al.*, 2006, 371). According to Sosik and Jung, "*transformational leadership is all about creating a larger leadership capacity for the whole organization through active mentoring and developmental opportunities*" (Sosik & Jung, 2010, 344). This leadership style has four components inter-correlated (5 I's) and they are: i) Idealized Influence (by Attributes - IIA and the behaviors. IIB); ii) Motivation Inspirational – IM; iii) Stimulation Intellectual – IS; iv) Individual consideration - IC (Bass, 1997, 133). The transactional leadership focuses on achieving the goals. The leader bases its action on power and formal authority conferred upon it (Gomes and Cruz, 2007, 152). This leadership style has two distinct components, and they are: i) Contingent Reward - CR, and ii) Management by Exception - Active - MBEA. The laissez-faire or passive leadership is considered by the authors as a component of non-leadership (Bass, 1997, 134). This style consists of two components, and they are: i) Laissez-Faire – LF; and ii) Management by Exception - Passive - MBEP. Each component is defined in *Table 2*.

According to the model of Bass and Avolio, the optimal leadership profile is characterized by low frequencies of Laissez-Faire, followed by greater use of transactional style, including increased Contingent Reward and Management by Exception - Active and finally, a greatest demonstration of the components of transformational leadership style (Avolio & Bass, 1988 cited by Gomes & Cruz, 2007; B. Avolio et al., 1999). Over the years, the research findings have shown that the components of transformational leadership have a high correlation (between 0.5 and 0.8) between each of them, but a lower correlation with Transactional Leadership specifically with the contingent reward component (between 0.30 and 0.5). Also is found in some studies, the correlation with the Management by Exception is practically null and moderately negative with the Laissez-Faire Leadership or Passive. (Bass, 1997, 134).

Table 2. Dimensions of Transformational Leadership Model – Adapted from Bass and Avolio, 1997

Dims.	Components	Definitions
Transformational Leadership	Idealized Influence by Attributes	The Idealized Influence or Charisma is when the leader provides a vision and sense of mission, stimulates pride and earns the respect and trust of followers. When perceived by others, it is the highest level of transformational leadership style, because it takes a great identification among group members and the leader. The IIA refers to the attribution of charisma to the leader, while the IIB emphasizes a collective sense of mission and values.
	Idealized Influence by Behaviors	
	Inspirational Motivation	IM is the ability of the leader to provide meaning and challenge to perform tasks in order to motivate and inspire group members. Issues related to team spirit, enthusiasm and optimism are aspects that characterize this component.
	Intellectual Stimulation	IS is the component where the leader encourages others to be creative and innovative at work, wondering the principles adopted, reformulating existing problems and giving new suggestions on the tasks.
	Individual Consideration	IC is the concern of the leader with the needs of personal and professional fulfillment of followers. The leader supports the followers to develop their potential, providing feedback and delegating responsibilities to them.
Transactional Leadership	Contingent Reward	CR is when the leader specifies what reward will be given to the follower for the effort; there is no transformation of ideals or values.
	Management by Exception - Active	MBEA occurs when the leader monitors the followers' performance, taking the necessary corrective action when established standards are not achieved. These actions occur through an attitude of search and anticipation of deviations, mistakes or errors of followers
Laissez-faire Leadership	Laissez-faire	LF is characterized by a workplace without defined objectives, because the leader takes no action plan and defers important decisions, ignoring their responsibilities and authority.
	Management by Exception - Passive	MBEP occurs when the leader reacts to the emergence of problems.

There are some authors who criticize the model of Bass and Avolio noting that there is ambiguity concerning the differentiation of the subdimensions of transformational leadership (Bryman, 1992; Yukl, 1999 cited by Rafferty & Griffin, 2004). Empirically, this issue has been reflected in a lack of support for the hypothesized factor structure of the transformational model and for the discriminant validity of the components of the model with each other (B. Avolio et al., 1999; Rafferty & Griffin, 2004). The higher-order factors of transformational leadership and transactional leadership should be examined rather than the individual components of the model (Carless, 1998; Tepper and Percy, 1994 cited by Rafferty & Griffin, 2004). To address these issues, Rafferty & Griffin identify a set of more focused and theoretically distinct subdimensions of transformational leadership. The empirical properties of measures selected to assess these subdimensions are examined, relating the leadership factors with theoretically selected outcomes, is developed and tested (Rafferty & Griffin, 2004).

Other studies have been conducted on transformational leadership, not only at the individual level, but also at the team performance level. It can be seen that transformational leadership is positively related to job satisfaction of followers and team performance (Braun, Peus, Weisweiler, & Frey, 2013). In this study, the relationship between supervisors' individual perceptions of transformational leadership and job satisfaction was mediated by trust in the supervisor and the team. However, trust in the team did not mediate the relationship between supervisors' perceptions of transformational leadership and team performance. Other studies of transformational leadership that analyze organizational performance, emotional intelligence, organizational learning, and innovation demonstrate the positive relationship with this style of leadership (García-Morales, Jiménez-Barrionuevo, & Gutiérrez-Gutiérrez, 2012; Harms & Credé, 2010; McCleskey, 2014; Pieterse, Knippenberg, Schippers, & Stam, 2010; Wang, Oh, Courtright, & Colbert, 2011).

Among other theories, we are witnessing a greater concern for the human being and the social issues. In this context, there are some leadership styles that arise from theories - Relational Leadership, Authentic Leadership, Servant Leadership, Humane Leadership and Ethical Leadership.

Following the Hollander's framework (1978) and other researchers, it is necessary to combine the different domains of leadership - Leader, Follower and Relationship. The traits and behaviors approaches are focused in the leader's domain. When we analyze the perspective of the Followers in the leadership process, we have the contingency approaches. According to the Leader-Member Exchange Theory, the concept of leadership changes in three domains: i) Leader-based Leadership – Appropriate behavior of the person; ii) Follower-based Leadership – Ability and motivation to manage one's own performance; and, iii) Relationship-based Leadership - Trust, respect, and mutual obligation that generates influence between parties (Graen & Uhl-Bien, 1995, 224). This approach yields a new term in the leadership literature - Relational Leadership. The concept is still unclear, however, relational leadership is "*a social influence process through which emergent coordination (evolving social order) and change (new values, attitudes, approaches, behaviors, and ideologies) are constructed and produced*" (Uhl-Bien, 2006, 655). More recently, Relational Leadership is associated with ethical issues (Nicholson & Kurucz, 2019) and Ethical Leadership (Brown & Treviño, 2006; Jensen, Cole, & Rubin, 2019).

Regarding authenticity, it is largely defined by what people see in the leader. There are consistent steps that help others to perceive the leader as authentic - to gain a better understanding of themselves, others, and to better connect with the organizational context (Goffee & Jones, 2005). George et al. report that over the past 50 years, various leadership studies have focused on determining the styles, characteristics, or personality traits of great leaders. According to the authors, being authentic is not trying to imitate others. It is possible to learn from the experiences of others, but success is not achieved by being equal to others. "*People trust you when you are genuine and authentic, not a replica of someone else*" (George, Sims, McLean, & Mayer, 2007, 1). One of the skills to be developed by leaders was recommended by 75 members of the Stanford Graduate School of Business's Advisory Council as self-awareness, which is the emotional competence associated with the emotional intelligence competency model. These and other researchers believe that authentic leadership emerges from leaders' life stories. "*The life-story provides followers with a major source of information on which to base their judgments about the leader's authenticity*" (Shamir & Eilam, 2005). In this approach, studies are found from the perspective of the attributes and characteristics of the leader (Goffee & Jones, 2005; Harvey, Martinko, & Gardner, 2006), however, there is a fundamental role of followers, particularly in its development. (Gardner, Avolio, Luthans, May, & Walumbwa, 2005). The antecedents of the concepts 'authentic leadership' and 'followership' are the personal stories of leaders and followers. However, life experiences are not expected to develop authenticity, so the distinction between the terms 'Authentic Leader Development' and 'Authentic Leadership Development' is found in the literature. This approach to authentic leadership continues to be studied along with the ethical issues associated with leadership (Crawford, Dawkins, Martin, & Lewis, 2019).

A servant leader is one who is a servant first. This leader has the natural feeling that one wants to serve first. Most of the servant leadership literature is philosophical. This approach has a theoretical framework that advocates a leader's primary motivation and role as service to others. However, it is not possible find enough scientific evidence (Russell & Stone, 2002, 145). These authors reviewed the literature on servant leadership. Agreeing with these authors, Avolio, Walumbwa and Weber (2009, 437) refer that it is necessary to examine how the personal values of servant differ from those of other leadership styles, such as transformational. According to Dingman & Stone (2007), one business process which holds potential to reflect the impact of servant leadership is succession planning. The case study conducted by these authors showed a positive relationship between servant leadership principles and the succession process.

More recently, Dimitrov (2015) realized the first empirical case study about Humane Leadership. The author explored how leadership influences an organization to become humane through its features and behaviors. One of the conclusions of the case study is that traits and behaviors of some modern leadership theories such as authentic leadership, transformational leadership and charismatic leadership were combined under the concept – humane leadership; certain types of leadership features and behaviors are similar. This study sums all these leadership styles in humane leadership.

In the most recent studies, two themes emerge linked to leadership styles. These studies address the ethical issues of leadership, more specifically the impact of ethical and moral behavior of the leader (Jensen et al., 2019; Nicholson & Kurucz, 2019).

Leadership Development

Leadership development occurs in a complex and dynamic context due to issues related to globalization, change in organizational structure, knowledge-based economy and diversity (Carbery & Garavan, 2014, 390). Moreover, leadership is "*a composite of multiple aspects and experiences*" (McGuire, 2014, 197). Consequently, a single theory is not enough to understand the leadership phenomenon. Leader development is "*a complex process and remains something of an art*" (McGuire, 2014, 197). All these issues make sense only if leadership development was considered a serious process. Only in this context leaders "*recognize that building their organization's leadership potential is going to be a major differentiator for future success*" (Kets de Vries & Korotov, 2010).

In *Tables 3 and 4*, we present some concepts and the main differences between leadership development and leader development.

Leadership development is a wider process that includes the development of leader. All authors believe that leadership development is a collective process that covers the organization and leader development (focused on the individual). It is also common concern that leader development must be in keeping with the needs and strategies of the organization. On the other hand, leadership development must consider the development needs of the leader and the organization's needs. Also note that in the last decade, leader development has piqued the interest by the authors. Leader development is focusing on the human capital development and leadership development is oriented towards the social capital development. Human capital corresponds to individual behaviors, such as self-awareness, self-regulation, and self-motivation (intrapersonal competence). The social capital emphasizes the development of reciprocal obligations and commitments on a foundation of trust and mutual respect (interpersonal competence). Leadership development is a relational leadership perspective.

It is necessary to identify and develop flexibility, results orientation, feedback, motives, values, attitudes and behaviors of the futures leaders, in order to analyze the technical and cognitive skills, and also what the author calls "*the ability to learn from experience*" (Christensen, 2006, 12). The lifelong learning process is only possible when organizations promote leadership development practices. Although Day considers that many practices have been developed and implemented for other purposes, he examined the practices used in the organizational context. The practices are described in *Table 5*.

Table 3. Definitions of Leadership Development and Leader Development

LEADERSHIP DEVELOPMENT	LEADER DEVELOPMENT
Leadership development refers to "(...) *development of collective leadership processes and social capital in the organization and beyond, involving relationships, networking, trust, and commitments, as well as an appreciation of the social and political context and its implications for leadership styles and actions.*" (Iles & Preece, 2006, 325)	"*Leader development refers to the training and development of individual competencies, skills and attributes of a leader. These training programs include skills models, team management, performance evaluation and conferences.*" (Iles & Preece, 2006, 322)
"*Leadership development involves relationships, networking, trust and commitments, as well as an appreciation of the social and political context an its implications for leadership styles and actions.*" (Iles, 2012, 56)	Leader development refers to "(...) *developing individual-level intrapersonal competencies and human capital (cognitive, emotional, and self-awareness skills).*" (Iles & Preece, 2006, 325)
"*Leadership development focuses on the social dimensions of leadership and includes such issues as interpersonal awareness and skills, team development processes and the processes involved in gaining commitment for vision and strategy.*" (Carbery & Garavan, 2005, 388)	"*Leader development focuses on the development of a leader or manager's self-awareness and understanding of self as a leader.*" (Carbery & Garavan, 2005, 388)
Leadership development is defined as "(...) *expanding the collective capacity of organizational members to engage effectively in leadership roles and processes.*" (McCauley *et al.* cited by Day, 2001, 582)	Leader development is defined as "*the expansion of a person's capacity to be effective in leadership roles and processes*" (Van Velsor & McCauley, 2004 cited by Day, 2011, 38)
"*Leadership development as a type of human development, takes place over time; it is incremental in nature, it is accretive; and it is the result of complex reciprocal interactions between the leader, others and the social environment. Leadership requires that individual development in integrated and understood in the context of others, social systems, and organizational strategies, missions, and goals.*" (Olivares *et al.*, 2007 cited by McGuire, 2014, 183)	Leader development is about "*the development of the leader's skills and abilities. These skills and abilities are often referred to as leader competencies, and many organizations have articulated a competency model that lists and describes their assessment of the capabilities individuals need to lead effectively in the organization.*" (Benson, 2007 cited by Mccauley, 2008, 8)

Table 4. Leader Development and Leadership Development - Adapted from Day, 2001

	Target Development	
Dimensions	**Leader**	**Leadership**
Type of Capital	Human	Social
Leadership Model	Individual (Personal Power, Knowledge, Reliability)	Relational (trust, mutual respect, commitment)
Competence-based	Intrapersonal	Interpersonal
Type of Skills	**Self-awareness** (Emotional Awareness, Self Confidence, Self-image)	**Social Awareness** (Empathy, Guidance, Awareness Policy)
	Self-regulation (Self control, Reliability, Adaptability, Personal Responsibility)	**Social Skills** (Building ties, Directing Team, Managing Conflict)
	Self-Motivation (Initiative, Commitment, Optimism)	

Table 5. Practices in Leadership Development - Adapted from Day, 2001

Practice	Description	Target Development	HC	SC
Feedback 360°	Performance Evaluation, organized and presented to the individual	Self-Knowledge, Behavior Change	√	x
Coaching/ Executive Coaching	Practical, focused on individual learning goals	Self-Knowledge, Behavior Change, Career Development	√	?
Mentoring	Counseling / Advising Relationship to support the development, usually with the more experienced manager	Broader understanding, Catalyst Progress, Lessons Learned / Prevent Errors	√	?
Networks	Contact with other functions and in different areas of the organization	Better problem solving, learning whom to consult to help the project, Socialization	?	√
Job Assignments	Provides broader and challenging assignments in terms of roles, function or geography; rotation functions / tasks	Skills Development, more comprehensive understanding of the business	√	?
Action Learning	Based learning projects targeted to business problems	Socialization, Teamwork to implement the strategy	√	√

Note: HC = Human Capital; SC = Social Capital; √ = intended target for the development; x = not intended target for the development; ? = possible development target;

Training is the first formal way to 'train' leaders. However, it is complemented with other activities - 360° Feedback, Coaching/Executive Coaching, Mentoring, Networks, Job Assignments and Action Learning. Most practices have their focus on human capital, except Networks. It is possible but the focus is on social capital and only Action Learning has focused on both (human and social capital). Coaching involves customized learning ways focused on the goals leading to behavioral change (Hall *et al.*, cited by Hernez-Broome & Hughes, 2012, 25). Mentoring allows the development of new leaders, through the influence of the older leaders (mentor) of the organization due to their own personal and professional experiences. Today, mentoring and coaching are the most simple and inexpensive investments in people and that provide higher returns and faster (Chiavenato, 2002, 183). According to Hamlin, Ellinger, & Beattie (2008, 288), the growth of an emergent coaching industry in various countries appears to be expanding rapidly and becoming an extensive new field of practice. Within the context of business and organizations, coaching could have much in common with the intent and purpose of contemporary HRD.

Human capital is what differentiates organizations, hence the importance in developing it. Action Learning is a set of development practices in which important organizational issues are addressed in real time (Hernez-Broome & Hughes, 2012, 25), for the following purposes: i) to find measurable results; ii) to develop targeted communications to specific contexts; and, iii) to develop skills and leadership abilities in general. Job Assignments is a systematic program of the job rotation. The assignment of challenging tasks is a powerful way of leadership development because it offers development opportunities for organizations; it produces benefits in labor and competitive advantage. The level of involvement and participation of the organization in this practice depends on the leadership development process; it depends on the amount of information provided in relation to development opportunities in your current role for a systematic program of job rotation. Finally, 360º Feedback has been the most widely used method to evaluate skills development of the leader. The purpose of this practice is to evaluate the different perceptions - supervisor, peers, suppliers, and internal customers - to obtain a more complete picture of individual performance.

The study of Broome and Hughes shows that individual development is not the main focus, although it is a critical issue in the development of leaders (Hernez-Broome & Hughes, 2012, 27). The purpose of leadership development involves action and not just knowledge, because it can support the performance and application of skills in organizations, through methods such as "(…) *training programmes, coaching, mentoring, action learning and developmental assignments*" (Hernez-Broome & Hughes, 2012, 27).

According to Dugan and O'Shea (2014, 1), organizations spend a lot of money on leader development. It is critical to know the return on investment. Kincaid and Gordick tried to know the Return on Investment (ROI) and concluded that leadership development is correlated with profitability and "(…) *can influence bottom line profit margins by as much as 47%*" (Kincaid & Gordick, 2003, 50). When coaching is used as leadership development practice, the programs focused on leadership development increase productivity, sales and reduce turnover. Accordingly, to the Goleman' research, only one third of ROI is due to the technical skills, because most of the variation is due to interpersonal and emotional competences. This variation goes to 80% when considering the senior leaders (Goleman, 1998 cited by Kincaid & Gordick, 2003, 50).

From the literature review we conclude that succession planning is effective only if it is beyond the identification of potential future leaders. According Day, succession planning and leadership development "*are inherently intertwined in the identification and development of leadership talent*" (Day, 2011, 45). In summary, the *Figure 2* outlines the theoretical model.

The research objective is to identify the leadership style that promotes succession planning by implementing leadership development practices. In Figueiredo' research, it was found that the transformational leadership style promotes Coaching/Executive Coaching and the laissez-faire leadership style promotes Networks and Action Learning (Figueiredo, 2013, 44).

Figure 2. Theoretical Model

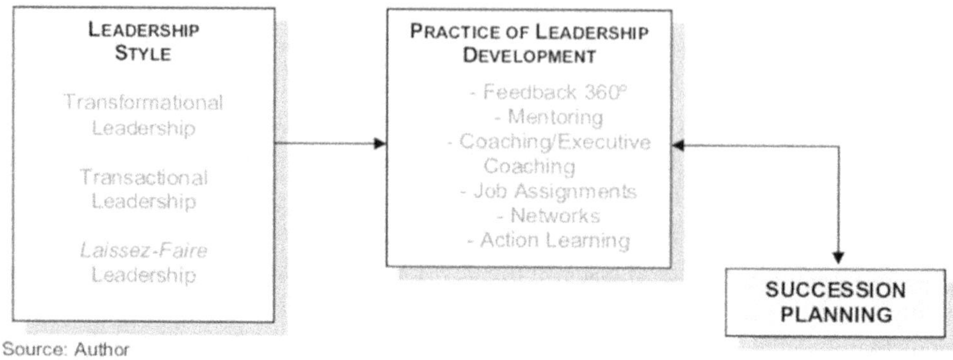

Source: Author

METHODOLOGY

The research methodology is quantitative, and the dependent variable is the existence/nonexistence of succession planning. The independent variables are: i) Leadership styles - Transformational, Transactional and Laissez-Faire; and ii) The existence/nonexistence of leadership development practices defined by Day - 360° Feedback, Coaching/Executive Coaching, Mentoring, Networks, Job Assignments and Action Learning. Most of the variables are dichotomous because the target population is composed of the leaders of several organizations and there is no advance information if organizations do some succession planning or implementing leadership development practices. It was the way found to check their existence within organizations.

The choice of research strategy was difficult for the resources available. The choice was to delimit the economic industry and get the first conclusions on the theme neglecting their possible generalization because the sample used is not representative. The services industry is the main economic industry, and it was the industry with the highest growth in turnover and employment created. The idea of this research was to conduct a pilot study to examine the perception of the leaders about succession planning in Portugal, because we do not find other scientific studies. The Portuguese business structure consists of 98% of small and medium-sized companies (up to 250 employees). In this sense, it was hard to get a pilot study in a large company. The choice was to use a database of service industry companies to get a bigger number of participants in the study. The selection of companies considered the following activities: i) Banking; ii) Insurance; iii) Consulting and Management Support; iv) Distribution; v) Media/Telecommunication; and vi) Construction. The research strategy adopted is questionnaire (Yin, 2002), using a database of 243 leaders from the services industry. Corroborating with the approach of Quivy and Campenhoudt (2008, 158), the field of analysis is limited to three groups: i) CEO/Director/Managing

Director/Manager; ii) HR Directors; and iii) Other Department Directors. The middle and top leaders are important in the identification and development of new leaders within the organization.

The survey was the technique of data collection chosen. The survey was developed in 3 parts: i) Characterization of the Organization ii) Characterization of the Leader; and iii) The Leadership style self-perceived. The last part of the survey is composed by the Multifactor Leadership Questionnaire[1] (MLQ - Form 5X-Short) developed by Bass and Avolio. The choice of MLQ was because according to Sosik and Jung, "*human resources staff can administer the MLQ on a yearly basis to facilitate the development of aspiring transformational leaders. By providing feedback from the MLQ report to these managers, the quality of mentoring and coaching typically increases, and you can accelerate your associates' leadership development*" (Sosik & Jung, 2010, 344). The questionnaire was presented in Portuguese. The obtained data were statistically analyzed by SPSS version 18.

ANALYSIS OF RESULTS

The survey was available on the platform *Zoomerang*. The survey recorded 145 visits which resulted in 65 completed surveys and 18 partially filled. Only 61 were considered valid because four surveys were not filled out properly. The number of participants is low. It is believed that participants do not conclude the survey due to it being too long.

Before starting the analysis and discussion of the results, we present a frequency analysis to characterize organizations, the profile of leaders and the leadership style perceived by the leaders. (*Table 6*).

Analyzing the components of transformational leadership model, it appears that follow the same trend presented by the authors. The most effective leader is the one that gets the highest score in the categories of transformational leadership (3,15) then the components of Contingent Reward (3,06) and Management by Exception - Active (2,13) and then Passive (1,34). Finally, the component with the lowest score is Laissez Faire (0,62). (Table 7)

As the variables related to the model components are quantitative, we can analyze correlations between them (Appendix 1). As the number of observations is greater than 30, we used the Pearson correlation coefficient (r) and the significance level (ρ-value). Across them it appears that the components of transformational leadership (IIA, IIB, IM, IS and IC) show a positive correlation between them. This correlation is moderate in most cases. The IIA and IM components are those that have the highest correlation (0.67). The LTRANSF variable also presents a positive linear correlation with the components of Results (EE, EEF and SAT) and negative with the LF variable

Table 6. Characterization of organizations, Leader Profile Leadership Style and self-perceived - Frequency Analysis

Organizations' characteristics	Leaders' profile	The leadership style self-perceived by the leader
i) 72% are companies that have fewer than 150 employees; ii) 85% are companies that are in business for over 5 years; iii) 43% are business consulting and support to management; iv) 61% are companies that have no succession planning; v) 77% are companies that choose leaders from within the organization; vi) 89% of companies consider "important" and "very important" the leadership development practices"; vii) 74% of companies have leadership development practices, and, viii) 46% of companies have used Coaching internally.	i) 76% are leaders aged from 31 and 50 years; ii) 74% of leaders are male; iii) 90% are leaders with higher education and 44 % are leaders with MBA /Graduate /MsC/PhD; iv) 49% are CEO/Director/ Managing Director /Manager and 20% are Human Resources Director; v) 60% are leaders that are in business for over 6 years; vi) 69% are leaders that play leadership roles for more than five years; vii) 89% prefer internal leaders viii) 99% of leaders consider "important" and "very important" the leadership development practices"; ix) 79% of leaders consider "very important" the development of their leadership skills and the other leaders consider "important".	i) 84% are leaders that perceive "fairly often" and "Frequently, if not always" their Transformational leadership style; ii) 58% are leaders that perceive "fairly often" and "Frequently, if not always" their Transactional leadership style; iii) 42% are leaders that perceive "not at all" and "once in a while" their Laissez-faire leadership style; and, iv) 76% are leaders that perceive that achieves the leadership results "fairly often" and "Frequently, if not always."

Source: Author

(Laissez-Faire). The LF variable stands out for having a negative linear correlation with all the variables of Transformational Leadership, Transactional Leadership and Results (RL). The RL variable has a strong positive linear correlation with its components (0.91, 0.88 and 0.86, respectively), as well as with all categories of Transformational Leadership. It also highlights the correlation coefficient of 0.77 with the CR variable belonging to Transactional Leadership and a negative linear correlation with the LF variable belonging to Laissez-faire leadership.

According to the Bass' assumptions, the Transformational Leadership components have a high correlation between them (0,5 - 0,8), except for the IIB variable. According to the author, the CR variable presents a moderate correlation (0,3 - 0,5) with the Transformational Leadership. It also notes that the MBEA / P variables have almost no correlation and moderately negative with the Laissez-Faire Leadership.

Research Question: Is there any relationship between the leadership styles and succession planning within the organization?

Table 7. Result of survey according to the scoring scale Model Bass and Avolio

Dimensions	Components	Abrev.	Results	
Transformational Leadership - **LTRANSF**	Idealized Influence by Attributes	**IIA**	3,16	**3,15**
	Idealized Influence by Behaviors	**IIB**	2,97	
	Inspirational Motivation	**IM**	3,32	
	Intellectual Stimulation	**IS**	3,16	
	Individual Consideration	**IC**	3,17	
Transactional Leadership - **LTRANS**	Contingent Reward	**CR**	3,06	**2,60**
	Management by Exception - Active	**MBEA**	2,13	
Laissez-faire Leadership - **LL**	Laissez-faire	**LF**	0,62	**0,98**
	Management by Exception - Passive	**MBEP**	1,34	
Results - **RL**	Extra Effort	**EE**	3,00	**3,08**
	Effectiveness	**EFF**	3,22	
	Satisfaction of leader	**SAT**	3,01	

Source: Author

We choose Binary Logistic Regression model to identify the leadership style perceived by leaders who promote succession planning in organizations. This model is used when the dependent variable is dichotomous and the independent variables are continuous and/or dichotomous (Osborn, 2008, 569).

There were obtained the results shown in the following tables using SPSS:

In *Table 8*, it is possible to evaluate of the quality of the model by the percentage correct answers that is 78,7%. By adding the variables, we can predict with 78,7% accuracy. The model seems to be good, but we need to evaluate the model fit and the significance level as well.

Table 8. Classification Table[a]

Observed			Predicted		
			Succession Planning		Percentage Correct
			No	Yes	
Step 1	Succession Planning	No	34	3	91,9
		Yes	10	14	58,3
	Overall Percentage				78,7

a. The cut value is 0,500

The '-2 Log likelihood' ratio varies between zero and infinity and measures the inability of the model to explain the dependent variable (*Table 9*). The ratio is 58,262. Additionally, the output shows the reduction of '-2 Log likelihood' when entering the independent variables: 23,510 (*Table 10*). This reduction is calculated using the reference model with only one constant. This model shows the ratio of 58,262 + 23,510 and the model with the independent variables translates into a reduction of 23,510. The ratio has a chi-square distribution and p-value (0,015) indicates that all the independent variables have explanatory power for any higher significance than 0,015.

Table 9. Omnibus Tests of Model Coefficients

		Chi-square	df	p-value
Step 1	Step	23,510	11	0,015
	Block	23,510	11	0,015
	Model	23,510	11	0,015

Note: df= Degrees of freedom; p-value= level of significance

Table 10. Model Summary

Step	-2 Log likelihood	Cox & Snell R Square	Nagelkerke R Square
1	58,262[a]	0,320	0,433

a. Estimation terminated at iteration number 6 because parameter estimates changed by less than 0,001.

The 'Cox & Snell R Square' and 'Nagelkerke R Square' coefficients are indicators of logistic regression like R Square (the linear model). The first evaluates the overall fit of the model and the other refers to the explanatory power of the model. The results indicate that the degree of fit is hardly satisfactory (0,320) and the results show a moderate explanatory power (0,433).

Finally, in *Table 11*, there are the estimates of the coefficients (βs) and the significance of the corresponding parameters. The Transformational Leadership was automatically removed. The Wald statistic has a chi-square distribution, and it is equal to the *t* ratio in the linear model. The results indicate the rejection of the hypothesis H_0, i.e., the significance of the Laissez-faire leadership style variable (LL) and its components - Laissez-faire (LF) and Management by Exception - Passive

(MBEP) -, contribute significantly for the explanation of the dependent variable, i.e., Succession Planning.

To understand the relationship between succession planning and leadership development practices, it is necessary to analyze the results of contingency tables because the variables are dichotomous (qualitative). In *Table 12*, it appears that the distance between the observed and expected values are large. There is evidence of association between them. With the results of the chi-square test, it appears that the p-value equals 0,05, so we reject the hypothesis H_0 - with a confidence level of 95%, the variables are associated (χ^2=3,86; df=1; ρ-value=0,05). The V. Cramer coefficient tells us that the intensity of association is weak (0,35), but acceptable.

Table 11. Variables in the Equation

		B	S.E.	Wald	df	ρ-value	Exp(B)
Step 1[a]	IIA	1,227	0,975	1,584	1	0,208	3,412
	IIB	-1,320	0,760	3,014	1	0,083	0,267
	IM	0,294	1,150	0,065	1	0,798	1,342
	IS	1,224	1,100	1,237	1	0,266	3,400
	IC	0,907	0,901	1,015	1	0,314	2,477
	CR	21,200	81,689	0,067	1	0,795	1,61E
	MBEA	23,423	81,804	0,082	1	0,775	1,48E
	LF	269,940	93,289	8,373	1	**0,004**	0,000
	MBEP	270,747	93,536	8,379	1	**0,004**	0,000
	LTRANS	-44,000	163,478	0,072	1	0,788	0,000
	LL	540,144	186,572	8,382	1	**0,004**	3,81E
	Constant	-9,440	4,485	4,431	1	0,035	0,000

a. Variable(s) entered on step 1: IIA, IIB, IM, IS, IC, CR, MBEA, LF, MBEP, LTRANS, LL.

Table 12. Crosstab – Succession Planning vs Leadership Development Practices

			Leadership Development Practices		Total
			No	Yes	
Succession Planning	No	Count	13	24	37
		Expected Count	9,7	27,3	37,0
	Yes	Count	3	21	24
		Expected Count	6,3	17,7	24,0
Total		Count	16	45	61
		Expected Count	16,0	45,0	61,0

Chi-Square Tests	Value χ^2	df	ρ-value
Qui-Quadrado Pearson	3,86	1	0,05

V.Cramer Coefficient	Value	ρ-value
V. Cramer	0,35	0,05

Note: df= Degrees of freedom; ρ-value= level of significance

Doing the same analysis for each practice, it appears that only 360° feedback and Coaching / Executive Coaching are associated with succession planning. (*Tables 13 and 14*) The V. Cramer coefficient shows that the intensity of association is weak, but acceptable (0,27 and 0,30, respectively).

Table 13. Crosstab – Succession Planning vs 360° Feedback

			360° Feedback		
			No	Yes	Total
Succession Planning	No	Count	27	10	37
		Expected Count	23	14	
	Yes	Count	11	13	24
		Expected Count	15	9	
Total		Count	38	23	61
		Expected Count	38	23	61

Chi-Square Tests	Value χ^2	df	ρ-value
Qui-Quadrado Pearson	4,56	1	0,03

V.Cramer Coefficient	Value	ρ-value
V. Cramer	0,27	0,03

Note: df= Degrees of freedom; ρ-value= level of significance

Table 14. Crosstab – Succession Planning vs Coaching/Executive Coaching

			Coaching/Executive Coaching		
			No	Yes	Total
Succession Planning	No	Count	29	8	37
		Expected Count	24,9	12,1	37,0
	Yes	Count	12	12	24
		Expected Count	16,1	7,9	24,0
Total		Count	41	20	61
		Expected Count	41,0	20,0	61,0

Chi-Square Tests	Value χ^2	df	ρ-value
Qui-Quadrado Pearson	5,32	1	0,02

V.Cramer Coefficient	Value	ρ-value
V. Cramer	0,30	0,02

Note: df= Degrees of freedom; ρ-value= level of significance

CONCLUSIONS AND IMPLICATIONS

Throughout time, leadership development has become increasingly important to HRD. There are many reasons that induce a greater concern for leadership development. Theoretically, many authors reported several reasons - the complexity, the strong commitment to innovation that is reflected in the need for greater adaptation to new contexts and the need for constant knowledge updating. These authors have a wider view because the focus is not only the leader but throughout the organization and team of leaders. Other authors focus on the leader, including the competence of leaders. A main concern is the existence of leaders who can quickly ascend to the leadership roles. For them, organizations must have the leadership pipeline and succession planning. This study was performed to middle leaders and not merely the CEO, because we believe that succession planning is transversal to the organization.

The research findings are outlined in Figure 3, and are the following:

1. The laissez-faire leadership style is related to the existence of succession planning; when leader adopts a passive leadership style, not involved in the processes, the succession planning is positively influenced by the leadership style;
2. The existence of leadership development practices in the organization is related to the existence of succession planning;
3. The 360º Feedback and Coaching/Executive Coaching separately are related to the succession planning; Coaching is a practice that promotes the human capital development, so it is assumed that succession planning may be related to leader development.

In Figure No 3, we seek to schematize the findings of this study with the research undertaken by Figueiredo (2013), about the relation between leadership styles and leadership development practices. Thus, the leadership styles that seem to have a relation to the leadership development practices are the Transformational Leadership and Laissez-faire Leadership. The transformational leadership style

Figure 3. Research Results

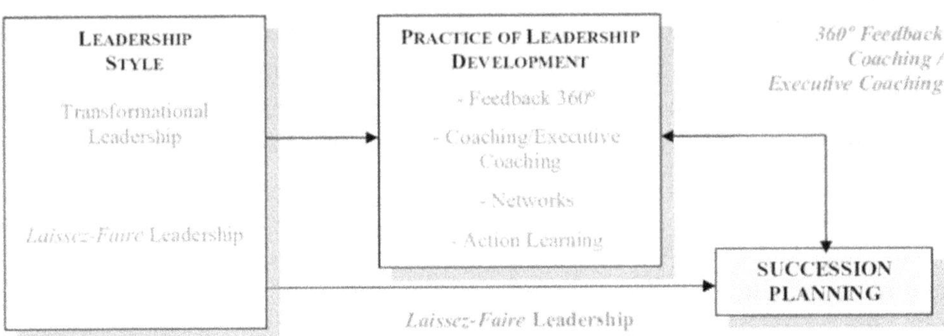

Source: Author

tends to promote Coaching/Executive Coaching and the laissez-faire leadership style tends to promote Networks and Action Learning (Figueiredo, 2013). Regarding the succession planning, the findings indicate a positive relationship with the Laissez-faire leadership style, as well as the following leadership development practices: 360 ° Feedback and Coaching / Executive Coaching.

One reason for these results can be found in theory. The transformational leadership style can be used in the context of organizational change and unstable environments and the transactional leadership style it turns the reverse. Although the sample was not representative and cannot be generalized without doing further research, the findings of this study point to two important ideas: i) the concern to promote succession planning occur when leader perceives that is not focused on defining objectives and action plans, delegating and not taking responsibility. Organizations should always have a leadership pipeline in order to have leaders available and prepared to assume leadership positions: and ii) the leader takes a passive style within the organization he cares about the promotion of succession planning. In the organizational context, this leader behavior jeopardizes the continuity and survival of the organization, because this concern should be ongoing.

These ideas are interesting, but we need to promote their validity particularly in the context of an organization. Even considering other more recent leadership styles found on literature review.

Within the field of leadership, this study adds to a greater awareness of the leaders on the impact of leadership style on the organization's daily life. In addition, the concern for developing leadership within the organization is not enough. It is necessary to understand the perceptions and expectations of several generations of leaders. The new theories of leadership emphasize leadership styles which focus more on the human element, even considering the human organizations. Increasingly, the leadership must be an 'interactive' process between the leader, the followers, and the relationship between them.

Leadership development and succession planning need to be integrated and work together since they are arguably essential to the future of organizations. The leadership development practices do not produce outcomes without a specific development plan and appropriate to the leader needs. Organizations that promote leadership development practices and do not have a succession planning are wasting resources, as well as organizations that have a succession planning and do not promote the most appropriate leadership development practices.

A greater awareness of leaders for these issues is required because leadership development and succession planning must be integrated into the strategy and organizational culture.

This study has a great interest for the HRD. First, it concerns to perception of the leaders on the need to develop human capital within organizations. On the other hand, the study raises awareness of the urgent need to promote leadership development in organizations. This development requires the development of leaders not only from the top of the pyramid but also at middle levels. Thus, the main implication for HRD can be summarized in the following sentence: Leaders who cares about the development of his followers are organizations with active measures of HRD and competitive and sustainable organizations.

RECOMMENDATIONS AND FUTURE RESEARCH

Without the chance of generalize, we believe that these findings are close to reality because organizations studied are like the Portuguese entrepreneurial structure. It is important in the next research reproduce the analysis in a single organization and considers the followers' perception too. The study considers only the leaders' perception. Increasingly, the followers' perception and the comparison with the leaders are essential for the social sciences. If the followers' perception is important, then the context and the environment in which research occurs is another of limitations.

We see that it is necessary to deepen the idea that succession planning is related to the leader development (human capital) instead of leadership development (social capital) due to the association found with the Coaching/Executive Coaching. Thus, we see the need to continue to conduct research in this field.

Finally, it is necessary to assess the level of satisfaction with the succession planning and leadership development practices used in the organization. It is important to realize the displeasures and the difficulties experienced with the process.

Only in this way it is possible to think about possible solutions to help organizations in promoting leadership development and, in turn, the succession planning. This is the road that organizations must go through to maintain effective leadership.

REFERENCES

Avolio, B., Bass, B., & Jung, D. (1999). Re-examining the components of transformational and transactional leadership using the Multifactor Leadership. *Journal of Occupational and Organizational Psychology*, *72*(4), 441–462. doi:10.1348/096317999166789

Avolio, B., Walumbwa, F., & Weber, T. (2009). Leadership: Current theories, research, and future directions. *Annual Review of Psychology*, *60*(1), 421–449. doi:10.1146/annurev.psych.60.110707.163621 PMID:18651820

Bass, B. (1990). From Transactional to Iransformational Leadership : Learning to Share the Vision. *Organizational Dynamics*, *18*(3), 19–32. doi:10.1016/0090-2616(90)90061-S

Bass, B. (1997). Does the transactional–transformational leadership paradigm transcend organizational and national boundaries? *The American Psychologist*, *52*(2), 130–139. doi:10.1037/0003-066X.52.2.130

Bass, B., & Avolio, B. (1993). Transformational Leadership and Organizational Culture. *Public Administration Quarterly*, (Spring), 112–121.

Behan, B. A., Kirschner, J., & Snyder, S. M. (2009). Succession in practice. *Chief Executive*, *239*(Mar/Apr), 28.

Brant, J., Dooley, R., & Iman, S. (2008). Leadership succession: An approach to filling the pipeline. *Strategic HR Review*, *7*(4), 17–24. doi:10.1108/14754390810880499

Braun, S., Peus, C., Weisweiler, S., & Frey, D. (2013). Transformational leadership, job satisfaction, and team performance: A multilevel mediation model of trust. *The Leadership Quarterly*, *24*(1), 270–283. doi:10.1016/j.leaqua.2012.11.006

Brown, M. E., & Treviño, L. K. (2006). Ethical leadership: A review and future directions. *The Leadership Quarterly*, *17*(6), 595–616. doi:10.1016/j.leaqua.2006.10.004

Christensen, C. (2006). Identifying and Developing Capable Leaders. *Harvard Business Review*, 1–12.

Crawford, J. A., Dawkins, S., Martin, A., & Lewis, G. (2019). Putting the leader back into authentic leadership: Reconceptualising and rethinking leaders. *Australian Journal of Management*, 1–44.

Day, D., Gronn, P., & Salas, E. (2004). Leadership capacity in teams. *The Leadership Quarterly*, *15*(6), 857–880. doi:10.1016/j.leaqua.2004.09.001

Day, D. V. (2001). Leadership development: A review in context. *The Leadership Quarterly*, *11*(4), 581–613. doi:10.1016/S1048-9843(00)00061-8

Day, D. V. (2011). Leadership Development. In A. Bryman, D. Collinson, K. Grint, B. Jackson, & M. Uhl-Bien (Eds.), The Sage Handbook of Leadership (pp. 37–50). SAGE Publications Ltd.

Deal, J. J. (2014). Leadership for All Ages. *Chief Learning Officer*, (December), 66–68.

Dimitrov, D. (2015). Leadership in a humane organization. *European Journal of Training and Development*, *39*(2), 122–142. doi:10.1108/EJTD-07-2014-0051

Dingman, W. W., & Stone, A. G. (2007). Servant Leadership's Role in the Succession Planning Process : A Case Study. *International Journal of Leadership IStudies*, *2*(2), 133–147.

Drotter, S. (2010). Leadership Pipeline. *Leadership Excellence*, *27*(8), 11.

Dugan, B., & O'Shea, P. (2014). Leadership Development: Growing Talent Strategically. *Society for Human Resource Management (SHRM) and Society for Industrial and Organizational Psychology (SIOP) Science of HR White Paper Series*, 1–17.

Dutra, A., & Griesedieck, J. (2010). Succession Success. *Leadership Excellence*, *27*(5), 14.

Erickson, T. (2010). The leaders we need now. *Harvard Business Review*, (May), 1–4. PMID:20429251

Field, A. (2007). When the boomers leave, will your company have the leaders it needs? *Harvard Business Review*, (April), 1–6.

Figueiredo, P. (2013). Planning and Developing Leadership within the Organization. *Organizational Cultures -. International Journal (Toronto, Ont.)*, *12*(3), 31–48.

García-Morales, V., Jiménez-Barrionuevo, M., & Gutiérrez-Gutiérrez, L. (2012). Transformational leadership influence on organizational performance through organizational learning and innovation. *Journal of Business Research*, *65*(7), 1040–1050. doi:10.1016/j.jbusres.2011.03.005

Gardner, W., Avolio, B., Luthans, F., May, D., & Walumbwa, F. (2005). "Can you see the real me?" A self-based model of authentic leader and follower development. *The Leadership Quarterly*, *16*(3), 343–372. doi:10.1016/j.leaqua.2005.03.003

Garman, A. N., & Glawe, J. (2004). Succession Planning. *Consulting Psychology Journal*, *56*(2), 119–128. doi:10.1037/1061-4087.56.2.119 PMID:15524307

George, B., Sims, P., McLean, A., & Mayer, D. (2007). Discovering Your Authentic Leadership. *Harvard Business Review*, (February), 1–8. PMID:17345686

Giambatista, R., Rowe, W., & Riaz, S. (2005). Nothing succeeds like succession: A critical review of leader succession literature since 1994. *The Leadership Quarterly*, *16*(6), 963–991. doi:10.1016/j.leaqua.2005.09.005

Goffee, R., & Jones, G. (2005). Managing authenticity: The paradox of great leadership. *Harvard Business Review*, *83*(12), 86–94. PMID:16334584

Goldsmith, M. (2009). Internal Successors. *Leadership Excellence*, *26*(8), 15.

Goleman, D. (1998). What makes a leader? *Harvard Business Review*, 82–91. PMID:10187249

Goleman, D. (2000, Mar.). Leadership that gets results. *Harvard Business Review*, 78–90.

Gomes, A. R., & Cruz, J. (2007). Abordagem carismática e transformacional: Modelos conceptuais e contributos para o exercõcio da liderança. *Psicologia USP*, *18*(3), 143–161. doi:10.1590/S0103-65642007000300008

Graen, G., & Uhl-Bien, M. (1995). Relationship-based approach to leadership: Development of leader-member exchange (LMX) theory of leadership over 25 years: Applying a multi-level multi-domain perspective. *The Leadership Quarterly*, *6*(2), 219–247. doi:10.1016/1048-9843(95)90036-5

Groves, K. S. (2007). Integrating leadership development and succession planning best practices. *Journal of Management Development*, *26*(3), 239–260. doi:10.1108/02621710710732146

Hamlin, R., Ellinger, A. D., & Beattie, R. S. (2008). The emergent 'coaching industry': A wake-up call for HRD professionals. *Human Resource Development International*, *11*(3), 287–305. doi:10.1080/13678860802102534

Harms, P. D., & Credé, M. (2010). Emotional intelligence and transformational and transactional leadership: A meta-analysis. *Journal of Leadership & Organizational Studies*, *17*(1), 5–17. doi:10.1177/1548051809350894

Harvey, P., Martinko, M., & Gardner, W. (2006). Promoting Authentic Behavior in Organizations: An Attributional Perspective. *Journal of Leadership & Organizational Studies*, *12*(3), 1–11. doi:10.1177/107179190601200301

Henderson, G. M., & Provo, J. (2006). A New World Ahead-Are We Ready? *Human Resource Development Review*, *5*(2), 274–277. doi:10.1177/1534484306287606

Hernez-Broome, G., & Hughes, R. L. (2012). Leadership Development: Past, Present, and Future. *Human Resource Planning*, 24–32.

House, R., & Aditya, R. (1997). The social scientific study of leadership : quo vadis? The social scientific study of leadership : quo vadis? *Journal of Management, 23*(3), 409–473. doi:10.1177/014920639702300306

Ingraham, P. W. (2006). The Challenge and the Opportunity. *American Review of Public Administration, 36*(4), 374–381. doi:10.1177/0275074006293630

Intagliata, J., Ulrich, D., & Smallwood, N. (2000). Leveraging leadership Competencies to produce Leadership Brand. *Human Resources Planning, 23*(4), 12–23.

Jensen, J. M., Cole, M. S., & Rubin, R. S. (2019). Predicting retail shrink from performance pressure, ethical leader behavior, and store-level incivility. *Journal of Organizational Behavior, 40*(6), 723–739. doi:10.1002/job.2366

Kesner, I., & Sebora, T. (1994). Executive succession: Past, present & future. *Journal of Management, 20*(2), 327–372. doi:10.1177/014920639402000204

Kets de Vries, M., & Korotov, K. (2010). *Developing Leaders and Leadership Development.* Academic Press.

Kincaid, S. B., & Gordick, D. (2003). The return on investment of leadership development: Differentiating our discipline. *Consulting Psychology Journal, 55*(1), 47–57. doi:10.1037/1061-4087.55.1.47

Kowalewski, S., Moretti, L., & McGee, D. (2011). Succession Planning: Evidence from "Best Companies in New York.". *International Journal of Management and Marketing Research, 4*(2).

Ludwick, P. (2007). The boomers are already gone. *Journal of Housing and Community Development, 64*(1), 22–26.

Manderscheid, S. (2008). New Leader Assimilation: An Intervention for Leaders in Transition. *Advances in Developing Human Resources, 10*(5), 686–702. doi:10.1177/1523422308322269

McCleskey, J. (2014). Situational, transformational, and transactional leadership and leadership development. *Journal of Business Studies Quarterly, 5*(4), 117.

McGuire, D. (2014). *Human Resource Development.* SAGE Publications Ltd. doi:10.4135/9781473906891

Morgan, G. (1986). *Images of Organization.* Sage Publication, Inc.

Morgeson, F., DeRue, D., & Karam, E. (2010). Leadership in Teams: A Functional Approach to Understanding Leadership Structures and Processes. Journal of Management, 36. doi:10.1177/0149206309347376

Nicholson, J., & Kurucz, E. (2019). Relational Leadership for Sustainability: Building an Ethical Framework from the Moral Theory of "Ethics of Care." *Journal of Business Ethics*, *156*(1), 25–46. doi:10.100710551-017-3593-4

O'Leary, N. (2009). In the Shadow of the Founders. *Adweek*, *50*(27), AM4.

Osborn, J. (2008). Logistic Regression. In *Best Practices in Quantitative Methods* (1st ed., pp. 568–588). Sage Publication, Inc. doi:10.4135/9781412995627

Pellet, J. (2008). What Can CEO's Do to Develop Leaders? *Chief Executive*, *234*(June), 50.

Pieterse, A., Knippenberg, D., Schippers, M., & Stam, D. (2010). Transformational and transactional leadership and innovative behavior: The moderating role of psychological empowerment. *Journal of Organizational Behavior*, *31*(4), 609–623. doi:10.1002/job.650

Rafferty, A. E., & Griffin, M. A. (2004). Dimensions of transformational leadership: Conceptual and empirical extensions. *The Leadership Quarterly*, *15*(3), 329–354. doi:10.1016/j.leaqua.2004.02.009

Ready, D. (2002). How storytelling builds next generation leaders. *MIT Sloan Management Review*, (Summer), 63–69.

Russell, R., & Stone, A. G. (2002). A review of servant leadership attributes:developing a practical model. *Leadership and Organization Development Journal*, *23*(3), 145–157. doi:10.1108/01437730210424

Santos, J. P., Caetano, A., & Tavares, S. (2015). Is Training Leaders in Functional Leadership a Useful Tool for Improving the Performance of Leadership Functions and Team Effectiveness? *The Leadership Quarterly*, *26*(3), 470–484. doi:10.1016/j.leaqua.2015.02.010

Shamir, B., & Eilam, G. (2005). "What's your story?" A life-stories approach to authentic leadership development. *The Leadership Quarterly*, *16*(3), 395–417. doi:10.1016/j.leaqua.2005.03.005

Sosik, J., & Jung, D. (2010). *Full Range Leadership Development - Pathway for people, profit and planet* (1st ed.). Routledge - Taylor and Francis Group, LLC.

Tomé, E. (2011). Human resource development in the knowledge based and services driven economy: An introduction. *Journal of European Industrial Training*, *35*(6), 524–539. doi:10.1108/03090591111150077

Uhl-Bien, M. (2006). Relational Leadership Theory: Exploring the social processes of leadership and organizing. *The Leadership Quarterly*, *17*(6), 654–676. doi:10.1016/j.leaqua.2006.10.007

Wang, G., Oh, I. S., Courtright, S., & Colbert, A. (2011). Transformational leadership and performance across criteria and levels: A meta-analytic review of 25 years of research. *Group & Organization Management*, *36*(2), 223–270. doi:10.1177/1059601111401017

Zaccaro, S., Rittman, A., & Marks, M. (2001). Team leadership. *The Leadership Quarterly*, *12*(4), 451–483. doi:10.1016/S1048-9843(01)00093-5

ADDITIONAL READING

Avolio, B. (2010). *Full Range Leadership Development* (2nd ed.). Thousand Oaks, Sage Publications.

Avolio, B., & Bass, B. (2004). *MLQ International Normative Samples*. Mind Garden, Inc.

Avolio, B., & Bass, B. (2008). *Multifactor Leadership Questionnaire: Manual and Sempler Set* (3rd ed.). Mind Garden, Inc.

Bass, B., Avolio, B., Jung, G., & Berson, Y. (2003). Predicting Unit Performance by Assessing Transformational and Transactional Leadership. *The Journal of Applied Psychology*, *88*(2), 207–218. doi:10.1037/0021-9010.88.2.207 PMID:12731705

Charan, R. (2008). *O líder criador de líderes* (1st ed.). Elsevier Editora.

Collins, J. (2007). *De bom a excelente* (3rd ed.). Casa das Letras.

KEY TERMS AND DEFINITIONS

Leader: Is someone who has the ability to influence, share, and inspire their vision on others; others live and feel this vision as their own.

Leader Development: Refers to the development of individual skills of the leader.

Leadership: Is a process of reciprocal influence between the leader and the follower.

Leadership Development: Refers to the development of leadership processes within the organization, involving the development of its human and social capital.

Leadership Style: Refers to the characteristic behaviors of a leader in directing, influencing, guiding, and managing a group of people.

Succession Planning: Is a process of identifying and developing people with characteristics to assume strategic positions within the organization.

Transformational Leadership: Is a leadership style based on the leader's charisma, in its concern to inspire and motivate others and in their willingness to encourage personal and professional development of its followers.

ENDNOTE

1 Available at www.mindgarden.com and permission on 03-07-2011

APPENDIX

Table 15. Correlation analysis between the MLQ variables

		IIA	IIB	IM	IS	IC	CR	MBE A	LF	MBE P	EE	EFF	SAT	L TRANSF	L TRANS	LL	R L
IIA	r																
	p-value	1															
IIB	r	0,33*															
	p-value	0,01	1														
IM	r	0,67**	0,27*														
	p-value	0,00	0,03	1													
IS	r	0,5 2**	0,42**	0,60**													
	p-value	0,00	0,00	0,00	1												
IC	r	0,51**	0,36**	0,52**	0,59**												
	p-value	0,00	0,00	0,00	0,00	1											
CR	r	0,58**	0,45**	0,54**	0,52**	0,52**	1										
	p-value	0,00	0,00	0,00	0,00	0,00											
MBEA	r	0,14	0,23	0,16	0,04	0,04	0,22										
	p-value	0,27	0,08	0,23	0,75	0,75	0,09	1									
LF	r	0,28*	0,18	0,33**	0,32*	-0,40**	-0,45**	-0,18	1								
	p-value	0,03	0,16	0,01	0,01	0,00	0,00	0,17									
MBEP	r	0,07	0,07	0,02	0,06	-0,09	0,05	0,36**	0,28*								
	p-value	0,62	0,61	0,87	0,67	0,50	0,70	0,01	0,04	1							
EE	r	0,63**	0,29*	0,64**	0,43**	0,56**	0,54**	0,17	-0,264*	0,14	1						
	p-value	0,00	0,03	0,00	0,00	0,00	0,00	0,19	0,04	0,30							
EFF	r	075 0**	0,34**	0,57**	0,45**	0,63**	0,61**	0,16	-0,39**	-0,08	0,71**						
	p-value	0,00	0,01	0,00	0,00	0,00	0,00	0,17	0,00	0,53	0,00	1					
SAF	r	0,58**	0,29*	0,62**	0,46**	0,52**	0,45**	0,16	-0,41**	0,11	0,65**	0,64**					
	p-value	0,00	0,02	0,00	0,00	0,00	0,00	0,23	0,00	0,40	0,00	0,00	1				
LTRANSF	r	0,79**	0,63**	0,80**	0,82**	0,78**	0,68**	0,060	-0,40**	-0,01	0,67**	0,72**	0,64**				
	p-value	0,00	0,00	0,00	0,00	0,00	0,00	0,65	0,00	0,96	0,00	0,00	0,00	1			
LTRANS	r	0,41**	0,40**	0,16	0,24	0,30*	0,69**	0,86**	-0,37**	0,29*	0,41**	0,45**	0,35**	0,40**			
	p-value	0,00	0,00	0,22	0,07	0,02	0,00	0,00	0,00	0,02	0,00	0,00	0,01	0,00	1		
LL	r	0,12	0,06	0,21	0,23	-0,30*	-0,24	0,13	0,77**	0,82**	0,07	-0,29*	-0,18	-0,24	-0,03		
	p-value	0,34	0,63	0,10	0,07	0,02	0,07	0,32	0,00	0,00	0,60	0,02	0,17	0,06	0,84	1	
RL	r	0,74**	0,34**	0,69**	0,51**	0,65**	0,60**	0,19	-0,40**	0,07	0,91**	0,88**	0,86**	0,77**	0,46**	-0,19	1
	p-value	0,00	0,01	,00	,00	0,00	0,00	0,14	0,00	0,61	0,00	0,00	0,00	0,00	0,00	0,14	

Note: * Correlation is significant at the 0,05 level; ** Correlation is significant at the 0,01 level.

Chapter 4
Five Critical Domains of Effective Leadership in Higher Education Administration

Deirdre M. Conway
https://orcid.org/0000-0002-6912-5974
Southern Methodist University, USA

ABSTRACT

Higher education today consists of a complex myriad of varying levels with individuals tasked to perform multiple roles and responsibilities. Faculty and staff find themselves tasked with multiple responsibilities and fewer resources. Many who embark on the journey of becoming academic administrators and leaders in higher education often do so based on their technical expertise and successes as a faculty member within the institution. Few organizations prepare faculty to step into leadership roles with the appropriate training. One area which often lacks training is in the area of individual leadership capabilities and connecting with others within the organization to accomplish a common goal. This chapter will provide insight into five critical domains necessary for individuals to focus on developing before entering into a leadership role within a higher education institution. Within each domain are central and core competencies which help to determine effectiveness in higher education leadership.

DOI: 10.4018/978-1-7998-2807-5.ch004

INTRODUCTION

Higher education today consists of a complex myriad of varying levels with individuals tasked to perform multiple roles and responsibilities. Faculty and staff no longer perform a single set of responsibilities; instead, they find themselves tasked with multiple responsibilities and fewer resources (Morris & Laipple, 2015). Many who embark on the journey of becoming academic administrators and leaders in higher education often do so based on their technical expertise and successes as a faculty member within the institution. Few organizations prepare faculty to step into leadership roles with the appropriate training (Leaming, 1998). One such area, which often lacks training, is in the area of individual leadership capabilities and connecting with individuals to accomplish a common goal.

The job of any leader requires an incredible amount of stamina, often feels taxing, and might take an emotional and physical toll if one fails to look after their individual health and well-being. Bolman and Gallos (2011) stress the importance of this in their book *Reframing Academic Leadership*, when discussing the five steps to healthy academic leadership and healthy academic leaders. They point out that healthy leaders look for opportunities to create strategies which will "sustain confidence and leadership resolve during the darkest hours" (Bolman & Gallos, 2011, p. 191), and that one should work toward achieving this accomplishment by paying close attention to the five key areas: boundaries, biology, balance, beauty, and bounce.

This chapter will provide insight into five critical domains necessary for individuals to focus on developing before entering into a leadership role within a higher education institution. These critical domains include: 1) Personal and Ethical Leadership, 2) Academic Leadership, 3) Strategic and Organizational Leadership, 4) Policy and Political Leadership, and 5) Evidence-Based Leadership. Within each domain are central and core competencies that help to determine effectiveness in higher education leadership. This book chapter will examine each of these domains and competencies. The goal of this chapter is to provide evidence related to best practices and recommendations associated with these five critical domains of leadership as well as the core competencies in each of the domain areas.

Personal and Ethical Leadership

As a leader in higher education administration, the ability to act with integrity, take responsibility for ones actions, and be portrayed as honest, provides a strong base for those in the organization (Gmelch & Miskin, 2011). Understanding what this means as a leader will guide individuals looking to advance within higher education.

Without this type of leadership, many organizations may struggle with fulfilling the institution's mission and vision.

Leadership involves the ability to influence, to work with people, and looks for ways to facilitate effective goal accomplishments with the primary function of focusing on producing change and movement within the organization (Northouse, 2010). Tapping into these traits in order to lead an organization with honesty, integrity, and responsibility shows the importance of communicating and acting. Through open communication and actions, leaders create an organization on which to build trust. Beatty and Page (2007) noted, "Trust requires their appreciation of a long-term investment in their personal interest and agendas" (p. 201). This statement reflects that building trust takes time, and remains a critical component for those interested in a role within higher education administration as a leader.

As a leader, possessing self-awareness and understanding one's own strengths and weaknesses allows for opportunities of growth. As leaders in higher education, many consider themselves to be *lifelong learners*. Laal, and Salamati (2012) defined lifelong learning as "a whole range of learning that includes: formal, informal, and non-formal learning" (p. 399). In addition, this type of learning includes the skills, knowledge, attitudes, and behaviors acquired by individuals throughout their day-to-day experiences (Dunn, 2003). Many individuals may struggle to understand the value of lifelong learning or realize that even though it may be unintentional, they are indeed in situations that make them lifelong learners. Whether formally or informally, any time individuals take on a task to learn a new skill, tool, or way of doing things, they are expanding their abilities and learning (DeMeuse, et al, 2012). As a leader, individuals often find themselves relying on their own strengths, such as the ability to connect with people to gain trust and a common understanding. This ability allows individuals to work with others to accomplish goals. This strength could be utilized as a leader to advance the mission of the school, while also helping those within the organization to achieve success in their own roles.

One major weakness for some individuals seeking to enter into a leadership role may be in the ability to bring their own voice to the table. As a rising or new leader, one may be fearful of speaking up in group settings or providing thoughts and opinions around what they believed was an appropriate action to take in a situation. Oftentimes leaders lack the ability to speak openly and freely regarding problems without feeling as though someone might judge their ability. Barwick (2007) expressed this best when he referred to leaders as people who "give up the prerogative of acting and reacting like everyone else" (p. 160).

In 2011, Brian Yoder published a report titled *Engineering by the Numbers* for the American Society of Engineering Educators (ASEE), which laid out the challenges facing engineering schools today. Some of the statistics included issues associated with a diverse population studying engineering disciplines. During the 2010-2011 academic year, approximately 4% of students graduating with an engineering degree identified as African American, and 8.5% as Hispanic, with women making up a total of 18.2% of all engineering bachelor's degrees awarded. In addition, Yoder pointed out that only 13.8% of women held tenured and tenure-track faculty appointments as of fall 2011, and the total percentage for African Americans, (men and women), was even worse, at just 2.5% (Yoder, 2012). With so much focus on increasing diversity and equity in higher education, as well as in the engineering discipline, the percentages associated with women and all populations of underrepresented minorities in the engineering disciplines poses a frightening reality related to a lack of participation in this area.

As an academic leader, identifying the reasons underrepresented minority and women students choose not to study engineering persists. For those who enroll in an engineering discipline, leaders should work to engage these populations early to identify ways to retain them in the field. Understanding the reasons why these students fail to study, or leave engineering to study another discipline, remains an important factor to helping understand and address the low retention and persistence rates within this discipline (Mara, Bogue, Shen, & Rodgers, 2007).

Today, more than ever, institutions are focusing on diversity issues within their organizations. One metric, which some institutions are utilizing, focuses on the concept of Cultural Intelligence. The idea behind Culture Intelligence focuses on the ability for one to suspend judgment of another until all information becomes available beyond just the ethnicity of an individual, so that one accounts for varying personality attributes (Triandis, 2006). This concept works to allow individuals to "meet people where they are" and learn from their individual experiences to gain a better understanding of differences and backgrounds (Livermore, 2011). The role for those in higher education leadership is to work toward this common ground and understanding.

Gender and racial parity continues to be a top priority for many higher education institutions; however, this attainment of gender and racial parity also comes with challenges and, often times, many institutions fall short of this accomplishment for a variety of reasons. Academic leaders should focus on working with the school as a whole to create a safe and inclusive environment so that all faculty, staff, and students feel comfortable and welcome. Through training, conversation, trust, and willingness to understand all sides, leaders can become a resource and a knowledgeable expert (over time) to provide feedback and support for this important initiative (Gmelch & Miskin, 1993).

Understanding that most people operate with the best of intentions when working through problems or issues will help leaders to stop and think about how they can collectively work together to find solutions. Knowing that issues and concerns that may come to light arise from individual passion, and not individual personal attacks on one another, will help leaders understand the situation and realize the importance of their role. Possessing the ability to listen to a situation as an impartial observer and provide fair treatment to all parties involved helps leaders and those within the organization realize there is a strong desire to work toward solving problems and finding solutions without judgment. Critical listening skills and the ability to render impartial decisions provide leaders with insight and the ability for others to view them as a valuable resource within their organization (Lawrence, 2009).

Many people think the minute they receive a leadership position those around them will automatically consider them a leader that they will willingly follow. Unfortunately, leaders who feel this way often fail to find support in their institutions. As Peter Shapiro (2005) pointed out, "Leadership is an action, not a title, and the ability to lead can be found in every person. Each of us needs to claim our authority to lead at the right time and in the right place" (p. 1). This statement should resonate with those seeking to become leaders within their organizations. Current and future leaders should understand that their actions would speak louder than their words or their title when attempting to gain the trust of those within the organization. As a leader, the individual serves as a role model for others, acting with character, integrity, and honesty (Northouse, 2010). In addition, leaders should create and adhere to a personal code of conduct which will help guide them through the many challenges, obstacles, and temptations that they will encounter at different stages of their career (Plinio, 2009).

A major challenge for some may be in the ability to separate from those who used to be seen as peers. Good leaders take advantage of social opportunities for a variety of very good reasons; however, they also know the importance of keeping some distance between themselves and those in their organizations (Barwick, 2007).

Academic Leadership

As an extremely complex organization, higher education today needs strong leaders. With so many demands from students, faculty, staff, parents, government agencies, and even donors, academic leaders need to understand the role they play within the institution. Leadership definitions vary greatly by experts in the field. Over the years, what *defines* a leader seems to change again and again. Understanding that everyone can possess leadership skills and traits will help guide individuals through their careers. Following Peter Northouse's theory, the ensuing components will help define individual leadership: 1) Leadership involves a process, 2) Leadership influences others, 3) Leadership occurs in groups, and 4) Leadership involves a common goal (Northouse, 2010).

Attaining the necessary skills and traits to operate as a leader who successfully works through the components identified by Northouse will allow individuals, as academic leaders, opportunities to understand the vast differences within their respective organizations. It will also provide each with the ability and skills needed to adjust their leadership styles based on the group dynamics and those working on the project or problem (i.e., faculty, staff, students, donors).

Field, or technical, expertise will no longer suffice to bring a campus together to advance an institution's mission and goals. For individuals choosing to participate in academic leadership, there is a need to understand individual mindsets, preferences, and even biases. As a leader, one must learn about varying areas previously unfamiliar in order to provide all parties with valuable resources within their units.

Understanding that today's student body needs much more than a strong technical skillset in their field of study in order to achieve success once they graduate, will help educational leaders identify resources to support these students throughout their academic careers at the institution. Simply providing students with curricular expertise (developing subject matter knowledge and academic literacy) will not give them the leg up they need when entering what many describe as an extremely competitive job market (Deming, 2017). Students today can set themselves apart from others by participating in co-curricular opportunities (activities that tend to fall outside of the academic degree—sports, societies, part-time work, entrepreneurial activities, or volunteering). Encouraging students to recognize the value of this co-curricular activity as part of their development (Andrews, 2013) is a critical role for educational leaders.

When serving in a leadership role, individuals need to recognize situations in which others around them may not receive what some consider fair treatment. Historically in academia, this lack of fairness often surrounded women and underrepresented minorities. The history of higher education consists of a predominately white male profession which seems challenged to shift the tides which would allow anyone interested in pursuing a career in academia to easily break into the ranks (Thelin, 2011). As an educational leader it becomes imperative to recognize and acknowledge the injustices of the past and work to ensure that all parties receive the same opportunities regardless of their individual differences or attributes.

In the 2007, ASHE Higher Education Report, *Are the Walls Really Down*, the authors identify ten organizational barriers which affect the workplace. These barriers include; hiring, promotion and advancement, lack of support, failure to empower and include in decision making, differing expectations, stereotyping and organizational fit, lack of mentoring and access to formal and informal networks, isolation and soloing, tokenism, and the revolving door (Evans & Chun, 2007).

Faculty searches are often areas where these types of barriers present issues. With each faculty search organizational leaders and search committees should work to ensure that a broader range of potential candidates can be attracted to help create a more diverse and inclusive environment, without falling into the trap of hiring minority faculty to reflect a sense of *tokenism,* as discuss in the 2007 ASHE report. Tokenism refers to the assumption that the goal of diversity reaches satisfactory levels simply by hiring a few minorities into faculty positions just to *check a box* (Wijaya, 2020). The goal of every faculty search should be to find more effective ways to affect specific change in how minority populations are recruited to better represent a diverse and inclusive faculty body.

One way to change this lack of representation in underrepresented populations focuses on collaborative efforts. Leaders should look to identify unintentional biases within job postings, ad placements, and resume screening processes, which may be limiting for some underrepresented populations. For example, if hiring committees are reviewing applications and have an allegiance to specific institutions, they may not consider candidates from other institutions that they consider a *lesser institution.* Leaders could work toward preventing this unintended bias toward applications by requiring that all applicants' personal information (i.e. names, school attended, etc.) be de-identified during the screening process to select candidates for the first round of interviews. Working with faculty and central diversity offices, leaders can change the way ads are written, as well as identify areas for posting jobs that will draw a more diverse candidate pool as a way to aid in this change. This type of change and transformation could take many years before institutions see a shift toward a more diverse faculty population; however, these are critical to the success of creating a more diverse population within every organization.

A good leader can help others grow and expand their skillset, so they in turn gain leadership skills. Every organization is faced with good leaders and poor leaders, which can influence individual growth and mindset related to how organizations should operate. Some of the best leaders are those that believe in the ability of others, as they choose to serve as mentors and provided individuals with opportunities to grow and advance in their own careers. For educational leaders, the ability to serve in this role, as an inspiration and guide for others, remains paramount. Education, after all, according to Miller and Miller (1997) persists as, "the acquisition of knowledge and skills by the learner" (p. 3). If the role of the educator then focuses on ensuring that the learner receive the knowledge and skills necessary, why then would leaders not transfer this ability to *educate* those individuals working in higher education in order to better prepare them for positions to more effectively transfer leadership knowledge?

One way in which leaders can be successful in the shift to educate others in the organization is through what can be referred to as *employee empowerment.* The AMA Dictionary of Business and Management refers to employee empowerment as a way to provide motivational strategy to channel more responsibilities to employees (Kurian, 2013). What this means is as leaders, and in an organization, individuals are provided with an opportunity to advance and grow in their own careers. While many might say the path of least resistance would result in a swift solution, and that by giving people the answers all you accomplished was solving the current problem at hand. Leaders should work with individuals to teach them the tools and skills needed to arrive at answers or solutions to problems—this increased knowledge will provide for individual growth.

Serving as a mentor to others will also support individual growth and should be part of every leader's role within their organization. The first step in any mentoring plan requires meeting with the individual to be mentored as a way to discover what areas they want help in developing in their current role, or to understand what type of role they hope to grow into as they look to advance their careers. Once goals are identified, the leader (mentor) should work with the individual (mentee) to come up with a plan to realize those goals. This will require staff to understand whether the leader is willing and available to teach new skills or is just interested in serving as a sounding board.

Other challenges that many academic leaders face are related to facilities and resource allocations. This challenge remains one of the most critical components for just about any leader working toward attaining adequate space to support their organization. Today, in higher education, academic leaders often receive fewer and fewer resources—less money, less staff, less space—while at the same time, institutions ask these same individuals to perform greater tasks and to stretch the resources provided even further (Morris & Laipple, 2015). Understanding these pressure points and ways to work within the organization's constraints requires leaders to have a strong balance and understanding of the critical nature their institution is under at a particular point in time. Assessing status within the organization and planning for future growth, changes, or even reductions, will help determine the direction a leader needs to focus efforts related to facilities and resources.

Physical facilities and space allocations within a unit often appear extremely limited and scarce based on available land within the university and funds available to expand. Understanding the complexity and scarcity of physical assets in higher education, at times proves cost intensive or even prohibitive, (Musa & Ahmad, 2012) adding additional barriers to units looking to grow and expand. Many times, as a leader, individuals face challenges to identify additional facility resources and make expansion requests on behalf of the organization. As such, the institution may require unit leaders to make a case for why their unit should receive these scarce resources over another unit on campus. In addition, as a leader, the institution may require you to show that if given the facility or space, your unit possesses ample resources (funding and staff) to move quickly to renovate and maintain that space.

Personnel and staffing resource, at times, can seem even more contentious. With so much emphasis today being placed on cost cutting and limiting the number of staff within a unit, academic leaders need to work together to determine the best use of these limited resources. In depth analysis across all units can become problematic for some leaders, as staff within the organization may worry about the risk of losing their jobs as a result of these efforts. Leaders are faced with asking some hard questions. Some of these questions may include: "Should current roles and responsibilities change?" "Are there duties that are repetitive in the unit?" "Should tasks currently handled by unit staff occur in a central processing office instead?" Understanding staff job responsibilities will help determine if resource shifts should happen or if additional personnel needs exist in order to accomplish the goals of the unit.

Strategic and Organizational Leadership

From the early formation of higher education, institutions were run by faculty members who not only educated the students but also lived with them and served as mentors and guides through the maturation of the student as a whole person. As demand for education grew and more and more regulations saddled institutions, faculty simply lacked the bandwidth and possible administrative skillset to handle all the activities required (Thelin, 2011). Increased student population and new regulations brought about the role of support staff and administrators in higher education institutions. These individuals became experts in the administrative activities associated with the institution, freeing up faculty to focus on the classroom education of the students.

With the expansion of federal and state regulations came the need for these newly appointed administrators to fine tune their skillsets and become experts in specific areas, (much like a faculty member serving as an expert in their academic discipline). Today, administrators handle issues related to Title IX, business and finance, student affairs, residential life, and other areas related to the administrative functions of the institution. These individuals are tasked with not only overseeing activities within their own organizations but also staying on top of both federal and state regulations. For academic leaders to achieve success in higher education, one important factor relies on the ability to understand the complexities and inner workings of the institution (Thelin, 2011). One area leaders may struggle with is in the area of staff performance and evaluations.

Performance issues associated with staff resources often can limit organizations and cause issues with the ability to move the organization forward. Individuals preparing or aspiring to enter into a leadership role should gain the skills necessary to deal with personnel and performance management. There are many training opportunities and resources available for leaders to utilize in order to build this skillset along with volumes of books and articles on building leadership skill and capacity, thus reiterating the need for leaders to be life-long learners. In order to stay on top of human resources issues one should participate in refresher training every few years to stay abreast of the changing dynamics associated with personnel issues as a way to continually improve and serve the institution. Without continued training, a leader may fail to understand changes to labor laws and current trends in the workforce that could affect how they manage and supervise others.

In looking at the various concepts associated with organization leadership, three particular theories appear to resonate with many researchers. These theories include, 1) the trait theory—a theory of leadership which focuses on personal qualities and characteristics, 2) behavioral theory—leadership capabilities (behavior) learned over time, and 3) contingency theory—the belief that leadership styles may change given a particular situation (Robbins & Judge, 2012). As a leader in higher education great importance falls on these individuals to understand varying theories related to organizational leadership in order to determine the best method to use when addressing a particular situation. Understanding that leadership comes easy for some and more difficult for others who need to work at learning this skill—developing relationships that work for all parties involved, benefits the institution. Adaptability, the willingness to adjust one's methods depending on the situation or the individual, creates a valuable asset for any leader in higher education and a skill that everyone should continually work to improve in order to achieve effectiveness in their role (Calarco, 2020).

As leaders develop in their own roles and skillsets, it is important to manage their own expectations. Oftentimes, the most effective leaders are those that do not have to have their hands in every activity or every decision. Balancing the variety of responsibilities thrust upon leaders in higher education can, at times, be a daunting task. Leaders should be able to rely on the staff members within their organization to own more of the processes and day-to-day activities. This is a concept reflected as a *managing up* method of organizational leadership (Palmer, 1998). By empowering those within the organization, each individual has the opportunity to learn their own behavioral organizational skills, which will serve to help them advance in their careers just as current leaders have done throughout their careers.

A critical piece of working toward a clear focus for any organization hinges on a strong strategic plan and planning process. The leadership within an organization should not take this process lightly and needs adequate preparation to invest a significant amount of time and resources into the planning process should they wish to create a successful plan for others within the organization to follow.

A 2013 study performed by the Hanover Research Group identified two interrelated steps considered keys for a successful strategic planning effort. These steps consisted of: 1) the ability to formulate goals, objectives, and action steps based on institutional values and mission, and 2) the ability to monitor implementation, track progress, and revise the plan as necessary (Hanover Research, 2013).

A shared vision gives organizations strength when looking to move forward and advance their mission (Northouse, 2010). If the members of the organization fail to agree on a vision and mission, success will not come easily. For educational leaders to obtain success in their roles, they should work to ensure that everyone in the organization understands the institutional vision and mission while remaining transparent throughout the process in order to gain buy-in and support from everyone within the organization.

Building a vision takes time, patience, and persistence. Leaders will need to work together to determine the current culture of the organization when constructing their new vision. A clear vision with a strong mission and shared values provides organizations with the opportunity to achieve high levels of success. Many people think that a vision statement and a mission statement are the same. While both of these statements may possess similar components, each provides institutions and those interested in the institution with good insight into the purpose and driving factors of the organization. A leader's vision helps create a clear organizational picture related to whom the organization aspires or hopes to represent. The vision statement also creates a clear picture to let people know what the leadership within the organization cares about and how they will work to achieve the vision set forth—who/what the organization will look like when their vision is achieved.

Developing and growing an organization requires a considerable amount of time as well as an inordinate level of responsibility from the leaders within the organization (Leaming, 1998). Identifying ways to improve services, such as improving the ways in which students receive information in the classroom, or improving the tenure process for faculty on campus can all help advance the institution. Process improvement happens through collaborative work within a unit as well as across campus. The more resources and buy-in gained for any type of change in process or service, the more likely the change will succeed and persist (Cohen, 2005).

Educational leaders are often tasked with finding new opportunities to expand programming and funding for their institutions. If schools remain static with their program offerings, then eventually enrollments will start to decline and students will select other institutions that offer cutting-edge programs or a wider variety of programs. Funding also plays a key role in advancing an institution. Another area affecting leaders focuses on donor relations and interactions. Potential donors play an important role within the institutions and leaders should understand this dynamic in order to find ways to connect donors to initiatives within their school (Leaming, 1998). This type of interaction and connection often leads to the introduction of new ideas, which happen due to the donor's willingness to fund the opportunity. Given all of these critical components to advancing the institution and ensuring future success, the ability of leaders to possess the skills necessary to balance the demands of their roles, as well as the demands of the institution, creates an incredible need at the leadership level.

Policy and Political Leadership

With a strong lack of public confidence in higher education today, academic leaders face many challenges and an immeasurable amount of work in order to restore this public confidence. Resources continue to shrink, tuition increases persist, student loan debt is out of control, retention and completion issues remain at the forefront, and the federal and state governmental agencies continue to put more and more pressure on higher education to improve (Brown, Kurzweil, & Pritchett, 2017). With the cards seemingly stacked against institutions, the change agents, known as academic leaders, need to find solutions collectively, in order to make significant and lasting changes in how the public, as well as government agencies, view higher education. Mettler (2014) discussed why this matters and pointed out the role of higher education to be "more necessary than ever to foster economic progress and growth, as well as innovations that benefit society as a whole" (p. 192).

Each student comes to their institution from different backgrounds and with different skills. While the number of international students across the US remains relatively small—5.5% of all students enrolled in US institutions as of 2015—(Digest of Educational Statistics, 2016), their needs on campus continue to grow. Adjustments to the US culture, at times, challenge and overwhelm these students, with many of them living far away from their families and homes for the first time. Because of these stresses, student affairs professionals and academic leaders need to understand the cultural differences of their students and work to find ways to help them adjust to their new academic and social setting (Conway, 2016). Recent challenges within the political landscape of the US have proven problematic for many institutions as it relates to international student enrollment.

The impact policies pose to institutions can determine not only funding levels, but also student enrollment and institutional growth. The success of any educational leader depends on understanding policies that affect their own higher education institution and the industry as a whole. Understanding implications associated with new policies and policy changes will allow leaders to prepare for these changes and prepare their institutions for the best way to handle these policies.

Continuing to focus on international students, one recent policy which reflects a major impact on student enrollment known as Executive Order 13780, which instituted a temporary travel ban on six countries: Iran, Libya, Somalia, Sudan, Syria, and Yemen. Initially executed in January 2017, and revised in March 2017 (removing Iraq from the original ban), it was in place for a 90-day period. The 2017 Executive Order 13780 restricted all travelers from these countries from entering the United States. In March 2020, the global COVID-19 pandemic issued a shockwave through the entire country. Higher education was not immune. With lockdowns across the nation and travel bans implemented to prevent travel not only within the

US but also from other regions of the world, higher education was immediately affected. Institutions pivoted to virtual learning platforms and saw large drops in enrollment from international students beginning in the fall of 2021. While the long-term impact to higher education institutions remains unclear at present time, a report by *Inside Higher E*, found that nearly 4 in 10 universities reported drops in overall international student applications (Redden, 2017). This statistic should send up red flags and alarm educational leaders as they work to increase enrollments, specifically with international student populations.

Understanding current policies associated with higher education at both the state and federal level will provide leaders with the necessary insight to gain success in their roles and provide their institutions with a valuable resource. In addition, should a policy implementation take place that could adversely affect higher education (i.e., Executive Order 13780), administrators should garner the necessary skills to analyze this policy and make recommendations to those above them as a way to take proactive action toward the policy and any issues which may arise as a result of the policy.

Well-trained, seasoned professionals in policy analysis start to anticipate policy directions before agencies implement them, and these professionals work to better prepare their institutions for changes in the event new policies take effect. One example related to this type of proactive action focuses on a campus-carry gun policy in the State of Texas. For several years, politicians attempted to pass this policy, which would allow individuals with gun permits to legally carry weapons on college campuses. During the 2015 legislative session, the bill passed and campus-carry went into effect on August 1, 2015 (Senate bill 11, 2015).

Once campus leaders saw the bill would likely pass during the session, institutions across the state came together to discuss how they would handle this new policy once the bill was in place. Policy analysts and lobbyists came together and fought hard against the bill. However, when the bill obtained enough support to pass, state institutions started looking for ways to mitigate the impact on their campuses. Private institutions achieved greater success in ensuring protections from the campus-carry bill and, in fact, lobbied for the bill to include an *opt-out* clause for private institutions. Section 411.2031.e outlines the rights of private institutions to opt-out of this policy, by stating:

A private or independent institution of higher education in this state, after consulting with students, staff, and faculty of the institution, may establish rules, regulations, or other provisions prohibiting license holders from carrying handguns on premises that are owned or leased and operated by the institution and located on the campus of the institution (Senate bill 11, 2015).

Without this proactive stance and ability to analyze the recommended policy, private institutions may not understand the implications or what they may need in order to fully prepare for the impending bill passage and requirements to adhere to the new regulations.

Every year, thousands of parents entrust their children to higher education institutions across the country. As a leader in higher education, understanding the relationship between student and institution helps to guide individuals through their roles and responsibilities. Until the 1961 court case, *Dixon v. Alabama State Board of Education*, higher education institutions served students in a capacity known as *In Loco Parentis*—in place of the parents. In 1999, Bickel and Lake noted:

With the fall of in loco parentis, the American College was no longer insular: it entered a new era of accountability in the courts. The fall of in loco parentis and the new role of the legal system on campus facilitated important developments in legal relations between students and administrators (and others) on campus (p. 8).

With the demand today for due process and the focus on constitutionality, the academic leader should possess a clear understanding of the landscape associated with the current student (and parent) relationships at their institution. Educating oneself on how students and parents view the role of higher education will help guide academic leaders in how to interact with students, how to deal with issues which may arise, and what to expect from the students and parents related to the laws and regulations in place for student protections.

Understanding students' mindsets today allows leaders in higher education to prepare for any incident that may occur—incidents such as the Virginia Tech shootings in 2007, the murder and rape of Jeanne Clery in 1986, and many other incidents, which changed and continue to shape the landscape of higher education. While incidents have occurred on college campuses throughout history, the way in which society addresses these issues and the magnitude of some of the incidents over time worked to change the public's perception of higher education as well as the institutional responses. Possessing the ability to prepare for a more litigious population through education and awareness will help leaders move forward within their institutions.

Another type of legal incident involved not a student issue, but an employment issue. Many times employee complaints trickle down and become more of a *he said/ she said* situation in which academic leaders will need to make a best judgment call to resolve the issue. A multitude of reasons exist as to why employees may file complaints, or even lawsuits against their employers. In higher education, the institution and its leaders may also deal with the public image associated with any sort of bad press that may arise as a result of employee or student complaints.

Employee complaints often come with many challenges. When an employee files a complaint against an individual or the institution, a leader's responsibility rests on the fact that they need to protect the institution. Administrative leaders work to identify potential problems that may interfere with institutional goals or the accomplishment of the mission, or that create threats to the health and safety of the campus community. They work to identify the causes of problems, any contributing factors, and levels of risk associated with the problems created (Kaplin & Lee, 2007).

Legal issues within higher education, whether student, faculty, or staff-related, takes an enormous amount of knowledge, time, energy, and patience. Kaplin and Lee (2007) indicated that, "despite the attempts of institutions and their national associations to limit the impact of federal regulations and federal funding conditions on postsecondary education, the federal presence on campus continues to expand" (p. 614). With this growing federal presence on campus, leaders need to understand how this will affect not only students, but also faculty and staff. Will federal government mandates exist that go against the institution's mission? If so, how will the leaders of the institution handle this situation? Many concerns and issues face leaders today related to federal regulations that require strong knowledge and expertise in this area.

With any new regulation, policy of mandate, leaders need to understand the impact and implications for their schools and institutions as a whole. Commanding a strong understanding of the rules handed down by not only the federal government, but also the state government, will help to ensure an institution is able to adhere to all regulations. This expertise and knowledge will protect students, faculty, and staff from improper actions and potential legal actions because of failure to comply with such regulations. In order to grow in this area a leader will need to review and analyze current regulations and policy, both at the federal and state levels, so that as these regulations or policies change, or as new policies and regulations get enacted, there is a clear understanding of how the changes may impact the institution (Kaplin & Lee, 2007). This gained knowledge in the area of federal and state policy will help provide the leaders with a level of expertise needed to prepare their institution for policy changes in the future.

Evidence-Based Leadership

Student learning outcomes continue to bubble to the top of current events and topics in higher education today. The demand for quality education seems higher than ever before (Brown, Kurzweil & Pritchett, 2017). Many institutions feel the pressure to improve the quality of teaching and overall student learning. With these increased demands comes a strong need for an assessment plan to ensure institutions achieve strong student learning outcomes.

Regarding Student Learning Objectives (SLOs), Carriveau (2016) noted that "an integral part of developing SLO statements is to determine the most important (key) topics that need to be covered and map them on a timeline of when they would be addressed during the course" (p. 3). This statement appears to describe a course syllabus—mapping out the topics based on specific times throughout the semester. Carriveau's developmental strategy goes on to lay out a three-level model—goals, topics, and clarifying statements—to help guide individuals through the process of setting up learning outcomes (Carriveau, 2016). Using a syllabus to outline the expectations of the course will help new faculty make sure they meet the expectations for institutional learning outcomes.

Using available case studies to understand SLO processes will help guide faculty and academic leaders through the process of SLO creation, assessment, and working through any necessary adjustments or modifications to current content. Galle and Galle (2010) provided a journal article focused on three different cases of institutions integrating SLO assessment into their general education curriculum. Each institution performed an in-depth analysis of the current situation associated with SLOs on their respective campuses, followed by a sustainable development plan on how to implement the SLOs, and finally the institutions worked to align upper-level courses and program outcomes to ensure consistency across all courses and programs. After analyzing the experiences from these three institutions, Galle and Galle described a three-stage process for designing and integrated SLOs into the general education curriculum through:

1. Establishing initial discussions that lead to alignment of key university SLOs with key general education SLOs.
2. Training and workshoping with faculty groups and administrators whose first task usually focuses on key general education outcomes and select the appropriate measures for them.
3. Training and workshoping with faculty groups who teach the junior and senior courses that most majors take to develop and establish course-embedded assessment in the assessment plans of the degree programs (Galle & Galle, 2010).

In order to develop this skillset, leaders will need to attend seminars and workshops that focus specifically on student learning outcomes and ways to assess these outcomes. Building off of the importance of developing strong student learning outcomes (SLOs) in coursework, institutional leaders should also create program evaluation plans to ensure SLOs developed will garner the best possible outcomes for students in the school's academic program. Program evaluations take place either informally or formally to provide leadership with information to support the methods used or help provide insight into changes to implement for improvement. Buller (2012) pointed out that a solid program evaluation includes data collected from not only evaluation and assessment standards, but also other sources that will help determine the quality of instruction. One way to create solid program evaluations includes aggregating scores on student course evaluations or external peer reviews.

According to Dunsworth and Billings (2012), a straightforward program evaluation process consists of five steps. These steps include:

1. Creating and completing a blueprint to define the purpose and scope of the evaluation.
2. Data gathering needed to assess the program's effectiveness.
3. Analysis of the data in order to identify strengths and weaknesses.
4. Using the results to plan for next steps.
5. Communicating results to stakeholders in order to build support and buy-in.

Having this clearly defined process will help leaders develop an understanding of how to work on creating a structured program evaluation for future work.

Educational leaders need the ability to scrutinize literature in order to determine whether the information presented provides a valid representation of the situation. There are often claims that data manipulation occurs and that some researchers work with data to tell whatever story they feel needs to fit the conclusion drawn (Ioannidis, 2005). Well-trained and educated leaders should have the ability to analyze literature and the findings within the literature to determine validity and usefulness for their specific needs. This ability to analyze the literature takes practice and training—a skill learned and developed over time.

Today's academic leaders often possess four major functions related to their role in higher education: decision making, problem solving, conflict resolution, and consensus building (Fincher, 2003). Each component takes an extraordinary amount of time, energy, and resources. As a leader in higher education, the ability to consider specific details and analyze the entire situation in order to make an informed decision may make or break a leader's ability within the organization. For example, if a leader makes poor decisions, support for the leader quickly diminishes and those around the leader lose trust in their ability to guide the team toward success (Wergin, 2007). Looking at each of these four functions, leaders might select varying ways to approach decisions and resolutions based on the situation occurring at the time.

Looking specifically at the financial aspects and responsibilities of leaders in higher education may require a cost-benefit analysis to determine whether the decision appears sound for the school or institution. As Buller (2012) pointed out, "traditional cost-benefit analysis consists of weighing the negative implications of a decision (the cost) against the positive implications (the benefits)" (p. 115). Many times the analysis completed consists of a simple calculation and instinct, while other times, spreadsheets and an in-depth review of historical information to determine outcomes may take more time and require other parties' involvement. A majority of the time, financial decisions contain highly confidential information and, most of the time, provide little opportunity to share with those outside of the leadership team.

FUTURE RESEARCH

Higher Education today is faced with a myriad of challenges—from increasing costs to higher demands from society for a more equitable solution—– institutions and institutional leaders require the skills to navigate so many demands. Understanding how strong leadership skills specific to each of the domains outlined in this chapter can enhance an individual's ability to lead and organization, regardless of current issues or trends, can ensure leaders have the skillset needed for success. While this chapter focused broadly on each of these domains, researchers can utilize this information to dig deeper into the specific needs for various entities; such as, Higher Education Centers, and two and four year colleges and universities.

Higher Education Centers

In looking at the five critical domains for effective leadership in higher education—personal and ethical, academic, strategic and organizational, policy and political, and evidence based leadership—future research on how each of these domains influences those interested in becoming leaders at a Higher Education Center can provide valuable insight into the values and skills needed for success. Utilizing qualitative methods to understand roles and responsibilities of those currently serving as leaders within Higher Education Centers will guide researchers toward specific skills needed for this type of organization. Grounding research on each of these five critical domains will provide researchers with a deeper understanding of leadership skill alignment for this type of center as organizations look to hire future leaders.

Two-Year Colleges

Two-year colleges— sometimes referred to as community colleges or junior colleges—have transitioned dramatically over the past few decades. Initially these institutions were focused on preparing students for trades and skills that would provide them with better jobs. Associate degrees and certificates were awarded to provide students with new skills to prepare for the workforce. Two-year institutions served individuals within the community or nearby communities. Today two-year colleges not only enroll students from areas outside of the community but they also enroll large populations of international students. In addition, many two-year colleges are now offering 4 year degrees and dual credit courses for high school students. Understanding the needs of the current student population within two-year colleges is important for any academic leader's success. Future research on those currently in leadership roles at two-year colleges utilizing the five critical domains of effective leadership identified in this chapter will help guide and influence organizations on the skills needed for this type of institution.

Four-Year Colleges and Universities

With the rising costs of four-year institutions, the current demands from society and government for more access, and the pressures on institutions related to new policies and regulations, institutional leaders must be well attuned to the needs of their students, faculty, staff and community. Future research on individuals currently serving in a leadership capacity within a four-year college or university will help guide these institutions. Utilizing qualitative methods, researchers can ground their research on the five critical domains outlined in this chapter to guide their research toward a stronger understanding of the skills needed for effective leadership within their organizations.

CONCLUSION

Diving into one's background and experiences associated with leadership skills makes individuals realize that while they may possess an incredible amount of knowledge on how to handle tasks and work with people, there remains a large amount of information and skills to learn in order to be effective as a leader. This chapter looked at five critical domains that higher education administrators should build capacity around in order to be effective leaders within their roles. Expertise in each of these domains requires dedication and commitment. In order to continue to grow as a leader and show an ability to handle the many challenges higher education institutions face, it becomes critical for leaders to continue to seek out training and education related to growth and best practices. Through formal training and working with others leaders, leaders can continue to grow and develop their personal skillset while lifting others up to grow as well. All administrators and academic leaders need to find a balance—they should understand and experience the classroom or experience working directly with students in another capacity to better understand the true operational activities of higher education. Without this knowledge and skill, academic leaders simply focus on one side of the equation and fail to see the full picture.

REFERENCES

Andrews, M. (2013). Why our students need co-curricular, not extra-curricular, activities. *The Guardian*. http://www.the guardian.com/higher-education-network/blog/2013/jan/22/student-development-university-curriculum-design

Barwick, J. (2007). Following the leader and leading the followers. *Leadership in place: How academic professionals can find their leadership voice,* 149-168.

Beatty, E. R., & Page, R. (2007). Leadership as place. In J. F. Wergin (Ed.), *Leadership in Place: How academic professional can find their leadership voice* (pp. 192–223). Jossey-Bass.

Bickel, R. D., & Lake, P. F. (1999). *The rights and responsibilities of the modern university: Who assumes the risks of college life?* Carolina Academic Press.

Bolman, L. G., & Gallos, J. V. (2011). *Reframing academic leadership.* Jossey-Bass.

Brown, J., Kurzweil, M., & Pritchett, W. (2017). *Quality assurance in U.S. higher education: The Current landscape and principles for reform.* ITHAKA. https://sr.ithaka. org/publications/quality-assurance-in-u-s-higher-education/ doi:10.18665/sr.303620

Buller, J. L. (2012). *The essential department chair: A comprehensive desk reference.* Jossey-Bass.

Calarco, A. (2020). *Adaptable leadership: What it takes to be a quick-change artist.* White Paper. Center for Creative Leadership.

Carriveau, R. S. (2016). *Connecting the dots.* Stylus Publishing, LLC.

Cohen, D. S. (2005). *The heart of change field guide: Tools and tactics for leading change in your organization.* Harvard Business Press.

Conway, D. (2016). *International students issue report.* Unpublished report. Dallas, TX: Department of Education Policy and Leadership, Southern Methodist University.

DeMeuse, K. P., Dai, G., Swisher, V. V., Eichinger, R. W., & Lombardo, M. M. (2012). Leadership development: Exploring, clarifying, and expanding our understanding of learning agility. *Industrial and Organizational Psychology: Perspectives on Science and Practice*, *5*(3), 280–286. doi:10.1111/j.1754-9434.2012.01445.x

Deming, D. J. (2017). The value of soft skills in the labor market. *NBER Reporter*, *4*, 7–11.

Dunn, E. (2003). Life Through Learning: Learning Through Life. In *The Lifelong Learning Strategy for Scotland: Summary* (p. 3). The Scottish Government. Retrieved from: http://www.scotland.gov. uk/Resource/Doc/47032/0028820.pdf

Dunsworth, M., & Billings, D. (2012). *Effective program evaluation*. Solution Tree Press.

Evans, A., & Chun, E. B. (2007). *Are the walls really down? Behavioral and organizational barriers to faculty and staff diversity*. Josey-Bass.

Executive Order 13780. (2017, March 6). *Protecting the nation from foreign terrorist entry into the United States*. The White House. https://www.whitehouse.gov/the-press-office/2017/03/06/executive-order-protecting-nation-terrorist-entry-united-states

Fincher, C. (2003). *Administrative leadership: In academic governance and management*. University Press of America, Inc.

Galle, J. K., & Galle, J. (2010). Building an integrated student learning outcomes assessment for general education: Three case studies. *New Directions for Teaching and Learning*, *2010*(121), 79–87. doi:10.1002/tl.390

Gmelch, W. H., & Miskin, V. D. (1993). *Leadership skills for department chairs*. Anker Publishing Company, Inc.

Gmelch, W. H., & Miskin, V. D. (2011). *Department chair leadership skills*. Atwood Publishing.

Ioannidis, J. P. (2005). Why most published research findings are false. *PLoS Medicine*, *2*(8), e124. doi:10.1371/journal.pmed.0020124 PMID:16060722

Kaplin, W. A., & Lee, B. A. (2007). *The law of higher education*. Jossey-Bass.

Kurian, G. (2013). *The AMA dictionary of business and management*. Amacom Publishing Div of the American Mgmt Assn. http://proxy.libraries.smu.edu/login?url=http://search.credo reference.com/content/entry/amadictbm/employee_empowerment/0

Laal, M., & Salamati, P. (2012). Lifelong learning; why do we need it? *Procedia: Social and Behavioral Sciences*, *31*, 399–403. doi:10.1016/j.sbspro.2011.12.073

Lawrence, F. L. (2009). *Views from the presidency: Leadership in higher education*. Transaction Publishers.

Leaming, D. R. (1998). *Academic Leadership: A Practical Guide to Chairing the Department*. Anker Publishing Company.

Livermore, D. (2011). *The cultural intelligence difference: Master the one skill you can't do without in today's global economy*. AMACOM, Div of American Mgmt Assn.

Mara, R., Bogue, B., Shen, D., & Rodgers, K. (2007). Those who leave-Assessing why students leave engineering (AC 2007-86). *Proceedings of American Society for Engineering Education*. http://search.asee.org /search/fetch

Mettler, S. (2014). *Degrees of inequality: How the politics of higher education sabotaged the American dream*. Basic Books.

Miller, W. R., & Miller, M. F. (1997). *Handbook for college teaching*. PineCrest Publications.

Morris, T. L., & Laipple, J. S. (2015). How prepared are academic administrators? Leadership and job satisfaction within US research universities. *Journal of Higher Education Policy and Management*, *37*(2), 241–251. doi:10.1080/1360080X.2015.1019125

Musa, M. F., & Ahmad, Z. (2012). Higher education physical assets and facilities. *Procedia: Social and Behavioral Sciences*, *50*, 472–478. doi:10.1016/j.sbspro.2012.08.051

National Center for Education Statistics. United States. Digest of Education Statistics. (2016, February). *Office of Educational Research, Improvement*. Retrieved May 27, 2017, from https://nces.ed.gov/programs/digest/ d15/tables/dt15_105.20.asp?current=yes

Northouse, P. G. (2010). *Leadership: Theory and practice*. SAGE Publications, Inc.

Palmer, P. J. (1998). Leading from within. *Insights on leadership: Service, stewardship, spirit, and servant-leadership*, 197-208.

Plinio, A. J. (2009). Ethics and leadership. *International Journal of Disclosure and Governance, 6*(4), 277–283. https://doi-org.proxy.libraries.smu.edu/10-1057/jdg.2009.20

Redden, E. (2017). Nearly 4 in 10 universities report drop in international student applications. *Inside Higher Ed*. https://www.insidehighered.com/news/2017/03/13/nearly-4-10-universities-report-drops-international-student-applications

Research, H. (2013). *Strategic planning in higher education–Best practices and benchmarking*. Hanover Research.

Robbins, S. P., & Judge, T. A. (2012). *Essentials of organizational behavior*. Prentice Hall.

Senate Bill 11. (2015). Retrieved June 15, 2021, from https://capitol.texas.gov/tlodocs/84R/ billtext/pdf/SB00011F.pdf#navpanes=0

Shapiro, P. (2005). Too many leaders? ... or do we use the term "leader" too freely? *News & Tools Leadership*, *1*(2), 1–2.

Thelin, J. R. (2011). *A history of American higher education*. Johns Hopkins University Press.

Triandis, H. C. (2006). Cultural intelligence in organizations. *Group & Organization Management*, *31*(1), 20–26. doi:10.1177/1059601105275253

Wergin, J. F. (2007). *Leadership in place: How academic professionals can find their leadership voice*. Ankor Publishing.

Wijaya, S. (2020). *How much diversity at work is needed to avoid tokenism?* SHL Blog. https://www.shl.com/en/blog/how-much-diversity-at-work-is-needed-to-avoid-tokenism/

Yoder, B. L. (2012). Engineering by the Numbers. In *American Society for Engineering Education* (Vol. 37). Retrieved June 4, 2016, from American Society of Engineering Educators:www.asee.org/ papers-and-publications/publications/college-profiles/11 EngineeringbythNumbersPart1.pdf

KEY TERMS AND DEFINITIONS

Academic Administrator: An individual who serves an institution in an administrative capacity to support the institution and further the mission and vision of the organization.

Academic Leadership: An individual who serves as a leader to create and support the vision and mission of the organization, providing direction and oversight for units within the institution.

Core Competencies: Basic skillset and foundation of knowledge related to a specific area of expertise.

Cultural Intelligence: The skill or ability to relate to and work with groups of individuals from diverse backgrounds and experiences.

Evidence-Based Leadership: The utilization of a leader to use evidence/data to guide their decision-making and management practices.

Personal and Ethical Leadership: The ability to model moral behavior within an organization and to lead by promoting and exuding appropriate ethical conduct.

Policy and Political Leadership: The ability to understand policy implications within the organization and provide support to those within the institution as it relates to the current policy and political climates.

Strategic and Organizational Leadership: The ability to think strategically to develop a clear mission and vision for the organization while seeing the "big picture."

Tokenism: The idea or assumption that the goal of diversity is reached simply by hiring a few individuals to check a box or satisfy a requirement.

Chapter 5
Leadership Lessons From Ratan N. Tata

Sriya Chakravarti
https://orcid.org/0000-0002-5396-0318
Higher Colleges of Technology, UAE

ABSTRACT

Ratan Tata is an Indian industrialist and philanthropist. He is a visionary leader and managing change is second nature to him. His leadership exudes confidence in others and has inspired many to become leaders in his own company, and through his service-oriented nature, influenced several others outside of his organizational space. Tata's leadership commands respect throughout the world, which is highlighted by the numerous prestigious awards bestowed upon him. This chapter aims to present and explain his leadership practices through case scenarios. These lessons on leadership are transferable and may guide future leaders of tomorrow to lead our world with wisdom, dignity, humility, and authenticity.

INTRODUCTION

Leadership is the elevation of human condition. Peter F. Drucker, also known as the father of modern management, defined Leadership as lifting an individual's vision to higher sights, raising of performance to an advanced standard and building an individual's personality beyond their normal limitations. He argued that leadership is about knowing when to give an order and when to treat someone like a partner (Drucker, 2002). For Drucker (1992), a leader should view leadership as a responsibility rather than a rank and privilege. He further stated that leaders of tomorrow would have a complex job. They would not be able to lead by charisma

DOI: 10.4018/978-1-7998-2807-5.ch005

alone but will need to think through the fundamentals so that other people can work effectively under their guidance.

Adding to the above, according to the article, Understanding Leadership in Harvard Business Review (2004), leadership is "the accomplishment of a goal through the direction of human assistants." Any individual who successfully organizes human collaborators to achieve a particular end is a leader. Therefore, a great leader is someone who can do the above on a consistent basis, day after day, year after year, in a wide variety of circumstances. An influential leader is one who understands his or her fellow workers and the relationship of their individual goals to group goals.

Therefore, this book chapter intends to present leadership lessons of a seasoned business leader from India. Through examination of mini organizational case studies, his leadership approaches will be put forth in this research. Tata group is the organization chosen for this study. The aim of the research is to present lessons from Mr. Ratan Tata's (Emeritus Chairman, Tata group) esteemed leadership. This knowledge may support contemporary managers in improving their leadership practices and better navigate the VUCA (Volatile, Uncertain, Complex, and Ambiguous) world of business.

The purpose of this research is to educate managers and inform their practices on how to lead with an impact, wisdom, dignity, humanity, efficiency and effectiveness. Ultimately, ideal leadership is an individual's ability to take a group and drive them towards a common shared purpose. Such leaders raise and develop other under their tutelage to become future leaders of tomorrow. This research suggests approaches to exemplary leadership, so that managers can lead suitably in challenging circumstances.

To understand the environment and context of Mr. Ratan Tata's leadership, the following section of this research presents a brief overview on contemporary India and the organization background of the Tata group.

OVERVIEW OF CONTEMPORARY INDIA

India is a country in South Asia. It covers the seventh-largest area by land. Being a peninsula, the Indian Ocean, the Arabian Sea, and the Bay of Bengal surround it. Andaman and Nicobar Islands of India share a maritime border with Thailand, Myanmar and Indonesia. Additionally, India shares land borders with Pakistan, China, Nepal, Bhutan, Bangladesh and Myanmar.

This sophisticated land, self-contained its political and cultural arena since the Indus valley civilization. Its present day capital is New Delhi, and the government is a constitutional republic representing a diverse population. One-sixth of the world's total population resides in India and it is the second most populous country in the world after China. While India suffers from various external (security threats) and internal challenges (poverty, unemployment, population explosion, pending justice, poor policing and economic inequality) it continues to shine its light to the rest of the world (Calkins, 2021).

Modern India is a vibrant society with an increasing influence in the world. It is the beacon of hope for democracies around the world. The nation continues to prosper through a diversified industrial base, scientific knowledge, cultural dynamism and agricultural expansion. The information on present-day India gives a glimpse on its journey to development. Tata group of companies has been a partner of modern India before independence from the British in 1947. After the 1991 Indian economic reform of liberalization, privatization and globalization, through its services and products Tata group has been able to put India on the global map.

Traditionally a conservative business conglomerate, the Tata's embraced the change after the launch of economic reforms in 1991. They acquired global brands and strived to perform better with every victory. The Tata group grew from USD 5 billion to USD 100 billion in size when Ratan Tata took over the reins in 1992 as chairman of Tata Sons. The company is a true pioneer of India with a strong global footprint and a wide interest that ranges from salt to software. Being a futuristic organization with sustainable development, philanthropy and innovation as its key goals indicate it as a robust company, which is governed by a wise leadership team.

ORGANIZATION BACKGROUND

Tata group is an Indian company making global waves today. It comprises of 30 companies in ten business verticals and this conglomerate operates in six continents around the world. In 2018, the Tata group had 28 publicly listed companies with a market capitalization of $145.3billion. Collectively, Tata group employs roughly 700,000 people. Tata Sons is the principal investment holding company and promoter of Tata companies. Each Tata company operates independently under the guidance of its Board of Directors. "66% of the equity share capital of Tata Sons is held by philanthropic trusts, which support education, health, livelihood generation, and art and culture." (TATA, 2021) This is indicative of the Tata group's benevolent mindset.

The governance philosophy of the Tata group stems from the speech of JRD Tata, where he said (TATA, 2021):

The Tata philosophy of management has always been, and is today more than ever, that corporate enterprises must be managed not merely in the interests of their owners, but equally in those of their employees, of the consumers of their products, of the local community and finally of the country as a whole.

The above indicates that Tata group is not merely interested in making money for its shareholders but also want to do holistic contributions towards sustainable development and wellbeing of the communities. Tata group has always been a values-driven organization. The five core Tata values are integrity, responsibility, excellence, pioneering and unity.

Tata aims to be a sustainable and resilient enterprise. It strives to "ensure fair, transparent, accountable and ethical management in order to protect the interests of all stakeholders, including shareholders, employees, customers, vendors, regulators and society. As a responsible corporate citizen, Tata Sons follows the laws of the land in letter and spirit. Tata Sons also goes beyond mere compliance to highlight certain behaviors and norms to Tata group operating companies." (TATA, 2021)

Leadership with Trust is the success mantra for the Tata group. The Tata Code of Conduct is another way by which the Tata brand ensures that it keeps building trust within the community. The Tata Code of Conduct provides an ethical road map for Tata employees and companies. All Tata group representatives are obliged to follow the tenets of the code of conduct. Following are the key pillars on which the Tata Code of Conduct is placed: (TATA, 2021)

- the highest moral and ethical standards;
- highest standards of corporate governance;
- respect for human rights and dignity;
- professionalism, honesty, fairness and integrity
- the economic development of communities;
- highest standards of safety;
- maintaining a balance in the interest of stakeholders and treating them fairly to avoid discrimination;
- not engaging in unfair or restrictive trade practices, and compliance with applicable laws, rules and regulations;
- creating an environment free of the fear of retribution; thereby allowing all stakeholders to raise ethics-related queries or concerns

Applying these practices has made the Tata group grow stronger year after year and has brought it the recognition it truly deserves. It has also helped the organization attract and retain talent long term and has built loyalty among employees. Tata group's code of conduct and governing philosophy are a recipe for business success. All organizations and affiliations that aspire to reach the top in India adopt Tata's framework of code of conduct to remain sustainable, innovative and involved in the community. Due to the above philosophy, Tata Consultancy Services (TCS), Tata Motors, Tata Steel, Tata Chemicals, Tata Global Beverages, Titan, Tata Capital, Tata Power, Tata Advanced Systems, Indian Hotels Company Limited (IHCL) and Tata Communication are some very well recognized brands in India and around the world (TATA, 2021).

Tata thrives on innovation. The group's involvement of stakeholders for better communication, recognition of innovative ideas, learning from other companies, and support for collaborative research and partnerships with academia confirm their approaches to advanced and sustainable systems. Moreover, Tata group invest in building research facilities and partnerships with academic and research organizations to promote creativity and innovation. Tata Chemicals Innovation Center, Tata Steel Europe Research, Development and Technology, Tata Consultancy Services (TCS) Innovation Labs, Tata Motors European Technical Center are some examples of research facilities that work on thinking creatively and finding innovative solutions for a better quality of life (TATA, 2021).

The above information clearly points out that the Tata group is innovative; community oriented, sustainable, and philanthropic in nature. The next section of this book chapter introduces the pioneer, trailblazer, entrepreneur and leader, Mr. Ratan Tata (Emeritus Chairman), of the Tata group.

LEADER'S INTRODUCTION

Ratan Naval Tata was born on December 28, 1937, Bombay (now Mumbai, India). A member of a prominent family of Indian industrialists and philanthropists, he was educated at Cornell University, Ithaca, New York. Mr. Tata earned a B.S. in architecture (1962) before returning to work in India. He gained experience in a number of Tata Group businesses. In 1971, he was named director in charge of the National Radio and Electronics Co. He became the chairperson of Tata Industries a decade later and in 1991 succeeded his uncle, J.R.D. Tata, as chair of the Tata Group.

Upon assuming leadership, Mr. Tata aggressively focused on globalizing the businesses. In 2000, the Tata group acquired London-based Tetley Tea for $431.3 million. In 2004, it purchased the truck-manufacturing operations of South Korea's Daewoo Motors for $102 million. In 2007, Tata Steel completed the biggest corporate takeover by an Indian company when it acquired the giant Anglo-Dutch steel manufacturer Corus Group for $11.3 billion (Encyclopedia Britannica, 2021).

Mr. Ratan Tata has outstanding business acumen and a strong ability to sense business opportunities. He is not only an Indian industrialist but also a philanthropist and praised for business ethics. He is India's brand ambassador and has an interest in almost everything from tea to steel. He was the Chairman of Tata Sons, the holding company of the Tata Group until retirement. Since 2012, Mr. Tata has been conferred the honorary title of Chairman Emeritus of Tata Sons, Tata Industries, Tata Motors, Tata Steel and Tata Chemicals. During his tenure, Tata group's revenues grew manifold, totaling over $ 100 billion in 2011-12 (TATA, 2021).

Mr. Tata serves on the international advisory boards of multinational companies like JP Morgan Chase and Mitsubishi Corporation. He is the Chairman of the Tata Trusts, which are amongst India's oldest, non-sectarian philanthropic organizations that work in several areas of community development. In addition, he chairs Allied Trusts, and the Sir Dorabji Tata Trust. Furthermore, he is the Chairman of the Council of Management of the Tata Institute of Fundamental Research and serves on the board of trustees of Cornell University and the University of Southern California (TATA, 2021).

From the above information, it can be established that Mr. Tata's leadership commands respect throughout the world. For his exemplary work in business and development of societies, he has been decorated with numerous positions, titles and prestigious awards. In 2014, he was awarded the Honorary Knight Grand Cross of the Most Excellent Order of the British Empire by the United Kingdom. He was also presented with the Padma Bhushan in 2000 and Padma Vibhushan in 2008 (highest civilian honors) awarded by the Government of India. The Rockefeller Foundation has conferred him with the Lifetime Achievement Award. Moreover, Mr. Tata is also an honorary fellow of the Institution of Mechanical Engineers, Royal Academy of Engineering and a foreign associate of National Academy of Engineering. He has received honorary doctorates from several universities in India and overseas. These awards are in recognition of his ability to foresee economic trends, manage change, take bold initiatives, and sustain values and for his contributions to business, industry and society (TATA, 2021). Some of his notable achievements include acquisition of Tetley by Tata Tea, Jaguar Land Rover by Tata Motors and Corus by Tata Steel in an attempt to turn Tata group into a global business enterprise.

Mr. Tata's legacy has the power to inspire great leadership and motivate anyone beyond words. He practices authentic leadership and is a transformational leader of India. He turned Tata Group into a global brand, while maintaining high standards on corporate social responsibility. He is a visionary and managing change is second nature to him. His leadership exudes confidence in others. It has inspired many to become leaders in his own company. Through his service-oriented nature, he has influenced a couple of Indian generations to serve others outside of his organizational space.

Mr. Tata's response to the COVID 19 pandemic on business operations was to be sensitive towards employees who have served their organizations. He stated further that companies have a moral responsibility towards their employees. Mr. Tata emphasized that it is impossible to survive as a corporation if one is not sensitive to the stakeholders of the society (Express Healthcare, 2020). Mr. Ratan Tata's response to the pandemic outbreak teaches business communities lessons on maintaining ethical conduct and building relationships in challenging times of the VUCA (Volatile, Uncertain, Complex and Ambiguous) world through authentic leadership.

Per Authentic Leadership Theory, Authentic Leaders are leaders who know who they are and who are true to themselves. Authentic leadership is a pattern of leader behavior that promotes positive psychological capacities and an ethical climate in the work place, to foster greater self-awareness, an internalized moral perspective, balanced processing of information, and relational transparency on the part of leaders working with followers, fostering positive self-development (Walumba & Lawler, 2003). Generally, authentic leaders are positive people with truthful self-concepts who promote openness. Authentic leaders need to be true to their leadership position, with a strong ethical dose of moral courage for the greater good of all (Wulfers, 2017). The above qualities of an authentic leader showcased in Mr. Tata's response to the pandemic business handling. Therefore, it can be concluded that Mr. Ratan Tata is an authentic business leader of India.

The lesson for contemporary leaders and managers in these times is to practice authentic leadership. They should be agile and resilient to respond appropriately to catastrophic and extraordinary events. They need to become the change they wish to see by developing self-awareness and what is meaningful to them. Furthermore, to be successful they need to be inclusive and genuinely care and relate to all stakeholders.

The next section of this research sets the stage to explain leadership practices of Mr. Ratan Tata through selective organization cases in India and abroad.

SETTING THE STAGE

This book chapter aims to present and explain leadership practices of Mr. Ratan Tata through application of leadership theories on Tata group of companies' case scenarios. These lessons on leadership are transferable and may guide future leaders of tomorrow to lead our VUCA (Volatile, Uncertain, Complex, and Ambiguous) world with wisdom, dignity, humility and authenticity. The following sections of this book chapter will present case scenarios of Mr. Ratan Tata's leadership. Through this chapter on Mr. Ratan Tata's leadership, the modern day managers can inform and improve their own practices in their respective organizational context.

CASE 1: Tata Nano

Tata Motors was founded in 1945 as a manufacturer of locomotives, but soon moved on to the automotive industry based on several international cooperation agreements. In 2003, Mr. Ratan Tata announced the development of a small four-wheel vehicle that would be affordable for the growing middle class in India. His vision was to provide a safe alternative for a single scooter carrying an entire family. The car was touted as the dream of a million Indians. The cheapest car prior to the launch of the Tata Nano was Maruti Alto sold at approximately INR 2,50,000 (Agrawal & Wadia 2008).

Tata Nano made automotive history when it was launched in 2008. It created a global excitement putting India on the world map of being able to produce a $2,500. The company had received orders for about 300,000 cars and a waiting list of close to two years. It was the world's cheapest auto, called "The People's Car". The environmentalists called it an eco-disaster. However, after Nano's debut, three Tata competitors started working on Nano copycats.

Internationally, Tata Nano was an innovative and transformational consumer product of the century. It started the trend of frugal and value based innovation strategy for emerging markets across the globe (Breuer & Upadrasta, 2017). Tata Nano was an ambitious project that had attention from potential customers, stakeholders, industry managers and academics. It was radical, economic and a disruptive innovation for the scooter markets (Tiwari & Herstatt 2012). The Tata Nano Development started without many fixed assumptions or benchmarks (Breuer & Upadrasta, 2017). The developers succeeded to create this low cost frugal innovation at a price less than 50 percent of a standard car in the current car segment (Agrawal & Wadia 2008). The peak volumes clocked by Tata Nano were in the year 2012 at 74,524 units. Over the years, small cars went out of vogue and style. Since then it has been a downhill journey for Tata Nano. While the Nano seems to have lost the edge, even after reinventing itself in 2015, it did not boost sales. Therefore, the car may be phased out in the coming years.

The Nano is still a controversially discussed case within the Tata Group as well as for managers and the academic community because it created significant financial loss. On the opposite side, the company gained reputation of developing frugal innovation in one of the world largest emerging economies. Mr. Ratan Tata's vision to make the company an international player, building advanced competencies and capabilities in technology and marketing and engaging in new ventures and relationships were key takeaways for the company (Chacko, 2010).

The frameworks and case studies on Nano pay little attention to the values and the vision that directed the development and marketing of the world's cheapest car. Hence, individuals and organizations have limited understanding on the unique development and marketing of the Nano (Breuer & Upadrasta, 2017).

Tata Motors continuously adapts to the new car trends. It is in this context that the company is no more trying to keep Nano alive by making upgrades to it. While some cars produced by Tata have not lasted the test of time, its latest models such as Tiago, Tigor, Nexon, and Hexa are doing quite well. The company recorded a 61% growth in sales of its passenger vehicles at 17,489 units in May compared with the same month last year (Arora, 2018).

Mr. Ratan Tata in the case of Nano emerges as a charismatic, innovative, ahead of his time, visionary kind of a transformational leader. Moreover, Mr. Tata can be categorized under charismatic leadership also because he was able to articulate an inspirational vision of a desirable future that motivates followers to sacrifice their self-interests and devote exceptional effort to the causes advocated by the leader (Anderson & Sun, 2017). According to Transformational Leadership Theory, Transformational Leadership is a process that changes and transforms individuals (Northouse, 2001). In Transformational Leadership the leader enhances the motivation, morale, and performance of followers through a variety of mechanisms (Dhingra, Gupta & Gupta, 2013).

After examining the above case, it is clear that Mr. Tata envisaged a low cost car that would be a safer option for future middle class. Through the development of this frugal innovation priced at USD 2,000, owning a car became an affordable option for the growing middle class of India. Hence, the car was publicized as the dream of a million Indians. Internationally, the Tata Nano was an innovative and transformational consumer product of the century. It started the trend of frugal and value based innovation strategy for emerging markets across the globe (Breuer & Upadrasta, 2017). As a result, it can be concluded from the above case that Mr. Ratan Tata has Transformational Leadership abilities because he was able to motivate his to team to think differently, pioneer technology, develop a growth mindset and at the same time address the needs of the society.

The next section of the research study discusses Tata Trusts, a nonsectarian, philanthropic organization overseen by Mr. Ratan Tata.

CASE 2: Tata Trusts (Philanthropy, Generosity and Humanity)

India is a pluralistic, multilingual and multi-ethnic society and a home to the world's second-largest population. While witnessing tremendous growth, India has been able to lift 133 million people out of poverty. However, the United Nation estimates that 28% of India is still poor. The government is committed to eradication of poverty and calls it the greatest unfinished business of the 20th century (UN India). Aiding the government's vision of poverty free India, the Tata group works to support communities through Tata Trusts.

Tata Trusts is the oldest philanthropic minded organization that is a symbol of hope and sustainable future for many deprived communities of India. The Tata group stand for humanitarian efforts and personifies the phenomenal force that advances new frontiers of social and economic development. The organization is not only charitable, benevolent but also non-sectarian. They work throughout the country in several areas of community development. Mr. Ratan Tata presides over Tata Trusts and areas of work include digital transformation, environmental and energy, sports, skill development, migration and urban habitat, social justice and inclusion, arts and culture, disaster relief and rehabilitation, institutions, individual grants, healthcare, nutrition, water, sanitation and hygiene, livelihood and education. Tata Trusts is ruled by the mantra, "Infinite progress – infinite happiness" (TATA TRUSTS, 2021).

At (Stanford Social Innovation Review (SSIR)) Mr. Ratan Tata said:

Working on the shop floor as a young man, I saw close up the misery and hardship of the less fortunate and thought about how one makes a difference to improve lives. As I moved up through departments and divisions, I continued to see hardship and had more opportunity to do something about it. Now I am trying to take the Tata Trusts to a different level of relevance in the 21st century to maximize the benefits the trusts seek to bring to disadvantaged communities.

In early charity, the Tata group was involved in alleviating individual hardships and supporting NGOs. Under Mr. Ratan Tata's leadership, philanthropy for Tata Trust has found a new meaning. The projects are large scale with maximum impact and the interventions are sustainable for better serving humankind. The Saathi Internet program is an example where Tata Trust teamed up with a corporation like Google to help rural women understand the Internet and give them a means of securing a livelihood. It was a new model of philanthropy and not the kind of project the trust invested in prior to Mr. Ratan Tata's leadership (Stanford Social Innovation Review (SSIR)). Following are few case in point examples chosen by the researcher on the philanthropic, humanitarian and benevolent acts that Tata Trust has worked on in the local and global setting under the leadership of Mr. Ratan Tata:

Example 1: Assistance and Relief for COVID 19

Tata Trusts and the Tata group's companies have in the past risen to the needs of the nation. Tata Trusts pledged to protect and empower all affected communities, and committed INR 500 crores to cope with the needs of fighting the COVID 19 crisis, which is one of the toughest challenges the human race is currently facing (Express Healthcare, 2020). The Tata group joined local, global partners and the government's fight on a united public health collaboration platform. It reached out to various sections of underprivileged and deprived communities.

Example 2: Funding Research and Knowledge Transfer for Growth and Sustainability

Clemson University's International Center for Automotive Research (ICAR) benefitted financially from India's Tata business empire. Tata Trusts, a collection of charitable trusts that Ratan Tata chairs, provided fellowships for five students from India to study automotive engineering at (ICAR). Each scholarship was worth $26500 per year. The fellowships covered tuition, fees, housing, books and other expenses associated with attending (ICAR). The chair of the automotive engineering department called the fellowships a golden ticket for the Indian students that need support to finish their graduate education. The university hopes the fellowships will further establish the university and ICAR as world leaders in automotive engineering. Furthermore, the university hoped that Tata Motors would establish their office and fund research or sponsor programs in engineering where students develop a car based on their education. In addition, the universities spoke about a broader collaboration for faculty exchange for technical knowhow and knowledge transfer (Bell & Coyne, 2016).

Example 3: Support and Encouragement for Digital India

Tata Trusts and Prodea Systems reported that 75 million residents will benefit through their partnership on DRUV – the North Star. The project combines the philanthropic vision of Tata's and technological expertise of Prodea to promote the Digital India initiative. The aim is to bring deprived communities of the state of Rajasthan online and provide access to important information and services in the areas of health, finances, agriculture, farming, education and entrepreneurship. The Government of Rajasthan and other Non-Government Organizations (NGOs) fully supported the above initiative (Entertainment Close-up, 2015).

Example 4: Scholarship for Indian Students

The Tata Trust collaborated with the University of Edinburgh to offer a joint scholarship to students wishing to pursue a Master's programme at the University in the field of developmental economics, public health and science-technology-society studies. Eligible Indian nationals, domiciled in India, with an excellent academic record, some evidence of extra-curricular achievement and work experience in the selected field of study were preferred for these scholarships. The value of the scholarship was £20,000 per year and covered tuition fees and living expenses (The Hindustan Times, 2011).

From the above illustrations, it can be noted that the Tata group believes in making a difference in the communities they serve. Another way is through sponsoring events that promote sports, art, culture, wellness and education. Tata Mumbai Marathon, Tata Steel Chess Tournament, TCS New York City Marathon, Invictus Games, Tata Crucible, Tata Literature Live, First Book, Tata Ultra Marathon and Tata Better Soles are some examples of events that are sponsored by the Tata group.

The above examples of humanitarian work highlight Mr. Ratan Tata's servant leadership towards his Indian community in various capacities. While terms like servant and leaders are common and have over 700 definitions (Thompson, 2015). For the purpose of this academic research, servant leadership theory posits that the leader is a servant, focused on the development of others (Greenleaf, 1977). He is the "one who influences others toward the accomplishment of group goals primarily by making sure their highest-priority needs are met" (Greenleaf, 2008, p. 7). Furthermore, Chu (2011) explains that a servant leader in context of an organization is a style of leadership that places the good of the organization above the self-interest of the leader.

Servant leadership is an altruistic calling within a leader to make a positive difference in the lives of others (Barbuto and Wheeler, 2006). Servant leadership theory is different from transformational leadership. In servant leadership the leader has the desire to serve and prepare others to serve as well. In transformational leadership the leader has the desire to inspire the followers to perform well. (van Dierendonck et al., 2014). As mentioned previously, Mr. Ratan Tata through his work with his group of companies exhibits servant and transformational leadership styles. Moreover, Mr. Tata as a servant leader displays characteristics like Listening, Empathy, Healing, Awareness, Persuasion, Conceptualization, Foresight, Stewardship, Commitment to the growth of people and Building community in his leadership, which are mark the character of servant leader (Heyler & Martin, 2018).

Greenleaf (1997) states that the best test of whether a person is a servant leader is, if the people he or she serves grow as individuals. Do these followers, while being served, become healthier, wiser? Are they more likely themselves to become servants? (Heyler & Martin, 2018). Analyzing Mr. Tata's through the above lens and test his true servant leadership, it is evident that he is servant leader because he inspires many of whom he serves to become servants of others. Moreover, the Guiding Principles of Tata Trusts, "what advances a nation or community is not so much to prop up its weakest and most helpless members, but to lift up the best and the most gifted, so as to make them of the greatest service to the country" indicates a service oriented and servant leadership focus (TATA TRUSTS, 2021).

The following section of the research presents the case of acquisition of global brands and putting Tata on the global map.

Case 3: Tata Acquisition of Global Marquee Brands (Jaguar and Land Rover)

Tata Motors acquired the iconic Jaguar and Land Rover (JLR) businesses from Ford Motor Co. at a price of US$2.3bn in the year 2007. Initially these brands struggled but soon under the ownership and leadership of Tata these two globally recognized marquee brands started doing exceedingly well. The revenues for JLR jumped to GBP 21.8bn in 2014-2015 from a mere GBP 4.9 billion in 2008-2009.

Tata Motors rationale for the acquisition was to enter the luxury cars and premium sports utility vehicles (SUV) segments to complete its product portfolio. Moreover, the Tata brand was largely limited to the Indian market. Acquisition of JLR gave global recognition and additional benefits included JLR's strong product pipeline, manufacturing expertise, design capabilities, and an extremely loyal global dealership network.

At first, the acquisition seemed like a mistake because of the global financial crisis and its effect on sales of luxury vehicles worldwide. JLR was strapped for cash and the first 18 months under Tata were difficult. JLR was for the first time responsible for its own money -- and the new company needed plenty of it. Unfortunately, JLR's prospects looked bleak when it could not negotiate a suitable access to credit (Truett, 2018). However, Tata Motors was patient. With the help of consultants it focused on cost control and improving profitability and liquidity. Moreover, it kept investing in product development initiatives (Pathak, 2016).

JLR posted a loss of about $540 million in its 2008-09 and Tata had to inject $1.2 billion into JLR to keep the company on course. JLR CEO Ralf Speth stated that the 2008 recession was a really a tough time and one of the most difficult recession in human memory (Truett, 2018). However, Ratan Tata stood by his word, kept faith and gave resources to JLR for improving the health of the company. With a warm personality and a patient ear, Mr. Ratan Tata won over quickly the anxious hearts of two orphaned luxury brands (Chappell, 2008).

Tata understood that the JLR vehicles succeeded worldwide because of their high quality design, engineering and manufacturing. Therefore, JLR's operations were allowed to remain in UK. It invested in two plants and UK employee numbers doubled in four years. In addition, Tata did not impose its culture on JLR and very few high-level management changes were made. This worked hugely in favor of the acquirers. Tata kept the two businesses apart and only shared knowledge on selected aspects. Mr. Tata's decision relating to JLR operations, and culture management indicate that he knew how to tackle or avoid obvious organizational icebergs and hidden organizational blackbergs (Wilde,2012).

The JLR acquisition has been a great success for Tata Motors. JLR has helped the company improve financial results when the Tata Motors commercial vehicles segment was underperforming in the Indian market. The Tata Motors' acquisition of Jaguar and Land Rover (JLR) is an excellent example of a difficult cross-border acquisition by an emerging market based company. While the acquisition was cumbersome, it has yielded excellent dividends to the parent company over the long term. Success of the acquisition depend on both internal (under the control of the company) and external factors (political, economic, social, technological, legal, environment) are under the control of the acquirer's management. Patience and luck are required ingredients for success in such contexts (Pathak, 2016).

No business is without flaws and risks but what is achieved in the fields of engineering, brands, design capabilities in the Tata JLR acquisition is remarkable. JLR continues to remain an independent business under the Tata ownership. They keep moving quicker than their competitors. They are seen as a very credible car manufacturer, and will get to 1 million units a year in some foreseeable future. That is a good enough size to be strong around the world and to fight the challenges of markets and products changing, from diesel to petrol to electric (Truett, 2018).

The success for this acquisition goes to Mr. Ratan Tata because not only is he humble but a fully engaged entrepreneur and these global brands had not been run by an entrepreneur since the beginning of time. (Chappell, 2008). Mr.Tata can be categorized as a visionary leader because he was able to spot the opportunity to make his company global expand during the worst world recession. He was able to see potential in the new world that might emerge as a result of the recession, and took appropriate steps to get there. He showed leadership resilience, ethical leadership in the VUCA (Volatile, Uncertain, Complex, and Ambiguous) world (Elkington, 2017).

Mr. Ratan Tata is a visionary leader and no one would have any doubts about it if they glance through his stint in Tata (Babu, 2017). He is a futuristic leader who looked ahead with a powerful vision. Thirty years ago, he authored a document that was called the Tata Plan which included restructuring, international operations and innovative solutions to improve the quality of life.

Visionary leaders are innovative, creative and bold. They imagine a better reality and improved quality of life for all. They are positive, aligned to a calling and share a sense of purpose. They think strategically and are social innovators and change agents. The case above on globalizing Tata Motors is an attempt to display the visionary leadership of Mr. Ratan Tata.

The subsequent section of this research discusses the leadership lessons from this research study.

LESSONS ON LEADERSHIP

From Case 1, Tata Nano, we learned that Mr. Ratan Tata is a transformational leader. He was able to articulate an inspirational vision of a desirable future with the launch of the Tata Nano. Through the case, it can be observed that Mr. Tata envisaged a low cost car that would be a safer option for future middle class on roads of slippery water clogged cities. Through the development of this frugal innovation priced at USD 2000, owning a car became an affordable option for the growing middle class of India. Hence, the car was publicized as the dream of a million Indians.

Internationally, the Nano was an innovative and transformational consumer product of the century. It started the trend of frugal and value based innovation strategy for emerging markets across the globe. As a result, Mr. Tata can be viewed as Mr. Transformational. Through his leadership abilities, he was able to motivate his to team to develop a growth mindset, dream big, improve quality of life and at the same time address the needs of the society. Through his leadership on the Nano, modern managers and leaders can understand transformational leadership in action. Mr. Tata's leadership also teaches us to be courageous, solve the needs of many and be futuristic to sustain a competitive advantage.

From Case 2, Tata Trusts philanthropy examples display the Tata group's belief in making a difference in the communities they serve. While in early charity, the Tata group was involved in alleviating individual hardships and supporting NGOs. Under Mr. Ratan Tata, philanthropy found a new meaning. The projects were large scale with maximum impact and the interventions sustainable for better serving humankind. The examples in the case highlight not only Mr. Ratan Tata's servant leadership towards his Indian community in various capacities but also the massive impact and sustenance it carries. His philanthropic involvement extends outside of India as well. Analyzing Mr. Tata's through the lens of true servant leadership, it is evident that he is servant leader because he inspires many of whom he serves to become servants of others. Moreover, the Guiding Principles of Tata Trusts, "what advances a nation or community is not so much to prop up its weakest and most helpless members, but to lift up the best and the most gifted, so as to make them of the greatest service to the country" indicates a service oriented and servant leadership focus (TATA TRUSTS, 2021). There is ample amount of evidence in Case 2 that highlights the above statement. Mr. Ratan Tata's advice to contemporary managers and leaders is to do thorough research before deciding where to get involved. This is because tremendous amounts of money is used poorly than it could be because an organization has not done enough research (Stanford Social Innovation Review (SSIR)).

From Case 3, Tata Acquisition of Global Marquee Brands (Jaguar and Land Rover) we learned that during mergers and acquisitions, leaders must continue to support and invest in the acquired entity. They need to be clear in their vision and be risk takers. Leaders should integrate only those aspects of business that make sense to assimilate. Furthermore, extensive research is always beneficial from a long-term perspective. Additionally, cultural ideologies at the organization level, if managed efficiently can improve the success rates of mergers and acquisitions. Patience and a long-term perspective on any deal is necessary for any leader in mergers and acquisitions. Finally, staying positive and vigilant for opportunities in the future for growth is a sign of a visionary leader. To become a visionary leader in business or any other setting, the individual must be innovative, creative and bold. They must think strategically, and be agents of change wanting to improve the quality of life for all.

Ratan Tata believes that a person's attitude and mindset can make or break them. His leadership style is situational. Through the cases above it can be observed that he practices authentic, charismatic, transformational, servant and visionary styles of leadership. He was able to turn Tata Group into a global brand amidst the global recession of 2008, while maintaining high standards on corporate social responsibility. This depicts his visionary and transformational nature. Through his humbleness and service-oriented nature, he has won many hearts and influenced a couple of generations to serve others outside the organizational space. Mr. Ratan Tata is known as a value based leader "who operates from a higher purpose that is beyond the balance sheet." Being a visionary leader without authenticity, self-awareness and self-knowledge is recipe for leadership failure. Therefore, alignment of values to action is the most important leadership trait. Mr. Ratan Tata demonstrates the above with ease and finesse (Babu, 2017).

CONCLUSION

Leaders in these times of the VUCA (Volatile, Uncertain, Complex and Ambiguous) world have to be agile, ethical, authentic and resilient. They need to respond appropriately to catastrophic and extraordinary events like Mr. Ratan Tata. They need to become the change they wish to see by developing self-awareness and what is meaningful to them. They need to do extensive research before joining or supporting a philanthropic cause. Furthermore, they need to genuinely care and relate to all stakeholders if they wish to thrive in business for the long term.

While there are many models on leadership, all successful leaders have a vision and purpose; they add value and create a new possibility. They build next-in-line leaders and are role models. Mr. Ratan Tata is a fine mix and an ideal example of a leader demonstrating all the above mentioned. Therefore, it is imperative for contemporary managers and leaders to be informed of his approach and practices.

REFERENCES

About Tata Trusts. (n.d.). Retrieved April 08, 2021, from https://www.tatatrusts.org/about-tatatrusts

Agrawal, S., & Wadia, J. (2008). *Tata Nano: the 'big' wonder.* Tata Motors. https://www.tata.com/article/inside/pJI3huSRc!$$$! 0=/TLYVr3YPkMU=

Anderson, M. H., & Sun, P. Y. T. (2017). Reviewing Leadership Styles: Overlaps and the Need for a New "Full-Range" Theory. *International Journal of Management Reviews, 19*(1), 76–96. doi:10.1111/ijmr.12082

Arora, K. (2018, Jun 6). *Tata motors may say goodbye to nano, ratan tata's pet project, in 2019*. Financial Express. Retrieved from http://ezproxy.hct.ac.ae/login?url=https://www-proquest-com.ezproxy.hct.ac.ae/newspapers/tata-motors-may-say-goodbye-nano-ratan-tatas-pet/docview/2050324206/se-2?accountid=1215

Babu, S. (2017, November 22). *Ratan TATA: The visionary*. Retrieved April 08, 2021, from https://www.thehindubusinessline.com/news/variety/Ratan-Tata-The-visionary/article20545504.ece

Barbuto, J. E. Jr, & Wheeler, D. W. (2006). Scale Development and Construct Clarification of Servant Leadership. *Group & Organization Management, 31*(3), 300326. doi:10.1177/1059601106287091

Bell, R., & Coyne, A. (2016, Jul 20). Tata funds fellowships for indian students. *The Greenville News*. Retrieved from http://ezproxy.hct.ac.ae/login?url=https://www-proquest-com.ezproxy.hct.ac.ae/newspapers/tata-funds-fellowships-indian-students/docview/1805513518/se-2?accountid=1215

Breuer, H., & Upadrasta, V. (2017). *Values-based product innovation – the case of tata nano*. Manchester: The International Society for Professional Innovation Management (ISPIM). Retrieved from http://ezproxy.hct.ac.ae/login?url=https://www-proquest-com.ezproxy.hct.ac.ae/conference-papers-proceedings/values-based-product-innovation-case-tata-nano/docview/1920222446/se-2?accountid=1215

Calkins, P. (2021). India. *Encyclopædia Britannica*. https://www.britannica.com/place/India

Chacko, P., Noronha, C., & Agrawal, S. (2010). *Small Wonder. The Making of the Nano*. Tata Sons Limited.

Chappell, L. (2008). In U.S. tour, mr. tata gives jaguar and rover dealers a hug. *Automotive News, 82*(6314), 3-37. Retrieved from http://ezproxy.hct.ac.ae/login?url=https://www-proquest-com.ezproxy.hct.ac.ae/trade-journals/u-s-tour-mr-tata-gives-jaguar-rover-dealers-hug/docview/219504170/se-2?accountid=1215

Chu, M. (2011). *Conflict management styles of pastors and organizational servant leadership: A descriptive study* (Unpublished doctoral dissertation). Southern Baptist theological Seminary, Louisville, KY.

Dhingra, G., Gupta, M., & Gupta, H. (2013). Study of transformational leaders in business and qualities required being a successful business leader. *Journal of Commerce and Management Thought*, *4*(3), 692–703. http://ezproxy.hct.ac.ae/login?url=https://www-proquest-com.ezproxy.hct.ac.ae/scholarly-journals/study-transformational-leaders-business-qualities/docview/1523932379/se-2?accountid=1215

Drucker, P. (1992). *Managing for the Future: The 1990s and beyond*. Truman Talley Books/Dutton.

Drucker, P. (2002). *Managing in the Next Society*. St Martin's Press.

Elkington, R., van der Steege, M., Glick-Smith, J., & Moss Breen, J. (2017). *Visionary leadership in a turbulent world: Thriving in the new VUCA context*. Emerald Publishing Limited. doi:10.1108/9781787142428

Greenleaf, K. (2008). The servant as leader (rev. ed.) Westfield, IN: Greenleaf Center for Servant Leadership.

Greenleaf, R. K. (1977). *Servant Leadership: A Journey Into the Nature of Legitimate Power and Greatness*. Paulist Press.

Heyler, S. G., & Martin, J. A. (2018). Servant leadership theory: Opportunities for additional theoretical integration 1. *Journal of Managerial Issues*, *30*(2), 230. http://ezproxy.hct.ac.ae/login?url=https://www-proquest-com.ezproxy.hct.ac.ae/scholarly-journals/servant-leadership-theory-opportunities/docview/2186639350/se-2?accountid=1215

Leadership Team & the Tata Group. (n.d.). Retrieved April 05, 2021, from https://www.tata.com/management-team

Northouse, P. G. (2001). *Leadership: Theory and Practice*. Sage Publications.

Pathak, A. A. (2016). Tata motors' successful cross-border acquisition of jaguar land rover: Key take-aways. Strategic Direction, 32(9), 15-18. doi:10.1108/SD-05-2016-0083

Poverty eradication programmes and urbanisation in India – UN India. (n.d.). Retrieved April 16, 2021, from https://in.one.un.org/poverty-and-urbanisation/

Prentice, W. (2004). *Understanding leadership*. Retrieved April 30, 2021, from https://hbr.org/2004/01/understanding-leadership

PTI. (n.d.). We changed our 'conservative' ways after economic reforms in 1991: Ratan Tata - Times of India. *The Times of India*. https://timesofindia.indiatimes.com/business/india-business/we-changed-our-conservative-ways-after-economic-reforms-in-1991-ratan-tata/articleshow/12135103.cms

Q&A With Ratan TATA (SSIR). (n.d.). Retrieved April 16, 2021, from https://ssir.org/articles/entry/qa_with_ratan_tata

Ratan N tata, chairman, tata sons, tata group statement on tata trusts COVID-19 strategy. (2020). *Express Healthcare*. Retrieved from http://ezproxy.hct.ac.ae/login?url=https://www-proquest-com.ezproxy.hct.ac.ae/trade-journals/ratan-n-tata-chairman-sons-group-statement-on/docview/2384128486/se-2?accountid=1215

Ratan Tata. (2021). In *Encyclopædia Britannica*. Retrieved from https://academic-eb-com.ezproxy.hct.ac.ae/levels/collegiate/article/Ratan-Tata/474479

Sir Ratan Tata - University of Edinburgh Scholarship. (2011, May 25). *The Hindustan Times*. Retrieved from http://ezproxy.hct.ac.ae/login?url=https://www-proquest-com.ezproxy.hct.ac.ae/newspapers/sir-ratan-tata-university-edinburgh-scholarship/docview/868433740/se-2?accountid=1215

Tata nano relocation from bengal hit marketability: Ratan tata. (2014, Aug 8). *Oncars India*. Retrieved from http://ezproxy.hct.ac.ae/login?url=https://www-proquest-com.ezproxy.hct.ac.ae/magazines/tata-nano-relocation-bengal-hit-marketability/docview/1552129635/se-2?accountid=1215

Tata Trusts Corporate Standee - Areas of Work. (n.d.). Retrieved from https://www.tatatrusts.org/Upload/Content_Files/tata-trusts-corporate-standee-areas-of-work.pdf

Tata Trusts Corporate Standee - Guiding Principles. (n.d.). Retrieved from https://www.tatatrusts.org/upload/pdf/tata-trusts-corporate-standee-guiding-principles.pdf

Tata trusts partners with prodea systems. (2015, Dec 5). *Entertainment Close – Up*. Retrieved from http://ezproxy.hct.ac.ae/login?url=https://www-proquest-com.ezproxy.hct.ac.ae/wire-feeds/tata-trusts-partners-with-prodea-systems/docview/1739244215/se-2?accountid=1215

The hindu business line: Ratan tata to receive MMA amalgamations leadership award. (2014). Chatham: Newstex. Retrieved from http://ezproxy.hct.ac.ae/login?url=https://www-proquest-com.ezproxy.hct.ac.ae/blogs-podcasts-websites/hindu-business-line-ratan-tata-receive-mma/docview/1636185039/se-2?accountid=1215

Thompson, B. (2015). Servant, leader, or both? A fresh look at Mark 10:35-45. *The Journal of Applied Christian Leadership*, *9*(2), 54–65. http://ezproxy.hct.ac.ae/login?url=https://www-proquest-com.ezproxy.hct.ac.ae/scholarly-journals/servant-leader-both-fresh-look-at-mark-10-35-45/docview/1766243034/se-2?accountid=1215

Tiwari, R., & Herstatt, C. (2012). *Open global innovation networks as enablers of frugal innovation: propositions based on evidence from India*. Hamburg University of Technology, Technology and Innovation Management, Working Paper (72).

Truett, R. (2018). The Empire Strikes Back: In its 10 years under tata, jaguar land rover has proved all of the naysayers wrong -- so far. *Automotive News, 92*(6831), 1. Retrieved from http://ezproxy.hct.ac.ae/login?url=https://www-proquest-com.ezproxy.hct.ac.ae/trade-journals/empire-strikes-back/docview/2047407272/se-2?accountid=1215

van Dierendonck, D. (2011). Servant Leadership: A Review and Synthesis. *Journal of Management*, *37*, 1228–1261.

Walumbwa, F. O., & Lawler, J. J. (2003). Building effective organizations Transformational leadership, collectivist orientation, work-related attitudes, and withdrawal behaviors in three emerging economies. *International Journal of Human Resource Management*, *14*, 1083–1101.

Wilde, R. K. (2012). Steering clear of organizational icebergs. *Public Management*, *94*(9), 14–18. http://ezproxy.hct.ac.ae/login?url=https://www-proquest-com.ezproxy.hct.ac.ae/trade-journals/steering-clear-organizational-icebergs/docview/1118126339/se-2?accountid=1215

Wulffers, T. (2017). *Authentic leadership effectiveness: For individuals and teams - A coaching approach*. KR Publishing.

KEY TERMS AND DEFINITIONS

Acquisition: A company buys most shares to gain control of the other company.

Eco-Disaster: Is a catastrophic event in the natural environment due to human activity.

GBP: The British pound sterling referred to as the GBP.

Growth Mindset: It means that with effort, it is possible to increase intelligence levels, talents, and abilities.

INR: The official Indian currency is the Indian rupee and referred to as the INR.

Organizational Culture Iceberg: The organizational culture iceberg model that you know of consists of the surface culture and the larger deep culture.

Recession: Refers to a significant decline in economic activity in a designated region.

USD: The US Dollar is the currency of United States.

VUCA World: It describes the situation of constant and unpredictable change.

Chapter 6
Leadership and Followership in the Context of Trade Unionism

Adekunle Theophilius Tinuoye
https://orcid.org/0000-0002-7500-8619
Micheal Imoudu National Institute for Labour Studies, Nigeria

Sylvanus Simon Adamade
Michael Imoudu National Institute for Labour Studies, Nigeria

Victor Ikechukwu Ogharanduku
https://orcid.org/0000-0003-1839-9358
Center For Peace and Strategic Studies, University of Ilorin, Nigeria

ABSTRACT

Trade union leadership and followership are complimentary and symbiotic. Pragmatic followership serves to engender effective trade union leadership. Union leaders are expected to work with and stand by their members in order to attain union mandates. Union ethos demands that leaders must place the interest and welfare of workers as their most paramount goal and work assiduously towards satisfying them. Union members must consider the antecedents and pedigree of aspirants and ensure that only unionists with track records of tenaciously and selflessly championing the union's cause should be elected as leaders. Through leadership by example, trust, integrity, and candor, union leaders can bring about positive changes to both workers and their union. Finally, the authors called on union leaders to be alive to their responsibilities and demonstrate ethical and servant forms of leadership in order to cope with the challenges of giving vent to the aspirations of their members.

DOI: 10.4018/978-1-7998-2807-5.ch006

1.0 INTRODUCTION

Most modern organizations comprise of two categories of people those who lead (leaders) and those who follow (followers). The success of any organization is predicated not only on the basis of how well the leaders lead *(Overbeck & Park, 2001; Schmid, Jonas, & Hall, 2009; Bourke & Dillion, 2016; Rihal, 2017)*, but also greatly on how well their followers tag along. So much emphasis is placed on the role of a leader, yet leadership alone does not contribute to success. Followers also play major part. Followership is integral to leadership and vice versa. In a way, leadership to a certain extent is also hinged on the quality and orientation of its followers. Drucker (1986) in reinforcing this said a leader is someone who has followers. The relationship between both parties is symbiotic *(De Hoogh & Den Hartog, 2008)*. Leaders and followers interact to form a dynamic and purposeful relationship, an essential ingredient in today's world. As stressed earlier, leadership is paramount to organizational success and sustainability leading to the great importance attached to the theme of leadership in modern enterprises. Likewise, Bendixen, Campbell, Criswel & Smith (2016) averred that *leadership is the major driver of organizational change*." What a leader does or his actions especially when championing change initiatives demonstrates the presence of effective leadership with great multiplier effects on organizational growth. More than ever, today's organizations need to squarely tackle changes in technological innovation, competitive strategy and internal organizational operations. Leadership is a crucial factor in confronting, addressing and designing actionable solutions to these issues and or changes that can improve organizational performance (*Morris & Seeman, 1950)*. This can be attained by leading, showing the way or motivating others to channel efforts towards a new or desired direction. *(Bryson, 1989; Goleman, 2000; Josephson, 2002; Lindeman & Rono, 2011)*

The First Industrial revolution which brought about changes in the dynamics of work led to the emergence of a boss in the workplace whose major focus was to get the job done fast and the need for an association(Trade Union) to advance the interests of workers in the new milieu. For workers and their families, this was a good event given the centrality of work to individual flourishing and stability. In the last century, International Labour Organization (2017a) noted that work became not only a means of material fulfillment, but also a fundamental tool for personal development and community participation. Thus, the need for the existence of trade unions as highlighted by Bivens et al.,(2017) is that the freedom of workers to join together in unions is a widely recognized fundamental human right across the globe. Trade unions are all about raising human well-being through the creation of jobs with humane conditions of employment, the emergence of thriving workplaces and prosperous and inclusive economies. The growing determination by workers to end their exploitation by employers, fight against the deprivation of their basic rights and to combat the plethora of unfair labour practices against them makes today's trade unions essential commodities.

Emerging challenges and developments in the work of world cumulatively threaten the long-term prosperity of workers and trade union relevance. For trade unions, these issues require the concerted efforts by both leaders and members. Industrial democracy which places emphasis on popular participation and the ability of workers to freely choose their representatives presupposes that workers decide who will lead them. Hence, workers should elect the right caliber of leaders that can advance their interests *(Batson, 2011)*. From this perspective, highly conscious union members are obligated to produce credible union leaders that would abide by the ethos of trade unionism in advancing their welfare and wellbeing.

Leadership and followership relations are getting increasingly intricate and the emergence of dynamic workplaces with divergent interests, motivations, backgrounds has made the issue of trade union leadership very germane. Successful leadership requires a modicum of active followership since it is the willingness of individuals to follow that makes elected executives union leaders. However, for people to simultaneously believe, accept and follow the leader, a key element called trust is mandatory. Maxwell (2007) noted that to build trust, a leader must exhibit competence, connection and character. Maxwell added that character makes trust possible and trust makes leadership possible. Trust engenders a sense of bonding, commitment and belief in the leader. As an addendum, trust can only be generated by a pedigree and record of selflessness and dedication. Trade union leaders foster understanding and commitment among their followers with regards to upholding and adhering to union values and rules. True leaders communicate their values with the people they lead, creating an atmosphere of certainty and trust *(Anderson, 2015)*. The leader can have background knowledge about all these if he has a firm grasp about the needs of followers which reflects in the type of workplaces they desire, the kind of union they want and how they can participate. The symbiotic interactions between followers and leaders requires leaders to help their followers to understand their overall vision, inspire them to know how they can contribute to achieving key objectives and sharing information about progress and prospects.

A central theme in union growth is the quality and foresightedness of leadership and followership. Effectively defending worker and union interest is emblematic of pragmatic union leadership and followership. Leadership entails responsibility and responsiveness. The possession of union power confers a sense of responsibility on the possessor in this case the union leader. This ideal promotes power as a source of freedom to be used to serve selflessly. That is the authors stated earlier that followers should choose leadership with track records of service. What is the role of the followers and how does it affect leadership behavior? How can union executives generate the required participation to create a truly dynamic partnership with their followers? Does the leader put the interest and welfare of his constituents first in all matters ? How can followers be more guided to ellect better leaders?, How does the leader respond to feedback or unfavorable comments? How can Leaders galvanize workers to do great things at work and in the society? How can leaders be more responsive and sensitive to the aspirations of their members?, the provision of critical answers to the above questions and more forms the major objective of this book chapter proposal.

1.1 Background

The importance of decent work, social justice, peace and worker prosperity was underscored by the establishment of the International labour organization (ILO) in 1919 and the fact that it is the first agency of the United Nations. The Declaration of Philadelphia highlighted the war against want, material wellbeing of workers and the popular maxim that poverty anywhere constitutes a danger to prosperity everywhere. But political conflicts, humanitarian catastrophes, economic crises, threats of war, policy instabilities at all levels and poverty etc are counterproductive to the long-term sustainability of enterprises, development of workplaces and relevance of trade unions. Workplace policies that promote equity and inclusion are beneficial to organizational progress, worker prosperity and trade union growth. But the regulation of the working-week, working-day and working hour on the one hand, and the varying modes of remuneration of work on the other, have been the source of major struggles within capitalist production relations has they have impinged upon the everyday lives of workers, and shaped both working and managerial practices at the point of production. (*Georg August University Gottingen, 2017*). More devastating to mostly least developing economies are Austerity measures. Reiterating the negative social impacts of austerity measures, Ortiz and Cummins (2019) declared that **a**usterity will affect approximately 5.8 billion people by 2021—about 75 per cent of the global population. They opined that for billions of people, the persistence of a long jobs crisis and austerity mean a deterioration of living conditions, rising inequalities and social discontent. International World of Workers (2015) viewed that within the labour movement, there are, broadly speaking, two main tendencies that are as far apart as two worlds--the world of the slave who yearns to be free and the world of the master who wants to keep him in chains. This is quite relevant because as Giroux (2011) pointed out that besides a growing inability to translate private matters into public concerns, what is also being lost is the very idea of the public good, the notion of connecting learning to social change and developing modes of civic courage infused by the principles of social justice. The authors accept that the quest for collective rights is essential to consolidate the actualization of individual rights and building and sustaining social solidarity which emphasizes the same common good. This speaks to what trade unions are all about and stand for.

Through strategic partnerships, unions contribute to improving enterprise efficiency by suggesting proficient means through which organizations can derive maximum mileage from their resources and revenues. Unions also boost the abilities of workers to ensure that their voices are heard and interests are protected. The union's intervening services have also facilitated the development of encompassing labor laws and stable social and economic systems that have enhanced employee welfare and promoted organizational progress. Galinsky et al., (2014) pointed out that a heightened sense of accountability can keep power in check. A key aspect of trade unions is their capacity to demand transparent processes in private and public sector institutions. For instance, trade unions like Senior Staff Association of Nigerian Universities, Nigeria Civil Service Union, Association of Senior Civil Servants of Nigeria and Medical and Health Workers Union of Nigeria have been consistent advocates for transparency in the administration of tertiary institutions, hospitals and ministries, departments and agencies.

MAIN FOCUS OF THE CHAPTER

2.0 Leadership

Leadership is a pervasive expression and phenomenon with diverse meanings. It is a word that speaks to everybody regardless of age, sex, religion, ethnicity, race, culture and education. Leadership to Brodbeck et al., (2000) is the ability to influence, motivate and enable others to contribute towards the effectiveness of a working group. Leadership in this perspective entails considerate utilization of power and focus on salient issues that positively affect the lives of others. To do this effectively, good leaders must understand the attitudes, standards, diversity and needs of the followers. Montgomery (n.d) noted that leadership is simply the capacity and will to rally men and women to a common purpose and character which inspires confidence. It requires drawing people close and generating followership based on shared values and ideas. It emphasizes empathy and collectivism that willingly gets the best out of followers. This is close to leadership by example which requires responsiveness and altruism. The Barefoot Collective (2009) accepted that leaders who strive to help others to see and hear themselves and each other more clearly, are in touch with their own thoughts, feelings and desires and walk their own talk

The issue of vision is also connected with Leadership. It illustrates an important issue such as the necessity of creating a vision, getting the followers to key into the vision, transforming followers through articulation of this vision, and attaining the goals set out in the vision through the mobilization of followers. Leaders may lead, but to successfully mobilize their followers to work towards attaining his or her vision and readily accept their leadership, they must first demonstrate their level of competence and capacity to lead. Because, eventually what makes a leader effective is the positive difference they make.. Importantly, leadership should design a picture of the future they desire through an articulate and inclusive vision, enlighten their followers about its advantages, strive to translate the vision into reality and endeavor to sustain it. In addition, the authors believe that leadership can strengthen or elicit the desired reaction and dedication from followers by the above and enabling the vision through viable ideas that can ensure the unselfish and mutually beneficial utilization of power and resources. A leader's effort to develop a shared vision has been described as bonding by Sergiovanni (1990) where leaders and followers with a shared set of values and commitment get bonded together in a common cause to meet a common goal.

Leadership is essential to facilitate the required interaction that can realize a group's objectives and improve performance through strategies and techniques. Jacobs & Jacques (1990) talked about leadership in terms of giving purpose to collective effort, and causing willing effort to be expended to achieve purpose. Leadership sparks productive environments and innovative workers. Accordingly, UNDP (2015) pointed out that work unleashes human potential, human creativity and human spirit. What is required in this instance is purposeful leadership that can bring out the best from its followers by designing and applying techniques that will optimize follower skills and competence for the overall progress of the group.

Richards & Engle (1986) saw leadership in terms of articulating visions, embodying values, and creating environments to accomplish things. The ability of organizations to respond effectively to various challenges, maximize opportunities and effect sustainable development depends largely on leadership. With effective leadership, transparent environments and fair regulations, followers willingly commit themselves to facilitating organizational vision. World Bank (2019) added that the presence of clear and coherent rules: that…..can promote growth and development when they are efficient, transparent and accessible to those for whom they are intended. Leadership encompasses organizing and structuring activities and functions that can foster the needed effective coordination and smooth interaction between and among stakeholders. Leadership is essentially influencing others to achieve goals, accomplish tasks, common purpose and objectives *(Hersey & Blanchard, 1988;Cohen, 1990; House et al., 1997; Yukl 2006)* Influence can also be linked with persuading an audience, bringing people on board, cultivating their camaraderie, winning their hearts, swaying their minds and having an effect them. This can be generated by leaders using the power of ideas, ideals and innovations to give direction, establish vision, obtain commitment, organize people, embody strong values and create environments that facilitate group cohesion and the achievement of results. Another perspective is caring, to which Stückelberger & Mugambi (2007) typified leadership as caring for life in dignity of all, strengthening justice and developing technological skills and political mechanisms for individual and community well-being and the obligation to protect. Leadership is a continuous process, with the accomplishment of one goal becoming the basis for the formulation and implementation of newer goals. The authors suggested that leadership is not a strait jacket endeavor and leaders need to exercise power in various ways and differing circumstances in order to accomplish various goals.

2.1 Trade Unions

Aiyelabola(2010) defined trade unions as organizations of workers who come together with the aim of bettering their lots. He also identified five major substantive issues which are at the heart of the workers' quest in combining, these being: wages and other material remuneration; working conditions; job security; working time and; respect and dignity. The ILO (2006) defined a trade union as an organization based on membership of workers in various trades, occupations, and professions. It then added that the organization is to be free, open, independent, democratic, and responsible. Yesufu (1984) defined a trade union as an economic organization whose primary concern is with the terms and conditions of work. He further noted that one of the (union's) main functions is to oversee the rates of pay of its members, to ensure that wages are adequate by reference to the cost of living and accepted living standard generally. Forrester (2010) defined trade unions as institutions that primarily mediate between their members and opposing social interests such as the state and employers. From the four definitions outlined above, the authors concluded that trade unions are institutions established to protect workers' rights, articulate workers demands, champion workers interests and defend the general cause of workers.

The actualization of the rights to join unions and bargain collectively for decent pay and good conditions of employment are core planks of the International Labour Organization and are also critical to entrenching fair workplaces and equitable societies. Trade unionism is about guaranteeing and meeting the needs of workers. Talking about needs, Fasset(2012) outlined four basic needs of humans:-the need to be understood and heard, to feel welcome and have a sense of belonging and inclusion, to feel important and be acknowledged when they do well and lastly the need for comfort and re-assurance. Working class individuals have both personal and organizational needs like continuity in employment, safe and healthy workplaces, work-life balance, career progression, learning and development opportunities which can make both life and work meaningful for them. These are issues that are best suited to be advanced and championed by trade unions. For example, Nigerian trade unions have a rich pedigree of contributing immensely to national development in diverse ways. Offiong & Olatuyi (2012) pointed out that the efforts of the union has most of the time paved way for the gradual increase in wage earnings, improvement in the employment conditions of workers, change in draconian government policies, election of popular political representatives, installation of popular mandates and the adjustment of harsh economic policies, like the recent fuel subsidy withdrawal. They further opined that the collective action of the labor movement has tried to make socio-economic policies in Nigeria more humane and supportive of the lives and economic interests of the generality of citizens. In cognizance of this, it becomes vital for trade union leaders to have detailed knowledge and understanding of the diverse needs of their members and endeavor to harmonize these needs in order to meet them. People join trade unions and remain members for different reason such as better pay and working conditions and union protection and support at work *(Margetts, 1998),* representation and treatment as human beings *(ILO & Gallup Inc, 2017*) and equality, health and safety and solidarity *(Industriall-union, 2019).* However, trade union membership is always motivated by the prospects of deriving some tangible and or non tangible benefits because the trade union is a beneficial society. Various studies have shown a correlation between trade unionism and better workers' wages and or welfare. *(Freeman & Medoff, 1984; Dollard & Neser, 2013; UNIFOR 2014; Peetz, 2015; Wood & Gallasso, 2015;Bucknor. 2016'; ILO & Gallup Inc, 2017)*

2.2 Trade Unions and the World of Work

Paradoxically, unions are misunderstood and unappreciated by majorities of rank and file members and even the generality of Nigerians. But this isn't surprising given the antecedents and opulent lifestyle of some union leaders in Nigeria. Workers perceive them as too aristocratic, removed from their everyday experiences, distant, disconnected and appearing unperturbed and unconcerned about their plight or situation. Based on this, workers responses have been apathy to union activities, perception of the union in wrong light and stereotyping of union leaders as self-serving giving rise to high distrust of what trade union officials truly represent or stand for. But no matter the perception, the union has come to be regarded as a necessity in the workplace. Supporting this, Ryder (2017) noted that left unprotected by trade unions workers are exposed to unbridled dehumanization, exploitation and misery without end by employers and their representatives. On another front, employers perceive unionists as irritants and trouble makers that are inimical to the enterprise growth. To most managers, trade unions are meddlesome interlopers that are clogs in the wheels of workplace progress. Several organizations in Nigeria engage in deliberate and systematic frustration of trade unionism through individual bargaining policies, extraction of commitments to contract out of union membership, unwritten, unofficial and invisible codes and insertion of non-unionization clauses in employment letters. They have also perfected the art of capitalizing on economic downturns and recessions to perpetually pauperize workers through reduced wages and conditions of work. Salazar (2016) mentioned others like refusing to bargain collectively, denying the unions participation in obtaining improvements for workers and all the strategies used to convince workers that unionizing is prejudicial. To some of them, the panacea is to render unions effete. Kent (2017) also spoke about situations of economic exploitation where mostly employers and managers benefit much of the value produced by workers who are left in marginal conditions and are deprived of their dignity and their identity as distinct individual personalities.

Oxfam (2017) observed that while the heads of corporations and the super-rich smile home with huge bonuses and dodge their taxes, the workers are paid peanuts. The main focus of multinationals and big businesses is to garner profits at the expense of workers welfare, thus widening the already large global inequality gap and pay disparity between executives and workers. To compound the woes of workers and unions, Oxfam (2017) also added that governments sing to the tune of big business and wealthy elites. State authorities claiming to be interested in attracting jobs through the provision of incentives to encourage inflow of foreign direct investments and industrialization, propose and design restrictive laws to curb unionism. This situation made Thomas (2011) to opine that trade unions are fast losing relevance in today's increasingly globalized world where private-sector companies can easily move production to escape unions, where unionized jobs are disappearing because of technological change, and where states are passing laws to reduce the power of organized labor. The grim consequences of this development for workers and their unions respectively attracted Ryder (2017) who called for considerations of humanity, social justice and peace. This is reminiscent of the position of Schulman (2012) who spoke about the development of a culture of transformative personal, organizational and social change that can foster high human qualities and practices including empathy, altruism, peaceful conflict resolution and restorative justice. But on the contrary, the world of work is witnessing the gradual whittling down of the power of unions and the ability of workers to obtain just and decent jobs and conditions.

According to UNIFOR (2014) today's trade unions are in a unique position to challenge inequality, demand redress for past wrongs, and push for a better future as instruments for building working class power in workplaces, communities, and in the political, economic, and cultural affairs of society. They have the tools, legislative backing, people power, and democratic structures in place. In agreement, ILO (2017b) noted the pressing need to improve conditions for the some 780 million women and men who are working but not earning enough to lift themselves and their families out of the US$2 a day poverty threshold. The authors maintained that to achieve this calls for ethically strong unions and leadership that can negotiate with, engage and compel the employer to recognize and bargain with it, oblige the employer to reach an acceptable agreement with it and serve as a vehicle to shift the balance of power between them and management more to their favor. Burrow (2017) opined that the union mean less inequality, more sustainable work practices and economic security and added that the same collective strength that delivers better wages also makes work safer and healthier. The union and its constitution must be founded on the principles of social justice and stimulating equality fairness and inclusion in its activities. The union as an organization that fights for the rights of workers, must not only be union by mere platitudes, name and on paper, but also by demonstrable practices, tangible action and leadership effusions. The struggle for the emancipation of workers in today's world of work has assumed a very herculean dimension that is neither for the light nor faint hearted and this is where the issue of strong ethical background to withstand all forms of negative and deleterious pressures arises.

New developments in the emerging world of work require virile and grounded leadership that can create a culture that promotes unity and cohesion, encourages ideas generation and implementation for problem solving, reinforces trade union consciousness and check the unsavory antics of adverse forces. Hordijk(1978) also averred that trade unionism is concerned with ethical attitudes and values despite the consideration of people that because trade unions are necessary countervailing forces against the power of employers, ethics should not be linked with trade union activities. The authors concurred with Ciulla (2005) that an ethical leadership may lead the organization (union) in a manner that respects the rights and dignity of others. Ethical leadership is reputed to enhance followership satisfaction with leaders. But Brown & Mitchell (2010) said both leaders and employees should behave ethically to enhance the positive aspects on organizational effectiveness. For effective balancing, ethics should be a two way thing. When both leaders and followers act ethically, they are on the same page and this stimulates cordiality and cooperation to achieve goals.

3.0 LEADERSHIP AND TRADE UNIONISM

Trade union leadership personifies the trade union as an institution that focuses on the dignity of labour, craves harmonious workplaces and desires good quality of (worker) work-life. Their utility comes from the impacts in the lives of both working and non working class people and their families. A point reemphasized by Eaton(1992) that union leaders who are elected democratically must respond to their membership base and lead their members to see beyond their own interests to the concerns of those who are not members but may be, and whose well-being affects both the members and the society. Trade Union leaders are expected to introduce pragmatic programmes and newer approaches to meeting the demands of the 21st century world of work and workers. Trade union leadership must take urgent steps to promote equality, avoid cabals, prevent discrimination, address issues that border on workers welfare and ensure that union policies have the desired impact on the lives of workers.

Like any formal organization, trade unions are facing enormous challenges from and on all fronts. It is becoming clearer that the success of the trade union as an agglomeration of workers groups is becoming increasingly dependent on the abilities of union leaders to identify and optimize its strengths, weaknesses, threats and opportunities. Ibarra & Hansen (2011) noted that research has shown that in today's workplace diverse teams produce better results. Therefore, the authors suggested that leaders should seek to bring people together from different backgrounds, disciplines, cultures and generations and leverage all they have to offer. **Nye** (2008) noted that in an era when the information revolution has dramatically changed the playing field, the urgency to attract, inspire, engage and persuade members as a leader has become most paramount. Leadership now require harnessing member skills, developing members' potentials, empowering followership, enhancing group harmony and promoting partnership to accomplish overlapping and mutually inclusive tasks.

Effective trade union leadership holds cardinal prospects to solve problems emanating from socio-economic and political globalization on workers' collectives. The accentuation of management control over labour processes hampers the quest for freedom at work and respect of trade unionization rights. Hammer, Bayazit & Wazeter (2009) underscored the existence of a closer proximity between what a union leader does and the consequences of union membership on the rank and file. To attain this, leaders should connect constantly with their members and also be ready to navigate the terrains of the increasingly complex world of work. This is because the capacity of union leaders to influence developments at work is hinged on their detailed knowledge of the dynamics of work. A leadership that is not steeped in union ideology and not knowledgeable about the practice and dynamics of industrial relations would not be able to thoroughly engage management and get the best for workers. Armstrong (2006) pointed out that in fulfilling their roles; leaders have to satisfy task, individual and group maintenance needs. These needs require knowledge for performance and success. So the authors agreed that effective leadership is proportional to union participation *(Fullagar, Gallagher, Clark, & Carroll, 2004).*

Workers cannot have power in the workplace if they don't have power in the union *(Peetz, 2015)*.. Industrial democracy is an instrument for building solidarity, establishing accountability and determining strategies which are critical to advancing worker and union interests. To embody the tenets and ethos of trade unionism, union leaders are expected to be inclusive in decision making and policy formulation and promote participation in charting the strategic direction for unions. The quality of worker democratic participation is vital to union success and continued relevance. The structuring of the trade unions and also the provisions of most union constitution vests power in the hands of workers. But at times, union leadership may be aloof and insensate. At times, power may become intoxicative and corruptive. For instance, some Nigerian trade unions have emperors and tin gods masquerading like trade union leaders. Many of them equate themselves with the union and believe they are bigger than the union, but still end up using the union platform to service their narrow agenda.*(DeCelles, DeRue, Margolis & Ceranic, 2012).* The leader's fortune is unavoidably linked with that of the followers.

3.1 Leadership Style

The trade union leadership is neither bestowed nor acquired by sheer rhetoric, but through action and ability to better the lot of workers and boost union prosperity. The leader is expected to foster a culture of high performance by nurturing the levels of solidarity, diligence and commitment required to facilitate the realization of the union objectives. But closely examined, union leadership mode and style falls within the purview of servant leadership (*Greenleaf, 1977; Hunter, 1998; Autry, 2004; Spears, 2010; Pritchard, 2013; Sendjaya, 2015; Keith, 2015; Jennings & West, 2016; Blanchard & Broadwell, 2018*). Since the main goal of servant leadership is to serve, the nexus between servant and union leadership is that union leadership connotes service to workers and the union. The servant leadership has been expressed and applied in many contexts over the years In the context of trade unionism, the authors regard it as a philosophy and set of practices that enriches the lives of workers, builds better trade unions and creates a more just and caring world of work. Greenleaf (2006) noted that servant leader is servant first. He continued that it begins with the natural feeling that one wants to serve/ A top priority for trade union leaders is to imbibe a cardinal aspect of servant leadership by making sure that other people's highest priority needs are served. In line the treatise of Greenleaf (2006) that the servant-leader focuses primarily on the growth and well-being of people and the communities to which they belong to, so union leaders must have in depth knowledge of their union's mission and vision goals, dynamics and constitution in order to unselfishly actualize membership aspirations.

Trade union leaders possess union power and are in leadership positions because they were elected by their members or in this context the followership for obvious reasons. Therefore, their actions or decision making processes should be guided by the best interests of their members. At the heart of this is the recognition that their decisions or choices affect the well-being of their followers. Bloomingdale (2016) effused that unity is what workers have always used to make the incredible contributions to our country, to our way of life and to society as a whole. Showing genuine concern and empathy for workers economic situation and associated challenges and working towards ameliorating should be key functions of union leadership. Pritchard (2013) describes a servant leader as one who values diverse opinions, cultivates a culture of trust, develops other leaders by teaching them to lead, providing opportunities for growth, demonstrates by example, helps people with life issues, thinks about others, thinks about others and acts with humility. Hunter (1998) in enthusing that the greatest leaders are the ones that serve the most illustrated the Servant Leadership model which has will at the bottom, service and sacrifice and leadership is at the top. This model dwells on service *and sacrifice* for others which eventually enable the leader to have *authority* and influence with people. A leader who intends to lead by example must be able and willing to sacrifice tangible things for the greater good of the group and it is at this stage that he earns his stripes and the right to be called a leader.

The Nigerian Humanist Tai solarin once said leadership is sacrifice. Kent (2017) defined sacrifice as the intensity of caring is indicated by the willingness to give up benefits to oneself in order to ensure benefits to others. Sacrifice entails the consciousness to put the union above individual goals in a bid to stimulate the creation of more conducive working environments. Speers (2010) noted that the concept of servant leadership is increasingly being viewed as an ideal leadership form that an untold number of people and organizations aspire. He added that servant leadership is strongly based in ethical and caring behavior which enhances the growth of workers while improving the caring and quality of organizational life. Keith (2008) shared the same perspective with Greenleaf (2006) that the desire to serve is natural and moral and that servant leadership is ethical, practical, and meaningful. Keith went on to describe a servant leader as a leader who is focused on serving others, who loves people and wants to help them. Therefore, the mission of the servant leader to identify and meet the needs of others is similar to the aspirations of trade union leadership. Loving and helping others gives a servant-leader meaning and satisfaction in life (Keith, 2008:.9). Correlated with this, Mathis & Jackson (2008) were of the view that the union's ability to foster commitment from members and remain as their bargaining agents depend on how well union leaders succeed in meeting member needs. Therefore, trade unions leaders should chart purposeful courses, develop feasible plans of action and work towards attaining member needs and at the core of these activities is servant leadership. In this guise, they should run inclusive unions that encompass all workers irrespective of gender, affiliation, religion, language etc, tolerate diverse, dissenting and unfavorable views and opinions and shun the proclivities for personal profiteering which eventually undermines and inhibits the capacity of the union to attain its goals.

The main resources of the trade union are its members. Organizations are successful and thriving because of their manpower and the value of leadership is to chart an actionable course and give the necessary directions towards achieving the desired results. Jennings & Stahl-West (2006) noted that the most effective leaders don't just stand in front of their people, they stand behind them too. They also argued that an individual can only qualify to be a leader only when they put other people first and outlined five key leadership actions upending the pyramid, raising the bar, blazing the trail, building on strength and running for great purpose. These actions can be coalesced by effective trade union leadership into promoting consistency, enhancing solidarity, espousing diligence, bargaining responsively negotiating reasonably, collaborating responsibly, mobilizing, organizing, directing and controlling the business of the union to accomplish workers aspirations (*Tinuoye, 2013*). Decision making processes are critical in any organization, trade union leaders must be guided by the prospects of making informed choices that will positively affect union members and boost union progress. Since trade unions operate a representative system that ensures that leadership reflect the wishes of members, members participation in decision making will reinforce this cardinal aspect of trade unionism..

3.3 Followership: Roles and Responsibilities of Trade Union Members

Several scholars have authored works and studies revolving around the theme of followership. (*Van Vugt, 2006; Baker, 2007; Kelley, 2008; Popper, 2011: Uhl-Bien, Riggio, Lowe & Carsten 2014: Bastardoz & Van Vugt, 2019*). For the purpose of this work, followers are defined as the rank and file members of the trade unions. They constitute the chunk of membership of trade unions and they are the basis for the presence of trade union leadership. Uhl-Bien, Riggio, Lowe & Carsten (2014) drew attention to the linkage between followership and leadership. They noted that leadership can only occur if there is followership—without followers and following behaviors there is no leadership. A main plank of their work is that following behaviors which represents a willingness to defer to another is a crucial component of the leadership process. Their work revolved around identifying followership theory as the study of the nature and impact of followers and following in the leadership process. Blankership (2018) examined followership from the perspective of inspiration, He explained that those people have something that others aspire to or at least want to aspire to. He came up with his working theory of Leadership which stated that people actively follows based on five factors of trust/relationship, competence, vision/purpose, admiration and the environment. Kellerman (2012) divided followers into five different types depending on their degree of engagement with the leader or leadership process i.e the isolates, bystanders, participants, activists or diehards. Based on the theme of this paper and the context of trade unionism, the authors will use the model of participative followership. This is because followers play the major role in the successful implementation of the plans, vision and mission of the leadership. A key component here is a cooperative synergy between the two parties, followers must not only be at the epicenter of the union programmes, but they should participate in its fashioning, key into it and play a vital part in its success. It is only after this that followers can willingly, conscientiously and sincerely work for its actualization.

Meindl (1995) viewed that both leadership and its consequences as largely constructed by followers and hence influenced by followers' cognitive processes. Union members must be courageous enough to voice their opinion as well as to help transform any situation, when he or she feels the leader is making a mistake, not toeing the correct path or deviating from the mission and goals of the union. This is because union leaders are not infallible; they have their own faults and imperfections. In concentrating so hard on leadership, people forget that the leader is human too. Leaders, like followers, need to be encouraged, supported and appreciated. Supporting the leader's cause means followers should deploy their skills, expertise, experience and competences to the attainment of the leader's vision and goals which are mutually agreed and enjoy the support of all rank and file members. Torbert (2004) underlined that the success of organizational transformation efforts are dependent upon the level of consciousness of both leaders and followers. The union and Leadership must continuously deepen and infuse the required union consciousness to the level that can yield positive benefits to the union.

The key to being effective as a follower is comprehensive understanding of the leader, and thorough evaluation of his mission and vision before keying into it. Followers should see themselves as partners in progress to the leaders with allegiance to the union and its goals for the major purpose of advancing common good. In doing this, they must keep on raising the bar or extending the borders of the leader's performance by asking questions continuously and seeking justifications or reasons for actions, policies or decisions. Developing strong followership is crucial to enhance the management and sustenance of a culturally diverse and integrated union and workplace.

4.0 SOLUTIONS AND RECOMMENDATIONS

In virile organizations like trade unions, the leaders and followers should serve common purposes, have common goals and share common aspirations . These are the ideals that serve to bond all parties together as they strive to advance, promote and defend workers interests in an inclement terrain. The concept of trade union leadership must be pursued from the perspective of a strong platform to enhance the socio-economic and political status of both working and non working class and their families with its positive impacts on national prosperity. Capable, qualified and experienced union leaders are critical to union effectiveness and their quest to broaden their goals to encompass social progress beyond the workplace and rediscover their capacity to mobilize workers and non workers in campaigns for national development. This is because only committed, dependable and ideologically sound union leaders can give vent to the aspirations of union members. The pursuit of enhancing leadership –followership relationships requires maximum cooperation and interaction, extraordinary efforts to emancipate mentalities, raise consciousness and mobilize the entire membership to work in tandem towards achieving the overall union vision and mission statement and goals. Trade union leadership must also understand that ultimate powers rest on union members—the workers and should be conscious of their responsibility to be loyal to and selflessly represent the interest of workers, value people and be committed to the union. Williamson(2017) noted that to establish a culture of servant leadership within your organization, in this case, the union let others see you serve and they will be naturally encouraged to join you. Most importantly, let them know that you care and they will be endeared to you. Lastly, invest in your people and don't place limitations on your service.

4.1 FUTURE RESEARCH DIRECTIONS

Union Leadership is neither a tea party nor a cake walk. Virile leaders emerge through a continuous process of self adjustment, knowledge acquisition, capacity building and experience gaining, Passing through the furnace of hard negotiations, moving through the tough road of organizing and mobilizing and constantly seeking to raise the bar of workers welfare and wellbeing makes union leaders worthy and inimitable. Leaders who take cognizance of and are in tune with the interests, aspirations and diversity of their followers will build strong unions and dedicated membership. (Blanchard, 2018). A union leader should keep up with, predict and anticipate changes in this ever changing and dynamic world of work especially against the backdrop of the coming of the fourth industrial revolution, lead the union in comprehending the changing contexts and proffer actionable programmes and strategies to correspond to these changes.

Workplaces are changing rapidly and giving rise to diverse forms of work, union leaders are obligated to generate new ideas, identify and seek opportunities and then translate these ideas into reality for both the union and workers. Trade union leaders in the words of *(Kent, 2017),* should be good shepherds and stewards respectively. Kent (2017) illustrated that a good shepherd and steward is expected to inspire others, build self-confidence, fight hopelessness and anxiety among people, overcome fear, initiate productive and life oriented actions, provide new light, define goals and provide a foundation for the future. Again, the authors re-emphasized the need for union leaders ensure that selfish interests have no place in union and the dominant thinking among leaders and followers is 'we' and not i. Vibrant and virile unions with servant leaders and participative followers have a surfeit of sacrifice, dedication, commitment, discipline and service that can be readily utilized in any meaningful struggle for the liberation and progress of workers.

The prevalent situation in Nigeria calls for ethically sound trade union leadership that can enhance the capacity of the labour movement to combat the magnitude of poverty, narrow the widening inequality gaps and foster social and economic justice nationwide.. The deplorable standard of living of workers, women, youths, physically challenged and migrant workers in Nigeria would be enhanced when trade union leaders pile more pressure on the Nigerian government to raise the minimum wage and introduce pro poor social programs. Johnson & Adams (2017) offered a useful guide by illustrating Immanuel Kant's *categorical imperatives* a set of leadership code of conduct that discourages or prevents behaviors or decisions which hurt the interests of the led or curtail benefits from union membership. Further research could be directed to study how leadership can engender the greatest benefits for the majority of followers and greater good of the union without prejudices. The research should focus on how and acsertain if trade union leadership policies and programmes are inclusive enough and are members deriving tangible or non tangible benefits that can accentuate union development?. Carrying out a study to generate sincere answers to these questions would shed considerable knowledge on the critical area of leadership and followsership in the context of trade unionism.

4.2 CONCLUSION

The pressures facing trade unions today require that trade union leaders and members should possess the prerequisite skills and abilities to deliver results in a very tough and challenging working environment. Effective training enables both leadership and followership to acquire new knowledge and ideals and update existing competences that will enable them to build virile and service oriented unions. Few union leaders and workers are well grounded on the dynamics, ethos and tenets of trade unionism. Building trade union solidarity, consciousness and membership loyalty is linked to the provision of comprehensive trade union education and training about the labour movement and working people, their history, struggles, milestones, challenges etc. Policy makers at all tiers should start recognizing the significance of followership and placing it on the same scale as leadership. Followership can help to compliment and construct leadership in productive and innovative ways that will be mutually beneficial to all parties. The strengthening of issues like followership development, skills and training etc should be place at the front burner of modern organizations. The importance of servant leadership and participative followership is further enhanced by the major finding of the study by DeCelles, DeRue, Margolis, & Ceranic, (2012) which demonstrated that those with strong moral self concepts, when given power, will increasingly behave in ways that benefit the common good. This is what lies at the heart of the importance and synergistic relationship between Leadership and followership in trade unionism.

REFERENCES

Aiyelabola, T. (2010, June). *Trade unionism and Trade unions: An Introductory perspective*. Retrieved from http://solidarityandstruggle.blogspot.com/2010/06/trade-unionism-and-trades-unions.html

Anderson, A. M. (2015). *The Characteristics of a True Leader*. Retrieved from https://www.forbes.com/sites/amyanderson/2015/03/01/the-characteristics-of-a-true-leader/#335df0372324

Armstrong, M. (2006). *A Handbook of Human Resource Management Practice* (10th ed.). Kogan Page Publications.

Autry, J. A. (2004). *The Servant Leader: How to Build a Creative Team, Develop Great Morale, and Improve Bottom-Line Performance*. Three Rivers Press.

Baker, S. (2007). Followership: The theoretical foundation of a contemporary construct. *Journal of Leadership & Organizational Studies*, *14*(1), 50–60. doi:10.1177/0002831207304343

Bastardoz, N., & Van Vugt, M. (2019). The nature of followership: Evolutionary analysis and review. *The Leadership Quarterly*, *30*(1), 81–95. doi:10.1016/j.leaqua.2018.09.004

Batson, C. D. (2011). *Altruism in humans*. Oxford University Press.

Bendixen, S. M., Campbell, M., Criswell, C., & Smith, R. (2016). *Change-Capable Leadership: The Real Power Propelling Successful Change*. White Paper. Greensboro, NC: Centre for Creative Leadership.

Bivens, J., Engdahl, L., Gould, E., Kroeger, T., McNicholas, C., Mishel, L., Mokhiber, Z., Shierholz, H., Zipperer, B. M., & Wilson, V. (2017). *How today's unions help working people Giving workers the power to improve their jobs and unrig the economy. Report*. Economic Policy Institute.

Blanchard, K. (2018). What is Leadership. In K. Blanchard & R. Broadwell (Eds.), *Servant Leadership in Action: How you can achieve great relationships and results* (pp. 7–13). Berrett-Koehler Publishers.

Blanchard, K., & Broadwell, R. (2018). *Servant Leadership in action: How you can achieve great relationships and results*. Berrett-Koehler Publishers.

Blankership, M. (2018, November 29). *A theory ofTechnical Followership*. Retrieved from https://medium.com/@marcusblankenship/the-diverse-and-dark-sides-of-followership-d9b9e6ad9836

Bloomingdale, S. (2016, August). *Unity is the tool workers have to gain power*. Speech presented at the 29th Biennial Convention of the Wisconsin state American Federation of Labour –Congress of Industrial Organizations, Madison, WI.

Bourke, J., & Dillion, B. (2016). *The six signature traits of inclusive leadership: Thriving in a diverse new world.* Retrieved from https://www2.deloitte.com/us/en/insights /topics/talent /six-signature-traits-of-inclusive-leadership.html

Brodbeck, F. C., Frese, M., Akerblom, S., Audia, G., Bakacsi, G., Bendova, H., & Wunderer, R. (2000). Cultural variation of leadership prototypes across 22 European countries. *Journal of Occupational and Organizational Psychology*, *73*(1), 1–29. doi:10.1348/096317900166859

Brown, M. E., & Mitchell, M. S. (2010). Ethical and Unethical Leadership: Exploring New Avenues for Future Research. *Business Ethics Quarterly*, *20*(4), 583–616. doi:10.5840/beq201020439

Bryson, J. M. (1989). *Strategic Planning for Public and Non Profit Organizations*. Jossey-Bass publishers.

Bucknor, C. (2016). *Black Workers, Unions and Inequality*. Center for Economic and Policy Research. Retrieved from http://cepr.net/images/stories/reports/ black-workers-unions-2016-08.pdf ?v=2

Ciulla, J. B. (2005). Integrating leadership with ethics; Is good Leadership Contrary to Human Nature? In J. P. Doh & S. A. Strumpf (Eds.), *Handbook of Responsible Leadership and Governance in Global Business* (pp. 122–138). Edward Elgar Publishing Limited. doi:10.4337/9781845425562.00017

Cohen, W. A. (1990). *The Art of a Leader*. Prentice Hall.

De Hoogh, A. H., & Den Hartog, D. N. (2008). Ethical and despotic leadership, relationships with leader's social responsibility, top management team effectiveness and subordinates' optimism: A multi-method study. *The Leadership Quarterly*, *19*(3), 297–311. doi:10.1016/j.leaqua.2008.03.002

DeCelles, K. A., DeRue, D. S., Margolis, J. D., & Ceranic, T. L. (2012). Does power corrupt or enable? When and why power facilitates self-interested behavior. *The Journal of Applied Psychology*, *97*(3), 681–689. doi:10.1037/a0026811 PMID:22250668

Dollard, M. F., & Neser, D. (2013). Worker health is good for the economy: Union density and psychosocial safety climate as determinants of country differences in worker health and productivity in 31 European countries. *Social Science & Medicine*, *92*(9), 114–123. doi:10.1016/j.socscimed.2013.04.028 PMID:23849285

Drucker, P. F. (1986). *The Practice of Management*. Harper Business.

Eaton, S. C. (1992, June). *Union Leadership Development in the 1990s and Beyond*. CSIA Discussion Paper 92-05, Kennedy School of Government, Harvard University.

Ford, J., & Harding, N. (2018). Followers in leadership theory: Fiction, fantasy and illusion. *Leadership*, *14*, 3–24.

Forrester, K. (2010). Labor Education. In *International Encyclopedia of Education* (3rd ed., pp. 139–143). Elsevier BV. doi:10.1016/B978-0-08-044894-7.00022-1

Freeman, R. B., & Medoff, J. L. (1984). *What do unions do?* Basic Book.

Fullagar, C., Gallagher, D. G., Clark, P. F., & Carroll, A. (2004). Union commitment and participation: A 10-year longitudinal study. *The Journal of Applied Psychology*, *89*(4), 730–737. doi:10.1037/0021-9010.89.4.730 PMID:15327358

Galinsky, A. D., Magee, J. C., Rus, D., Rothman, N. B., & Todd, A. R. (2014). Acceleration with steering: The synergistic benefits of combining power and perspective-taking. *Social Psychological & Personality Science*, *5*(6), 627–635. doi:10.1177/1948550613519685

Georg-August-University. (2017). *Call for papers, "Metamorphoses of the Political"/ Time and Money: Themes in Labour Relations International Workshop, 15 – 16 December 2017*. Centre for Modern Indian Studies: Georg-August-University.

Giroux, H. (2011, October 6). *Got Class Warfare? Occupy Wall Street Now!* Retrieved from https://truthout.org/articles/got-class-welfare-occupy-wall-street-now

Goleman, D. (2000). Leadership that gets results. *Harvard Business Review*, *78*(2), 78–90.

Greenleaf, R. K. (1977). *Servant Leadership A Journey into the Nature of Legitimate Power and Greatness*. Paulist Press.

Greenleaf, R. K. (2006). *Start here. What is Servant Leadership?* Retrieved from https://www.greenleaf.org/what-is-servant-leadership/

Hammer, T. H., Bayazit, M., & Wazeter, D. L. (2009). Union leadership and member attitudes: A multi-level analysis. *The Journal of Applied Psychology*, *94*(2), 392–410. doi:10.1037/a0013613 PMID:19271797

Hersey, P., & Blanchard, K. (1988). *Management of Organizational Behavior*. Prentice Hall.

Hordijk, A. (1978). Trade Unionism and Ethics. In C. V. Dam & L. M. Stallaert (Eds.), *Business Ethics* (pp. 43–50). Springer.

House, R. J., Hanges, P. J., Ruiz-Quintanilla, S. A., Dorfman, P. W., Javidan, M., & Dickson, M. (1999). Cultural influences on leadership and organizations: Project GLOBE. In W. F. Mobley, M. J. Gessner, & V. Arnold (Eds.), Advances in global leadership (Vol. 1, pp. 171–233). Academic Press.

Hunter, J. C. (2008). *The Servant: A Simple Story About The True Essence of Leadership*. Currency Publishers.

Ibarra, H., & Hansen, M. T. (2011). Are you a Collaborative Leader? *Harvard Business Review*, *89*(7/8), 68–74. PMID:21800471

ILO. (2006). *Manual for Indonesian Trade Unions on Trade Unions Administration*. International Labour Office.

ILO. (2017a). *The future of work*. Retrieved from http://www.ilo.org/global/topics/future-of-work/WCMS_541627/lang--en/index.htm

ILO. (2017b). *Organization of work and production*. Retrieved from http://www.ilo.org/global/topics/ future-of-work/WCMS_541635/lang--en /index.htm

Industrial-Global Union. (2019). *5 Reasons to Join a Union*. Retrieved from http://www.industriall-union.org/5-reasons-to-join-a-union

Industrial World of Workers. (2015). *Ethics and the Unions–Part 1*. Retrieved from https://iww.org/history/library/Dolgoff/newbeginning/1

International Labour Organization & Gallup Inc. (2017). *Towards a better future for women and work: Voices of women and men.* Retrieved from https://www.ilo.org/wcmsp5 /groups/public/---dgreports/---dcomm/---publ/documents/publication/wcms_546256. pdf

Jacobs, T. O., & Jacques, E. (1990). Military executive leadership. In R. Gal & A. D. Manglesdorf (Eds.), *Handbook of Military Psychology*. John Wiley & Sons.

Jennings, K. R., & Stahl-West, J. (2016). *The Serving Leader: Five Powerful Actions to transform your team, business and community, 10th Anniversary Edition.* San Francisco, CA: Berrett-Koehler Publishing.

Johnson, R., & Cureton, A. (2017). Kant's Moral Philosophy. *The Stanford Encyclopedia of Philosophy*. Retrieved from https://plato.stanford.edu/archives/spr2017/entries/kant-moral

Josephson, M. (2002). *Making ethical decisions. The Basic primer on using the six pillars of Character to make better decisions, and a better life*. Josephson Institute of Ethics.

Keith, K. M. (2015). *The case for servant leadership* (2nd ed.). The Greenleaf Center for Servant Leadership.

Kellerman, B. (2012). *The End of Leadership*. HarperCollins.

Kelley, R. E. (2008). Rethinking Followership. In R. E. Riggio, I. Chaleff, & J. Lipman-Blumen (Eds.), *The Art of Followership: How Great Followers Create Great Leaders and Organizations* (pp. 5–16). Jossey-Bass.

Kent, G. (2017). *On Caring*. Retrieved from https://www.transcend.org/tms/category /featured-- research-paper/

Lindeman, L. & Rono, P. (2011) Leadership Development in Africa. *Leadership and Transformation, 2*, 22-25.

Margetts, S. (1998). *Trade Unions*. Retrieved from http://www.revisionguru.co.uk/business/unions.htm

Mathis, R. L., & Jackson, J. H. (2008). *Human Resource Management* (12th ed.). South-Western Cengage Learning.

Maxwell, J. C. (2007) The 21 irrefutable laws of Leadership; Follow them and People would follow you. Nashville, TN: Thomas Nelson Publishing.

Meindl, J. (1995). The romance of leadership as a follower-centric theory: A social constructionist approach. *The Leadership Quarterly*, *6*(3), 329–341. doi:10.1016/1048-9843(95)90012-8

Montgomery, B. L. (n.d.). *Leadership Quote*. Retrieved from https://www.goodreads.com/quotes/713104-leadership-is-the-capacity-and-will-to-rally-men-and

Morris, R. J., & Seeman, M. (1950). The problem of Leadership: An interdisciplinary approach. *American Journal of Sociology*, *56*(9), 149–155. doi:10.1086/220696

Nye, J. S. (2008). *The powers to lead*. Oxford University Press.

Offiong, L. A., & Olatuyi, A. L. (2012, March). *Situation Country Report: Nigeria as Empirical Study*. Report presented at the workshop on Trade Union training in employment relations and the informal economy, Turin, Italy.

Ortiz, I., & Cummins, M. (2019, October). *Austerity the New Normal: A renewed Washington consensus*. ITUC, Initiative for Policy Dialogue, Public Services International, the Bretton Woods Project and the European Network for Debt and Developments collaboration. Retrieved from https://www.ituc-csi.org/IMG/pdf/austerity_the_new_normal_ortiz_cummins.pdf

Overbeck, J. R., & Park, B. (2001). When power does not corrupt: Superior individuation processes among powerful perceivers. *Journal of Personality and Social Psychology*, *81*(4), 549–565. doi:10.1037/0022-3514.81.4.549 PMID:11642345

Oxfam. (2017). *An Economy for the 99 percent*. Nairobi, Kenya: Oxfam International.

Peetz, D. (2015). *Are Australian trade unions part of the solution, or part of the problem?* Retrieved from http://www.australianreview.net/digest/2015/02/peetz.html

Popper, M. (2011). Towards a theory of Followership. *Review of General Psychology*, *15*(1), 29–36. doi:10.1037/a0021989

Pritchards, S. (2013, January 24). *9 Qualities of a servant leader*. Retrieved from https://www. skipprichard. com/9-qualities-of-the-servant-leader/

Richards, D., & Engle, S. (1986). After the vision: Suggestions to corporate visionaries and vision champions. In J. D. Adams (Ed.), *Transforming leadership* (pp. 199–214). Miles River Press.

Rihal, C. S. (2017). *The Importance of Leadership to Organizational Success*. Retrieved from https://catalyst.nejm.org/importance-leadership-skills-organizational-success/

Ryder, G. (2017, April) *Humanity and Social Justice, a Must for the Future of Work*. Paper presented at a Global dialogue on the future of work we want. An ILO Centenary Initiative, Geneva, Switzerland.

Salazar, A. G. (2016). *The battle to unionize Starbucks in Chile*. Retrieved from https://www.counterpunch.org/2016/01/20/the-battle-to-unionize-starbucks-in-chile-an-interview-with-andres-giordano-salazar/

Schmid, M., Jonas, K., & Hall, J. A. (2009). Give a person power and he or she will show interpersonal sensitivity: The phenomenon and its why and when. *Journal of Personality and Social Psychology*, *97*(5), 835–850. doi:10.1037/a0016234 PMID:19857005

Schulman, M. (2012). How to Combat a Culture of Violence and Maybe Save Lives. *Huffington Post: The Blog*. Retrieved from www.huffingtonpost.com/mark-schulman/combat-culture-of violence_b_2371661.html

Sendjaya, S. (2015). *Personal and Organizational Excellence through Servant Leadership: Learning to Serve, Serving to Lead, Leading to Transform (Management for Professionals)*. Springer. doi:10.1007/978-3-319-16196-9

Sergiovanni, T. J. (1990). Adding value to leadership gets extraordinary results. *Educational Leadership*, *47*(8), 23–27.

Speers, L. C. (2010). Character and Servant Leadership: Ten Characteristics of Effective, Caring Leaders. *The Journal of Virtues & Leadership*, *1*(1), 25–30.

Stückelberger, C., & Mugambi, J. N. K. (Eds.). (2007). *Responsible Leadership Global and contextual ethical perspectives*. WPP Publications.

The Barefoot Collective. (2009). *Barefoot Guide to working with organizations and Social change*. Community Development Resource Associates.

Thomas, M. (2011). *How Unions' Trickle-Down Effect Trickled Away*. Retrieved from https://www.thefiscaltimes.com/Columns/2011/03/01/How-Unions-Trickle-Down-Effect-Trickled-Away

Tinuoye, T. A. (2013). Trade Union Governance and Administration. In *Proceedings of Capacity building workshop on Leadership and Administration of Trade Unions* (pp 15-40). Ilorin, Nigeria: Felicity Press.

Torbert, W. (2004). *Action inquiry: The secret of timely and transforming action*. Berrett-Koehler.

Uhl-Bien, M., Riggio, R. E., Lowe, K. B., & Carsten, M. L. (2014). Followership theory: A review and research agenda. *The Leadership Quarterly*, *25*(1), 83–104. doi:10.1016/j.leaqua.2013.11.007

UNIFOR. (2014). *Policy on Human Rights, Workers' Rights*. Retrieved from http://www.unifor.org/sites/default/files/attachments/unifor_policy_paper_-_english_-humanworkers rights.pdf

United Nations Development Programme. (2015). Human Development Report 2015: Work for Human Development. New York: United Nations Development Programme.

Van Vugt, M. (2006). Evolutionary origins of leadership and followership. *Personality and Social Psychology Review*, *10*(4), 354–371. doi:10.120715327957pspr1004_5 PMID:17201593

Williamson, C. P. (2017). *Servant Leadership. How to put your people before yourself*. Retrieved from https://www.forbes.com/sites/forbescoachescouncil/2017/07/19/servant-leadership-how-to-put-your-people-before-yourself/#1e681cd766bc

Wood, M. E., & Galasso, N. (2015). *8 Ways to Reduce Global Inequality*. Retrieved from https://inequality.org/8-ways-reduce-global-inequality

World Bank. (2019). *Doing Business 2019 Training for reform comparing business regulation for domestic firms in 190 economies A World Bank Group Flagship Report*. World Bank.

Yesufu, T. M. (1984). *The Dynamics of Industrial relations. The Nigerian Experience*. University Press Limited.

Yukl, G. (2006). *Leadership in organizations* (6th ed.). Pearson-Prentice Hall.

ADDITIONAL READING

Burns, J. M. (1978). *Leadership*. Harper & Row.

Erdogan, B., & Bauer, T. N. (2014). Leader--member exchange (LMX) theory: The relational approach to leadership. In D. Day (Ed.), *Oxford handbook of Leadership and organizations* (pp. 407–433). Oxford University Press.

Flanders, A. (1974). *Management and Unions: The Theory and Reform of Industrial Relations*. Faber.

Hersey, P., Blanchard, H. B., & Dewey, E. J. (2008). *Management of organizational behavior: leading human resources* (9th ed.). Pearson Education.

ITUC. (2021). *ITUC Global Rights Index 2021: COVID-19 pandemic puts spotlight on workers' rights*. ITUC.

Lukman, M. S. (2021) *Labour issues and the need for reorientation in Nigeria*. https://www.thenewsnigeria.com.ng/2021/08/08/labour-issues-and-need-for-reorientation-in-nigeria/html

Sipe, J. W., & Frick, D. M. (2009). *Seven pillars of Servant Leadership: Practicing the wisdom of leading by serving*. Paulist Press.

Ubeku, A. K. (1983). *Industrial Relations in Developing Countries: The Case of Nigeria*. Macmillan Press. doi:10.1007/978-1-349-17265-8

Yates, M. D. (2009). *Why unions matter* (2nd ed.). Monthly Review Press.

KEY TERMS AND DEFINITIONS

Employer: A group of people who employ people to work and whose major objective is to make profits.

Enterprise: A business or undertaking that has specific areas of operation and engages people to perform certain activities in the area.

Influence: The ability or power to inspire or motivate an individual to act in one way or the other.

Leader: An individual who leads or directs the affairs of a group, organization, or activity.

Success: The ability to achieve stated or outlined goals, objectives and aims.

Sustainability: The ability to maintain a certain level of activity or perform a defined course of action over a period of time.

Trade Union: An agglomeration of workers formed for the sole purposes of articulating and defending their collective socio-economic and political interests.

Worker: An individual who exchanges his skills and experience to an employer in exchange for tangible and non-tangible benefits.

Workplace: A place where work is being performed collectively by a group of individuals.

Chapter 7
Positive Leader Development:
Theoretical Model Proposal

Paula Figueiredo
https://orcid.org/0000-0002-5267-546X
Universidade Lusófona, Portugal

Cristina Nogueira da Fonseca
Instituto Politécnico de Gestão e Tecnologia, Portugal

ABSTRACT

Organizations are increasingly investing in human resource development. The positive psychology approach warns of the importance of strengthening the forces. Leveraging the strengths is a way to achieve better results and even minimize the weaknesses of the leader. It is this assumption that positive psychology adds to the human resource development, which includes the leadership development. This chapter aims to propose a theoretical model about positive leader development supported by the positive psychology approach. This model comes from the literature to the evolution of leadership and organizational theories and the positive psychology. Positive leader development model seeks to enhance leadership development within an organization with a positive psychology approach. The literature shows the advantages of strengthening forces in the organizational context. So, it is necessary to systematize a theoretical model that facilitates the positive leader development in organizations. The proposed model is based on the study by Malinga, Stander, and Nell.

DOI: 10.4018/978-1-7998-2807-5.ch007

INTRODUCTION

The industrial revolution has changed the way we live and how we perceive the world. This historical landmark was the driving force behind the changes that occurred during the 20th century and keep going in the 21st century. The changes were reflected in management and leadership practices in organizations that quickly had to adapt to the context and market demands to ensure the survival. The change in focus was due to the perception of exogenous and endogenous factors and their influence on the organization's performance, the introduction of new technologies and their impact on people's lives and workplaces.

The beginning of the 21st century and the digital transformation has caused great challenges in the management and leadership of organizations (Bartsch, Weber, Büttgen, & Huber, 2021; Sainger, 2018; Van Wart, Roman, Wang, & Liu, 2019). There has been a search for new approaches, new ways of managing resources and ensuring the sustainability of organizations. With the COVID-19 era, the remote work environment, virtual teams and e-leadership were issues that stood out in the organizational environment and in research, namely the role of the leader in this context (Bartsch et al., 2021; Daraba, Wirawan, Salam, & Faisal, 2021; Zeuge, Weigel, Bjorn, Frederike, & Michael, 2020). This research seeks to systematize the contributions of the positive psychology approach to the development of leaders within organizations. Assuming that the positive psychology approach promotes positive performance results (Youssef & Luthans, 2007), both at the level of people and organizations, this study aims to define a model that facilitates the development of positive leadership in organizations.

The methodology is based on the literature review on the evolution of leadership and organizational theories and positive psychology approach. It is assumed as soon as the positive psychology approach can better answer to the current challenges of organizations. The research begins by addressing leadership theories and the impact of positive psychology in the organizational context. Then, the positive leadership and corporate happiness concepts are presented, ending with the proposal of a theoretical model for the development of positive leadership. It is intended that the model will lead to positive behaviors and that it allows building a positive culture and environment within the organization.

BACKGROUND

The Evolution of Leadership

Leadership is one of the topics that produces more scientific papers and specialty books throughout history. At the end of the 20th century, this was one of the conclusions of the study by House and Aditya (1997). The systematic approach to leadership began in the 1930s and the development of knowledge of the phenomenon has been cumulative, but with two major problems (House & Aditya, 1997): - the excessive focus on the boss-subordinate relationship instead of the performance of the leader and the organizational and environmental variables that contribute to the effectiveness of the leadership; and, the inadequate integration of the management and leadership literature as there has been greater concern with the generic functions of leadership (House & Aditya, 1997).

From very early on that there is a great controversy when trying to clarify the concepts of leadership and management (Zaleznik, 1977; Kotter, 1990). It is clearly assumed that the concepts are complementary and equally important in the organizational context. The fact that the management and leadership literature are not properly integrated is another assumption that leads to the need to analyze them in an integrated manner (Hamlin, 2004). More recently, Hamlin reports that the problem of management research has been the lack of agreement on management behaviors that are most associated with effective leadership practices (Hamlin & Hatton, 2013). Other researchers reinforce that there is a lack of agreement on the category of behaviors that are relevant and their significance for leaders (Yukl, Gordon, & Taber, 2002). Leadership is focused on change and management ensures some stability through planning, organizing and controlling situations. (Anderson, 2006).

Leadership was already studied by Aristotle while management emerged with the industrial revolution, with the need to organize, supervise and manage organizations more efficiently. The first management function was created by Fayol, at the beginning of the 20th century. Throughout the century, many other developments in the management have emerged. (McNamara, 2011). There have been major changes in the workplace because of technological changes and globalization. The most competitive organizations need to invest more in the development of management and leadership (Carbery & Garavan, 2005).

Leadership is a dynamic process of aligning, motivating, involving and encouraging people's participation in the vision and the future (Day, 2011; Kotter, 1990; Mccauley, 2008). There are also concepts that consider leadership as the ability to influence a group in order to achieve the established goals (Robbins, 2004). Given the complexity of the context, several researchers have identified the need to integrate the leadership concepts to get a closer concept of reality. Winston and

Patterson created an integrated definition of leadership using ninety dimensions that they found in the literature, thus showing the complexity of the concept (Winston & Patterson, 2006).

All leadership theories seek effectiveness or how to make leaders more effective. The focus of the theories is a fashion issue because when analyzing a long period of history, some thoughts common to the theoretical perspectives are verified, allowing a functional integration (Chemers, 2000). The evolution of 20th century leadership theories followed the evolution of organizations from the implementation of mechanization processes and mass production to automation through the introduction of computers and cyber systems; the systems we know, but no one sees. Today, organizations need to adapt to digital transformation and artificial intelligence. Leadership is not left out of the changes as people, working methods and work environments are changing.

Organizations evolved from a structural, mechanistic, and bureaucratic approach (Taylor, Ford, and Fayol), emphasizing the tasks and structure of the organization in which the leader was only seen according to his personal traits. Then with the humanistic approach (MacGregor, Maslow, Herzberg,), organizations emphasized the people and working conditions in which the leader assumes several styles due to the situations and maturity of the team itself. Followers are highlighted in the leadership process and the leader is seen as the element who listens and serves the team. In the last half of the twentieth century and early twenty-first century, organizations are considered 'living systems' integrated. Hence, the integrative approach of organizations emerges (Bertalanffy, Burns e Stalker, Emery e Trist). With a focus on people and strategy, the leader begins to worry about the personal and professional development of each member of the team and promotes constant feedback. The leader stands out from the others for his behavior, posture, and knowledge, namely for the technology he holds.

The 'Great Man' theory dominated in the 1940s and focuses on the leader's personality traits. Over the past three decades, research with an emphasis on the individual characteristics of leaders and their relationship to effective leadership has proliferated (Hoffman, Woehr, Maldagen-Youngjohn, & Lyons, 2011; Kirkpatrick & Locke, 1991; Yukl, 2010; Zaccaro, 2007). According to the literature about leadership effectiveness, Hoffman conclude that it is fragmented into two distinct focuses: - traits (personality and intelligence) and states (knowledge and skills). According to the researchers, the states' approach is less stable (Hoffman et al., 2011). This vision follows the three ways of growth throughout career and life presented by Boyatzis (Boyatzis, 1993; Boyatzis & Kolb, 1995). Traits theories are associated with personality and leadership (Judge, Bono, Ilies, & Gerhardt, 2002) and over time have had decades of prominence, skepticism and disinterest (Judge, Piccolo, & Kosalka, 2009). Other researchers refer to the difficulties of progressing this theory due to the lack of coherence and conceptual meaning (Zaccaro, 2007). The studies carried out show a modest correlation of each individual characteristic in isolation with effective leadership. Behavioral approaches, situational factors and their interaction with the characteristics of leaders are reinforced (Hoffman et al., 2011).

The lack of empirical evidence for the existence of a leadership traits profile led to the search of leadership effectiveness through leadership style. (Den Hartog & Koopman, 2001). One of the most contemporary approaches to behavioral theory is that of Ulrich, Zenger and Smallwood, which supports the assumption of results-based leadership; effective leadership is a function of personal attributes and the results achieved (Intagliata, Ulrich, & Smallwood, 2000; Safferstone, 2005). During the 50s and 70s of the last century, we witnessed the search for the behaviors of the leader and manager that are considered universal and that contribute to the leadership effectiveness. It was concluded that there is no single pattern in behavior that featured all managers and effective leaders. (Hamlin, 2004). Behavioral approach was considered insufficient due to inconsistencies in results, measurement problems, causality, informal and emerging leadership and the lack of situational analysis (Den Hartog & Koopman, 2001).

Situational and contingency approaches seek to resolve the deficiencies previously identified and to value environmental issues over variations in leadership effectiveness (Kets de Vries, Vrignaud, Florent-Treacy, & Korotov, 2007). According to these approaches, the leadership style is contingent on a concrete situation (Den Hartog & Koopman, 2001). Therefore, the leader's behaviors are effective in only a few situations. Chemers considers the research carried out unproductive in the context of personality traits and behaviors to be unproductive (Chemers, 2000). Contingency theories recognize the complex nature of leadership by considering the characteristics and behaviors of the leader in a context of situational parameters.

Other approaches also called New Leadership' seek to understand how the leader achieves extraordinary levels of motivation, admiration, commitment, respect, trust, dedication, loyalty, and performance by the followers. The emphasis on charisma reinforces the idea that the leader's personality has an extraordinary effect on his followers (Kets de Vries, Vrignaud, & Florent-Treacy, 2004) and on organizational success; the leader leads his followers to experience positive emotions. Leader plays an important role in the perceptions of the followers about the effectiveness of the leader, in attracting new leaders and in the mood of the followers (Bono & Ilies, 2006). Charismatic leadership is a meso-theory that emphasizes the relationship of a follower and leader and is the product of the leader, the follower and the situation (Klein & House, 1995). Transformational theory analyzes the interactions between the situation and the traits according to the perceptions of the leader and the followers. Transformational leadership measures leadership as a result and contingency theories tend to focus on the characteristics of the leader (Chemers, 2000). Transformational and transactional leadership are distinct but complementary processes in which the leader uses both in different situations (Bass, 1997). Bass and Avolio also studied the relationship between types of leadership and organizational contexts (Bass & Avolio, 1993). According to the charismatic and transformational leadership, it is possible to verify the effects of leadership on the followers (Shamir, House, & Arthur, 1993). Although some critics view transformational leadership as unethical, Bass and Steidlmeier present the four components of authentic transformational leadership. (Bass & Steidlmeier, 1999).

Leadership theories are also influenced by the development of Emotional Intelligence and the proliferation of studies associated with emotional competencies that contribute to the effectiveness (Goleman, Boyatzis, & Mckee, 2001; Goleman, 1998; Mayer, DiPaolo, & Salovey, 1990; Mayer & Salovey, 1997). To realize the differences between the organizations considered 'good' and 'great', Collins and his team concluded that organizations need a mechanism for training and development of internal leaders. Researchers found the existence of levers that accelerate the process of transforming organizations from good to great. Organizations that presented a set of characteristics, like ambition by the company and the preparation of competent successors, are considered "Level 5 Leadership" (Collins, 2001, 2007). Level 5 Leadership refers to the highest level in the hierarchy of executive skills and builds long-term optimum through a paradoxical blend of humility and personal determination (Collins, 2007).

At the end of the century, the follower's role is no longer seen as passive to integrate models of understanding the phenomenon of leadership, contributing to a relational concept of leadership (Hollander, 1992, 1995). Relational Leadership comes from the leader-member exchange theory and the theoretical approach to relationship-based leadership developed by Graen and his team (Graen & Uhl-Bien, 1995; Schriesheim, Castro, & Cogliser, 1999). Although the concept is not yet clear, it is a process of social influence through which emergent coordination (evolving social order) and change (new values, attitudes, approaches, behaviors and ideologies) are constructed and produced (Uhl-Bien, 2006). So leadership is seen as a social construction process that relationships are the key to new forms of leadership that explain why leaders act differently with those they lead and develop different types of relationships with them (Lunenburg, 2010).

The leader who serves first is a concept that was introduced into the organizational context by Greenleaf in 1977. Servant leadership was not only defined as a management technique but a way of life (Parris & Peachey, 2013). This approach has a theoretical framework based on the leader's motivation to serve others, however, there are some difficulties in operationalizing the variables (Winkle, Allen, Devore, & Winston, 2014), due to not finding sufficient scientific evidence (Russell & Stone, 2002). It is necessary to analyze how the personal values of this leadership style differ from others, such as the transformational (Avolio, Walumbwa, & Weber, 2009). Over the past 20 years, the servant leadership has progressed despite problems identified. For many authors, it is possible to advance the theory by solving problems and continuing to offer meaningful insights to the leadership field over the next 20 years (Eva, Robin, Sendjaya, Van Dierendonck, & Liden, 2019).

One of the problems pointed out to servant leadership is the proximity to ethical, transformational, and authentic leadership. The latter has proliferated since the beginning of the XXI century. According to Luthans & Avolio, authentic leadership is a process that is based on positive psychological capacities in a highly developed organizational context, resulting in greater self-awareness and positive self-regulated behavior on the part of leaders that promote positive self-development (Avolio et al., 2009). Authenticity is largely defined by what people see in the leader as there is no right way to establish and manage authenticity; there are consistent steps that help others to perceive the leader as authentic - to gain better knowledge of themselves and others and to improve their connection to the organizational context (Goffee & Jones, 2005). Being authentic is not trying to imitate others; it is possible to learn from the experiences of others, but success is not achieved when trying to be like others (George, Sims, McLean, & Mayer, 2007); thus, authentic leadership emerges from the life stories of leaders (Shamir & Eilam, 2005).

Avolio and Gardner systematized the authentic leadership theory presenting definitions, antecedents, contexts, and levels of analysis (Avolio & Gardner, 2005). The major concern was to accelerate the impact of leadership at individual, group, community and nation (Avolio, 2010). These researchers defined the components of Authentic Leadership and compared it with Charismatic, Transformational and Servant Leadership. In recent decades, researchers have sought to integrate more positive forms of leadership (Avolio et al., 2009), promoting the integration of leadership theories (Avolio, 2007). Dimitrov recently conducted the first case study on the concept of Humane Leadership looking for more humane leadership and organization (Dimitrov, 2015). Researcher explores how leader influences an organization to become more human through his characteristics and behaviors. This study highlights the traits and behaviors of modern leadership theories, such as authentic, transformational, and charismatic leadership, summing up all these styles in the concept of human leadership.

Taking up the leader's personal characteristics, there are several studies addressing the importance of humility previously reported by Collins (2007). Researchers who reborn the issues of leaders' humility seek to understand the impact on team performance, innovation, the leadership process and the organization as a whole (Owens & Hekman, 2016; Owens, Johnson, & Mitchell, 2013; Rego, 2019; Rego, Cunha, & Simpson, 2018). Humility means to have the feet on the ground, contributing to a healthy relationship between leaders and followers and to the individual and collective performance (Rego, 2019).

Throughout the evolution of theories, three important premises are verified: i) a current trend towards the humanization of organizations; ii) the need to integrate leadership styles to address the complexity of the organizational context; and iii) the search for new approaches that contribute to the development of effective leadership. These findings help to understand the trend of leadership theories over time. Currently, in addition to digital transformation and artificial intelligence, the world has suffered a pandemic with strong impacts on people and organizations (Chen & Sriphon, 2021). COVID-19 reinforced the importance of the leader's role in the virtual teams context (Bartsch et al., 2021; Daraba et al., 2021; Liao, 2017; Lilian, 2014; Sainger, 2018; Zeuge et al., 2020). These phenomena reinforce the emergence of transformational and authentic leaderships (Balthazard, Waldman, & Warren, 2009; Karam, Gardner, Gillifor, Tribble, & Li, 2017; Yavuz, 2019), as they contribute to engagement and the perception of support from leaders, namely when working from home (Daraba et al., 2021). It is important to consider the risks of perceiving traditional leadership or non-leadership (Contreras, Baykal, & Abid, 2020), with the growth of more flexible working methods in organizations. The positive approach can overcome these risks pointed out by the researchers.

Positive Psychology in the Organizational Context

Positive Psychology is the study of conditions and processes that contribute to the flourishing or the ideal functioning of people, groups and institutions (Gable & Haidt, 2005). According to the researchers, positive psychology has grown so quickly because it provides a more complete picture of human nature compared to traditional psychology. Martin Seligman, the father of positive psychology, began by emphasizing human strengths and promoting human development. The positive psychology approach arises because the so-called traditional psychology focuses more on treating 'disease' than on enhancing 'sanity'.

The focus of psychology on the negative issue was primarily due to historical and cultural reasons (Seligman & Csikszentmihalyi, 2000). Researchers state that the prior studies on the positive issues of human nature that did not prosper due to a lack of methodological rigor and inconsistent results, leading to the weakening of humanistic psychology (Seligman & Csikszentmihalyi, 2000). With the beginning of the 21st century, psychologists were expected to contribute to the flourishing of individuals, communities and societies (Cameron, 2010; Seligman & Csikszentmihalyi, 2000). As positive psychology focuses on the forces of human nature, it will promote an open and appreciative perspective on the potential, motivations and capabilities of the human being (Sheldon & King, 2001).

Following these assumptions, Seligman and Peterson created a manual for classifying the strengths and virtues of character in relation to psychological well-being (Seligman, Steen, Park, & Peterson, 2005). This classification aimed to describe and classify the strengths and virtues of character that allow people to flourish. *Figure 1* shows the 24 strengths of character, grouped into 6 virtues.

Figure 1. Seligman's strengths and virtues of character (2005)

1. Wisdom and knowledge	**2. Courage**	**3. Humanity**
Creativity, Curiosity Open-mindedness, Love of learning, Perspective	Authenticity, Bravery, Persistence, Zest	Kindness, Love, Social intelligence
4. Justice	**5.Temperance**	**6. Transcendence**
Fairness, Leadership, Teamwork	Forgiveness, Modesty, Prudence, Self-regulation	Appreciation of beauty and excellence, Gratitude, Hope, Humor, Religiousness

In the book Flourish: A Visionary New Understanding of Happiness and Well-being (2012), Seligman corrected and expanded his previous approach, due to the extreme complexity of the human being. Happiness was previously understood as the common end goal, being the only factor on which people based their choices. The researcher added other goals besides happiness, thus strengthening his theory. The developments known as the Theory of Well-being have five objectives: - happiness (positive emotions), relationships (positive social relationships), purpose (meaning), engagement (flow) and achievements (goals, persistence). Seligman defined that PERMA (Positive Emotion, Engagement, Relationships, Meaning, and Accomplishment) are the elements of well-being (Martin Seligman, 2018), and can be measured through the PERMA profiler (Butler & Kern, 2016). It was further demonstrated that there is strong evidence of the subjective well-being is the final common path of PERMA elements (Goodman, Disabato, Kashdan, & Kauffman, 2018).

As for positive emotions, Fredrickson states that do not fit the previously emotions models because they fail in their description, focusing on negative emotions (Fredrickson, 1998). Researcher proposes a model to describe the form and function of a subset of positive emotions, including joy, interest, and love.

There is also the concept of subjective well-being (SWB) associated with positive psychology. This is defined as a cognitive and affective assessment of a person's life (Diener, Lucas, & Oishi, 2002). These assessments include emotional reactions to events, as well as cognitive judgments of satisfaction and fulfillment. Subjective well-being is a broad concept that includes experiencing pleasant emotions, low levels of negative mood and high satisfaction with life. Positive experiences embodied in subjective well-being are a central concept of positive psychology because it make life rewarding (Diener et al., 2002). Results from a recent study suggest the factor underlying PERMA is capturing the same type of well-being (Goodman et al., 2018).

Positive psychology allows for the transition from healing to a perspective that emphasizes prevention. There are three main focuses of Positive Psychology (Gavin & Mason, 2004; Martin Seligman, 2002): i) Positive states of subjective well-being; ii) Positive individual/psychological traits; iii) Positive organizations. The movement of positive psychology was widely stimulated at the organizational level (Lopez & Snyder, 2012; Seligman & Csikszentmihalyi, 2000; Sheldon & King, 2001), with a concentration of research related to positive psychological capital (Avey, Reichard, Luthans, & Mhatre, 2011; Luthans, Avey, Avolio, & Peterson, 2010; Luthans & Youssef, 2004), which led to the creation of two approaches related to applied positivity and management based on forces in the workplace - Positive Organizational Scholarship (POS) and Positive Organizational Behavior (POB).

Positive Organizational Scholarship (POS) is based on the work of the University of Michigan that emphasizes positive organizational characteristics that can improve survival and organizational effectiveness in times of crisis. Cameron and other researchers note that the POS field was developed to study the positive skills and practices that lead to the flourishing of organizations. This school differs from traditional organizational studies in that it seeks to understand what it is and how it approaches the best of the human condition (Cameron, Dutton, & Quinn, 2013). To give credibility and reinforce the importance of a positive approach in the organizational context, empirical evidence was needed to demonstrate that these positive practices in organizations produce desirable changes in organizational effectiveness (Cameron, Mora, Leutscher, & Calarco, 2011). An instrument of positive practices was created and evidence was found that positive practices actually predict organizational performance and contribute to indicators of effectiveness over time (Cameron et al., 2011).

Positive Organizational Behavior (POB) applies the positively oriented psychological forces and capabilities that can be measured, developed, and managed to improve performance in the workplace. These capabilities include self-efficacy/confidence, hope, optimism, and resilience and are called Positive Psychological Capital (Cunha, Rego, & Lopes, 2013; Luthans & Youssef, 2004; Youssef & Luthans, 2007). This school also contributes to raising the honesty and integrity of people in the world (Cameron, Quinn, & Caldwell, 2017).

Based on positive psychology and positive organizational behavior, two studies test the hypotheses about the impact that positive capabilities (hope, optimism, and resilience) have on the employees' desired results in relation to work. These results include performance, job satisfaction, happiness at work and organizational commitment (Youssef & Luthans, 2007). Another study shows that organizations highlight positive organizational behavior due to its competitive and changing nature (Pouramini & Fayyazi, 2015). The findings reinforce that positive organizational behavior has a strong relationship with job satisfaction, organizational citizenship behavior and employee involvement, and these relationships will be strongest when positive organizational behavior is high.

According to a meta-analysis, positive psychological capital is made up of psychological resources of hope, effectiveness, resilience and optimism and is being used in human resource development and performance management (Avey et al., 2011). The results demonstrated the positive relationships between positive psychological capital and employees' desirable attitudes (job satisfaction, organizational commitment, psychological well-being), employees' desirable behaviors (citizenship) and performance measures (self-assessment, supervisor assessments and objectives). There was also a significant negative relationship between positive psychological capital and employees' undesirable attitudes (cynicism, turnover intentions, work stress and anxiety) and employees' undesirable behaviors (Avey et al., 2011).

A study of the role of positivity and connectivity in the performance of teams in organizations concluded that the great challenge is to create a liberating and enriching order so that teams can explore the liberating and creative power of positivity (Losada & Heaphy, 2004). Organizations need highly connected teams in which the polarity of the other and the self are integrated in a sense of 'we', leading to a productive and continuous dialogue. Thus, positivity based on constructive negative feedback can generate a state of realistic enthusiasm that drives organizations to achieve and maintain levels of excellence (Losada & Heaphy, 2004). Luthans and Youssef said that organizational decision making, and human resource management must undergo transformation, focusing on development approaches that consistently improve performance over time (Luthans & Youssef, 2004). The 157 predominantly negative theories that defend human behavior and motivation in organizations need to change to a force-based management (positively oriented), and focused on the development of human, social and psychological capital to reach full potential (Luthans & Youssef, 2004). Thus, the management of positive psychological capital can effectively lead people's talents, strengths and psychological capacities to achieve productive, ethical and sustainable results that are a competitive advantage for organizations. (Luthans & Youssef, 2004).

Positive Leadership and Corporate Happiness

Since the beginning of the 21st century, the integration of leadership theories and positive psychology approach has been at the same time as the emergence of the concepts of Positive Leadership and Positive Organizations.

Positive Leadership

Arakawa and Greenberg showed that if leaders exhibit positive leadership behaviors, they will promote the organization's success as a whole (Arakawa & Greenberg, 2007). Other researchers have expressed the view that positive leadership is crucial in organizations particularly in difficult times and also show that high performance is associated with high levels of positive affect (Youssef-Morgan & Luthans, 2013).

There are several concepts for positive leadership that show the lack of consensus regarding its conceptualization. Cameron was one of the researchers at the University of Michigan to highlight the importance of positivity in leadership. Positive leadership is a process of considering good and evil in individuals and organizations, emphasizing what elevates individuals and organizations, what works in organizations, what gives life, what is experienced as good, what is extraordinary and what is inspiring (Cameron, 2008). Another concept shows that positive leadership is seen as a process that focuses on the strengths of employees and the recognition of good work in order to help employees be more productive and committed to their work (Arakawa & Greenberg, 2007). Other researchers believe that positive leadership focuses only on the leader's behaviors and how they affect employees' positive emotions (Kelloway, Weigand, Mckee, & Das, 2013). A more comprehensive way is a concept of leadership positive considering the background and results of positivity as a systematic and integrated manifestation of leadership traits, processes, intentional behaviors and high, exceptional and affirmative performances of the leaders' strengths, employees and the organization itself (Youssef & Luthans, 2012).

Cameron has defined the four principles for developing the concept of positive leadership - Positive Climate, Positive Relationships, Positive Communication and Positive Purpose -, and the practices associated with each one (Cameron, 2008). The positive leader promotes a positive work climate by identifying positive energizers in tasks/functions and recognizing and supporting the teams; the positive leader also promotes positive communication through affirmative and supportive language, replacing negative and critical language; the leader does not fail to address the negative aspects, only takes a positive and constructive approach to weaknesses; the positive leader develops positive relationships between members by facilitating positive energy, modeling it and diagnosing and building positive energy networks; and, lastly, the positive leader guarantees work associated with a positive purpose that contributes to keeping everyone focused and motivated on significant goals (Fairlie, 2011).

Malinga and other researchers recently conducted a critical review of the literature to clarify the concept of positive leadership (Malinga, Stander, & Nell, 2019). Researchers have proposed an integrated definition of positive leadership that results in three proposals for positive leadership interventions: i) the traits that a positive leader should have (optimism and a mindset of 'can do' altruism, ethical guidance and motivational characteristics); ii) the specific leadership behaviors (creating a positive work environment, developing positive relationships, focusing on results and engaging employees through positive communication); and, iii) the leadership results (such as productivity and performance levels, organizational citizenship behavior and employee well-being) (Malinga et al., 2019). Through the leaders' narratives, other researchers concluded that positive leaders are crucial in creating organizational patterns regardless of the characteristics of the external context (Pina e Cunha, Campos e Cunha, & Rego, 2009).

Positive leadership is more ethically oriented and transformational leaders are more able to transform their followers and may even be a little abusive or unethical. Ethical leadership is like positive leadership because both encourage two-way communication between followers and seeks to involve them in decision-making. An ethical leader seeks to do the right thing and always act ethically as positive leaders, however, these tend to be more authentic than the ethical leader (Brown & Treviño, 2006). The positive leader is also perceived as being fair to his followers and tends to put the needs of others before his own needs as the servant leader. Both inspire their followers; however, the difference is in focus. The servant leader focuses on followers and positive leader focuses on organizational goals as well as inspire, motivate and encourage followers to achieve these goals (Stone, Russell, & Patterson, 2004). Authentic and positive leaders are both optimistic and hopeful about the future, but only the positive leader is ethically oriented and is both authentic and transformational. While the definitions of positive leadership are not explicitly the authentic traits (self-awareness, authenticity and genuineness) (Walumbwa, Avolio, Gardner, Wernsing, & Peterson, 2008), they are implicit in other traits (ethical orientation, motivational characteristics and altruism) that a positive leader should have (Malinga et al., 2019).

Previous research points to the lack of studies on the acceleration, emergence and development of positive leadership (Blanch, Gil, Antino, & Rodríguez-Muñoz, 2016; Zbierowski, 2016), and how it should be measured (Antino, Gil-Rodríguez, Rodríguez-Muñoz, & Borzillo, 2014). Previous studies show that the positive leader promotes a more collaborative, harmonious, and participative mind-set among team members in which people seek well-being and happiness in their personal and professional lives.

Positive Organizations

The new millennium began with the improvement of the Authentic Leadership Theory and the extension of its assumptions to organizations - Authentizotic Organization (Kets de Vries, 2001). There is a concern for human needs and how people are refreshed in their work, feeling a sense of balance and integrity (Kets de Vries, 2001). In a more comprehensive concept of Authentic Leadership and already integrating the assumptions of positive psychology, the leader uses and promotes positive psychological capacities and a positive ethical climate within the organization, through moral guidance, relational transparency, self-awareness and balanced processing information to promote positive self-development (Walumbwa et al., 2008; Walumbwa, Luthans, Avey, & Oke, 2011). Thus, the leader promotes the psychological capital and creativity of the follower (Rego, Sousa, Marques, & Cunha, 2012), and the organizational environment has an impact on the happiness of followers (Rego & Cunha, 2008).

To create positive teams and organizations it is not enough that individuals are positive because the individual effects of positivity are not reflected proportionally in the organizational effects; it is crucial to analyze the learning behaviors of work teams (Edmondson, 2008). The concept of psychological security consists of the group's shared belief that it is safe to take risks (Edmondson, 1999). Group members need to feel free to speak and participate openly, ask questions, receive feedback and recognition, discuss controversial issues, suggest and try new things and make mistakes and be able to learn from mistakes (Cunha et al., 2013). All this collaborative, participative and positive environment is essential for creating positive teams within organizations. The role of psychological security in creating positive teams is critical because openness, flexibility and interdependence are only developed in psychologically safe environments; thus, it is possible to give negative feedback and have difficult conversations that require trust and respect (Edmondson, 2008). Organizations that intend to develop a positive culture need to promote a collaborative and learning environment. Some researches show a relationship between the perception of the work environment and the organization's results (Harter, Schmidt, & Keyes, 2003). Other researchers had already looked for synergies between entrepreneurship and positive behavior (Palma, Cunha, & Lopes, 2007), but a new line of research has only recently opened (Zbierowski, 2016).

Corporate Happiness

Researchers refer to happiness as psychological well-being, a multidimensional construct that includes life satisfaction, positive emotional experiences, absence of negative emotional experience components (Diener, 2000; Haller & Hadler, 2006), as well-being affective, competence, aspiration, autonomy, integrative functioning (Daniels, 2000; Lyubomirsky, King, & Diener, 2005). Psychological well-being is the combination of feeling good and functioning effectively. Sustainable well-being does not require people to always feel good because negative or painful emotions are part of life and the ability to manage those emotions is essential for long-term well-being (Huppert, 2009). Another concept associated with happiness is affective well-being (frequent experience of positive affect and the rare experience of negative affect) (Daniels, 2000). This construct is also multidimensional and can be measured in relation to the work area. Studies show that happiness is a personality trait as subjective well-being (Weiss, Bates, & Luciano, 2008). Psychologists' knowledge of subjective well-being is rudimentary, and a stronger scientific basis is needed to make recommendations (to people and society in general) on how to increase happiness. Societies need to give greater importance subjective well-being, tracking the phenomenon, supporting research and educating people (Diener, 2000).

There is evidence of the positivity of organizational leadership in the well-being of employees (Kelloway et al., 2013). The positive psychology movement has helped people in the pursuit of genuine happiness every day (Gavin & Mason, 2004). Researches indicate that happiness is functional and generally leads to success (Oishi, Diener, & Lucas, 2007). Researchers have shown that people who experience the highest levels of happiness are the most successful in close relationships and volunteer work, and people who experience slightly lower levels of happiness are the most successful in income, education and political participation (Oishi et al., 2007). When people are moderately happy, the most effective level of happiness depends on the specific results used to define success as well as the resources available (Oishi et al., 2007).

Happiness as pleasant moods and emotions, well-being and positive attitudes have attracted all research in psychology in recent decades, and this interest has also extended to previously underestimated workplace experiences. Many discrete constructs of organizational behavior belong to the family of constructs related to happiness (Fisher, 2010). Happiness at work includes job satisfaction but it is much more, namely work involvement and affective organizational commitment. There is evidence that happiness has important consequences for individuals and organizations (Fisher, 2010). More specifically, there is evidence that happier employees are better able to 'expand and build' themselves, more creative, resilient, socially, physically and mentally healthy and more productive (Fredrickson, 2001). The impact of leadership on employee happiness has been studied and results showed that happiness was a significant predictor of affective commitment and mediator in the relationship between transformational leadership and affective commitment (Abdullah, Ling, & Peng, 2017). Other research shows that optimism and high resilience are positively related to positive leadership affecting flourishing, life satisfaction and subjective happiness (Zbierowski & Góra, 2014).

Researchers recommend that organizations put more emphasis on positive psychology to create and maintain healthier, happier and more productive workplaces (Gavin & Mason, 2004). Happy companies foster positive behaviors not only in leadership, but at all levels of the organization. There are some suggestions for a happy company:

Create a healthy, respectful and supportive organizational culture; Supply competent leadership at all levels; Provide fair treatment, security and recognition; Design jobs to be interesting, challenging, autonomous, and rich in feedback; Facilitate skill development to improve competence and allow growth; Select for person–organization and person–job fit; Enhance fit through the use of realistic job pre-views and socialization practices; Reduce minor hassles and increase daily uplifts; Persuade employees to reframe a current less-than-ideal work environment as acceptable; Adopt high performance work practices (Fisher, 2010).

A happy company reinforces individual differences by adding value to employees, information is not suppressed and the work itself is intrinsically rewarding and there are no stupid rules (Goffee & Jones, 2013). Researchers show that happy individuals are successful in many areas of life and suggest a conceptual model. By analyzing the happiness-success ratio, it seems that success makes people happy but positive affection also generates success (Lyubomirsky et al., 2005). Results suggest that positive affect can be the cause of many characteristics, resources and desirable successes related to happiness (Lyubomirsky et al., 2005). Cultural issues about national differences were not considered to improve national levels of happiness (Judge & Kammeyer-Mueller, 2011).

Some researchers reveal the concept of 'Relational Energy' and verify its impact on the organizational context (Owens, Baker, Sumpter, & Cameron, 2016). Energy has emerged as relevant to organizations, however, little is known about how energy can be useful at an interpersonal level to achieve goals in the workplace (Owens et al., 2016). Early results suggest that relational energy shows evidence of a relationship with engagement and job performance.

There are other concepts that are linked to the positive psychology approach, namely 'virtuous organizations' and 'regenerative organizations.' Associated with subjective well-being at work and ethical issues, the concept of virtuous organizations emerged. Business ethics has been emphasized over the past decade and organizations are aware of its influence on performance. The proliferation of studies on the influence of leadership on employees, examining job satisfaction, subjective well-being at work and satisfaction with life (Yang, 2014), and the moral and financial scandals in recent years across the world, strengthened the role of virtuousness in organizational environments (Rego, Ribeiro, & Cunha, 2010). Virtuousness is associated with what individuals and organizations aspire to be at their best and it is related to organizational performance (Cameron, Bright, & Caza, 2004). Virtuous organizations follow the assumption of positivity because the focus is on excellence, positive and virtuous (Cunha et al., 2013). Associated with sustainability issues, several studies have emerged that present a model for transforming people and organizations for sustainability into business, education and the community (Mang & Reed, 2012; Reed, 2007). The concepts of regenerative organizations and leadership emerged (Hardman, 2009; Sturnick, 2004). Both concepts have in common with the positivist approach the search for well-being at work and in life.

Positive Leader Development: Theoretical Model Proposal

Leadership is made up of multiple aspects and experiences so that a single theory is not enough to understand the phenomenon (McGuire, 2014). Leadership development should be seen as a serious process in which leaders recognize that it will be a differentiating factor for the organization's success (Kets de Vries & Korotov, 2010). This context is complex and dynamic due to issues of globalization, changing organizational structure, the knowledge-based economy and diversity (Carbery & Garavan, 2014).

Leadership development (social capital) has focused more on the development of leaders (human capital) more specifically on the development of leadership skills to achieve effective leadership (Day, 2001, 2011). Leadership development focuses on the social dimensions and includes awareness and interpersonal skills, team building and the processes involved in the commitment to vision and strategy (Carbery & Garavan, 2005). Leadership development focuses not only on collective leadership processes, involving relationships, networking, trust and commitments as well as an appreciation of the social and political context and its implications for leadership styles and actions (Iles, 2012; Iles & Preece, 2006).

Boyatzis takes a different position on leadership development. According to the intentional change theory, individuals, groups and organizations can create leaders through the sustainable desire for change (Boyatzis, 2006a, 2006b). Individuals only develop characteristics of effective leaders if they wish to be leaders; the dilemma lies in the leader 's desire to want to be and to invest energy and time to obtain the emotional, social and cognitive skills required for effective leadership. Boyatzis relies on complexity theory to understand sustainable change. Given the complexity, leadership development is a dynamic, discontinuous and non-linear system through a discontinuity between the current state and future states (Boyatzis, 2006b).

Organizations are currently still adapting to the changes caused by the COVID-19 pandemic (Kniffin et al., 2021). The impacts on organizations have been the object of study – at work and in human resource management practices (Carnevale & Hatak, 2020), well-being and work-life balance (Bellmann & Hübler, 2020; Xiao, Becerik-Gerber, Lucas, & Roll, 2021) and in the quality and satisfaction of work (Palumbo, 2020; Rodríguez-Modroño & López-Igual, 2021) -, are just a few example.

The leader's role is fundamental in these uncertain times where the authenticity of the leader and his proximity to the team members is fundamental and necessary. In addition to the unpredictability of organizational changes, virtual teams are the main challenge for leaders as it is necessary to strengthen everyone's belonging and engagement. In this context, positive leadership can be the solution to maintain levels of engagement, satisfaction, well-being, and performance in organizations.

Few interventions on the development of positive leadership are found in the literature and some interventions include: - the development of psychological capital (leaders and followers), creating hope, resilience, optimism and self-efficacy as leadership behaviors; the development of the emotional maturity of the leader (or Emotional Intelligence) as a characteristic of positive and successful leaders; the creation of meaning; building trust; humor in the workplace; empowerment; and mindfulness (Malinga et al., 2019). Following the integrated concept of positive leadership, interventions for a positive culture simultaneously improve the organization's results (Malinga et al., 2019). Leader development based on the positive psychology and coaching has been increasingly practiced with positive results in people's well-being, individual and organizational performance and organizational citizenship behavior (Cilliers, 2011).

Competence development is critical for organizations to meet the challenges of the future. Competent people must be developed and encouraged to develop their skills constantly. People development is currently a key competence of the leader (Giles, 2016). With a positive leadership strategy, it is critical that leaders have training in people development, however, not all leaders have this competence and perspective. Furthermore, the training of leaders is not enough, a global strategy of the organization through a positive leadership development model is necessary. More recently, some researchers have tried to define the key factors to encourage the development of this kind of leadership in organizations. Steelman and Wolfeld pointed out three important factors: - to develop specific behaviors (active listening, managing expectations, communication, facilitating and removing obstacles, supporting decision making, creative and challenging thinking); creating positive relationships with followers (trust and respect, integrity, commitment, support and development, genuine interest, and effective communication; and, favorable feedback environment (Steelman & Wolfeld, 2018). Organizations need a model that allows them to develop a positive culture consistent with leadership behaviors so that results are effective.

Based on the positive psychology (Seligman, 2002), researchers propose a more structured and systematic approach to positive leadership. Positive leader identifies each follower's strengths, adapts expectations, and encourages strengths. This process involves identifying the follower's strengths and preferences, adjusting the follower's expectations, encouraging the leader according to the strength profile of each follower, monitoring and promoting the personal brand of the followers in the organization (Malinga et al., 2019). Other researchers concluded that the positive leader is able to balance the followers' expectations and give them the encouragement to achieve exceptional performance (Arakawa & Greenberg, 2007).

Positive leader is able to promote a positive relationship between employees, developing trust and teamwork (Zbierowski & Góra, 2014). Followers trust leaders who care about getting to know them, build relationships and implement an open policy, sharing their work and life story and promoting informal moments with team members. The leader who promotes the development of the team emphasizes collaboration between the team members and encourages them to support each other (Zbierowski & Góra, 2014). Love, forgiveness and trust are the critical values of leaders who are committed to maximizing value for organizations while helping members of the organization to become the best (Caldwell & Dixon, 2010).

These interventions help to create a culture of positive leadership in the organization, promoting change and organizational effectiveness (Hartnell, Ou, & Kinicki, 2011). Organizational change processes are very complex because organizations are composed of people who are complex human beings. Any change process affects the bases of any organization and has strong implications for everything that is done and how it is done inside. Through a literature review and following the positive psychology approach and the integrated definition of positive leadership by Malinga, Stander, & Nell (2019), a proposal for a positive leadership development model is presented. This model emphasizes the following points: - the organizational culture; leaders that promoting positive traits and behaviors; and the positive results of excellence. This model seeks to integrate all the critical factors for the development

Figure 2. Positive leadership development model

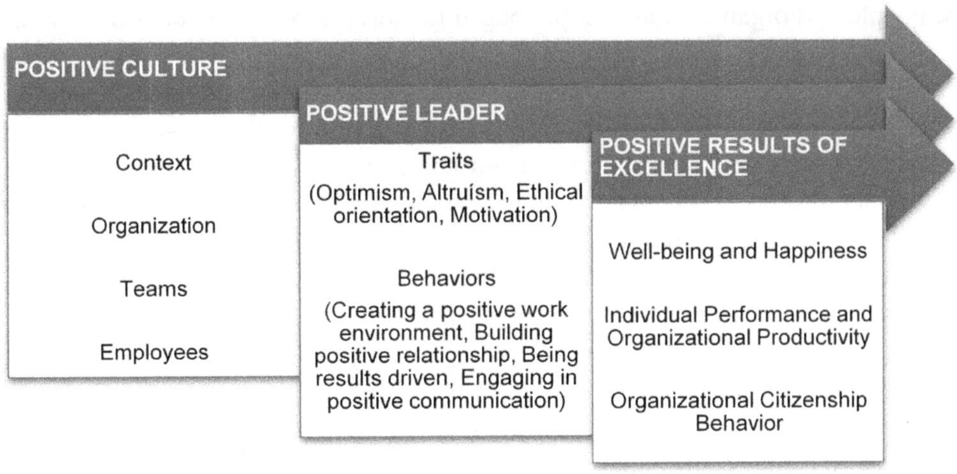

of positive leadership, covering not only training and skills development, but mainly the organization's culture. The model is outlined in *Figure 2*.

Building an organizational culture based on positivity, it is essential to emphasize the context, the level of entrepreneurship and internationalization, the promotion of organizational virtuosity and sustainability issues. After analyzing the contextual factor, positivity must be worked at the individual (employees), group (teams) and organizational (the organization as a whole) levels. This approach allows organizations to have a high human capital and a high social and psychological capital in teams and employees. According to Cameron, the positive leader is fundamental in promoting a positive organizational climate and communication, developing positive relationships and in the existence of a positive purpose to ensure the motivation and involvement of all. It is necessary for leaders to understand their positive qualities and make the correct strategic use of them. Given the awareness that the leader influences the commitment of team members and organizational performance, it is important to develop their positive traits and behaviors. Only if the leader believes in changing the organizational culture, the results of excellence will be achieved.

CONCLUSIONS AND RECOMMENDATIONS FOR FUTURE STUDIES

The evolution of leadership and organizational theories show a clear trend towards more humanistic approaches that promote the development of people and organizations. The complex and chaos context that characterizes the current world is a great challenge for all professionals in organizations. Training and development are a way to reduce anxiety caused by difficulties in understanding certain phenomena. COVID-19 highlighted the major weaknesses in the world that have become major concerns for people and organizations. People began to worry even more about their well-being and their personal life. Organizations need to consider the concerns of their people and should deal with alternative working methods and possible changes in the organizational culture and strategy. In this non-linear and difficult-to-understand scenario, leaders need to keep their team members engaged. Leaders should be present and listen to people and give them some security even in a world of chaos so that people remain committed and engaged with the organization's purpose.

The positive psychology approach applied to the organizational context focuses on a differentiating view based on the premise of valuing positive aspects to maximize the performance of individuals, teams, and organizations. This approach is presented as a possibility in relation to the needs of the current world, as research has shown that positive psychology practices have direct impacts on people management and organizational culture. The implementation of these practices requires a change in culture and values in which the leadership role is fundamental for this change, as the positivity and excellence of results should be aligned with the organization's culture and strategy.

Through the leadership and organizational theories, it seems that there has been a growing concern with human nature due to its complexity. The need for integrate various approaches is the way to find solutions that answer to the complexity of the human being and to the concrete situations of today's world. The integration of several approaches allows strengthen the knowledge generated over time. Positive leadership seems to be the style that best suits the challenges that leaders face in organizations due to constant changes in the workplace and the knowledge of human beings. Malinga and other researchers provided the categories of positive leadership through a critical review of the literature (Malinga et al., 2019). These results are essential to define an effective positive leadership development model. The benefits of a positive psychology approach in personal and organizational development are visible, so it is necessary to define a model that effectively promotes the development of a positive leader within organizations. The originality of the proposed model results from the holistic integration of leadership and organizational theories and the several studies carried out on the approach of positive psychology in an organizational context.

Positive Leadership Development Model is a working foundation for consultants, leaders, and human resources professionals. The model systematizes the main pillars for the implementation of a positive leadership development process based on a positive culture that leads to practical results for the organization. Thus, this model serves as a guideline for defining an organizational intervention plan based on the positive psychology approach. The investigation clearly shows the advantages of adopting a more positive vision in the day-to-day activities of organizations, but professionals do not always know how to intervene in a coherent and consistent way to achieve excellent results. The main limitation of the model is the lack of evidence regarding its applicability. The model is built through the contributions of several investigations carried out and the integration of existing theories. It is necessary in the future to promote a case study to operationalize the model. This research presents only a guide for professionals to develop positive leadership within organizations. Despite the model's limitations, the main contribution is to reinforce the importance of this approach in the organizational context, given the current state of the world and the need to adopt disruptive approaches.

The brittleness of the context caused by the chaos that characterizes daily life is verified while there is a growing trend towards sustainability issues in organizations. The mechanistic view gave rise to a more ecological view that led to a new paradigm - regenerative sustainability. (Mang & Reed, 2012; Reed, 2007). This thinking redefines the environment encompassing the culture, economy, and politics of communities.

'It redefines what sustainability means and requires within the context of a dynamic, interdependent, evolving world' (Mang & Reed, 2012). This paradigm implies major changes in the organizational culture and the leadership style. Positive leadership can be a great contribution to promote these changes, however, it is necessary to develop more research to integrate the principles of regenerative leadership with positive leadership. With this integration, it will be possible to strengthen the theoretical model of positive leader development.

REFERENCES

Abdullah, A., Ling, Y., & Peng, C. (2017). Workplace happiness, transformational leadership and affective commitment. *Advanced Science Letters*, *23*(4), 2872–2875. doi:10.1166/asl.2017.7588

Anderson, D. (2006). Is building relationship the key to leadership? *Performance Improvement*, *51*(2), 15–22. doi:10.1002/pfi.21245

Antino, M., Gil-Rodríguez, F., Rodríguez-Muñoz, A., & Borzillo, S. (2014). Evaluating positive leadership: Pilot study on the psychometric properties of a reduced version of the Positive Leadership Assessment Scale. *Revista de Psicología Social*, *29*(3), 589–608. doi:10.1080/02134748.2014.972705

Arakawa, D., & Greenberg, M. (2007). Optimistic managers and their influence on productivity and employee engagement in a technology organisation: Implications for coaching psychologists. *International Coaching Psychology Review*, *2*(1), 78–89.

Avey, J. B., Reichard, R. J., Luthans, F., & Mhatre, K. H. (2011). Meta-analysis of the impact of positive psychological capital on employee attitudes, behaviors, and performance. *Human Resource Development Quarterly*, *22*(2), 127–152. doi:10.1002/hrdq.20070

Avolio, B. (2007). Promoting more integrative strategies for leadership theory-building. *The American Psychologist*, *62*(1), 25–33. doi:10.1037/0003-066X.62.1.25 PMID:17209677

Avolio, B. (2010). Pursuing authentic leadership development. In N. Nohria & R. Khurana (Eds.), *Handbook of leadership theory and practice* (pp. 739–768). Harvard Business School Publishing Corporation.

Avolio, B., & Gardner, W. (2005). Authentic leadership development: Getting to the root of positive forms of leadership. *The Leadership Quarterly*, *16*(3), 315–338. doi:10.1016/j.leaqua.2005.03.001

Avolio, B., Walumbwa, F., & Weber, T. (2009). Leadership: Current theories, research, and future directions. *Annual Review of Psychology*, *60*(1), 421–449. doi:10.1146/annurev.psych.60.110707.163621 PMID:18651820

Balthazard, P. A., Waldman, D. A., & Warren, J. E. (2009). Predictors of the emergence of transformational leadership in virtual decision teams. *The Leadership Quarterly*, *20*(5), 651–663. doi:10.1016/j.leaqua.2009.06.008

Bartsch, S., Weber, E., Büttgen, M., & Huber, A. (2021). Leadership matters in crisis-induced digital transformation: How to lead service employees effectively during the COVID-19 pandemic. *Journal of Service Management*, *32*(1), 71–85. doi:10.1108/JOSM-05-2020-0160

Bass, B. (1997). Does the transactional–transformational leadership paradigm transcend organizational and national boundaries? *The American Psychologist*, *52*(2), 130–139. doi:10.1037/0003-066X.52.2.130

Bass, B., & Avolio, B. (1993). Transformational Leadership and Organizational Culture. *Public Administration Quarterly*, (Spring), 112–121.

Bass, B., & Steidlmeier, P. (1999). Ethics, character, and authentic transformational leadership behavior. *The Leadership Quarterly*, *10*(2), 181–217. doi:10.1016/S1048-9843(99)00016-8

Bellmann, L., & Hübler, O. (2020). *Job Satisfaction and Work-Life Balance: Differences between Homework and Work at the Workplace of the Company.* IZA Discussion Paper.

Blanch, J., Gil, F., Antino, M., & Rodríguez-Muñoz, A. (2016). Positive Leadership Models: Theoretical Framework and Research. *Psychologist Papers*, *37*(3), 170–176.

Bono, J., & Ilies, R. (2006). Charisma, positive emotions and mood contagion. *The Leadership Quarterly*, *17*(4), 317–334. doi:10.1016/j.leaqua.2006.04.008

Boyatzis, R. (1993). Beyond competence: The choice to be a leader. *Human Resource Management Review*, *3*(1), 1–14. doi:10.1016/1053-4822(93)90007-Q

Boyatzis, R. (2006a). An overview of intentional change from a complexity perspective. *Journal of Management Development*, *25*(7), 607–623. doi:10.1108/02621710610678445

Boyatzis, R. (2006b). Using tipping points of emotional intelligence and cognitive competencies to predict financial performance of leaders. *Psicothema*, *18*(SUPPL.1), 124–131. PMID:17295969

Boyatzis, R., & Kolb, D. (1995). From learning styles to learning skills the exec skills profile. *Journal of Managerial Psychology, 10*(5), 3–17. doi:10.1108/02683949510085938

Brown, M. E., & Treviño, L. K. (2006). Ethical leadership: A review and future directions. *The Leadership Quarterly, 17*(6), 595–616. doi:10.1016/j.leaqua.2006.10.004

Butler, J., & Kern, M. L. (2016). The PERMA-Profiler: A brief multidimensional measure of flourishing. *International Journal of Wellbeing, 6*(3), 1–48. doi:10.5502/ijw.v6i3.526

Caldwell, C., & Dixon, R. D. (2010). Love, forgiveness, and trust: Critical values of the modern leader. *Journal of Business Ethics, 93*(1), 91–101. doi:10.100710551-009-0184-z

Cameron, K. (2008). *Positive Leadership - Strategies for extraordinary performance* (1st ed.). Berrett-Koehler.

Cameron, K. (2010). Five keys to flourishing in trying times. *Leader to Leader, 2010*(55), 45–51. doi:10.1002/ltl.401

Cameron, K., Bright, D., & Caza, A. (2004). Exploring the Relationships between Organizational Virtuousness and Performance. *The American Behavioral Scientist, 47*(6), 766–790. doi:10.1177/0002764203260209

Cameron, K., Dutton, J., & Quinn, R. (2013). An Introduction to Positive Organizational Scholarship. In K. Cameron, J. Dutton, & R. Quinn (Eds.), *Positive Organizational Scholarship* (pp. 3–13). doi:10.1108/S2046-410X(2013)0000001004

Cameron, K., Mora, C., Leutscher, T., & Calarco, M. (2011). Effects of positive practices on organizational effectiveness. *The Journal of Applied Behavioral Science, 47*(3), 266–308. doi:10.1177/0021886310395514

Cameron, K., Quinn, R. E., & Caldwell, C. (2017). Positive leadership and adding value – a lifelong journey. *International Journal of Public Leadership, 13*(2), 59–63. doi:10.1108/IJPL-12-2016-0055

Carbery, R., & Garavan, T. N. (2005). Leadership and management development. In J. P. Wilson (Ed.), International Human Resource Development - Learning, education and training for individuals and organizations (3rd ed.). Kogan Page.

Carnevale, J. B., & Hatak, I. (2020). Employee adjustment and well-being in the era of COVID-19: Implications for human resource management. *Journal of Business Research, 116*(May), 183–187. doi:10.1016/j.jbusres.2020.05.037 PMID:32501303

Chemers, M. M. (2000). Leadership research and theory: A functional integration. *Group Dynamics*, *4*(1), 27–43. doi:10.1037/1089-2699.4.1.27

Chen, J. K. C., & Sriphon, T. (2021). Perspective on COVID-19 pandemic factors impacting organizational leadership. *Sustainability*, *13*(3230), 1–21.

Cilliers, F. (2011). Positive psychology leadership coaching experiences in a financial organisation. *SA Journal of Industrial Psychology*, *37*(1), 1–14. doi:10.4102ajip.v37i1.933

Collins, J. (2001). Level 5 leadership. The triumph of humility and fierce resolve. *Harvard Business Review*, *79*(1), 66–76. PMID:11189464

Collins, J. (2007). De bom a excelente (3a ed.). Lisboa: Casa das Letras.

Contreras, F., Baykal, E., & Abid, G. (2020). E-Leadership and Teleworking in Times of COVID-19 and Beyond: What We Know and Where Do We Go. *Frontiers in Psychology*, *11*(December), 1–11. PMID:33362656

Cunha, M. P., Rego, A., & Lopes, M. P. (2013). Comportamento organizacional positivo. *Análise Psicológica*, *31*(4), 313–328. doi:10.14417/ap.804

Daniels, K. (2000). Measures of Five Aspects of Affective Well-Being at Work. *Human Relations*, *53*(February), 275–294. doi:10.1177/a010564

Daraba, D., Wirawan, H., Salam, R., & Faisal, M. (2021). Working from home during the corona pandemic: Investigating the role of authentic leadership, psychological capital, and gender on employee performance. *Cogent Business and Management*, *8*(1), 1–17. doi:10.1080/23311975.2021.1885573

Day, D. (2011). Leadership Development. In A. Bryman, D. Collinson, K. Grint, B. Jackson, & M. Uhl-Bien (Eds.), The Sage Handbook of Leadership (1st ed., pp. 37–50). Sage Publications Ltd.

Den Hartog, D., & Koopman, P. (2001). Leadership in organizations. In *Handbook of Industrial, Work an Organizational Psychology* (pp. 167–187). Sage Publication, Inc.

Diener, E. (2000). Subjective well-being: The science of happiness and a proposal for a national index. *The American Psychologist*, *55*(1), 34–43. doi:10.1037/0003-066X.55.1.34 PMID:11392863

Diener, E., Lucas, R., & Oishi, S. (2002). Subjective Well-Being The Science of Happiness and Life Satisfaction. In C. Snyder & S. Lopez (Eds.), *Handbook of Positive Psychology* (pp. 63–73). Oxford University Press.

Dimitrov, D. (2015). Leadership in a humane organization. *European Journal of Training and Development, 39*(2), 122–142. doi:10.1108/EJTD-07-2014-0051

Edmondson, A. (1999). Psychological safety and learning behavior in work teams. *Administrative Science Quarterly, 44*(2), 350–383. doi:10.2307/2666999

Edmondson, A. (2008, July). The competitive imperative of learning. *Harvard Business Review,* 60–67.

Eva, N., Robin, M., Sendjaya, S., Van Dierendonck, D., & Liden, R. C. (2019). Servant Leadership: A systematic review and call for future research. *The Leadership Quarterly, 30*(1), 111–132. doi:10.1016/j.leaqua.2018.07.004

Fairlie, P. (2011). Meaningful work, employee engagement, and other key employee outcomes: Implications for human resource development. *Advances in Developing Human Resources, 13*(4), 508–525. doi:10.1177/1523422311431679

Fisher, C. D. (2010). Happiness at Work. *International Journal of Management Reviews, 12*(4), 384–412. doi:10.1111/j.1468-2370.2009.00270.x

Fredrickson, B. (1998). What good are positive emotions? *Review of General Psychology, 2*(3), 300–319. doi:10.1037/1089-2680.2.3.300 PMID:21850154

Fredrickson, B. L. (2001). The role of positive emotions in positive psychology: The broaden-and-build theory of positive emotions. *The American Psychologist, 56*(3), 218–226. doi:10.1037/0003-066X.56.3.218 PMID:11315248

Gable, S. L., & Haidt, J. (2005). What (and why) is positive psychology? *Review of General Psychology, 9*(2), 103–110. doi:10.1037/1089-2680.9.2.103

Gavin, J. H., & Mason, R. O. (2004). The virtuous organization: The value of happiness in the workplace. *Organizational Dynamics, 33*(4), 379–392. doi:10.1016/j.orgdyn.2004.09.005

George, B., Sims, P., McLean, A., & Mayer, D. (2007). Discovering Your Authentic Leadership. *Harvard Business Review,* (February), 1–8. PMID:17345686

Giles, S. (2016). The Most Important Leadership Competencies, According to Leaders Around the World. *Harvard Business Review,* (March), 2–7.

Goffee, R., & Jones, G. (2005). Managing authenticity: The paradox of great leadership. *Harvard Business Review, 83*(12), 86–94. PMID:16334584

Goffee, R., & Jones, G. (2013). Creating the best workplace on earth. *Harvard Business Review, 91*(5). PMID:23898736

Goleman, D. (1998). What makes a leader? *Harvard Business Review*, 82–91. PMID:10187249

Goleman, D., Boyatzis, R., & Mckee, A. (2001). Primal Leadership : The Hidden Driver of Great Performance. *Harvard Business Review*, (December), 42–51.

Goodman, F. R., Disabato, D. J., Kashdan, T. B., & Kauffman, S. B. (2018). Measuring well-being: A comparison of subjective well-being and PERMA. *The Journal of Positive Psychology*, *13*(4), 321–332. doi:10.1080/17439760.2017.1388434

Graen, G., & Uhl-Bien, M. (1995). Relationship-based approach to leadership: Development of leader-member exchange (LMX) theory of leadership over 25 years: Applying a multi-level multi-domain perspective. *The Leadership Quarterly*, *6*(2), 219–247. doi:10.1016/1048-9843(95)90036-5

Haller, M., & Hadler, M. (2006). How social relations and structures can produce happiness and unhappiness: An international comparative analysis. *Social Indicators Research*, *75*(2), 169–216. doi:10.100711205-004-6297-y

Hamlin, R. (2004). In support of universalistic models of managerial and leadership effectiveness: Implications for HRD research and practice. *Human Resource Development Quarterly*, *15*(2), 189–215. doi:10.1002/hrdq.1098

Hamlin, R., & Hatton, A. (2013). Toward a British taxonomy of perceived managerial and leadership effectiveness. *Human Resource Development Quarterly*, *24*(3), 365–406. doi:10.1002/hrdq.21163

Hardman, G. J. (2009). *Regenerative leadership: an integral theory for transforming people and organisations for sustainability in business, education, and community*. Academic Press.

Harter, J. K., Schmidt, F. L., & Keyes, C. L. M. (2003). Well-being in the workplace and its relationship to business outcomes: A review of the Gallup studies. In C. L. M. Keyes & J. Haidt (Eds.), *Flourishing: Positive psychology and the life well-lived* (pp. 205–224). doi:10.1037/10594-009

Hartnell, C. A., Ou, A. Y., & Kinicki, A. (2011). Organizational Culture and Organizational Effectiveness: A Meta-Analytic Investigation of the Competing Values Framework's Theoretical Suppositions. *The Journal of Applied Psychology*, *96*(4), 677–694. doi:10.1037/a0021987 PMID:21244127

Hoffman, B. J., Woehr, D. J., Maldagen-Youngjohn, R., & Lyons, B. D. (2011). Great man or great myth? A quantitative review of the relationship between individual differences and leader effectiveness. *Journal of Occupational and Organizational Psychology, 84*(2), 347–381. doi:10.1348/096317909X485207

Hollander, E. (1992). Leadership, followership, self, and others. *The Leadership Quarterly, 3*(1), 43–54. doi:10.1016/1048-9843(92)90005-Z

Hollander, E. (1995). Ethical challenges in the leader-follower relationship. In J. Ciulla (Ed.), Ethics: The Heart of Leadership (2nd ed., pp. 47–58). doi:10.2307/3857272

House, R., & Aditya, R. (1997). The social scientific study of leadership : quo vadis? The social scientific study of leadership : quo vadis? *Journal of Management, 23*(3), 409–473. doi:10.1177/014920639702300306

Huppert, F. A. (2009). Psychological Well-being: Evidence Regarding its Causes and Consequences. *Applied Psychology. Health and Well-Being, 1*(2), 137–164. doi:10.1111/j.1758-0854.2009.01008.x

Iles, P. (2012). Leadership Development and Talent Management. In M. Lee (Ed.), *Human Resource Development as we know it - Speeches that Have Shaped the Field* (1st ed.). Routledge Studies.

Iles, P., & Preece, D. (2006). Developing Leaders or Developing Leadership? The Academy of Chief Executives' Programmes in the North East of England. *Leadership, 2*(3), 317–340. doi:10.1177/1742715006066024

Intagliata, J., Ulrich, D., & Smallwood, N. (2000). Leveraging leadership Competencies to produce Leadership Brand. *Human Resources Planning, 23*(4), 12–23.

Judge, T., Bono, J., Ilies, R., & Gerhardt, M. (2002). Personality and leadership: A qualitative and quantitative review. *The Journal of Applied Psychology, 87*(4), 765–780. doi:10.1037/0021-9010.87.4.765 PMID:12184579

Judge, T., & Kammeyer-Mueller, J. (2011). Happiness as a societal value. *The Academy of Management Perspectives, 25*(1), 30–41.

Judge, T., Piccolo, R., & Kosalka, T. (2009). The bright and dark sides of leader traits: A review and theoretical extension of the leader trait paradigm. *The Leadership Quarterly, 20*(6), 855–875. doi:10.1016/j.leaqua.2009.09.004

Karam, E., Gardner, W. L., Gillifor, D., Tribble, L., & Li, M. (2017). Authentic Leadership and High-Performance Human Resource Practices: Implications for Work Engagement. *Research in Personnel and Human Resources Management, 35*, 103–153. doi:10.1108/S0742-730120170000035004

Kelloway, E., Weigand, H., Mckee, M., & Das, H. (2013). Positive leadership and employee well-being. *Journal of Leadership & Organizational Studies, 20*(1), 107–117. doi:10.1177/1548051812465892

Kets de Vries, M. (2001). Creating authentizotic organizations: Well-functioning individuals in vibrant companies. *Human Relations, 54*(1), 101–111. doi:10.1177/0018726701541013

Kets de Vries, M., & Korotov, K. (2010). *Developing Leaders and Leadership Development*. Academic Press.

Kets de Vries, M., Vrignaud, P., & Florent-Treacy, E. (2004). The Global Leadership Life Inventory: Development and psychometric properties of a 360-degree feedback instrument. *International Journal of Human Resource Management, 15*(3), 475–492. doi:10.1080/0958519042000181214

Kets de Vries, M., Vrignaud, P., Florent-Treacy, E., & Korotov, K. (2007). *360-degree Feedback Instruments: An overview*. doi:2007/01/EFE

Kirkpatrick, S. A., & Locke, E. A. (1991). Leadership: Do traits matter? *The Academy of Management Executive, 5*(2), 48–60.

Klein, K. J., & House, R. J. (1995). On fire: Charismatic leadership and levels of analysis. *The Leadership Quarterly, 6*(2), 183–198. doi:10.1016/1048-9843(95)90034-9

Kniffin, K. M., Narayanan, J., Anseel, F., Antonakis, J., Ashford, S. P., Bakker, A. B., ... van Vugt, M. (2021). COVID-19 and the workplace: Implications, issues, and insights for future research and action. *The American Psychologist, 76*(1), 63–77. doi:10.1037/amp0000716 PMID:32772537

Kotter, J. (1990). What leaders really do. *Harvard Business Review*, 85–96. PMID:10104518

Liao, C. (2017). Leadership in virtual teams: A multilevel perspective. *Human Resource Management Review, 27*(4), 648–659. doi:10.1016/j.hrmr.2016.12.010

Lilian, S. C. (2014). Virtual Teams: Opportunities and Challenges for e-Leaders. *Procedia: Social and Behavioral Sciences, 110*, 1251–1261. doi:10.1016/j.sbspro.2013.12.972

Lopez, S. J., & Snyder, C. R. (2012). The Oxford Handbook of Positive Psychology. In The Oxford Handbook of Positive Psychology (2nd ed.). New York: Oxford University Press.

Losada, M., & Heaphy, E. (2004). The Role of Positivity and Connectivity in the Performance of Business Teams: A Nonlinear Dynamics Model. *The American Behavioral Scientist*, *47*(6), 740–765. doi:10.1177/0002764203260208

Lunenburg, F. C. (2010). Leader-Member Exchange Theory : Another Perspective on the Leadership Process. *International Journal of Management. Business Administration*, *13*(1), 1–5.

Luthans, F., Avey, J. B., Avolio, B. J., & Peterson, S. J. (2010). The development and resulting performance impact of positive psychological capital. *Human Resource Development Quarterly*, *21*(1), 41–67. doi:10.1002/hrdq.20034

Luthans, F., & Youssef, C. M. (2004). Human, social, and now positive psychological capital management: Investing in people for competitive advantage. *Organizational Dynamics*, *33*(2), 143–160. doi:10.1016/j.orgdyn.2004.01.003

Lyubomirsky, S., King, L., & Diener, E. (2005). The benefits of frequent positive affect: Does happiness lead to success? *Psychological Bulletin*, *131*(6), 803–855. doi:10.1037/0033-2909.131.6.803 PMID:16351326

Malinga, K. S., Stander, M., & Nell, W. (2019). Positive Leadership: Moving Towards an Integrated Definition and Interventions. In L. E. Van Zyl & S. R. Sr (Eds.), *Theoretical Approaches to Multi-Cultural Positive Psychological Interventions*. doi:10.1007/978-3-030-20583-6_9

Mang, P., & Reed, B. (2012). Designing from place: A regenerative framework and methodology. *Building Research and Information*, *40*(1), 23–38. doi:10.1080/09613218.2012.621341

Mayer, J., DiPaolo, M., & Salovey, P. (1990). Perceiving affective content in ambiguous visual stimuli: A component of emotional intelligence. *Journal of Personality Assessment*, *54*(3&4), 772–781. doi:10.120715327752jpa5403&4_29 PMID:2348356

Mayer, J., & Salovey, P. (1997). What is Emotional Intelligence? In P. Salovey & D. Sluyter (Eds.), *Emotional Development and Emotional Intelligence* (pp. 3–31). Basic Books.

Mccauley, C. D. (2008). *Leader Development : A Review of Research*. Center for Creative Leadership.

McGuire, D. (2014). Human Resource Development (2nd ed.). SAGE Publications Ltd.

McNamara, D. E. (2011). From Fayol's Mechanistic To Today's Organic Functions Of Management. *American Journal of Business Education*, *2*(1), 63–78. doi:10.19030/ajbe.v2i1.4023

Oishi, S., Diener, E., & Lucas, R. (2007). The Optimum Level of Well-Being: Can People Be Too Happy? *Perspective on Psychological ScienceScience*, *2*(4), 346–360. doi:10.1111/j.1745-6916.2007.00048.x PMID:26151972

Owens, B., Baker, W., Sumpter, D., & Cameron, K. (2016). Relational energy at work: Implications for job engagement and job performance. *The Journal of Applied Psychology*, *101*(1), 35–49. doi:10.1037/apl0000032 PMID:26098165

Owens, B. P., & Hekman, D. R. (2016). How does leader humility influence team performance? Exploring the mechanisms of contagion and collective promotion focus. *Academy of Management Journal*, *59*(3), 1088–1111. doi:10.5465/amj.2013.0660

Owens, B. P., Johnson, M. D., & Mitchell, T. R. (2013). Expressed humility in organizations: Implications for performance, teams, and leadership. *Organization Science*, *24*(5), 1517–1538. doi:10.1287/orsc.1120.0795

Palma, P., Cunha, M., & Lopes, M. (2007). Comportamento organizacional positivo e empreendedorismo: Uma influência mutuamente vantajosa. *Comportamento Organizacional e Gestão*, *13*, 93–114.

Palumbo, R. (2020). Let me go to the office! An investigation into the side effects of working from home on work-life balance. *International Journal of Public Sector Management*, *33*(6–7), 771–790. doi:10.1108/IJPSM-06-2020-0150

Parris, D. L., & Peachey, J. W. (2013). A Systematic Literature Review of Servant Leadership Theory in Organizational Contexts. *Journal of Business Ethics*, *113*(3), 377–393. doi:10.100710551-012-1322-6

Pina e Cunha, M., Campos e Cunha, R., & Rego, A. (2009). Exploring the Role of Leader—Subordinate Interactions in the Construction of Organizational Positivity. *Leadership*, *5*(1), 81–101. doi:10.1177/1742715008098311

Pouramini, Z., & Fayyazi, M. (2015). The Relationship between Positive Organizational Behavior with Job Satisfaction, Organizational Citizenship Behavior, and Employee Engagement. *International Business Research*, *8*(9), 57–66. doi:10.5539/ibr.v8n9p57

Reed, B. (2007). Forum: Shifting from "sustainability" to regeneration. *Building Research and Information*, *35*(6), 674–680. doi:10.1080/09613210701475753

Rego, A. (2019). Liderança - Humildade e Soberba. Lisboa: Edições Sílabo.

Rego, A., & Cunha, M. (2008). Perceptions of authentizotic climates and employees happiness: Pathways to individual performance? *Journal of Business Research, 61*(7), 739–752. doi:10.1016/j.jbusres.2007.08.003

Rego, A., Cunha, M. P., & Simpson, A. V. (2018). The Perceived Impact of Leaders' Humility on Team Effectiveness: An Empirical Study. *Journal of Business Ethics, 148*(1), 205–218. doi:10.100710551-015-3008-3

Rego, A., Ribeiro, N., & Cunha, M. P. (2010). Perceptions of organisational virtuousness and happiness as prediction of organisational citizenship behaviours. *Journal of Business Ethics, 93*(2), 215–235. doi:10.100710551-009-0197-7

Rego, A., Sousa, F., Marques, C., & Cunha, M. P. (2012). Authentic leadership promoting employees' psychological capital and creativity. *Journal of Business Research, 65*(3), 429–437. doi:10.1016/j.jbusres.2011.10.003

Robbins, S. (2004). Fundamentos do Comportamento Organizacional (7a ed.). São Paulo: Prentice Hall.

Rodríguez-Modroño, P., & López-Igual, P. (2021). Job quality and work—Life balance of teleworkers. *International Journal of Environmental Research and Public Health, 18*(6), 1–13. doi:10.3390/ijerph18063239 PMID:33800995

Russell, R., & Stone, A. G. (2002). A review of servant leadership attributes:developing a practical model. *Leadership and Organization Development Journal, 23*(3), 145–157. doi:10.1108/01437730210424

Safferstone, M. (2005). Organizational Leadership: Classic Works and Contemporary Perspectives. *CHOICE: Current Reviews for Academic Libraries, 42*(6), 959–975.

Sainger, G. (2018). Leadership in digital age: A study on the role of leader in this era of digital transformation. *International Journal on Leadership, 6*(1), 1–6.

Schriesheim, C., Castro, S., & Cogliser, C. (1999). Leader-member exchange (LMX) research: A comprehensive review of theory, measurement, and data-analytic practices. *The Leadership Quarterly, 10*(1), 63–113. doi:10.1016/S1048-9843(99)80009-5

Seligman, M. (2002). Positive Psychology, Positive Prevention, and Positive Therapy. In C. Snyder & S. Lopez (Eds.), *Handbook of Positive Psychology* (pp. 3–12). Oxford University Press.

Seligman, M. (2018). PERMA and the building blocks of well-being. *The Journal of Positive Psychology, 13*(4), 333–335. doi:10.1080/17439760.2018.1437466

Seligman, M., & Csikszentmihalyi, M. (2000). Positive psychology. An introduction. *The American Psychologist*, *55*(1), 5–14. doi:10.1037/0003-066X.55.1.5 PMID:11392865

Seligman, M., Steen, T. A., Park, N., & Peterson, C. (2005). Positive psychology progress: Empirical validation of interventions. *The American Psychologist*, *60*(5), 410–421. doi:10.1037/0003-066X.60.5.410 PMID:16045394

Shamir, B., & Eilam, G. (2005). "What's your story?" A life-stories approach to authentic leadership development. *The Leadership Quarterly*, *16*(3), 395–417. doi:10.1016/j.leaqua.2005.03.005

Shamir, B., House, R. J., & Arthur, M. B. (1993). The motivational effects of charismatic leadership: A self-concept based theory. *Organization Science*, *4*(4), 577–594. doi:10.1287/orsc.4.4.577

Sheldon, K. M., & King, L. (2001). Why positive psychology is necessary. *The American Psychologist*, *56*(3), 216–217. doi:10.1037/0003-066X.56.3.216 PMID:11315247

Steelman, L. A., & Wolfeld, L. (2018). The Manager as Coach: The Role of Feedback Orientation. *Journal of Business and Psychology*, *33*(1), 41–53. doi:10.100710869-016-9473-6

Stone, A. G., Russell, R. F., & Patterson, K. (2004). Transformational versus servant leadership: A difference in leader focus. *Leadership and Organization Development Journal*, *25*(4), 349–361. doi:10.1108/01437730410538671

Sturnick, J. A. (2004). The Art of Regenerative Leadership: Language, Spirit, and Principles. *Education and Culture*, *20*(Spring), 42–47.

Uhl-Bien, M. (2006). Relational Leadership Theory: Exploring the social processes of leadership and organizing. *The Leadership Quarterly*, *17*(6), 654–676. doi:10.1016/j.leaqua.2006.10.007

Van Wart, M., Roman, A., Wang, X. H., & Liu, C. (2019). Operationalizing the definition of e-leadership: Identifying the elements of e-leadership. *International Review of Administrative Sciences*, *85*(1), 80–97. doi:10.1177/0020852316681446

Walumbwa, F., Avolio, B., Gardner, W., Wernsing, T., & Peterson, S. (2008). Authentic Leadership: Development and Validation of a Theory-Based Measure. *Journal of Management*, *34*(1), 89–126. doi:10.1177/0149206307308913

Walumbwa, F., Luthans, F., Avey, J. B., & Oke, A. (2011). Authentically leading groups: The mediating role of collective psychological capital and trust. *Journal of Organizational Behavior*, *32*(1), 4–24. doi:10.1002/job.653

Weiss, A., Bates, T. C., & Luciano, M. (2008). Happiness Is a Personal(ity) Thing - The Genetics of Personality and Well-Being in a Representative Sample. *Psychological Science*, *19*(3), 205–210. doi:10.1111/j.1467-9280.2008.02068.x PMID:18315789

Winkle, B., Allen, S., Devore, D., & Winston, B. (2014). The Relationship Between the Servant Leadership Behaviors of Immediate Supervisors and Followers' Perceptions of Being Empowered in the Context of Small Business. *Journal of Leadership Education*, 70–83.

Xiao, Y., Becerik-Gerber, B., Lucas, G., & Roll, S. C. (2021). Impacts of Working From Home During COVID-19 Pandemic on Physical and Mental Well-Being of Office Workstation Users. *Journal of Occupational and Environmental Medicine*, *63*(3), 181–190. doi:10.1097/JOM.0000000000002097 PMID:33234875

Yang, C. (2014). Does Ethical Leadership Lead to Happy Workers? A Study on the Impact of Ethical Leadership, Subjective Well-Being, and Life Happiness in the Chinese Culture. *Journal of Business Ethics*, *123*(3), 513–525. doi:10.100710551-013-1852-6

Yavuz, M. (2019). Transformational leadership and authentic leadership as practical implications of positive organizational psychology. In *Handbook of Research on Positive Organizational Behavior for Improved Workplace Performance* (pp. 122–139). IGI Global.

Youssef, C. M., & Luthans, F. (2007). Positive organizational behavior in the workplace: The impact of hope, optimism, and resilience. *Journal of Management*, *33*(5), 774–800. doi:10.1177/0149206307305562

Youssef, C. M., & Luthans, F. (2012). Positive global leadership. *Journal of World Business*, *47*(4), 539–547. doi:10.1016/j.jwb.2012.01.007

Youssef-Morgan, C. M., & Luthans, F. (2013). Positive leadership: Meaning and application across cultures. *Organizational Dynamics*, *42*(3), 198–208. doi:10.1016/j.orgdyn.2013.06.005

Yukl, G. (2010). *Leadership in organizations* (7th ed.). Pearson Prentice Hall.

Yukl, G., Gordon, A., & Taber, T. (2002). A Taxonomy of Leadership Behavior: Integrating a Half Century of Behavior Research. *Journal of Leadership & Organizational Studies*, *9*(1), 15–32. doi:10.1177/107179190200900102

Zaccaro, S. (2007). Trait-based perspectives of leadership. *The American Psychologist*, *62*(1), 6–16, 43–47. doi:10.1037/0003-066X.62.1.6 PMID:17209675

Zbierowski, P. (2016). Positive leadership and corporate entrepreneurship: Theoretical considerations and research propositions. *Entrepreneurial Business and Economics Review*, *4*(3), 73–84. doi:10.15678/EBER.2016.040306

Zbierowski, P., & Góra, K. (2014). Positive Leadership: Its Nature, Antecedents and Consequences. *Journal of Positive Management*, *5*(1), 85. doi:10.12775/JPM.2014.008

Zeuge, A., Weigel, A., Bjorn, N., Frederike, O., & Michael, S. (2020). Leading Virtual Teams -A Literature Review. *Project: ASTAR - Competence Transfer in a VR/AR-Based Environment for Work Design*, (August), 1–9.

ADDITIONAL READING

Bryman, A. (1996). Leadership in Organizations. In *Handbook of Organization Studies*. Sage Publication, Inc.

Bryman, A., Collinson, D., Grint, K., Jackson, B., & Uhl-Bien, M. (2011). *The SAGE Handbook of Leadership*. Sage Publication, Inc.

Ilies, R., Morgeson, F. P., & Nahrgang, J. D. (2005). Authentic leadership and eudaemonic well-being: Understanding leader-follower outcomes. *The Leadership Quarterly*, *16*(3), 373–394. doi:10.1016/j.leaqua.2005.03.002

Morgan, G. (1986). *Images of Organization*. Sage Publication, Inc.

Nelson, D., & Cooper, C. L. (2007). *Positive Organizational Behavior–Accentuating the positive at work*. Sage Publication, Inc.

Peterson, C., & Seligman, M. (2004). Character Strengths and Virtues: A Handbook and Classification. American Psychological Association / Oxford University Press.

Pfeffer, J. (1977). The ambiguity of leadership. *Academy of Management Review*, *2*(January), 104–113. doi:10.5465/amr.1977.4409175

Pfeffer, J. (1997). *New directions for Organization Theory - Problems and Prospects*. Oxford University Press.

Seligman, M. (2004). *Authentic Happiness: Using the New Positive Psychology to Realize Your Potential for Lasting Fulfillment*. Atria Books.

Seligman, M. (2012). *Flourish (A Visionary New Understanding of Happiness and Well-Being)*. Atria Books.

KEY TERMS AND DEFINITIONS

Corporate Happiness: It is the adoption of a set of practices that involve the organization's strategy and culture with the objective of ensuring the well-being and happiness of employees.

Leader: Is someone who has the ability to influence, share and inspire their vision on others; others live and feel this vision as their own.

Leadership Development: Refers to the development of leadership processes within the organization, involving the development of its human and social capital.

Leadership Theories: Are the various theoretical approaches to leadership over time.

Organizational Theories: Are the different theoretical approaches of organizations over time.

Positive Leadership: Are a set of positive practices with an impact on the work environment that promote desirable changes for greater organizational effectiveness.

Positive Psychology: It is a movement within psychology that focuses on human strengths, motivations, and capabilities that are critical to human well-being and happiness.

Chapter 8
Organizational Change:
Review of the Literature

Sajjad Nawaz Khan
https://orcid.org/0000-0003-1366-9080
Iqra University, Pakistan

Hafiz Mudassir Rehman
https://orcid.org/0000-0001-9114-0989
Universiti Tunku Abdul Rahman, Malaysia

Muhammad Muzammil Ghayas
Iqra University, Pakistan

ABSTRACT

Nearly no organizational phenomenon has garnered as much attention as organizational change. It appears as one of the fascinating and nearly eroticizing inducements for business organizations, and it has been highly acknowledging as a response. Highlighting the importance this phenomenon holds in the current environment, there is a huge and still growing body of research concentrating on organizational change. This chapter briefly explains the overview of the three major organizational change approaches (teleological approaches and evolutionary approaches and psychological approaches), which highlight organizational change through different models and theories.

DOI: 10.4018/978-1-7998-2807-5.ch008

INTRODUCTION

Nearly no organizational phenomenon has altered as much attention as organizational change. It appears as one of the fascinating and nearly eroticizing inducements for business organizations, and it has been highly acknowledging as a response. Highlighting the importance, this phenomenon holds in the current environment, there is a huge and still growing body of research concentrating on organizational change (Schwarz, 2012; Wetzel & Van Gorp, 2014). Change is a basic, notable and recurring part of life. As a result, it has become one of the big comforts in organization theory (Wetzel & Van Gorp, 2014). Generally, organizational change can be defined as "a new state of things, different from the old state of things" (French & Bell Jr 1999, p. 2). Furthermore, Huse and Cummings (1985) defined organizational change as "a state of transition between the current state and a future one, towards which the organization is directed". It shows that organizations are constantly engaged in change processes in order to survive in a competitive environment. Lewin (1947) was the first to propose that life is never without change, and organizations are constantly engaged in the change processes although the nature of change is not always the same, as change comes in different sizes and shapes (Hodges & Gill, 2014). Therefore, this chapter briefly explains the overview of the two major organizational change approaches (teleological approaches and evolutionary approaches), which highlight organizational change through different models and theories.

Background

In terms of size and shape, organizational change can further be divided into incremental (first order change) and transformational (second order/strategic) change. Incremental change pointed out the less-drastic and small-scale transformation that helps the organization to improve its efficiency and overcome inactiveness. Moreover, incremental change tends to be easy and quick to implement and therefore, having both will lower failure risk and allow return in terms of benefits. Conversely, transformational change impacts the organizational structure and the critical areas that form the organizational structure are culture, power distance, strategy, and control system (Tushman & Romanelli, 1985). The transformational change is also referred to as revolutionary or strategic change. Many researchers acknowledged that the success of any type of change depends on the people (employees) of the organizations, and it is more critical for the employees to alter their perspectives and values according to the overall perspective of the organization (Jacobs, van & Christe-Zeyse, 2013; Moran & Brightman, 2001). Therefore, it is supposed that social actors live in the zone of upheaval, and organizations try to gradually change and to manage its effects (Burke, 2008; Schwarz & Huber, 2008). This makes it more fascinating to explore and study organizational change. Previous studies focused on the "how" and "what" features of change or in other words the content and trends (Sashkin & Burke, 1987), explore change introduction (Pasmore & Fagans, 1992), summarize and categorize change developments (Woodman, 1989), assess change themes (Armenakis & Bedeian, 1999). This chapter also focused on the human aspects of organizational change by determining the content, context and process factors of employees' reactions towards organizational change.

Teleological Approaches

Conventional outlook to organizational change predominantly follows a rational, linear approach which focuses on the role of a leader as a steward to control organizational change. These approaches assume of planned change and popularity among change consultants as it follows the predefined or predictable steps towards organizational change implementation (Collins, 1998; Graetz & Smith 2010). The traditional or conventional approaches are also referred as the teleological, rational or strategic planning approaches. The organizational process is linear and rational, and a leader acts as the change agent or instigator of change that ultimately controls organizational processes. It is assumed that organizations are adoptive and purposeful. Change is evoked by the internal environment rather than external conditions (Carr et al., 1996; Kezar, 2001). Teleological approaches consist of Lewin (1947) model of unfreezing, change and refreeze, Kotter (1995) eight steps model of organizational change and Kanter (1992) Ten Commandments (Graetz & Smith 2010; Kezar, 2001). Moreover, planned change or teleological approaches deal with development as a repetitive chain of envisioned goal formation, implantation, evaluation and modification and that was accomplished by the people involved (Van de Ven & Sun, 2011).

In Lewin (1947) model of planned change: unfreezing simply means to identify the need for a change and break the employee's way of work. It means to encourage or forced employees to get out of their comfort zones, breaking the status quo. In this stage, the resisting forces need to be minimized rather than in increasing deriving forces of change (Cummings & Worley, 2009; Schein, 1996). During the changing stage, process comprises of problem identification, collecting information about relevant deriving and opposing forces, seeking alternative solutions, and selecting a desired course of action. Refreezing is the final step of planned change model this stage distinguished by changes to policies, culture, and practices of the organization for a new quasi-stationary equilibrium (Burnes, 2004; Cummings & Huse, 1989). The importance of refreezing is to make consistent the new behaviours to some degree with the rest of the employees' personality, environment, and behaviour. The employee satisfaction and acceptance of the new behaviour may be achieved through reinforcement or rewards like bonuses, promotion, greater authority or salary increase (Cummings & Worley, 2009; Schein, 1996).

Kotter's 8 steps model: first step is in establishing the sense of urgency: It means that the beginning of a successful change depends on some people or a group of people start to look deeply at the organization position in competitive environment, like market position, current technological trends and financial position (Cooney et al., 2016; Kotter, 1995). The second step is building coalition: According to Kotter (1995), renewal programme starts with the efforts of one or two individuals. In short, the base of successful transformation is the coalition of organization leaders when the sense of urgency developed within the managerial rank as it further helps in developing coalition or team together. The third step is creating a vision: Kotter (1995) and Cooney et al. (2016) argued that behind every successful transformation there is a picture of the future that is developed by the guiding coalition, and it can be easily communicable to all the stakeholders of the organization. The fourth step is communicating the vision: Organizations needs help and sacrifices of many people for successful organizational change and this is only possible through effective communication strategies (Kotter, 1995, 1996).

The fifth step is empowering others: Organizational transformation would be successful if more people are involved during transformation. The sixth step is creating short-term wins: According to Kotter (1995, 1996), successful transformation is a long process and most employees are fed up when there are no short-term wins thus setting short-term objectives during change process give employees hope that new transformation process is going according to desirable direction or vision. The seventh step produces a more significant change: After a few years of hard work and after the first achievement of a long-term transformation, managers are persuaded to declare victory. But after the first win, if individuals start realizing that the transformation process is almost done, it is a terrible mistake. Successful transformation needs 3 to 10 years. The final step is to institutionalize the new approach: In the final stage, the new approaches and strategies are embedded into the bloodstream of the organization like social norms, behaviour, and culture of the organization; because as the change pressure decreases, the new approaches degrade, so it is very important to institutionalize a new transformation (Cooney et al., 2016; Kotter 1995, 1996). Recently, Cooney et al. (2016) applied Kotter model to implement an appreciative advising model in a university in order to provide the best service to the students in light of outside factors. It has been concluded from the study that using Kotter model provides success to the office of student affairs and furthermore, it was also ensured that involving all students provides different voices and give vision to the student about the university. Chappell et al. (2016), conducted a qualitative study to test the Kotter model to explore the implementation of workplace health and wellbeing initiatives. The findings showed that during the implementation of healthy workplace initiatives, none of the workplaces utilizes the formal model of organizational change. It was further confirmed that all of the steps in Kotter model are not necessary and the order of the steps was challenged.

Much of the criticism that these approaches have attracted relate to overly linear and rational process of change described by teleological models (Dawson, 1994; Hock, 1999). Another major criticism is that these models overemphasized human thoughts, creativity, and decision. These models assume that leaders lead the organization from one state to another otherwise it operates on stable states, in other words, these approaches are more leader-centric (Kezar, 2001). Teleological studies ignore the content, context and process factors of employees' reactions towards organizational change (Pettigrew, 1985).

Evolutionary Approaches

Evolutionary approaches unlike teleological approaches are based on the biological investigation of change concentrated that change is a slow process of mutation periodically shaped by environmental conditions (Morgan, 1997; Van de Ven, & Poole, 1995). Evolutionists claim that organizational change and adaptation are not necessarily the outcome of managerial actions. In this framework, changes or variation can be intentional or unintentional and the selections of variations are not the results of intentions of those who generate variations but the results of their consequences (Demers, 2007; Langton, 1979). Thus, evolutionary theories originally concentrated on emergent changes as an alternative to the planned top-down organizational change theories (Burgelman, 1991; Miner, 1990). These approaches talked about the repetitive and progressive movement of variation, selection and retention activities (Campbell, 1969, as cited in Ven & Sun, 2011). Variation activities refer to the creation of unique and emerging forms of chances. Nevertheless, selection occurs mainly through competition among forms. For example, higher level decision makers or customers select those forms that are best suited for the resource base of an environmental niche. Retention activities explained the routines and forces that sustain and maintain some organizational forms (Aldrich & Ruef, 2006; Baum & McKelvey, 1999). Several different individual approaches come out from evolutionary tradition such as population ecology, contingency and system theory, resource dependency and life cycle theory (Graetz & Smith, 2010; Kazer, 2001).

Population ecology popularized by Hannan and Freeman (1977) argued that individual organization operates as a member of the population where all other organizations are considered as species. It concentrated on incremental changes within the industry, not on individual organizations. Also, ecologists focus on the biological view of industrial behaviour. They propose that Darwinian-like natural selections are the causes of change where organizations continuously evolve to match with the environmental conditions (Demers, 2007, Graetz & Smith, 2010). This approach dealt with the institutional environment where organizations operate, particularly the density of that environment and the number of resources it can provide. Population ecology does not overthrow the importance of agency relationship, goals, benefits or functions, but concentrate on the opportunities and constraints created by the institutional environment (Abbott et al., 2016).

Contingency approach dealt with the fit between organizational structure and environment in which the organization operates. The main assumption of contingency approach is that the organization's structural components must be integrated with each other in order to survive in the environment so that the changes in one structural part must be followed in another part by the adaptive way to maintain coherence (Demers, 2007; Jones & Jones, 2013). In other words, organizational internal structure must be designed in such a way that controls the external environment, and managers are the relational decision makers that are responsible to alter the organizational characteristics to respond positively to its environment (Demers, 2007). Dunphy and Stace (1988, 1993) proposed a model that pointed out the two dimensions; first is the scale of change and second is the style of leadership required for the change, the former related to incremental change; which considers small-scale routine changes and transformational change that pointed out a large-scale organizational transformation. The second dimension is the leadership style namely 'collaborative', 'consultative', 'directive' and 'coercive' (Andriopoulos & Dawson, 2009; Dunphy & Stace, 1988). Therefore, the type of change is the structural response of organizations to the environmental contingencies, nevertheless an organizational change is considered as a deliberate but reactive response to the periodical adaptation (Demers, 2007).

Resource dependency theory is another important evolutionary approach that described the interdependence of organizations and their environments. The organization ability to get resources effectively from the external environment is essential for survival (Aldrich & Pfeffer 1976; Pfeffer & Salancik 2003). Simply, organizations need resources from the environment and when organizations acquire those resources, it produces influence, power, and stability. Those organizations are in power position which acquires more necessary resources, while organizations which depend on others for resources can easily be controlled (Malatesta, & Smith, 2014; Marie-Pier, 2017). In some cases, like organizational change, organizations are interdependent on each other on the basis of resources that they have and what they need for their survival. Therefore, this works as powerful stimuli for creating alliances, mergers, joint ventures, and other collaboration among companies (Guo & Acar 2005; Sowa, 2009). To understand the inter-organizational relationship, power and dependence play a critical role, the balance of power mostly favours the organization that holds what other organizations' needs. Therefore, following resource dependency, managers find and compare different strategies, stressing the short term coordination cost along with a long-term plan for organizational growth and survival (Malatesta, & Smith, 2014).

The last but not the least, life cycle is another important evolutionary approach to organizational change. According to the life cycle theory, organizational change passes through the stages of birth, growth, maturity, decline, and death. The basic assumption is developmental in nature which compares continued progress and change in the organization by the metaphor of human life cycle (Kezar, 2001; Levy & Merry, 1986; Van de Ven & Poole, 1995; Van de Ven, & Sun, 2011). Many different life cycle models have been developed for instance Greiner, (1972) model of organizational growth, Miller and Firesen (1984) five-stage model, and Lester et al. (2003) five-stage life cycle model. The regulation and prescription of activities in life cycle models are natural, logical or institutional routines. The rules recommending the change process in life cycle models are based on previously learned routines for managing periodic changes in an effective and efficient manner. This model diverts attention from the leader as a change agent and focused on each individual role that is critical in the change process. This theory [model] concentrated on activities related to individual development, training and development, assessment of culture and monitoring of the environment and life cycle (Kezer, 2001).

The main criticism of evolutionary approaches is that these theories do not emphasize on the social capital or social phenomenon. Evolutionary approaches are lacking the assumption of human psychology despite the life cycle theory (Kezer, 2001). Population ecology is mainly concern with the environment and organizational inertia and in consequence, it does not explain the process of change and pointed out that organizational change takes time and is costly. Population ecology is a-processual and a-contextual approach at the organizational level of analysis (Demers, 2007). According to Hirsch and Lounsbury (1997) population ecology is not relevant to study organizational change because of its absence of concern for actions in the organization. Contingency approach also receives criticism about the assumption of extreme environmental constraints on managerial choice and for the underestimation of human agency (Child, 1972; Demers, 2007). Contingency framework has also been highlighted as limited in its approach because it sheds lights on outcomes without taking into account the process by which the outcome is reached (Kulkarni, 2017). In other words, evolutionary approaches have overemphasized on the external environment and overly deterministic in nature in order to study organizational change processes.

In conclusion, teleological and evolutionary approaches highlighted organizational change from the macro-perspective. These approaches focused on the external environment and leader-centric internal strategies of implementation. Furthermore, both approaches underestimate the role of individuals in the process of organizational change. Therefore, the following section briefly explained the importance of social capital or human agency in organizational change explaining the factors of employees' reactions to organizational change.

The Psychological Perspective Organizational Change

The bulk of studies focused on the macro-perspective of organizational change, highlighting the types of change implementation, development strategies and how to manage it. Psychological perspective deals with the human side of organizational change which explained how change looks and feels like from the standpoint of change recipients [employees] of the organization (Oreg et al., 2011, 2013). In last two decades, the realization of the importance of recipients' perspective is gently increasing and researchers are acknowledging the role of employees in the success of organizational change (Mdletye et al., 2013; Oreg, 2006; Rafferty & Restubog, 2010; Vakola & Nikolaou, 2005).

Oreg et al. (2011) has reviewed quantitative empirical studies of change recipients' reactions towards organizational change, which were published between 1948 and 2007, and developed a model (Figure, 2.1) revealing the relationship among antecedents, explicit reaction, and change consequences. According to Vogt and Johnson (2011, p. 2), antecedent refers to "*A condition that precedes another and is thought to influence or to cause it*". It explained the reasons for the reaction, not the reactions itself (Oreg et al., 2011). It predicts either change reactions or indirectly change consequences. Figure 1 depicts the five major categories of antecedents, (a) change recipient characteristics, (b) internal context, (c) change process, (d) perceived benefit/harm, and (e) change content. Among other categories of antecedents Oreg et al. (2011) revealed that content, context, and process are the important antecedents of employees' reactions. On the other hand, in a critical review of organizational change literature, Armenakis and Bedeian (1999) also identified that content, context and process factors are the main factors of employees' reactions in organizational change context.

Content of Change

Change content is one of the most important issues in public sector reform literature, but it has also received considerable attention in change management literature. It is concerned with the "employees to perceive what" question of the change initiative. Change content is represented by other terms in the literature such as "personal valence" and "appropriateness" (Armenakis, Harris, & Feild, 2000). According to Armenakis and Bedeian (1999), Burk (2017), Oreg et al. (2011), the substance of change also called 'content factor of change' refers to the "What" of the organizational

Figure 1. Antecedents, explicit reactions, and change consequences of organizational change. The variables in each box constitute only a sample of the relevant variables in each category.
Source: Oreg et al., (2011)

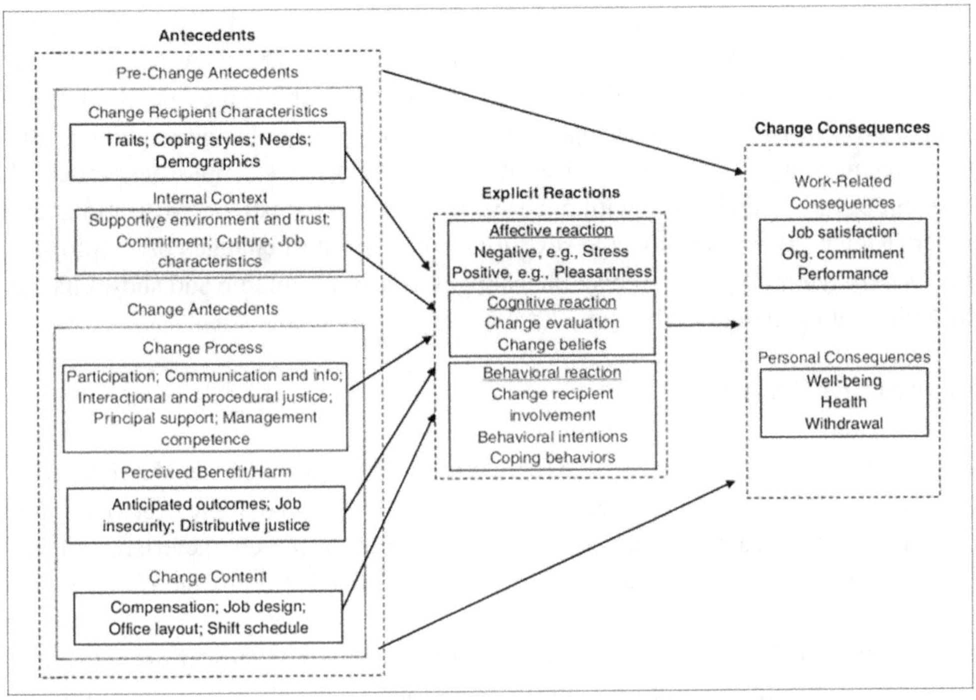

change. They pointed out the area where change occurs. Different authors use different terminologies to explain the content of change, like first-*order* and *second-order* changes (Bartunek & Moch, 1987), incremental change and transformational change (Sammut-Bonnici &Wensley, 2002). First order and incremental changes are those which aim to provide improvement. It pointed out the less-drastic and small-scale transformation that helps the organization to improve efficiency and overcome inactiveness. These changes happen incrementally through adjustments for the improvement of the organization without altering its core (Devos et al., 2007). A small number of studies pointed out the type and nature of change as a possible factor of employees' reaction to it. To analyse the impact of a content factor, studies compared employees' reaction with different pre and post-change situations, or with different types of changes (Oreg et al., 2011).

Few studies like Hatcher and Ross (1991), Latona and Van (1993), and Morgeson et al. (2006) identified positive work attitude and improved performance by analysing content factors such as compensation system, employees' involvement implementation programme, and job redesign. On the other hand, second order or transformational changes aimed changes in the organization's strategic directions, identity, and cultural assumptions also affect employee's reactions. Organizations major transformation is also called radical, strategic or revolutionary change (Hodges & Gill, 2014; Weick & Quinn, 1999). This type of change undergoes a fully new behaviour not only in a single organization but also in the whole sector that can be stated as a paradigm shift (Hodges & Gill, 2014). Contrary to the operationalized change content as a type of change, other studies identify change content as the perceived meaningfulness or the degree of change. For instance, employees perceived frequent or ongoing changes with negative reactions like mistrust, frustration, and anger (Kiefer, 2005). Because the severity of the impact of changes on employees has increased, employees perceive the changes as less acceptable and show change commitment to change (Self et al., 2007).

Context of Change

In their reviews of change research, Armenakis and Bedeian (1999) and Kuipers et al. (2014) found that what we did not sufficiently explore the role of the organizational context in which we embed a change. Context refers to the characteristics of the organization and its membership that precede organizational change (Oreg et al., 2014).

The contextual factors related to organizational change represent the pre-existing forces present in the internal and external surroundings. These surroundings are vital in analysing the success or failure of organizational change, it might also work as a catalyst for change or as an impeding factor that restricts transition to the attitude and/or behaviour in an organization. Context described the triggers that are expected to impact the process and content of change (Johns, 2006; Pichault 2007). Context factors explained the "Why" of organizational change (Armenakis & Bedeian, 1999; Johns, 2006). The external factors comprise of competitions, government regulations, social factors, technological advancement (Armenakis & Bedeian, 1999). However, internal context mostly constructs employee's reactions toward organizational change: it refers to a supportive environment and trustworthy management, organizational commitment, organizational culture and climate, and job characteristics (Oreg et al., 2011). According to Albrecht (2002), Oreg (2006) and, Stanley et al. (2005) trust in management is also a variables that are likely to influence employees' response to organizational change.

Supportive environment and trustworthy management: Change recipients who report that they maintain high levels of trust in management, who consider management as supportive and who feel respected, were receptive to suggested changes and reported a greater willingness to work on the change (Coyle-Shapiro & Morrow, 2003; Cunningham et al., 2002; Kiefer, 2005; Wanberg & Banas, 2000).

Organizational commitment: Change recipients who are committed to their organization, accept their values, are willing to make efforts on their behalf and want to stay there (Mowday, Steers, & Porter, 1979). Several studies have shown that committed recipients of change tend to report higher levels of acceptance and change (Iverson, 1996; Madsen et al., 2005; Shapiro & Kirkman, 1999).

Organizational culture and climate: Another factor that was found relevant to the responses of change recipients to change was the general atmosphere in which we applied change. Observing the work environment in positive terms was found to predict the willingness of change recipients for change, openness to change and change accordingly (V. D. Miller et al., 1994). Likewise, a positive communication climate, such as the existence of an "information environment," predicts the willingness of change recipients as well (Armenakis, Bernerth, Pitts, & Walker, 2007; Holt et al., 2007).

Miscellaneous factors: Besides the factors above, we have linked a variety of other organizational characteristics to positive responses to the change. Such factors include the degree of perceived participation in work and the existence of flexible policies (Eby et al., 2000); perceived organizational integrity (Bernerth et al., 2007; Walker et al., 2007); perceived organizational constraints, such as an unmanageable workload and lacking necessary information (Kiefer, 2005); perceived organizational capabilities and competencies (Holt et al., 2007; Stanley et al., 2005); and in the context of mergers, being a member of the acquiring, versus acquired, organization (Covin, Sightler, Kolenko, & Tudor, 1996).

Process of Change

The process factor of organizational change refers to the actions, reactions, and intersections from the different concern parties as they are keen to move the organization from its current to its desired future state. It refers to the "How" factor of organization change (Burke, 2017; Pettigrew, 1987). The internal process factors consist of quality of change communication, support by supervisors, the attitude of top management, and participation. The process of change is the area of study which deals with the manner (way) of change implementation (Bouckenooghe et al., 2009; Oreg et al., 2011). According to Andriopoulos, & Dawson (2009) politics or process factors of change pointed out the political activities had taken place at different levels in the inside and outside of the organizational setting. The external politics or process refers to competitor's alliances, governmental pressure or multinational corporation influence. This implies that process factors of change highlighted the manner or the way in which organizations implement changes. According to Oreg et al. (2011) employee participation is considered among the most prevalent variables in this category.

Communication and information: Closely related to participation, another researched variable had to do with the amount and quality of change information provided by the recipient of change. Additional information and realistic, supportive, and effective communication during change was associated with several positive responses, such as greater acceptance of change and support for change (Wanberg & Banas, 2000). However, in one study, contrary to what we hypothesize, additional information about the change corresponded with negative evaluations of the change (Oreg, 2006).

Principal support during change: The main influencers of organizational change are change agents and advisors. Some work highlighted the effect of principal support during a change on the responses to change recipients to change (Amiot et al., 2006; Eby et al., 2000). In a study, we associated principal support during change with a higher willingness to change and lower negative effects of change lower (Logan & Ganster, 2007). In addition, we considered mainstays to influence affective and behavioral resistance to organizational restructuring (Oreg, 2006).

Management change competence: Several studies addressed the extent to which we saw management as competent and effective in managing the change. Two studies found perceived management control for change and perceived effectiveness in managing it to deliver positive outcomes, such as the better implementation of change (Lok et al., 2005) and lower levels of stress for the recipient of change (Amiot et al., 2006).

LEADERSHIP AND ORGANIZATIONAL CHANGE

Leaders play a critical role in organizational change. It is primarily because of three major reasons. The first is that the leaders are the ones who decides on the question that whether there exists a need to change something or the status quo suits the organization. Secondly, leaders are the ones who decides that what should be changed or what kind of change the organization need. Last but not the least, leaders are the ones who are required to decide how and when to bring the change. Therefore, one can argue that leaders play a key role in the process of change.

Leadership Styles and Change

There are a number of types of leadership or leadership styles for instance transactional leadership, transformational leadership, paternalistic leadership, servant leadership, moral / ethical leadership, lessiz fare leadership and autocratic leadership etc.

In this regard, one can argue that there is a complete spectrum of leadership. On the one extreme of which is the tendency to assert authority and on the other extreme of which is the tendency to accommodate the people and in between them is the blend of concern about the production and the people. Furthermore, this leadership spectrum is not of 360 degrees but is that of 180 degrees. It is primarily because of the fact that followers' readiness and ability certainly affects the effectiveness of decisions made by the leaders. Hence, encompassing the remaining 180 degree of the leadership spectrum.

The problem with this leadership spectrum is that none of the point of this spectrum can be categorized as useless. Furthermore, greater emphasis to remain on one extreme of this leadership spectrum results in being at a greater distance from the other extreme of the leadership spectrum. This certainly results in compromising on the thing at the other extreme of this leadership spectrum. As a result, it argued that being on one extreme of this leadership spectrum is not of any benefit when it comes to managing the change.

In order to bring in and successfully implement the radical change, leaders are required to assume the responsibility of the change and are required to be the center of attraction or the gravitational point of the change. Hence, for this reasons, managers / leaders must understand that they need to carefully analyze the situation and identify the effect of being on one extreme of this leadership spectrum. In other words, on one hand, leaders must understand that they must not be as much concerned about the tasks that they lose the concern for the people or at-least the followers think so, and on the other hand they must not be as accommodating that they lose the authority or are considered as the weak leaders. This not only brings you at the center point of the 180-degree leadership spectrum but also at the center point of the remaining 180 degree half of the followers spectrums. Hence, brings the leaders at the center points of the entire 360-degree leader-follower equation.

However, being at the center of the circle does not necessarily mean that you act like a gravitational force that controls all the other elements revolving around the circle. For this reason, the center point must have the charisma that the other elements revolve around it. In the case of organizational change, a leader can become a true gravitational force only when he exhibits the qualities of being able to see what others are not able to, and articulating it in a manner that others may also understand the need or urgency of the change and the ability to take risk.

FUTURE RESEARCH DIRECTIONS

A bulk of researchers have studied organizational change; however, the world has not witnessed such a major change and the change of such magnitude as this pandemic has been in the last century. This pandemic has not only been able to brought in the threats and opportunities for the businesses but has also been able to change the way of thinking of the people across the globe. Furthermore, the pandemic and the resultant work from home policies in organizations have made it look that majority of the activities or tasks that businesses were performing were either useless or redundant in nature. Therefore, there exists a need to develop a mechanism that can help organizations in identifying and eliminating the redundant practices. Hence, future researchers who are interested in studying the change should first focus developing a mechanism on eliminating the non-critical tasks that are eating up the much-needed capital.

REFERENCES

Abbott, K. W., Green, J. F., & Keohane, R. O. (2016). Organizational ecology and institutional change in global governance. *International Organization*, *70*(2), 247–277. doi:10.1017/S0020818315000338

Albrecht, S. L. (2002). Perceptions of integrity, competence and trust in senior management as determinants of cynicism toward change. *Public Administration and Management: An Interactive Journal*, *7*(4), 320–343.

Aldrich, H. E., & Pfeffer, J. (1976). Environments of organizations. *Annual Review of Sociology*, *2*(1), 79–105. doi:10.1146/annurev.so.02.080176.000455

Aldrich, H. E., & Ruef, M. (2006). *Organizations Evolving* (2nd ed.). Sage.

Amiot, C., Terry, D., Jimmieson, N., & Callan, V. (2006). A longitudinal investigation of coping processes during a merger: Implications for job satisfaction and organizational iden-tification. *Journal of Management*, *32*(4), 552–574. doi:10.1177/0149206306287542

Andriopoulos, C., & Dawson, P. (2009). *Managing Change, Creativity and Innovation*. Sage.

Armenakis, A. A., & Bedeian, A. G. (1999). Organizational change: A review of theory and research in the 1990s. *Journal of Management*, *25*(3), 293–315. doi:10.1177/014920639902500303

Armenakis, A. A., Harris, S. G., & Feild, H. S. (2000). Making change permanent a model for institutionalizing change interventions. *Research in Organizational Change and Development*, *12*, 97–128. doi:10.1016/S0897-3016(99)12005-6

Ashford, S. J. (1988). Individual strategies for coping with stress during organizational transi-tions. *The Journal of Applied Behavioral Science*, *24*(1), 19–36. doi:10.1177/0021886388241005

Bartunek, J. M., & Moch, M. K. (1987). First-order, second-order, and third-order change and organization development interventions: A cognitive approach. *The Journal of Applied Behavioral Science*, *23*(4), 483–500. doi:10.1177/002188638702300404

Baum, J. A. C., & McKelvey, B. (Eds.). (1999). *Variations in Organization Science: In honour of Donald T. Campbell*. Sage.

Burgelman, R. A. (1991). Interorganizational ecology of strategy making and organizational adaptation: Theory and field research. *Organization Science*, *2*(3), 239–262. doi:10.1287/orsc.2.3.239

Burke, W. W. (2008). Organization Change: Theory and Practice (2nd ed.). Los Angeles, CA: Sage.

Burnes, B. (2004). *Managing change: A strategic approach to organisational dynamics*. Pearson Education.

Campbell, D. T. (1969). Variation and selective retention in socio-cultural evolution. *General Systems*, *16*, 69–85.

Carr, D., Hard, K., & Trahant, W. (1996). *Managing the Change Process: A Field Book for Change Agents, Consultants, Team Leaders, and Reengineering Managers*. McGraw-Hill.

Chappell, S., Pescud, M., Waterworth, P., Shilton, T., Roche, D., Ledger, M., & Rosenberg, M. (2016). Exploring the process of implementing healthy workplace initiatives: Mapping to Kotter's leading change model. *Journal of Occupational and Environmental Medicine*, *58*(10), 341–348. doi:10.1097/JOM.0000000000000854 PMID:27525528

Child, J. (1972). Organizational structure, environment and performance: The role of strategic choice. *Sociology*, *6*(1), 1–22. doi:10.1177/003803857200600101

Collins, D. (1998). *Organizational Change: Sociological Perspectives London*. Routledge.

Cooney, M. A., Pernick, J., Rice, K., & Monago, E. A. (2016). Utilization of Change Theory to Implement an Appreciative Advising Model. *Journal of Research, Assessment, and Practice in Higher Education*, *1*(1), 21–25.

Covin, T. J., Sightler, K. W., Kolenko, T. A., & Tudor, K. R. (1996). An investigation of post-acquisition satisfaction with the merger. *The Journal of Applied Behavioral Science*, *32*(2), 125–142. doi:10.1177/0021886396322001

Coyle-Shapiro, J. A., & Morrow, P. C. (2003). The role of individual differences in employee adoption of TQM orientation. *Journal of Vocational Behavior*, *62*(2), 320–340. doi:10.1016/S0001-8791(02)00041-6

Cummings, T. G., & Huse, E. F. (1989). *Organization Development and Change* (4th ed.). West Publishing.

Cummings, T. G., & Worley, C. G. (2009). *Organization Development and Change*. Cengage Learning.

Cunningham, G. B. (2006). The relationships among commitment to change, coping with change, and turnover intentions. *European Journal of Work and Organizational Psychology*, *15*(1), 29–45. doi:10.1080/13594320500418766

Dawson, P. (1994). *Organizational Change: A Processual Approach. Paul Chapman Publishing*.

Demers, C. (2007). *Organizational Change Theories: A Synthesis*. Sage.

Devos, G., Buelens, M., & Bouckenooghe, D. (2007). Contribution of content, context, and process to understanding openness to organizational change: Two experimental simulation studies. *The Journal of Social Psychology*, *147*(6), 607–630. doi:10.3200/SOCP.147.6.607-630 PMID:18314790

Dunphy, D., & Stace, D. (1993). The strategic management of corporate change. *Human Relations*, *46*(8), 905–920. doi:10.1177/001872679304600801

Dunphy, D. C., & Stace, D. A. (1988). Transformational and coercive strategies for planned organizational change: Beyond the OD model. *Organization Studies*, *9*(3), 317–334. doi:10.1177/017084068800900302

Eby, L. T., Adams, D. M., Russell, J. E., & Gaby, S. H. (2000). Perceptions of organizational readiness for change: Factors related to employees' reactions to the implementation of team-based selling. *Human Relations*, *53*(3), 419–442. doi:10.1177/0018726700533006

Eby, L. T., Adams, D. M., Russell, J. E. A., & Gaby, S. H. (2000). Perceptions of organiza-tional readiness for change: Factors related to employees' reactions to the implementation of team-based selling. *Human Relations*, *53*(3), 419–442. doi:10.1177/0018726700533006

French, W. L., & Bell, C. (1999). Organization development: Behavioral Science Interventions for Organization Improvement. Auflage: Prentice Hall.

Graetz, F., & Smith, A. C. (2010). *Managing organizational change: A philosophies of change*. Academic Press.

Greiner, L. E. (1972). Evolution and Revolution as Organizations Grow. *Harvard Business Review, 50*(4), 37-46. https://ssrn.com/abstract=1504482

Guo, C., & Acar, M. (2005). Understanding collaboration among non-profit organizations: Combining resource dependency, institutional, and network perspectives. *Nonprofit and Voluntary Sector Quarterly*, *34*(3), 340–361. doi:10.1177/0899764005275411

Hannan, M. T., & Freeman, J. (1977). The population ecology of organizations. *American Journal of Sociology*, *82*(5), 929–964. doi:10.1086/226424

Hatcher, L., & Ross, T. L. (1991). From individual incentives to an organization-wide gainsharing plan: Effects on teamwork and product quality. *Journal of Organizational Behavior*, *12*(3), 169–183. doi:10.1002/job.4030120302

Hirsch, P. M., & Lounsbury, M. (1997). Putting the organization back into organization theory: Action, change, and the" new" institutionalism. *Journal of Management Inquiry*, *6*(1), 79–88. doi:10.1177/105649269761015

Hock, D. (1999). *Birth of the Chaordic Age*. Berrett-Koehler Publishers.

Hodges, J., & Gill, R. (2014). *Sustaining Change in Organizations*. Sage.

Holt, D. T., Armenakis, A. A., Feild, H. S., & Harris, S. G. (2007). Readiness for organizational change the systematic development of a scale. *The Journal of Applied Behavioral Science*, *43*(2), 232–255. doi:10.1177/0021886306295295

Jacobs, G., van Witteloostuijn, A., & Christe-Zeyse, J. (2013). A theoretical framework of organizational change. *Journal of Organizational Change Management*, *26*(5), 772–792. doi:10.1108/JOCM-09-2012-0137

Johns, G. (2006). The essential impact of context on organizational behaviour. *Academy of Management Review*, *31*(2), 386–408. doi:10.5465/amr.2006.20208687

Jones, G. R., & George, J. M. (1998). The experience and evolution of trust: Implications for cooperation and teamwork. *Academy of Management Review*, *23*(3), 531–546. doi:10.5465/amr.1998.926625

Jones, G. R., & Jones, G. R. (2013). *Organizational Theory, Design, and Change*. Pearson.

Kezar, A. (2001). Understanding and facilitating organizational change in the 21st century. *ASHE-ERIC Higher Education Report*, *28*(4), 147.

Kiefer, T. (2005). Feeling bad: Antecedents and consequences of negative emotions in ongoing change. *Journal of Organizational Behavior*, *26*(8), 875–897. doi:10.1002/job.339

Korsgaard, M. A., Sapienza, H. J., & Schweiger, D. M. (2002). Beaten before begun: The role of procedural justice in planning change. *Journal of Management*, *28*(4), 497–516. doi:10.1177/014920630202800402

Kotter, J. P. (1995). Leading change: Why transformation efforts fail. *Harvard Business Review*, *73*(2), 59–67.

Kotter, J. P. (1996). *Leading change*. Harvard Business Press.

Kuipers, B. S., Higgs, M., Kickert, W., Tummers, L., Grandia, J., & Van der Voet, J. (2014). The management of change in public organizations: A literature review. *Public Administration*, *92*(1), 1–20. doi:10.1111/padm.12040

Kulkarni, V. (2017). Contingency Theory. In *The International Encyclopedia of Organizational Communication* (pp. 1–6). John Wiley & Sons, Inc. doi:10.1002/9781118955567.wbieoc041

Langton, J. (1979). Darwinism and the behavioural theory of sociocultural evolution: An analysis. *American Journal of Sociology*, *85*(2), 288–309. doi:10.1086/227011

Latona, J. C., & La Van, H. (1993). Implementation of an employee involvement program in a small, emerging high-technology firm. *Journal of Organizational Change Management*, *6*(4), 17–29. doi:10.1108/09534819310042713

Lester, D. L., Parnell, J. A., & Carraher, S. (2003). Organizational life cycle: A five-stage empirical scale. *The International Journal of Organizational Analysis*, *11*(4), 339–354. doi:10.1108/eb028979

Levy, A., & Merry, U. (1986). *Organizational Transformation: Approaches, Strategies, Theories*. Greenwood Publishing Group.

Lewin, K. (1947). Frontiers in group dynamics II. Channels of group life; social planning and action research. *Human Relations*, *1*(2), 143–153. doi:10.1177/001872674700100201

Logan, M. S., & Ganster, D. C. (2007). The effects of empowerment on attitudes and perfor-mance: The role of social support and empowerment beliefs. *Journal of Management Studies*, *44*, 1523–1550.

Lok, P., Hung, R. Y., Walsh, P., Wang, P., & Crawford, J. (2005). An integrative framework for measuring the extent to which organizational variables influence the success of process improvement programmes. *Journal of Management Studies*, *42*(7), 1357–1381. doi:10.1111/j.1467-6486.2005.00547.x

Madsen, S. R., Miller, D., & John, C. R. (2005). Readiness for organizational change: Do organizational commitment and social relationships in the workplace make a difference? *Human Resource Development Quarterly*, *16*(2), 213–233. doi:10.1002/hrdq.1134

Malatesta, D., & Smith, C. R. (2014). Lessons from resource dependence theory for contemporary public and non-profit management. *Public Administration Review*, *74*(1), 14–25. doi:10.1111/puar.12181

Marie-Pier, R. (2017). *What Are the Five Contemporary Organizational Theory Models?* Bizfluent. Retrieved from https://bizfluent.com/info-8544476-five-contemporary organizational-theory models.html

Mdletye, M. A., Coetzee, J., & Ukpere, W. I. (2013). Emotional Reactions to the Experiences of Transformational Change: Evidence from the Department of Correctional Services of South Africa. *Mediterranean Journal of Social Sciences*, *4*(14), 501–518. doi:10.5901/mjss.2013.v4n14p501

Miller, D., & Friesen, P. H. (1984). A longitudinal study of the corporate life cycle. *Management Science*, *30*(10), 1161–1183. doi:10.1287/mnsc.30.10.1161

Miner, E. R. (1990). *Comparative poetics: An Intercultural Essay on Theories of Literature*. Princeton University Press.

Moran, J. W., & Brightman, B. K. (2001). Leading organizational change. *Career Development International*, *6*(2), 111–119.

Morgan, G. (1997). *Imaginization: New Mindsets for Seeing, Organizing, and Managing*. Berrett-Koehler Publishers.

Morgeson, F. P., Johnson, M. D., Campion, M. A., Medsker, G. J., & Mumford, T. V. (2006). Understanding Reactions to Job Redesign: A Quasi-Experimental Investigation of the Moderating Effects of Organizational Context On Perceptions of Performance Behaviour. *Personnel Psychology*, *59*(2), 333–363. doi:10.1111/j.1744-6570.2006.00941.x

Oreg, S. (2006). Personality, context, and resistance to organizational change. *European Journal of Work and Organizational Psychology*, *15*(1), 73–101. doi:10.1080/13594320500451247

Oreg, S., Vakola, M., & Armenakis, A. (2011). Change recipients' reactions to organizational change: A 60-year review of quantitative studies. *The Journal of Applied Behavioral Science, 47*(4), 461–524. doi:10.1177/0021886310396550

Pettigrew, A. M. (1985). *Awakening Giant: Continuity and Change in Imperial Chemical Industries*. Blackwell.

Pfeffer, J., & Salancik, G. R. (2003). *The External Control of Organizations: A Resource Dependence Perspective*. Stanford University Press.

Pichault, F. (2007). HRM-based reforms in public organizations: Problems and perspectives. *Human Resource Management Journal, 17*(3), 265–282. doi:10.1111/j.1748-8583.2007.00041.x

Rafferty, A. E., & Restubog, S. L. D. (2010). The impact of change process and context on change reactions and turnover during a merger. *Journal of Management, 36*(5), 1309–1338. doi:10.1177/0149206309341480

Reg, S., & van Dam, K. (2009). Organisational justice in the context of organisational change. *Netherlands Journal of Psychology, 65*, 127–135.

Sammut-Bonnici, T., & Wensley, R. (2002). Darwinism, probability and complexity: Market-based organizational transformation and change explained through the theories of evolution. *International Journal of Management Reviews, 4*(3), 291–315.

Sashkin, M., & Burke, W. W. (1987). Organization development in the 1980's. *Journal of Management, 13*(2), 393–417.

Schein, E. H. (1996). Kurt Lewin's change theory in the field and in the classroom: Notes toward a model of managed learning. *Systems Practice, 9*(1), 27–47.

Schwarz, G. M. (2012). Shaking fruit out of the tree: Temporal effects and life cycle in organizational change research. *The Journal of Applied Behavioral Science, 48*(3), 342–379.

Self, D. R., Armenakis, A. A., & Schraeder, M. (2007). Organizational change content, process, and context: A simultaneous analysis of employee reactions. *Journal of Change Management, 7*(2), 211–229.

Shapiro, D. L., & Kirkman, B. L. (1999). Employees' reaction to the change to work teams: The influence of "anticipatory" injustice. *Journal of Organizational Change Management, 12*, 51–67.

Sowa, J. E. (2009). The collaboration decision in non-profit organizations: Views from the front line. *Nonprofit and Voluntary Sector Quarterly, 38*(6), 1003–1025.

Stanley, D. J., Meyer, J. P., & Topolnytsky, L. (2005). Employee cynicism and resistance to organizational change. *Journal of Business and Psychology, 19*(4), 429–459.

Vakola, M., & Nikolaou, I. (2005). Attitudes towards organizational change: What is the role of employees' stress and commitment? *Employee Relations, 27*(2), 160–174.

Van de Ven, A. H., & Poole, M. S. (1995). Explaining development and change in organizations. *Academy of Management Review, 20*(3), 510–540.

Van de Ven, A. H., & Sun, K. (2011). Breakdowns in implementing models of organization change. *The Academy of Management Perspectives, 25*(3), 58–74.

Van der Voet, J. (2015). Change leadership and public sector organizational change: Examining the interactions of transformational leadership style and red tape. *American Review of Public Administration, 46*, 660–682.

Van der Voet, J., Kuipers, B. S., & Groeneveld, S. (2015). Implementing change in public organizations: The relationship between leadership and affective commitment to change in a public sector context. *Public Management Review, 18*, 842–865.

Vogt, W. P., & Johnson, R. B. (2011). *Dictionary of statistics & methodology: a nontechnical guide for the social sciences: a nontechnical guide for the social sciences*. Sage.

Walker, J. H., Armenakis, A. A., & Bernerth, J. B. (2007). Factors influencing organizational change efforts: An integrative investigation of change content, context, process and indi-vidual differences. *Journal of Organizational Change Management, 20*, 761–773.

Wanberg, C. R., & Banas, J. T. (2000). Predictors and outcomes of openness to changes in a reorganizing workplace. *The Journal of Applied Psychology, 85*, 132–142.

Weick, K. E., & Quinn, R. E. (1999). Organizational change and development. *Annual Review of Psychology, 50*(1), 361–386.

Wetzel, R., & Van Gorp, L. (2014). Eighteen shades of grey? An explorative literature review into the theoretical flavours of organizational change research. *Journal of Organizational Change Management, 27*(1), 115–146.

Woodman, R. W. (1989). Organizational change and development: New arenas for inquiry and action. *Journal of Management, 15*(2), 205–228.

KEY TERMS AND DEFINITIONS

Change Agent: A person who helps in transformation of an organization for improvement and its development.

Cycle Theory: Society and history events generally repeat in cycles.

Incremental Change: (First Order) Incremental change pointed out the less-drastic and small-scale transformation that helps the organization to improve its efficiency and overcome inactiveness.

Organization Change: It is a process of changing structure, culture, technology, processes, or techniques.

Organization Culture: Includes principles and activities that contribute to environment of an organization.

Radical Change: Change that occurs relatively fast and adapts the principle of organizational practices.

Transformational Change: (Second Order) Referred as revolutionary or strategic change impacts the organizational structure and the critical areas that form the organizational structure are culture, power distance, strategy, and control system.

Chapter 9
Innovation Leading Organizations

André Nogueira
Portuguese Naval Academy, Portugal

Pedro B. Agua
https://orcid.org/0000-0003-1886-9938
Portuguese Naval Academy, Portugal

Anacleto C. Correia
https://orcid.org/0000-0002-7248-4310
Portuguese Naval Academy, Portugal

ABSTRACT

Innovation is one of the most likely factors to boost effectiveness, efficiency, and sustainability of an organization, regardless of its sector of activity, as for instance, the armed forces. The absence of innovation can affect the organizations in different ways, from suboptimal operational effectiveness and improvement of organization processes (administrative, operational, or logistics), bringing with it negative impacts on human resources motivation – the main keepers of knowledge, institutional culture, and organizational values. Innovative organizations also generate a stronger sense of belonging across their ranks and structures and fosters effectiveness in fulfilling organizations' missions. Hence, fostering innovation across any typology of organization is crucial and requires a proper approach to promote the desirable involvement of the entire workforce. This text, based on a review of some relevant literature, exposes critical enabling factors. Based on a cause-and-effect analysis, it proposes some recommendations for the practitioner as well as the academic.

DOI: 10.4018/978-1-7998-2807-5.ch009

INTRODUCTION

Nowadays, organisations need to add value to their assets, as to be profitable they need to reduce expenditure. After so many budget reductions, however, this approach does not look like an option anymore for many organizations. To respond to the needed increase in value, a new trend has emerged – innovation - specifically innovation whose source are the employees themselves.

Despite the will to innovate, not all organisations are able to do so, that is, the more traditional organisations do not normally cultivate a culture that facilitates innovation. Therefore, this text presents some ideas for organising for innovation in such a way that organizations may become more innovative. Hence, incentives, new forms of communication, values to be taken into account by the leadership, are suggested in starting this task of making their organisations more innovative. Literature and research points to two essential factors for the success of innovation in an organisation: (1) an innovation process suitable to the needs of the organisation, and (2) a culture that facilitates innovation.

The Theory of Constraints (TOC), a methodology based on logic and cause-effect, is used to arrive at some solutions. TOC provides a set of tools, *Thinking Processes,* which help in analysing the system under study through a sequence of logic diagrams, named logic trees. Hence, the current state of the organization (i.e., system of interest) is analysed, then solutions to the system are presented and, finally, the requirements to implement such solutions are verified.

In order to respond to the challenge posed, this chapter is divided into four parts. besides this introductory section, where the need to address the topic of organising for innovation is introduced, as well as the solution design method, section two addresses some key background. The third section summarises the used methodology. In the fourth section the solutions will be presented and justified. Finally, a conclusion provides some remarks.

BACKGROUND

Innovation may have distinct definitions, however, it is undoubtedly about challenging the *status quo* and introducing new and better products, processes, services or management approaches that add value (Deschamps, 2008). Innovation is a capability that is evident in an innovative organisation, and distinguish them from others, by constantly seeking change through innovative solutions to the problems and challenges presented to them.

When an organisation seeks the ability to innovate, it should design and implement a strategy aiming at better results than the current state (Looy et al.,

2005). These outcomes will foster innovations that add value to the organisation after implementation (Miller & Brankovic, 2010). They can, however, be differentiated taking into account the type of innovation the organisation is aiming for. That is, incremental or radical innovations may arise. According to Tushman and O'Reilly (2004), incremental innovation consists of small improvements to existing products and operations. These will make their use more efficient and add value to the organisation. On the other hand, if the organisation seeks radical innovation, it must select ideas that have the power to change the basis of competitive advantage and alter the economic structure of the industry (Skarzynski & Gibson, 2008).

An enterprise may be organised in such a way that the two types of innovation can coexist. Looy et al. (2005), proposes the term *ambidextrous organisations,* to refer to organisations consisting of two structures, where each one deals with one type of innovation. Hence, one of the structures focuses on incremental innovation, where commitment, convergence and dependence of actions is required. The second structure, which is dedicated to radical innovation, is designed to be more flexible, divergent and explore new paths. According to Tushman and O'Reilly (2004) ambidextrous organisations may be the solution because there is no contamination effect, but rather fertilisation, from the radical to the incremental structure. According to Looy et al. (2005), however, such organisations may be at a disadvantage because they are quickly overtaken by competition that focus on just one approach.

Innovation can also be focused on processes, products or business models. Process innovation is associated with the introduction of new elements into the production or service operations in order to increase efficiency (Çokpekin & Knudsen, 2012). Regarding product innovation, this is defined by new technologies or combination of technologies introduced at a commercial level to meet a user or market need. Innovation at the business model level is defined as a new creative way of doing the business by the organization (Deschamps, 2008).

Structuring an organisation so that it can be more innovative can be carried out in two different ways. These are more effective when executed simultaneously, since they complement each other. The first way to stimulate innovation is from the top to bottom of the organisation, through leadership, and the second being a bottom-up approach. In the first approach it requires organisational discipline, imposed by leadership through the innovation process, while in the second approach of stimulus is intrinsic to creativity and innovative cultures, and is promoted by employees.

An innovative culture has the members of the organisation, individually or in groups, coming up with innovative solutions to existing problems (Miller & Brankovic, 2010). According to Deschamps (2008) an innovative culture is one of exploration, experimentation and entrepreneurship, and where there is an emphasis on learning, optimisation, knowledge sharing (Love et al., 2007) together with tolerance for failure and risk acceptance (Cheltenham, 2016).

Creativity predominates within innovative organisation, and is an effect of the freedom which is normally experienced in such environments (Boeddrich, 2004; Çokpekin & Knudsen, 2012). Creativity is the source of ideas, and without ideas there will be no innovation (Boeddrich, 2004). Nowadays, ideas have several origins, due to the fact that people are more connected, and consequently share their knowledge faster and more frequently (Água & Correia, 2020). In this way several types of innovation have emerged, taking into account the source of ideas: (1) collaborative innovation (Bogers et al., 2016; Ollila & Yström, 2016), open innovation (Back et al., 2019; Goglio-Primard & Crespin-Mazet, 2015; Tushman et al., 2012; Winsor et al., 2019) and worker-driven innovation (Tirabeni et al., 2016).

Each source corresponds to an endeavour where freedom is provided, sharing and communication exists, and where networks were formed. These networks give rise to ideas, which after going through the whole innovation process are transformed into innovations (Mascia et al., 2015). Such networks lead to the creation of so-called innovation networks, which are structures that support the development and implementation of innovations through cooperation and coordination (Goglio-Primard & Crespin-Mazet, 2015).

Leadership is fundamental for innovation to succeed within the organisation, which may be helped by transformational leadership (Ashoor, 2021). Therefore, it is critical to select leaders with the right qualities to take the lead in innovation in the organisation. Such qualities include: (1) acceptance of risk, failure and uncertainty, (2) commitment to the mission of innovation, (3) influence within the organisation, and (4) trust in employees providing them the adequate freedom. According to Deschamps (2008), to lead innovative organizations, it is necessary to give a purpose to innovation, to give a direction to the employees, and to introduce a sense of focus.

In order to introduce the values of innovation, leadership has to build a vision to the organization according and provide evidence to the employees that the decision-making processes are in line with innovation (Palmisano et al., 2005). With this stance leaders will create a culture based on the values, attitudes, policies and processes they practice (Deschamps, 2008; Schmiedel et al., 2017; Sull et al., 2020).

An innovative culture is based on the values of creativity, improvisation, trust, humility, reward and collaboration, which should be stimulated by the leadership. Therefore, creativity and improvisation should be enhanced by the freedom that leadership should provide to employees. Collaboration should be promoted by increasing interactions among employees, especially those who are physically distant. Reward and trust should be fostered by leadership by encouraging innovative initiatives and allocating resources to them, showing the organization's trust on employees who experiment and explore.

Another important factor in making a culture more innovative is related to training on innovation. It is essential to explain to employees the importance of innovation in creating value for the organisation. It is also necessary to show employees the facilities that the organisation has in the innovation area, specifically the steps inherent to the established innovation process. Within the organisation the levels of innovation training may be different, so that all employees should have basic training, while training should be more intense according to the involvement across the innovation structure of the organisation.

The innovation process is the stimulus from the top to the bottom of the organisation, regarding the objective of organising for innovation. Each organisation should have its own innovation process, i.e., rules and steps suitable to its needs and aligned to its objectives. The innovation process is a balance between supporting the quality of ideas and directing the focus of employees' creativity towards the organisation's goals (Ende et al., 2015). Despite the dynamics and due adaptation to each organization, all processes should have three distinct stages: (1) idea solicitation, (2) idea selection and (3) innovation implementation. These phases shall be transparent and structured, without restricting creativity or discouraging innovators (Boeddrich, 2004).

The first stage in the innovation process, idea gathering, supports the rest of the process by keeping a sustainable flow of ideas (Boeddrich, 2004). Leadership should promote such flow through incentives, rewards, and competition; however, it is not healthy for the flow to put too much pressure on sources of ideas because it can counteract creativity, and consequently the ideas may be of little value (Manso, 2017). Hence, it is critical to provide time for employees to share knowledge, explore and experiment their ideas or recombine them with other employees, as Google already does by providing 20% of time for its employees to work on new ideas. Mandal, (2020) research also supports this standing. Hence, it is necessary to manage the portfolio of ideas, starting by defining the strategic lines that guide the ideas, by predefining criteria to select ideas.

Since the main sources of innovation in organisations are their frontline employees, or those who are in contact with customers, it is important to support such personnel in their innovation initiatives. Hence, the figure of "innovation champions" is becoming common. These champions are people qualified in innovation and who help other employees to progress their ideas through the innovation process. As a result, employee' motivation will increase because they feel supported and will come up with more new ideas. Innovation champions help speed up the innovation process, accelerating it through idea gathering and selection.

The second stage involves the selection of ideas, according to predefined criteria. This stage is important due to resources allocation for those ideas that are in line with the organizational objectives. The first factor in selecting ideas should be the content, i.e., whether the idea is in line with what is intended by the organisation. To this end, the organisation should communicate to its stakeholders what the objectives and criteria for the ideas are. The second factor is to map ideas on a risk matrix, where ideas shown as too risky should be removed from the innovation process (Day, 2007; Jay, 2016). The risk associated with an idea, is related to the number of resources an organisation is willing to spend on it, and the added value of the idea. The third factor is the experimentation of the idea itself, that is, testing the idea in "islands of experimentation" a concept which promotes rapid learning and resource savings by experimenting with innovations in smaller units (Rao & Weintraub, 2013).

The acceptance of innovations by customers or employees is essential in the implementation stage, and may be an obstacle. Implementation brings uncertainty, and a difficult part of transforming an organisation to become more innovative is cultural resistance. Therefore, it is sometimes necessary to create an environment of constant change, which demands leadership to take the initiative. Leading change within organisations is an operation that takes into account many variables, and initiatives must be planned in advance so that the process takes place gradually. Kotter (2012) listed eight essential steps for effective change management:

1. Establish a sense of urgency
2. Create a leading coalition
3. Develop a vision and strategy
4. Communicate the vision of change
5. Empower others to act according to the vision
6. Plan and create quick wins
7. Consolidate improvements and bring about more change
8. Institutionalise new approaches in organisational culture

METHODOLOGICAL APPROACH

The used methodology to develop solutions is the Theory of Constraints. This methodology uses cause and effect logic chains to optimise systems in accordance with a previously determined objective. By system it is meant any organisation, department or section. Any system may have problems, which may originate from constraints, and prevent it from achieving its objectives or goals. TOC tools are known as *Thinking Processes,* which through basic questions investigate and identify a system's constraints, find solutions to eliminate them, and help speed up their implementation.

TOC basic questions are: (1) "Why Change?", (2) "What to change?", (3) "What to change to?" and (4) "How to cause the change?". Moreover, the *Thinking Processes* help in finding a flexible strategy, easy to understand by all employees of an organisation (Cox III & Robinson, 2017). The graphs used are known as logic trees, which reflect the logical connections across the system of interest, which help identifying the constraints to be eliminated, and implementing the solutions found. Each tree type is associated with a question, which in turn corresponds to a step in the process (Dettmer, 2000). Table 1 shows the relationship between the steps of the model, the basic questions and the logic trees.

Table 1. Relationship between the steps of the model, the basic questions and the logic trees, (Dettmer, 2000)

Steps of the Dettmer Model	Basic questions	Logic Trees
1.Defining the paradigm	Why change?	IO-MAP
2. Analyse the differences	What to change?	CRT
3. Creating changes	What to change to?	CDR
4. Designing the future	What to change to?	FRT
5. Planning the implementation	How to cause the change?	PRT
6. Implementing the strategy	How to cause the change?	TT

Logic trees are applied in order to carry out a complete analysis of a complex system, providing a path towards change by answering the basic questions (Mabin, 1999). Originally, Goldratt conceived only five types of trees: the Current Reality tree (CRT), the Conflict Resolution Diagram (CRD), the Future Reality Tree (FRT), the Prerequisite Tree (PRT) and the Transition Tree (TT). However, later Dettmer (2011), added the Intermediate Objectives Map (IOMAP).

Trees are based on two types of logic. Sufficiency logic which is derived from cause-effect, expressing its relationships through "If...then..." is used in the CRT, FRT and TT. Arrows indicating the logical relationships between the conditions are used in the construction of these trees. The second type of logic used is the logic of necessity, which is done when setting necessary conditions to achieve something. This logic uses the language "In order to reach A we must have B". PRT and CRD use this type of logic (Dettmer, 1998).

When analysing a system through cause-and-effect relationships it is necessary to have a deep knowledge of the system. The more knowledge one has about the system, the easier it is to identify its constraints, and to make a more accurate prediction about the impact of a decision on the system. Cause-and-effect logics used in trees differs from correlation. On the one hand, cause-and-effect is the verifiable relationship between an element, condition or action that causes another to arise, when the latter would not have occurred by itself. On the other hand, correlation is the observation of a change when another change occurs, which does not mean that there is a causal relationship established between the two recorded events (Dettmer, 1998).

To test the logical relationships embedded in the trees, the Categories of Legitimate Reservation (CLR) are used. CLRs test the logic in the trees by examining meaning, legitimacy and clarity of the existing entities, relations and assumptions (Mabin et al., 2006). This test consists of eight rules, upon which trees should be built and reviewed (Dettmer, 1998).

In this chapter, only the CRT, FRT and PRT types will be used. Since the objective is to make organisations more innovative, the IO-Map is dispensed. Regarding the TT, it has to be adapted, like all the others, to the reality of each organisation, however, it needs a temporal analysis that should be done by the organisation's leadership.

The *Current Reality Tree* is the beginning of the logical analysis sequence. The representation of current reality in a diagram makes it possible to clarify what is preventing the system from achieving its goal. Hence, undesired effects emerge which will give rise to root causes through cause-effect links. Therefore, to achieve the objective it is necessary to eliminate the root causes, which by its side will allow the system to achieve desirable effects. This will enable the building of the *Future Reality Tree*, the tree that follows in the logical sequence of system's analysis. Having concluded the first phase, "What to change?", it is necessary to move on to the question of "What to change to?", where the system's change strategy is idealised. The construction of the *Future Reality Tree* involves actions named as "injections", which are solutions found, through creativity, conflict resolution or by eliminating root causes. The injections allow the system to achieve the desirable effects and, consequently, the main goal.

The last tree in the logical sequence is the *Pre-Requisite Tree,* this corresponds to the question of "How to cause the change?". This diagram intends to demonstrate the necessary conditions, as well as the obstacles, to which each injection is subject. The implementation of the injections is more robust if it takes into account the conditions mentioned in the *Pre-Requisite Trees.* To build these trees, it shall be taken into account all the factors inherent to the implementation of envisioned. Thus, a form of verification, may be the frame DOTMLPFI (Doctrine, Organization, Training, Material, Leadership, Personnel, Facilities and Interoperability); used in order to clarify if additional constraints will be in the way of the identified solution.

Diagnosing an Organization Innovation Capability

This text presents a systems analysis, considering organisations as the system of interest, that want to become more innovative. Therefore, the aim is to suggest solutions applicable to any organisation, regardless of some needed tailoring on a case-by-case basis. In formalizing solutions, it is first necessary to analyse the current state of the system of interest, in this case organisations that intend to become more innovative. Hence, the first tree to be built is the CRT, which starts by the identification of the undesired effects, i.e., events currently occurring in the organisation that prevent it from achieving the goal. In this case, the goal is to promote the systematic capacity to innovate throughout the organisation. Therefore, a core question is related to what, in most organisations, prevents this objective from being achieved.

Identifiable unwanted effects are typically as follows:

1. Culture that does not facilitate innovation
2. Incomplete innovation processes
3. Collaborative innovation with little impact on problem solving
4. Values followed by the organisation have little aligned with innovation
5. Leadership misaligned with innovation
6. Unclear internal communication regarding the objectives defined for innovation
7. Lack of innovation training

The initiative to make an organisation more innovative has to come from the leadership, however it should be a task in which all employees should be involved. Hence, the organization's leadership team should be the first part of the company's structure to adopt behaviours and values that are aligned with innovation. If the leadership team does not make decisions that have the values of innovation into account, then these values do not pass to the lower hierarchical levels, so the organisation is not align with the values of innovation culture. Such, is identified as an undesired effect, whenever the values followed by the organisation are poorly aligned with innovation.

In order to design a strategy to make organisations more innovative, it is necessary that the leadership team presents and clarifies its objectives to the whole organisation. In this way, all employees and *stakeholders* will be aware of them and, consequently, they will all head in the same direction. Clear internal communication is essential so that information is conveyed by all and quickly. If internal communication is not clear and effective, the information does not reach all employees and *stakeholders, which* undermines the dissemination of the objectives set by the leadership team.

Lack of innovation training is another impediment for organisations in achieving the capability of innovating systematically. Innovation training is essential to shape the actions of employees, as well as their abilities to solve problems in different, more innovative ways. Such training in innovation, should initially be done outside the organisation, where the scholar and specialists in this field are located. However, when the innovation maturity level of the organisation becomes higher and the innovation process is properly implemented, the training should be provided inside the organisation. This is important because all employees should have a minimum knowledge level about innovation and know the platforms and processes that the organisation has for valuing their ideas.

If all employees have innovation knowledge and know the organisation's enablers to value their ideas, then their contributions will add value to the organisation by solving problems in innovative ways. However, collaborative innovation has been found to have little impact on problem solving. This unintended effect undermines employee motivation and the achievement of the main goal. If employees are not taken into account in the problem-solving process, then the difficulty in solving such problems will be greater and consequently no value will be added to the organisation.

Given these undesired effects, it can be stated that in many organisations there is a culture that does not facilitate innovation, which greatly hinders the achievement of objectives. Without any kind of training in innovation it is difficult to build an innovation process that is able to comply with the three phases (gathering, selection and implementation of ideas). Hence, the innovation process is incomplete and the achievement of the goal is compromised.

1. Vertical communication is not clear about innovation
2. The objectives for innovation are not clearly displayed to all employees
3. Little expressive *networking* in connecting employees
4. Little use is made of multifunctional and multidisciplinary teams
5. Existence of conservatism in the face of risk
6. Low fault tolerance
7. Islands of experimentation concept not implemented
8. Initial resistance to innovations from employees
9. Absence of "innovation champions"
10. Little publicised recognition mechanisms for innovative initiatives
11. Little encouragement for the exposure of ideas

The identified root causes represent the constraints that prevent a system from achieving its goal. In this sense, they are the answer to the question "What to change?".

A critical root cause often at play is the vertical communication about innovation, that may not be done clearly (Figure 1). A second common root cause is the inability to expose the objectives for innovation to all employees. Together these two root causes give rise to unclear internal communication about the objectives defined for innovation, which is an undesirable effect.

Another set of root causes worth mentioning is about organizational connection and knowledge sharing, essential for creativity, which in turn is essential for ideas to emerge. When employees are more connected, more and better ideas will be exposed to the innovation process. Oftentimes organizations provide few facilities

Figure 1. Current Reality Tree of a non-innovative organisation.Once the undesired effects (UDE) have been detected, it is necessary to make logical connections that enable the identification of the root causes responsible for the current state of an organisation. The following list suggests some common root causes:

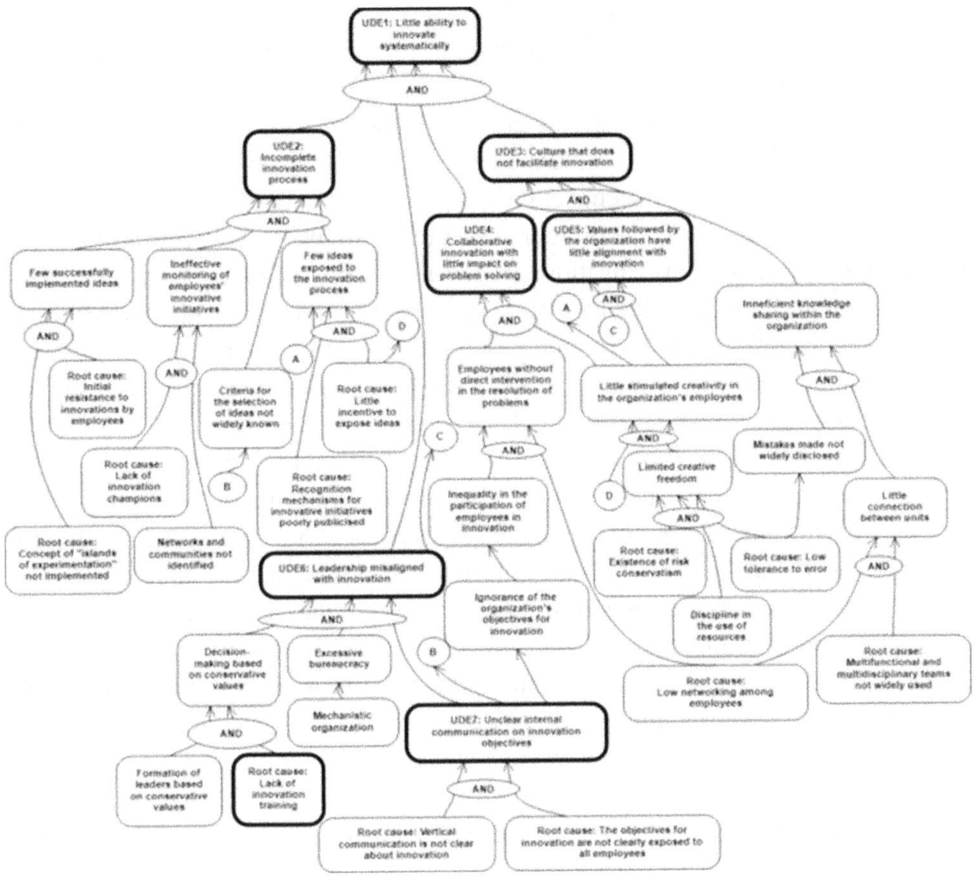

to their employees to connect and share knowledge with quality, time and quickly. Hence, suggested root causes are a little expressive use of networking in connecting employees and the lack of multidisciplinary and multifunctional teams that gather regularly. These teams are used by organisations with proven innovative potential and tend to produce quick results with greater quality.

The leadership team's posture towards innovative initiatives is fundamental for employees to buy in. Two common root causes that take into account the posture of leadership in organisations: (1) the low tolerance to error, and (2) the existence of conservatism towards risk. The inhibition of creativity due to lack of support from leadership is one of the main obstacles to innovation and cause demotivation on employees.

Changing the organizational culture is a task that requires a considerable amount of commitment and persistence. However, a culture that facilitates innovation, coupled with an innovation process tailored to the organisation's needs and with committed resources, are essential factors for the organisation to succeed in the ability to innovate systematically.

Organisations should promote incentives for the exposure of new ideas to the innovation process, in order to motivate employees to interact with the innovation structure. However, it can be seen that most organisations still do not have incentives for employees to expose their ideas. Therefore, the potential creativity from employees is wasted and thus such organisations do not get value from this source. Another root-cause in this context is the lack of recognition for innovative initiatives, which in itself is an incentive to the exposure of ideas. Recognition can be done in different ways: financial, personal or symbolic. Organisations cannot stop at the creation of these mechanisms. To achieve the goal, these acknowledgements must be widely disseminated, both in their presentation and afterwards during execution.

The ideas selection phase is carried out in accordance with the objectives of the organisation for innovation, so the ideas selection criteria should also be widely disseminated so that the employees are able to focus their creativity. Hence, this stage of the process is directly connected with the root cause related to the communication of the objectives for innovation.

The lack of support for employees during the innovation process is also a problem for organisations towards innovation, and is more critical when in the absence of "innovation champions". These employees are specialised in innovation and should be previously selected according to their profiles. Their role will be to help the most creative employees across organizational ranks, during their passage through the innovation process, so they should have good connections within the organisation and, ideally, there should be one innovation champion per organizational unit.

The implementation phase of innovations has little success if organisations have not implemented a standard procedure that allows the introduction of innovations in an easy and effective way. The concept of "islands of experimentation" fits this phase as a general procedure for implementing innovations. This concept presents itself as an effective solution, but it is still not spread enough. Still at this stage there may be some resistance to implementation of ideas by employees or customers. Such resistance should be mitigated, so that innovations can start adding value to the organisation as soon as possible.

The referred root causes related to the innovation process are more susceptible to adaptation to each reality, since different solutions can be found for the same problems.

Designing a Solution

The second tree to be built is the Future Reality Tree. This tree derives from the logical analysis of the system under consideration and intends to answer the question "What to change to?". Thus, the goal of this tree is to present solutions and verify their impact on the rest of the system. These solutions are named injections, as they are actions to "inject" into specific areas in order to neutralize the undesirable effects originated from root causes. Some injections are found to make organisations more innovative:

- Train employees in innovation
- Enable employees to take sustainable risks in helping innovation
- Incentives for long-term innovation
- Mechanisms for recognition of innovative initiatives
- Definition of objectives for innovation
- Networking established as a form of communication within the organisation
- Form multidisciplinary and cross-functional teams to spread knowledge within the organisation
- Adoption of the concept of "islands of experimentation"
- Process re-engineering with a view to reduce bureaucracy across the organisation

The suggested injections will give rise to desirable effects, which when present, will enable the achievement of the main objective. An injection to be inputted to the system is innovation training. Innovation training should be initially provided to elements of the organisation selected for that purpose. After that, these people together with the leadership team shall build the innovation process for the organisation. When the innovation process is complete, some of these people will return to their previous positions and others will join the innovation structure of the organisation. Those who return to their previous positions will be the so-called innovation champions (Figure 2).

Long-term incentives are an important solution for organisations that want to innovate, as they commit the organisation to the employee, being tolerant to employee to make mistakes as a way of learning and innovate. This freedom to make mistakes gives employees the opportunity to innovate in a more disruptive way. If employees feel pressured not to make mistakes, they will not take risks, so their ideas will tend to be more incremental or a recombination than disruptive. In this way, the injection that allows employees to take sustainable risks in innovation emerges. Organisations have finite resources, so it is necessary to make a sustainable use of them, especially with regard to innovation. It is necessary to have sustainable budgets for innovation.

Figure 2. Future Reality Tree of an organisation that wants to innovate

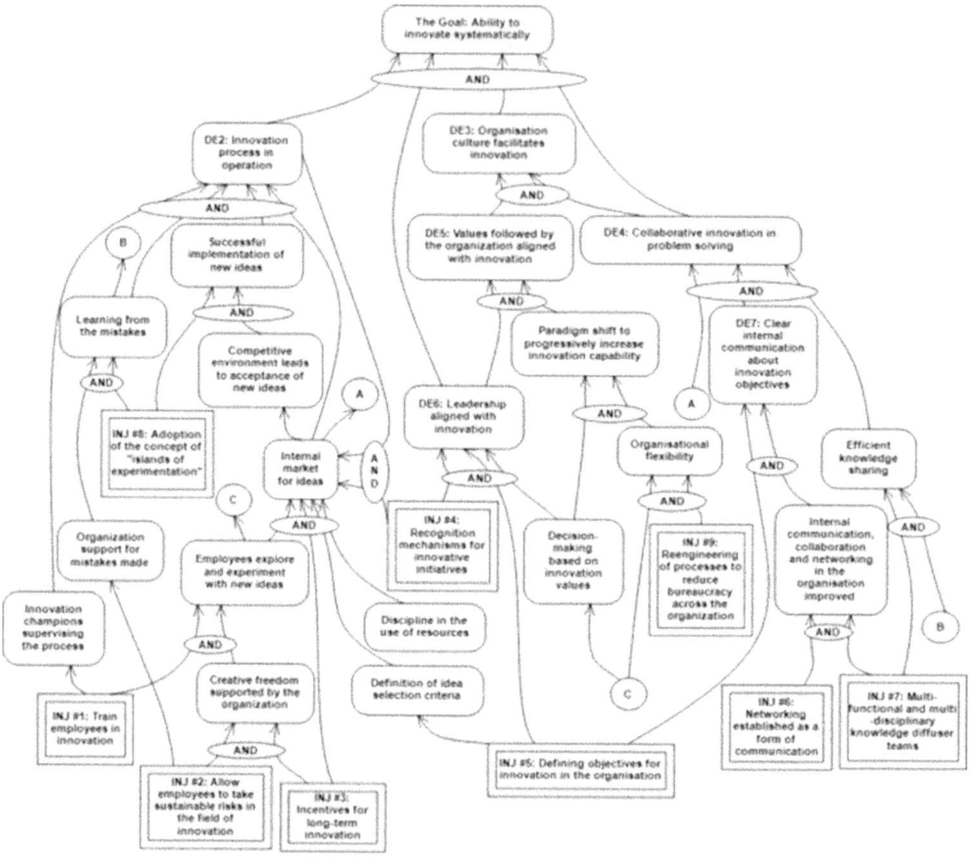

However, the leadership has to take into account that innovation wins are slow, so its fruits will come in the long term. Still, it is possible and necessary to give space to employees to innovate in a sustainable way by allocating resources to their initiatives.

In the case of initiatives that succeed through innovation processes, it is necessary to use recognition mechanisms to praise them. These recognition mechanisms are important to motivate other employees and showing that the innovation process is functioning. The fact that there are recognition mechanisms also reveals that leadership is aligned with innovation, since it rewards employees who add value to the organisation through the capability that is being integrated.

Leadership has a role in the initial impetus of innovation in the organisation, in order to define the objectives for innovation. In this way it is one of the injections adequate for organisations that want to be more innovative. The definition of clear and unambiguous objectives is essential to create criteria for the selection of ideas. Once these criteria are defined, employees will start to be creative and expose their ideas to the innovation process. Now, if too many ideas come in at the gathering stage of the innovation process, competition between employees will start to take place. In this phase an internal market of ideas will emerge, where the goal will be to get an idea selected. It is necessary that the selection criteria are fulfilled in order to bring credibility to the innovation process. In this competitive environment the acceptance of innovations will be facilitated, because after so many steps, the innovation that reaches the implementation phase will be respected and credible in the eyes of employees and customers.

Still regarding the innovation process, it is necessary that organisations adopt a procedure for implementing innovations. The literature suggests the concept of islands of experimentation, as a procedure that allows for quick learning from mistakes and their consequent correction.

In the field of internal communication, two need injections emerge. The first injection is to foster networking as a form of communication within organisations. Networking enables even physically distant employees to share their ideas in forums, which leads to the creation of knowledge, which is essential for the quality of ideas produced. The second injection to take into consideration is the formation of multifunctional and multidisciplinary teams. These teams bring quick and efficient knowledge sharing to the organisation, as well as sharing of mistakes made. Another objective of these teams is focused innovation, i.e., after these teams are formed, they can be assigned existing problems in organisation in order to come up with innovative solutions to those problems.

The last suggested injection to insert in the FRT is process reengineering in order to reduce bureaucracy. The main objective of this injection is to make the organisation more flexible, and improve continuously. Thus, the capacity to innovate systematically will be implemented progressively according to the speed of paradigm change to which each organisation best adapts. If there is less bureaucracy, resources will be more easily allocated to innovation initiatives.

The suggested solution enables the desirable effects in the organization according to the aimed objective, in this case to make organisations more innovative. This will bring the following desired effects:

- Leadership aligned with innovation
- Organisational culture that facilitates innovation
- Collaborative innovation present in problem solving
- Values followed by the organisation in line with innovation
- Clear internal communication regarding the objectives defined for innovation
- Innovation process in operation

The first desired effect that must be achieved is the alignment between leadership and innovation. If leadership is aligned with innovation, it will make possible for innovative initiatives to emerge. This desired effect is verified when the values practiced by the leadership team are framed by innovation. That is, if leadership is willing to take risks, tolerates mistakes and encourages knowledge sharing, then the implicit values in leadership decision-making are in line with innovation. The leadership at any organization is taken as an example by the rest of the employees, so the contagion of these values will be made across all employees, and as a consequence, the values followed by the organisation will be aligned with innovation.

Clear communication about the objectives set for the organisation is one of the foundations for successful innovation. If employees are aware of the goals for innovation they can start their creative thinking, and from there develop their ideas. Communication, together with a marketplace of ideas and the sharing of knowledge are fundamental to collaborative innovation.

The organisation should use networking as a way to expose its employees to the current problems, with the aim of creating innovative solutions. This type of solution is very viable, since it is employees who face many problems on a daily basis and know the strengths and limitations of the organisation. Therefore, it is important that information reaches all those who are part of the organisation, in order to gather many and diverse ideas. In other words, the objective here is to include as many brains as possible in order to have the largest possible flow of input into the innovation process. However, knowledge sharing should also be efficient, so that all employees are aware of what is being produced throughout the organisation.

In an organisation where employees, when faced with problems, try to find innovative solutions and the values practised within the organisation are aligned with innovation, it is possible to consider that the organisation has a culture that facilitates innovation. The change in organizational culture, whether towards a more innovative one or any other, is a long process, which requires persistence and planning, together with change management and adaptation.

With the desired effects achieved, the organisation can reach the proposed goal, or become a more innovative organisation. Achieving this goal takes usually time and resources, where small victories should be celebrated so that everyone feels motivated and does not lose focus of the goal.

A further last tree from the theory of constraints to be used to make the solution viable would be the PRT. Such tree answers the question "How to cause the change?" and intends to clarify the actions required for the injections to be successfully inserted in the system. It is derived through the verification of the DOTMLPFI dimensions, referred before. It is not dealt with here as it is specific to each organization's paradigm, circumstances, including available resources.

The first injection, "Train employees in innovation", needs as necessary conditions to identify the training needs in innovation. Secondly, to contract the training with competent entities capable of training the employees in innovation subjects. At this point, it must be taken into account that there will be financial resources spent on training employees in innovation – so resources shall be provided upfront. Finally, it is necessary to select the employees who will receive the training. This selection should take into account the profiles of employees as well as their willingness to participate in the innovation structure of the organisation.

The second injection, "Enable employees to take sustainable risks with innovation", requires the leadership team to be committed to providing employees with opportunities to experiment with their ideas. This requires creating spaces where there is room for experimentation within the organisation without having to spend excessive resources. Finally, it is necessary to allocate resources to innovation, so that employees can experiment with their ideas.

The third and fourth injections demand similar necessary conditions to be realised. For there to be incentives and recognition mechanisms the leadership team has to define what types of stimuli they should use for innovation, as these should be adapted to the circumstances of each organisation. Then these should be widely disseminated so that all employees become aware of the opportunities given by the organisation. Thus, it is fundamental to take into account and communicate to all employees in the same way and in a timely manner.

Injection five, "Define objectives for innovation in the organisation", has to be among the first to be put into practice, since it is from these objectives that the organisation's strategy will emerge to make it more innovative. For this injection to materialise it is necessary to ascertain what the intentions of the leadership for innovation are. Once these intentions have been declared, the leadership should meet with experts in organising for innovation, and design a plan for the integration of innovation in the organisation. This way, the last step will be to define specific objectives for innovation, which will then be communicated to the rest of the organisation in order to guide all employees in the same direction.

The sixth injection, "Networking established as a form of communication", intends to connect all employees even if they are physically far apart. To carry out this injection, it is necessary to engage employees with computer skills to build a platform that allows the organisation to communicate problems to its employees, so that they can come up with innovative solutions. Then, it is necessary to implement the online platform and communicate its existence to the rest of the organisation.

The seventh injection is the establishment of "Multi-functional and multi-disciplinary knowledge diffuser teams". It is necessary that employees gather knowledge and share it within these teams. In this way, a culture of sharing between all units of the organisation will be implemented. The last necessary condition for this injection focuses on the integration of elements across these teams with the ability to lead and manage the elements involved in them.

The eighth injection "Adoption of the concept of "islands of experimentation"", aims to introduce a procedure for implementing innovations. For this concept to be successful, it is necessary to explore it and adapt it to a particular organisation's needs. Then, to put it into practice, it will be necessary to allocate resources so that experimentation can be carried out in the places provided.

The last injection, number nine, "Reengineering of processes with a view to reducing bureaucracy in the organisation", requires the organisation to have employees specialised in process reengineering. If the organisation does not have employees with such skills, it should buy these services.

CONCLUSION

An organization designed for innovation aims at introducing new and better products, processes, services or management approaches that enable the organisation to deliver greater value. Such organisation is based on a culture of innovation, an appropriate innovation process as well as the correct management of change in the organisation.

A culture of innovation demands proposals for innovative solutions to existing problems, through exploration, experimentation and entrepreneurship, with an emphasis on learning, optimisation, knowledge sharing, some risk taking and tolerance for failures that may occur during the innovation process. For a culture of innovation, the existence of a leadership team willing to innovate is critical, together with a strategy encompassing adequate training.

The innovation process is the set of actions aimed at fostering innovation in the organisation, under the leadership of top managers. The implementation of the innovation process is carried out in phases: (1) gathering of a portfolio of ideas, (2) selection of suitable ideas according to criteria of added value for the organisation, (3) the risk involved in the development, and the success of prototyping and proofs of concept, and (4) their implementation safeguarding the barriers, internal or external to the organisation.

A transformation has to occur for innovation to become a systemic capability in organisations. Therefore, an organisation must go through a process of change which must be properly planned and managed. It is essential that this process is led in a chained and comprehensive way throughout the organisation. In view of the solution proposed, it is necessary to emphasise the focus on internal and external communication, as well as on the way in which it is communicated, the attitude of the leadership team towards the values practised and the employees' initiatives in the field of innovation.

Any study or research always has some limitations, among them and thinking in practical applied terms, there would be a gap between the application of the suggested models and the observable results. As the model implies changes to organizational culture, such timespan could last for several years.

However, as for further research related with this chapter, one could follow one or more of three possible domains: (1) the substantive domain, (2) the conceptual domain, and (3) the methodological domain. As for the substantive domain or the extension to the tangible application this study could be further investigated towards the inclusion and risk sharing with third party organizations. Additionally, and taking the conceptual domain, one could further study the impact of organizational values on the proposed organization for innovation. Finally, as for the methodological domain, and taking into account that organizations are socio-technical systems, further research on the subject of organization for innovation would benefit from a systems approach, specifically, through the use of complex systems modelling, of which systems thinking and systems dynamics modelling are adequate approaches.

REFERENCES

Água, P. B., & Correia, A. (2020). Innovation governance in practice: A business policy approach. *Corporate Board: Role. Duties and Composition*, *16*(2), 54–64. doi:10.22495/cbv16i2art5

Ashoor, W. A. (2021). Transformational Leadership and Innovation for Competitive Advantage in Large Firms and SMEs. *International Journal of R&D Innovation Strategy*, *3*(1), 1–12. doi:10.4018/IJRDIS.20210101.oa2

Back, A., Werro, T. M., & Peter, L. M. (2019). Practical Implications On How Established Companies Innovate With Startups: Tools and Guidelines for Innovation Managers. *International Journal of R&D Innovation Strategy*, *1*(2), 1–20. doi:10.4018/IJRDIS.2019070101

Boeddrich, H. J. (2004). Ideas in the Workplace: A New Approach Towards Organizing the Fuzzy Front End of the Innovation Process. *Creativity and Innovation Management*, *13*(4), 274–285. doi:10.1111/j.0963-1690.2004.00316.x

Bogers, M., Ollila, S., & Yström, A. (2016). Designing and being designed: Organizing complex collaborative innovation in a societal challenge. *Best Paper Proceedings of the Academy of Management.*

Cheltenham, E. E. (2016). Corporate Venturing: Organizing for Innovation. *Science & Public Policy*, *43*(4), 576–578. doi:10.1093cipolcv066

Çokpekin, Ö., & Knudsen, M. P. (2012). Does Organizing for Creativity Really Lead to Innovation? *Creativity and Innovation Management, 21*(3), 304–314. doi:10.1111/j.1467-8691.2012.00649.x

Cox, J. III, & Robinson, E. (2017). Applying Goldratt's thinking processes to prevent mistakes. *Human Systems Management, 36*(4), 315–340. doi:10.3233/HSM-17116

Day, G. S. (2007). Is it real? Can we win? Is it worth doing. *Harvard Business Review, 85*(12), 110–120. PMID:18283921

Deschamps, J. P. (2008). *Innovation Leaders: How Senior Executives Stimulate, Steer and Sustain Innovation*. Jossey-Bass.

Dettmer, H. W. (1998). *Breaking The Constraints To World-Class Performance. Milwaukee*. ASQ Quality Press.

Dettmer, H. W. (2000). Constraint Management. Quality America Ed.

Dettmer, H. W. (2011). *Strategic Navigation*. ASQ Quality Press.

Ende, J. V. D., Frederiksen, L., & Prencipe, A. (2015). The front end of innovation: Organizing search for Ideas. *Journal of Product Innovation Management, 32*(4), 482–487. doi:10.1111/jpim.12213

Goglio-Primard, K., & Crespin-Mazet, F. (2015). Organizing Open Innovation in Networks- the role of boundary relations. *International Management, 19,* 135-147.

Jay, J. (2016). Sustainability-Oriented Innovation: A Bridge to Breakthroughs. In *The Sustainability Learning Forum*. CSR Academy.

Kotter, J. P. (2012). *Leading Change*. Harvard Business Review Press.

Looy, B. V., Martens, T., & Debackere, K. (2005). Organizing for Continuous Innovation: On the Sustainability of Ambidextrous Organizations. *Creativity and Innovation Management, 14*(3), 208–221. doi:10.1111/j.1467-8691.2005.00341.x

Love, J. H., Roper, S., & Mangiarotti, G. (2007). Organizing innovation: Complementarities between cross-functional teams. *Technovation, 29*(3), 192–203. doi:10.1016/j.technovation.2008.07.008

Mabin, V. (1999). Goldratt's «Theory of Constraints» Thinking Processes: A Systems Methodology linking Soft with Hard. *History (London)*.

Mabin, V., Davies, J., & Cox, J. III. (2006). Using the Theory of Constraints Thinking Processes to complement system dynamic's causal loop diagrams in developing fundamental solutions. *International Transactions in Operational Research, 13*(1), 33–57. doi:10.1111/j.1475-3995.2006.00532.x

Mandal, P. C. (2020). Generating Ideas for New Product Development: Strategies and Initiatives. *International Journal of R&D Innovation Strategy*, *2*(1), 1–21. doi:10.4018/IJRDIS.2020010101

Manso, G. (2017). Creating Incentives for Innovation. *California Management Review*, *60*(1), 18–32. doi:10.1177/0008125617725287

Mascia, D., Magnusson, M., & Björk, J. (2015). The Role of Social Networks in Organizing Ideation, Creativity and Innovation: An Introduction. *Creativity and Innovation Management*, *24*(1), 102–108. doi:10.1111/caim.12111

Miller, P., & Brankovic, A. (2010). Building a "Creative Culture" for Sustainable Innovation. IESE Business School.

Ollila, S., & Yström, A. (2016). Exploring Design Principles of Organizing for Collaborative Innovation: The case of an Open Innovation Initiative. *Design Principles for Collaborative Innovation*, *25*(3), 363–377. doi:10.1111/caim.12177

Palmisano, S. J., Hemp, P., & Stweart, T. A. (2005). Liderar a mudança quando o negócio corre bem. *Harvard Business Review*, *82*(12), 60–70. PMID:15605566

Rao, J., & Weintraub, J. (2013). How Innovative is your company's culture? *MIT Sloan Management Review*, •••, 29–38.

Schmiedel, T., Spiegel, M., & Brocke, J. V. (2017). What Makes Change Harder - or Easier. *MIT Sloan Management Review*.

Skarzynski, P., & Gibson, R. (2008). *Innovation to the Core: A Blueprint for Transforming the Way Your Company Innovates*. Harbard Business Press.

Sull, D., Sull, C., & Turconi, S. (2020). When it comes to culture, Does your company walk the talk? *MIT Sloan Management Review*.

Tirabeni, L., Soderquist, K. E., & Pisano, P. (2016). Driving Innovation by Enhancing Employee Roles: The Balancing Act of Employee-Driven Innovation. *International Scholarly and Scientific Research & Innovation*, *10*(1), 148–156.

Tushman, M. L., Lakhani, K. R., & Lifshitz-Assaf, H. (2012). Open innovation and organizational boundaries: task decomposition, knowledge distribution and the locus of innovation. *Journal of Organizational Design,* 355-382.

Tushman, M. L., & O'Reilly, C. A. (2004). The Ambidextrous Organization. *Harvard Business Review, 82*(4), 74–81. PMID:15077368

Winsor, J., Paik, J., Tushman, M., & Lakhani, K. (2019). Overcoming cultural resistance to open-source innovation. *Strategy and Leadership, 47*(6), 28–33. doi:10.1108/SL-08-2019-0114

ADDITIONAL READING

Christensen, C. M. (1997). *The Innovator's Dilemma. When new technologies cause great firms to fail.* Harvard Business Press.

Christensen, C. M., & Raynor, M. E. (2003). *The Innovator's Solution. Creating and sustaining successful growth.* Harvard Business Press.

Gauthier, V. (2014). Leading with Sense. Stanford, CA: Stanford Business books.

Goldratt, E. M. (1990). *What is this thing called Theory of Constraints and how should it be implemented?* The North River Press.

Goldratt, E. M. (1992). *The Goal.* North River Press.

Goldratt, E. M. (2000). *Necessary but not sufficient.* North River Press.

Luecke, R. (2003). *Managing Creativity and Innovation.* Harvard Business Press.

Miller, P., & Wedell-Wedellsborg, T. (2013). *Innovation Business as Usual. How to help your people bring great ideas to life.* Harvard Business Press.

Utterback, J. M. (1996). *Mastering the Dynamics of Innovation.* Harvard Business Press.

KEY TERMS AND DEFINITIONS

Change Management: A term for all approaches to prepare, support, and help individuals, teams, and organizations in making organizational change.

Constraint: A condition that prevents a system (or organization) to achieve its goals.

Desirable Effects (DE): A concept from the Theory Of Constrains (TOC), that represents effects that contribute to enable the organization or system of interest to achieve its goal.

Disruptive Innovation: An innovation that creates a new market and/or a value network and eventually displaces established market-leading firms, products, and alliances.

Incremental Innovation: A series of small improvements made to a company's existing products, services, or processes.

Innovation: The practical implementation of ideas that result in the introduction of new goods or services or improvement in processes.

Leadership: A practical skill encompassing the ability of an individual, group, or organization to "lead," influence, or guide other individuals, teams, or entire organizations.

System: A grouping of parts that operate together for a common purpose.

Theory of Constraints (TOC): The theory of constraints is a management paradigm that views any socio or technical system as being limited in achieving its goals by a certain number of constraints.

Undesirable Effect (UDE): A central concept from TOC thinking processes, which represents effects that prevent the system of interest, or organization, from achieving its goal.

Chapter 10
Following Through the Good and the Bad?
Building a Positive Change Culture With Authentic Followers

Joseph Crawford
https://orcid.org/0000-0002-2191-6216
University of Tasmania, Australia

Sarah M. Young
https://orcid.org/0000-0003-3384-670X
University of Tasmania, Australia

Matthew Knox
https://orcid.org/0000-0002-6092-071X
University of Tasmania, Australia

ABSTRACT

Followers are underrepresented in the organizational change literature despite their considerable influence on change success. Politics, culture, motivation, communication, and readiness have a large impact on change success, and these influences are examined in the change context. Each of these are influenced by leaders and followers. The role of authentic followers in enabling positive change through their organizational engagement is explored in depth. This chapter demonstrates that while the influential role of leaders in change is established, the authentic follower represents a large body of potential change agents with the capacity to positively influence the success of change. Many behaviors of the authentic follower make them an ideal candidate for this role, including moral potency, high levels of engagement in organizational structure, and flexibility. Further research highlighting the value of the authentic follower is warranted.

DOI: 10.4018/978-1-7998-2807-5.ch010

INTRODUCTION

Change is a facet of daily life and should be an expectation rather than a surprise. The rapid rate of innovation and evolution in contemporary beliefs, influenced in part by globalization, has brought with it a period of significant transformation. Organizational change, however, is still poorly understood, and the rate of change failure is one indicator of such. Some studies indicate rates of failure as high as 80 percent (Strebel, 1996) and others found that of 125 mergers, 40 percent failed to achieve anticipated savings (Doucet, 2000). In fact, there appears to be a consensus that most organizational change initiatives fail (e.g. Franken et al., 2009; Gilley et al., 2008; Pasmore, 2011; Sterling, 2003). Considering how common change has become in society and organizations, such a high rate of failure is problematic.

Scholars have turned their attention to exploring the antecedents of successful organizational change practice and have begun to document the extensive complexity associated with organizational change (Lewis et al., 2005). For example, recent studies identify that psychological capital (Nwanzu & Babalola, 2019), individual readiness (Haffar et al., 2019), and motivation (Ryan & Danaher, 2019) have a positive influence on organizational change. Perhaps one of the most effective predictors of organizational change is leadership (Agote et al., 2016) and the organizational culture such leaders can cultivate.

The weakness in organizational change literature is the dearth of understanding of the role of the follower. Research supports the effect of employee involvement (Morgan & Zeffane, 2003), cynicism (Stanley et al., 2005), and commitment (Turner Parish et al., 2008) on organizational change. However, while these studies should inform our understanding of followership, the followership context is underdeveloped within the contemporary leadership domain (de Zilwa et al., 2014). The organizational change context is no exception, despite the integral role that employee resistance can have on the success or failure of change implementation (Piderit, 2000). It is not surprising then, that evidence indicates around 70 percent of change initiatives fail (Meaney & Pung, 2008).

The importance of follower behaviors becomes more pertinent when considering that many change agents emerge from employee groups. That is, followers sometimes become leaders or enact leadership in periods of change. Leader-follower fluidity does tend to occur when individuals are required to utilize different behaviors in multiple environments (Crawford et al., 2018). The behaviors of the change agent are important in facilitating organizational change (Specht et al., 2017). Where the individual characteristics of the follower are important in the leader-follower relationship, so too are these behaviors important when the follower is taking on a temporary leadership role such as a change agent. Indeed, the follower becomes the leader, for at least a time. Therefore, scholars need to consider followers who are active in their engagement with the organization and can demonstrate some degree of responsibility beyond a 'sheep follower' (Kelley, 1988).

The follower to work with during change also needs to display ethical tendencies. In a post-GFC world, the unethical cultures that created the 2008 world economic collapse have not been erased from existence. Building and maintaining ethical cultures during change, however, is an important step (By et al., 2015). The inclusion of the examination of moral potency in organizational change research is an important step to responding to this challenge (By et al., 2015). Moral potency is composed of moral ownership, moral efficacy, and moral courage (Hannah & Avolio, 2010). Ethics is a key part of positive change (Tanno & Banner, 2018).

The authentic follower (Crawford et al., 2018) offers such a proposition, by being ethical with a psychological propensity for authenticity, and active by their positive organizational engagement. This follower style offers a method by which individuals can transcend their employee role to a change agent role fluidly. Consideration of the authentic follower should begin with deliberation around them as individuals, and understanding what it means to be a follower. Subsequently, it would be appropriate to consider the follower in the context of change and leadership. At present, there is recognition that authentic followers are important in the authentic leadership process (Avolio & Gardner, 2005), yet there is still minimal research which genuinely values the authentic follower (de Zilwa, 2016).

To further explore the role of the follower in enabling positive organizational change, we begin with a summary of our research method followed by a brief literature review on organizational change. For this critical review, we begin with an overview of the role of politics and culture, motivation, communication, and readiness in the organizational change process. Next, we highlight authenticity, the authentic leader, and the authentic follower as they relate to change. We follow by considering what a positive change climate looks like. To conclude this chapter, we provide a synthesis of these three domains of research: organizational change, authentic followers, and positive organizational climates. We do so to address the following research question: *what is the role of the authentic follower in enabling positive organizational change?*

CRITICAL REVIEW METHOD

The term 'critical review' has been adopted by scholars to define a form of semi-structured literature review. Critical reviews "aim to demonstrate writer has extensively researched literature and critically evaluated its quality" (Grant & Booth, p. 94). Our intention with this critical review is to consider the quality of existing literature in each of the elements of our Chapter, in their independence and in relation to their role in organizational change. This is similar to existing critical reviews (e.g. Dichev & Dicheva, 2017; Hughes et al., 2018). We critically review each component, and synthesize these highly varied collections of literature in our discussion.

ORGANIZATIONAL CHANGE

Organizational change requires no introduction to contemporary management scholars, with change being a new norm in enabling efficient and effective organizations. The models of effective organizational change are as diverse as the change they seek to respond to. Many of these adopt a process approach that includes some form of problem identification, diagnosis, planning, implementing, evaluation, and normalising (Hayes, 2014). One of the oldest models, is the three-phase Lewin model that emphasizes periods of unfreezing, movement, and refreezing. In this model, leadership style has a significant effect on organizational change processes (Hussain et al., 2018). In a review, Van de Ven and Poole (1995) identify four ideal developmental theories of change processes: lifecycle theory, teleological theory, dialectical theory, and evolutionary theory. Life cycle theories identify change as a sequential stage-based process with each stage contributing to the outcome. Teleological theories suggest that change is an emergent learning process with goals formed, implemented, and evaluated. Dialectical theories adopt a dialectic approach with conflicting goals that highlight change emerging from conflict, and periods without change emerging from stability. Evolutionary theories suggest a quality improvement style of change that recognizes a continuous cycle of variation, selection, and retention.

Pardo del Val and Martinez Fuentes (2003) identify elements of inertia in the formulation and implementation stage of change. These include a wide array of challenges from myopia and denial to capability gaps and leadership inaction. We have extracted four broad themes from the sources listed to include: politics and culture, motivation, communication, and readiness, and discuss these further independently.

Politics and Culture

Political behavior is an inevitable accompaniment of organizational change. Changes in power relationships are common during large scale systematic change. These power changes can stem from deeply political systems that exist prior to change emerging. The desire for those 'in power' and who overvalue power may act to create barriers to change as a mechanism to maintain power status. Political skills in organizations can include social astuteness, interpersonal influence, networking ability, and apparent sincerity (Ferris et al., 2005). Social astuteness manifests in an awareness of others' ability to engage in organizational politics, with negative actor behavior including leveraging less skillful political actors for their personal benefit. Interpersonal influence is the degree to which subtle and convincing style persuades others. Agents can use their interpersonal influence to hinder change or enable it, and the degree to which individuals have strong networks influence their ability to affect change.

Exhibiting political influence over large networks can have rapid implications for change effectiveness. Social networks evolve, collapse, and/or reform through the lived experience of organizational change (Burkhardt & Brass, 1990). Likewise, apparent sincerity is the ability to be perceived as authentic and sincere, despite unethical intentions. In periods of change, politics can be both a critical success mechanism and a point of resistance (Kotter, 2007). In the short-term, apparent sincerity can have positive implications for change if leveraged effectively. However, long-term change resistance is likely to ensue for two reasons: a failure to create authentic reasons for change, and the lack of development of sincere relations with those who will be affected by current and future change.

Culture, likewise is critical in understanding how to enable success (Hansen, 2007). If the individuals within the organization are not adequately prepared for implementation, they will be resistant (Klein & Sorra, 1996). Likewise, underlying cultural norms and artefacts that are not incorporated into change will have a negative effect on the change process. Organizations are social by nature, and this needs to be recognized in the way the organizational culture affects the implementation and planning of change. This is particularly true when discussing deeply held beliefs or long-standing assumptions. Historical narratives are a building block to organizational culture, and this type of building block has direct implications for organizational change (Hansen, 2007). Leadership and politics are key components to enabling an organizational climate conducive to change (Bass & Avolio, 1993), particularly when the narratives of the organization are not naturally compatible with transformative change.

Motivation

Undertaking developmental changes in an organization requires a growth mindset built on creating a motivational work environment (Gilley et al., 2009). Likewise, motivation more generally has a role in enabling or inhibiting change success (Wright et al., 2013). Managers and employees that seek consensus on mutually agreeable performance build positive work-group spirit that subsequently creates enhanced motivation (Appelbaum et al., 1998). An exception to this situation occurs when managers and employees differ in their beliefs surrounding change. For example, the failures of past organizational change can create cynical attitudes towards change from employees causing motivational declines (Wanous et al., 2000).

There are costs of change that can have negative implications for motivation. The direct costs of change are varied but could include personnel costs (e.g. recruitment, selection, temporary staff, redundancy: Morrell et al., 2004) and maintaining multiple redundant systems in the interim (Abdinnour-Helm et al., 2003). There is also the potential for cannibalization during change, that is, enabling the success of one element of the business to the detriment of another. Cannibalization often occurs when new and more innovative competitor products hit the market (Velu & Stiles, 2013). For example, organizations like Marriott International are currently undergoing changes to combat sharing economy competitors such as Airbnb (El-Bawab, 2019). On the one hand, employees involved in the new move could feel motivated to engage in a new pursuit. However, on the other, existing employees may begin to fear for their job security, or see declines in trade from consumers transferring across to the alternate division of the company. Similarly, cross subsidy comforts may exist where one high performing side of the business funds another, so motivation to engage in the change is diminished (Pardo del Val & Martinez Fuentes, 2003).

Communication

Communication and change success have been intertwined in their respective disciplines (Taylor et al., 2001), from communication of an effective strategic vision across an entire organization, to identification of needs through internal and external environmental scanning by employees and management (Johansson & Heide, 2008). In identifying change, employee voice and sincere interactions between leaders and followers is critical (Morrison & Milliken, 2000). The follower has a role to play in identifying the need for change.

During change, followers also have a role. A follower self, including their insecurities and attachment, has an impact on change (Collinson, 2003). Thus, where a follower may feel excluded from a change conversation, or insufficiently aware of their change context, they may demonstrate resistance. Genuine two-way communication is key to enabling organizational change (Reichers et al., 1997). Middle-managers (who serve as followers to senior managers, and leaders to front-line employees/supervisors) experience uncertainty during organizational change due to this dual role, and sincere communication is one method to respond to such ambiguity (Herzig & Jimmieson, 2006).

Beyond two-way communication is the need to mitigate and prevent organizational silence from occurring. Organizational silence is the reluctance to share information, speak freely, and provide feedback that others may not agree with (Beer & Eisenstat,

2000). Fear of job loss and adverse effects on power dynamics are just two antecedents of organizational silence (Appelbaum et al., 2000). While some degree of organizational silence is expected in organizations and indeed during change, silence is exacerbated by a climate of silence, reduced employee voice behaviors, and poor organizational culture (Vakola & Bouradas, 2005).

Readiness

Organizational change readiness is often defined structurally (e.g. Bloom et al., 2000; Lehman et al., 2002) and psychologically (e.g. Cunningham et al., 2002). We explore both perspectives here, for parity, but focus on the psychological perspective in our discussion. We believe both have significance, however, each needs sufficient independent consideration, and we consider the latter. Some antecedents to change readiness, however, have ambiguity. For example, a capabilities gap could be representative of poor structure of training and development, or individual failures to engage in learning.

From the psychological perspective, change readiness is recognized as the synthesis of change commitment (built on change valence) and change efficacy (Weiner, 2009). Consistent leadership communication and actions through social exchange is key in enabling change readiness (Klein & Kozlowski, 2000). Implicit assumptions of change, individuals involved in change, or assumptions predating change can be enablers or detractors for change. If individuals in the organization have been well communicated with, formally and informally, and their implicit assumptions of the change are positive, employees will be more willing to engage in the change. If their implicit assumptions are negative, they may be indignant or resigned from the process of change, demonstrating low change readiness. Next, we consider structural and contextual factors, but note that many of these are influenced by follower behaviors.

Structural and contextual factors that affect readiness include culture, policies, experience, and resources (Weiner, 2009). Individuals in the organization have embedded routines that they procedurally deploy based on long-standing organizational structures, policies, and strategies (Amis & Aïssaoui, 2013). When change practice is not effectively embedded into these routines, there can be general lack of readiness enabled (Wee & Taylor, 2018). In change, resources and schemas inform actions, except that these resources are considered as sources of energy rather than stable and independent of context (Feldman, 2004).

AUTHENTIC LEADERS AND FOLLOWERS

Authenticity

The notion of authenticity has proliferated contemporary society. The collapse of the modernist and structural periods has led to a desire to feel 'real' and 'genuine' in a fast-paced and digitally connected world. The term itself originated in Greek philosophy with phrases like 'be true to oneself' (Harter, 2002), and scholars have consistently challenged the fluidity of being authentic. Some existential philosophers articulate self-actualization, awareness of morality (Heidegger, 1962), and inherency of constant redefinition of self (Sartre, 1956). Camus (1942) represents an alternative field of thought that argues individual authenticity is exclusive of objective morality and purpose. One of the popularized explications of authenticity stems from the scene in Shakespeare's *Hamlet* (1954, p. 31):

This above all: to thine own self be true, and it must follow, as the night the day, thou canst not then be false to any man.

Contemporary scholars appear to align with adoption of developmental assumptions of authenticity, building multidimensional constructs leveraging awareness of self, ability to think without bias, actions consistent with self, and truthfulness in relationships (Kernis & Goldman, 2004). The complication with authenticity is its 'sister construct', sincerity. The two are often conflated, with sincerity generally being considered relational with others, and authenticity relational with self (Crawford et al., 2019; Trilling, 2009). In a seminal piece on authenticity and sincerity, Trilling (2009) identifies sincerity as the congruence between avowal and feeling. Being authentic, that is, true to ones' true self, is not confined by societal expectations; instead, the actions of an authentic person are confined by societal expectations. Humans, on many occasions have dark thoughts manifesting from some component of their current self. The action is refined by socially-constructed roles, not the thought. For this paper, we adopt the intrapersonal and developmental foundations of authenticity, with a view that sincerity is best understood as the outward expression legitimized by others.

Considering authenticity in organizational change, authenticity has a mediatory effect on organizational culture and engagement (Reis et al., 2016). Experiencing and engaging in genuine work is affected by periods of organizational change (Kira et al., 2012). Cultivating individual and team authenticity during change is important to enable honest and open conversations about the change process (Doorewaard & Benschop, 2003). Take, for example, an empirical study of mergers that identified a lack of organizational authenticity leads to lower productivity, and affects long-term merger performance (Cording et al., 2014). During a period of change, staying true to self has direct implications for organizational performance. This is explainable, perhaps, by the revitalizing effect that authentic behaviors have in organizations (Bunker & Wakefield, 2004).

In some cases of organizational change, there is a willingness to sacrifice efficiency to enable authenticity. The economic assumption is that the creation of a "kind of satisfying authenticity" will counter the loss of efficiency gains (Liedtka, 2008, p. 243). The ability to acknowledge the current reality and a shared consensus surrounding the desirable future is a gold standard in organizational change. Organizational change lends itself to state-like levels of organizational authenticity (van den Bosch & Taris, 2013). The assumption made by van den Bosch and Taris (2013) that authenticity is also state-like lead to asking whether this is authenticity, sincerity, or a failure to capture either on a tool. Authenticity is the psychological capacity to be true to one's self (de Zilwa et al., 2014), how we choose to manifest our authenticity is best understood as sincerity. Our faces change, as Goffman (1959) highlights, but our core self develops slowly.

Leaders

Authentic leadership was conceptualized in response to significant global issues (e.g. 9/11 and the dotcom bust: Luthans & Avolio, 2003). Authentic leadership has been applied to diverse contexts including work-life balance (Lyu et al., 2019) and building high performance teams (Shirey et al., 2019). Authentic leadership was posited to be the root of all positive forms of leadership (Avolio & Gardner, 2005), with recent calls cautioning about the excessiveness of positivity in leadership research (Alvesson & Einola, 2019). The outcomes of enacting authentic leadership have been well documented to include psychological capital, follower empowerment, performance, satisfaction, commitment, and openness to present a few (Gardner et al., 2011). More recently, and in response to growing critiques of the model, authentic leader behaviors were reconceptualized as the synthesis of five key behaviors (see Table 1).

Authentic leaders build supportive organizational climates through their sincere interactions with others, considering all relevant information, working for collective benefit, and having a strong moral compass. In an organizational change climate, authentic leaders seek to create readiness for change, develop organizational commitment to the change, and facilitate behavioral change (Bakari et al., 2017). Authentic leaders are posited as a mechanism to enable and support organizational change when multiple age demographics are affected (Mhatre & Conger, 2011), and to engender change supportive behaviors (Kim & Huh, 2019).

Table 1.

Authentic leader	Influences and motivates followers to achieve goals through their sincerity and positive moral perspective, enabled through heightened awareness and balanced processing.
Awareness	Having insight into the behaviours of one's self, other individuals, and groups.
Sincerity	Presenting one's true self to others, honestly and openly in all relationships and with consideration for the context.
Balanced processing	The tendency to consider all relevant information available, and using this to make decisions that benefit the collective (e.g. followers).
Positive moral perspectives	The commitment to one's intrinsic ethical framework, and a willingness to subdue personal interests and ego to facilitate collective interests.
Informal influence	The ability to inspire and motivate individuals to accomplish goals of their own volition, regardless of rank or position.

Definitions quoted from multiple pages in Crawford et al., (2019b).

Leadership during organizational change is recognized as a critical component of successful communication, mobilizing, and evaluation of change (Battilana et al., 2010; Gilley et al., 2009). For communication, the leader must destabilize the status quo and articulate a desired future. Resistance because of communication may stem from emotional distress, or the stress of uncertainty. The authentic leader seeks to overcome such resistance with sincere communication established on foundations of honesty and transparency. Authentic leaders recognize the inherent stress and decline in productivity during periods of change, which often cannot be eliminated during change. Thus, their sincere interactions seek to minimize the tension and acknowledge openly that change is inherently stressful.

In the mobilizing stage, the leader must overcome personal and professional goals (of their own, and others) to enable acceptance of the change (Battilana et al., 2010). The authentic leader leverages their own positive moral perspectives to transcend their own ego and narcissistic tendencies (e.g. Grijalva et al., 2015) and thereby minimize their potential to leverage change for career progression over organizational growth. This could be as simple as recognizing that a valuable employee may be best enabled by being provided with the desirable the corner office (organizational-interest) that the leader coveted (self-interest). It could be as complex as renegotiating employee agreements (e.g. Enterprize Bargaining Agreements in Australia) to provide staff whose jobs were being eliminated during downsizing with flexible part-time work for a generous interim period. The action, while difficult for the leader, could result in less remaining employees experiencing 'survivors' guilt' because of being chosen to retain their jobs after the downsizing.

In the evaluation of change, leaders must have the capacity to think critically and carefully, and the self-awareness to understand their own limitations and indeed their biases in the evaluation process. Authentic leaders are reflective, and have a desire to better understand their own behaviors, emotions, and cognitions (Avolio & Gardner, 2005). Indeed, authentic leaders are reflexive in their thinking (Eriksen, 2009) and seek relevant information before making decisions (Crawford et al., 2020). The ability to be balanced in their processing of information should not, however, be overtly slow, given authentic leaders still enable rapid innovation and creativity in their workforces (Černe et al., 2013).

Followers

The authentic leadership domains of leadership, followership, leader, and follower have been inconsistently researched. The dominance has been on leadership, often treating the leader and leadership as synonymous. Indeed, questions about the origins of followership are not often posed in psychology with the general assumption that leader and follower objectives are the same (Van Vugt, 2006). Followers, however, have importance within the enabling and hindering of leaders and organizational objectives. Actions such as followers' whistleblowing provide justification for the divergence of leader and follower goals at times. Followers have a key role to play in either obeying or challenging their leaders (Carsten & Uhl-Bien, 2013).

Early literature on leadership identified heroic and idealized leaders (e.g. Burns, 1978; Carlyle, 1993). These leaders were to be found, placed in a position of power, and obeyed. Obedience required passive followers, and the literature primarily focused on such an assumption. Kelley (1988) classified these as 'sheep' followers (passive and dependent). Kelley (1998) also articulated the categories of 'yes people' (positive, leader-dependent, and active), 'alienated' (independent thinkers and negative), 'pragmatics' (fence sitters), and 'star' (independent, active, and positive) followers. The difference among these is their ability to think independently (versus await the leader to think for them), their active engagement (or lack thereof), and their positive (or negative) energy (Kelley, 2008).

In the early 20th century, followers were rarely considered in the management literature, but some psychoanalytic and psychology researchers began to examine the follower (e.g. Freud, 1921). Indeed, social exchange, attribution and small group theories have since been applied to explain how the active follower emerges and is sustained (Baker, 2007). Despite continued recognition in the following century, the role of the follower is still marginalized in contemporary leadership literature. The authentic follower has been one of the first genuine steps towards such recognition (de Zilwa, 2016). Crawford et al. (2018) conceptualize authentic followers by their psychological capacity to be authentic (awareness, sincerity, balanced processing, and a positive moral perspective) and their positive organizational engagement. Moreover,

An authentic follower is an individual who, through their capacity for authenticity and positive organisational engagement, are self-managing and follow leaders with whom they share values (p. 274).

Spiritual followership has also been discussed in the emerging literature, with the assumption that leadership and followership are paradoxical and intersubjective (Frye et al., 2007). Communicative practices and participative structures are identified as a key action necessary to develop and nurture such followers. Such antecedents offer insight into the broader mechanism with which to develop ethical and proactive follower behaviors within a change context. That is, creating open and transparent channels of communication and soliciting and acting based on feedback are likely to reduce change resistance from followers.

Within change environments, there is an overemphasis on the role of the leader. The leader, in much research, overshadows the follower (Baker, 2007). However, followers are not all mere sheep wishing to be herded, but can demonstrate highly independent behaviors, think critically, and be active within their organization (Kelley, 1991). Followers play an important role in maintaining ethical cultures within organizations (Carsten & Uhl-Bien, 2013), and we posit that this extends to organizational change.

The role of the leader is unquestioned in having an influence on the motivation of employees to undergo change. However, Collinson (2005) notes that the follower role has multiple identities that can be enacted, some of which may include resistant selves. Gleeson and Shain (2003) explore the middle manager and their role as both a leader, and a follower. This complexity during change leads to middle managers adopting a willing, unwilling, or strategic perspective to the change process. Constructions of follower identities are likely created and enabled or hindered during organizational change contexts (Bligh, 2011).

POSITIVE CHANGE CULTURE

In early psychology, the focus was on the assessment of psychological issues and the prescription to cure it. This bias to the negative, termed 'negative psychology', led to short-term responses to challenges, rather than building up human capability to provide long-term solutions (Gillham & Seligman, 1999). Adopting an appreciative perspective to the human condition through the study of human strengths and virtues was a way to counter the reductionist perspectives of the then normative approach to psychology (Sheldon & King, 2001). The emergence of positive psychology has led to the growth in a wide range of new theories of management, organizations, and organizational change.

Positive organizational scholarship (POS) was one such emergence, with an emphasis on going beyond current organizational literature to consider "that which is positive, flourishing, and life-giving in organizations" (Cameron & Caza, 2004, p. 734). The POS field led to a growth in theoretically-driven affirmative bias research focusing on the enhancement of organisational processes and dynamics (Cameron & Dutton, 2003). Some of the emerging works from the POS discipline include psychological capital (Dawkins et al., 2015), prosocial motivations (Grant, 2008), and virtuousness (Rego et al., 2011).

Positive organizational behaviour (POB) followed, with critique of the emergence of theories without empirical rigor as mainstream books compared to the lack of rigorous academic theories (Luthans, 2002). The POB discipline led to the emergence of authentic leadership (Luthans & Avolio, 2003) as the root of positive leadership theories (Avolio & Gardner, 2005). Other theories in this field include core self-evaluations (Judge & Bono, 2001), self-efficacy (Bandura, 2010), and hope (Youssef & Luthans, 2007).

In organizational change literature, the role of positivity is less pronounced. Some scholars discuss the role of positive organizational development (Cooperrider & Godwin, 2010) and appreciative inquiry models of change management (Cooperrider & Srivastva, 2017). The appreciative inquiry model seeks to explore the best within the organization, and amplify such practice (Hayes, 2014). The adoption of deficiency perspectives of organizational change leads to change agents focusing on fixing the negative, rather than promoting the positive.

Approaches to enabling positive organizational cultures that foster a willingness for change have been diverse in the literature. Leading by example, training and development (Schraeder et al., 2004), charisma (Beyer, 1999), and effective motivation strategies are some examples of enablers of positive change cultures. Significant among these is the role of the individual employee: the follower. Leading by example is made possible by followers who are willing to role model behavior. A pragmatic follower avoids picking a side until the majority take the first step. These employees will not respond to a positive role model unless others do as well. Alienated followers are likely to be negative about the change regardless, and be less affected by motivation strategies and reasons.

An employee, or follower, during organizational change is required to be committed to the organization (Turner Parish et al., 2008), be engaged in the change (Fugate et al., 2012), and possess the ability to regulate emotions (Klarner et al., 2011). These behavioral elements will have a direct influence on their ability to buy into or involve themselves in the change. For some subordinates, the desire to disengage is based on their perceptions of the leader, disenfranchisement as a result of previous changes, perceptions of the organization, or other factors distinguishable from the existing organizational change practice. These ongoing cultural elements will influence the effectiveness of change implementation, management, and communication.

A positive change culture is established with developmentally ready followers, and leaders with a genuine desire to engage with such followers on the change. A leader, during change, must be sincere in their communication to minimise organizational cynicism (Atwater et al., 2000). A change leader also needs to be fair in their decisions (Bernerth et al., 2007), and possess sufficient emotional intelligence to understand the disruptive effect the change will have on productivity, wellbeing, and short-term outcomes (Groves, 2005). Such leaders will be able, and willing, to work with subordinates who are disenfranchised from other elements of the organization. This may include higher levels of engagement with some employees, and less with others. Leaders are required to provide due consideration to typical in-groups and whether the barriers between in-groups and out-groups are influencing employee resistance (Stevens et al., 2008).

Positive change cultures are made up of leaders and followers willing to engage with each other sincerely, and with the pursuit of presenting their authentic selves. This may mean engaging in difficult conversations or seeking to develop employees that have exhibited extra-role behaviors. In developing and recognizing the importance of their authentic and sincere interactions, engagement can be fostered, and positivity and openness to new experiences can be increased (Fredrickson & Joiner, 2002).

DISCUSSION

Thus far, this paper has examined a series of disparate component parts, and this discussion aims to tie these together with several caveats. Up until this point, we have discussed authentic leaders and authentic followers. This discussion on the authentic leaders is only to the extent of their role with followers in the change process, and preliminary discussion on the role of the authentic leader in four differing process models. The primary focus of this Chapter is on the authentic follower. We do so, not because of the lack of importance of leadership in organizational change, but because of the dearth of exploration of followers in the organizational change literature. There are numerous works on the leader in organizational change, but there is far less research on followers, and even less on authentic followers.

Process Models

The authentic leader and authentic follower adopt differing roles in organizational change, dependent upon the assumptions made in the process of change (see Van de Ven & Poole, 1995). This section provides some discussion and theorization on the possible linkages between the authentic leader, authentic follower, and specific philosophical assumptions underlying different process models of change.

In a lifecycle theory, the authentic leader engages in careful and considered processing of information in the planning and diagnosis stage, involving a wide range of stakeholders to gain accurate information. The authentic follower contributes through actively engaging in reflection of their department or discipline regarding the relevant knowledge to share with their leader (Edú-Valsania et al., 2016). This could include soliciting, supporting, or challenging the ideas of other followers within the workplace, as well as challenging or supporting the perceived value their leader has on the information.

The teleological theory recognizes the importance of learning during the process of change and being willing to change perspectives as new information emerges. Managers can enable organizational learning through enacting authentic leader behaviors and authentic dialogue (Mazutis & Slawinski, 2008). Outside of a change environment, employees often exhibit defensive behaviors that can inhibit their openness to learn. Within change environments, these defensive behaviors are likely exacerbated by their change-based resistance. An authentic follower is more open to experience through a secure relationship with their leader (Popper & Amit, 2009), and therefore less resistant to learning opportunities and change.

The dialectical theory articulates a case for recognizing that change emerges from conflict, however, this does not completely align with the authentic leader and authentic follower. Like all relationships, the authentic relationship has conflict. This conflict may not always result in change, and likewise, change does not always emerge from conflict. The appreciative inquiry approach to change (Cooperrider & Srivastva, 2017) recognizes value in identifying what is working well and promoting that best practice. As a developmental approach to leadership (Avolio & Gardner, 2005), authentic leaders actively seek to better understand their environment to find opportunities to improve. Authentic leaders respond to conflict, and authentic followers may create reasonable conflict when their views and values are not in alignment with their leader's. Such activity may lead to change, but it may also lead to individual learning or opportunities to clarify.

The evolutionary theory of change identifies that change is a continuous cycle of variation, selection, and retention. This approach aligns closely with authentic leadership and followership. The relationships between followers and leaders create continuous opportunities to learn of better practice and to improve organizational practice and policy where appropriate (Caldwell et al., 2011). In a model of leadership, where followers are empowered to make decisions, it is possible that variation in practice will occur among teams and different departments of an organization. Such variation creates an opportunity to understand what works, what does not, and to make improvements accordingly.

Authentic Leaders

The authentic leader has a significant role in enabling positive organizational change, through role modelling, enabling positive spirals, and fostering positive behaviors in others. The research on the effects of authentic leaders is limited, compared to other leadership styles (e.g. transformational, charismatic, and distributed). The role of the authentic leader in change has been discussed so far, as an enabler of environmental conditions conducive to positive change attitudes. Authentic leaders transcend Machiavellian and power-driven cultures to enable sincere and moral interactions with others (e.g. Sendjaya et al., 2016). Authentic leaders go beyond the pursuit of political skills to engage in careful consideration of relevant information, active decision-making, and action with integrity. Apparent sincerity and forms of network-based power form critical elements of political skill (Ferris et al., 2005), and the authentic leader veers away from leveraging such activities.

The authentic leader's largest contribution to the short-term component of organizational change is their ability to motivate others. While they engage in activities to build a culture that is conducive and adaptive, their engagement can prepare followers to positively engage with their organization (Crawford et al., 2018). Individuals who report to authentic leaders are more motivated and committed to their organization, even when formal authority lines do not exist (e.g. board chairs and non-executive directors). Such relationships have been found to be stronger when the directors rated their relationship as being of high-quality (Guerrero et al., 2015).

Authentic leaders facilitate a growth mindset by seeking to develop those around them, recognizing the role this has in motivating, empowering, and enabling others in the organization generally. This has an additional benefit of creating individual behaviors conducive to engagement with organizational change, without resignation or cynicism. While authentic leaders recognize that their subordinates may share views divergent from their own, there is the recognition that the authentic self is to be nurtured in followers. In practice, this leads to conversations about differences rather than resentment and the ability to discuss, with earnestness, how to move forward with divergent views.

Authentic Follower

The relationships that exist between the authentic leader and authentic follower are most conducive to positive and sustained organizational change in a world where change is a norm. These relationships characterised by authenticity create a natural platform for open and honest communication and decision-making, as was discussed in the above section on authenticity. However, there is recognition that authentic followers are not always paired with authentic leaders. That is, an authentic leader may be a direct report to a charismatic or servant leader or be in a place to be reporting to a corporate psychopath. In these scenarios, it is critical that scholars and practitioners seek to understand how an authentic follower will respond, and how the process of authentic followership evolves.

Authentic followers can serve as everyday employees in an organization undergoing change, and they can also act as change champions or change agents. However, as active and authentic individuals, they can also serve as detractors where they genuinely believe the decision for change is immoral or irreconcilable. As detractors, an authentic follower would first engage with their manager to discuss differences with openness and transparency. In such a time, the authentic follower would seek solutions to reconcile differences with their manager, embodying the action of a detractor as a last resort.

Through a genuine desire for open and honest communication, authentic followers are unlikely to engage in organizational silence with a desire to share information with others and to provide feedback despite the potential that others may not agree. This leads to a willingness to subvert group think and recognize when group think is occurring. A sheep follower would join in with the consensus, while an authentic follower would seek to engage to enable others to understand their differences (at the very least).

In organizations, authentic followers do not always report to an authentic leader. It is possible for an authentic follower to report to a Machiavellian leader, and in this case, there is some long-term incompatibility associated with the relationship. However, in the short-term, there are potential implications for organizational change. Authentic followers are not immune to the fear of job loss and the adverse effects of change, and the way in which they engage with the issues is different, sometimes to their detriment. An authentic follower may have some degree of attachment to their leader (de Zilwa et al., 2014), however, they can also be independent and think critically like a star follower (Kelley, 2008). Some followers may stay quiet and wait out the change, to see where they fall, others are more likely to seek knowledge to make a considered decision about their options. Therefore, an authentic follower may not have success in seeking to gain knowledge from their leader, if Machiavellian, but this enables them to gain knowledge elsewhere and potentially decide to leave or to be active in the change.

Authentic followers also tend to be more ready to engage with change. Their high baseline positive organizational engagement (Crawford et al., 2018) creates the conditions to be willing to forego embedded personal and professional routines for alternative options. They desire to grow and develop, facilitated by their leader where necessary (Avolio & Reichard, 2008). While authentic followers hold implicit assumptions, like all other humans, they possess the ability to seek out and process information in a balanced way, recognize their own biases, and be willing to change their position on a topic as new information arises.

FUTURE RESEARCH DIRECTIONS

This review provides a foundation outlining the importance of authentic followers, and therefore justifies further research in this area. The authentic follower has been shown to have as much significance to positive change as the authentic leader, an area that has been covered considerably by previous research. We encourage future scholars to understand the role of the follower as an emergent leader in change, or as an enabler *and* indeed inhibitor of change. Authentic followers have an important role in change, and we should provide them significantly more attention than currently provided in the change literature.

CONCLUSION

Change is a vital and inevitable part of human existence, and yet organizational change remains poorly understood and is troubled by high rates of failure. Leadership plays an important role in cultivating positive organizational change, but what we often fail to recognize is the role of the follower. This lack of understanding exists despite followers comprising most of the workforce. Because change agents almost inevitably emerge from employee, or follower, groups, their importance in this arena is solidified.

This critical review explored the existing inertial barriers to positive organizational change, which were categorised into four broad themes: politics and culture, motivation, communication, and readiness. Authenticity was also explored as a concept relating to leaders and followers, and the value and role of authentic followers was explored in terms of successful positive change. The attributes of authentic followers that make them valuable contributors to positive change include flexibility in their roles (the ability to move between their position as employee to leader, even temporarily), strong ethical tendencies, and a willingness to act.

REFERENCES

Abdinnour-Helm, S., Lengnick-Hall, M., & Lengnick-Hall, C. (2003). Pre-implementation attitudes and organizational readiness for implementing an enterprise resource planning system. *European Journal of Operational Research, 146*(2), 258–273. doi:10.1016/S0377-2217(02)00548-9

Agote, L., Aramburu, N., & Lines, R. (2016). Authentic leadership perception, trust in the leader, and followers' emotions in organizational change processes. *The Journal of Applied Behavioral Science, 52*(1), 35–63. doi:10.1177/0021886315617531

Alvesson, M., & Einola, K. (2019). *Warning for excessive positivity: Authentic leadership and other traps in leadership studies. Leadership Quarterly.*

Amis, J., & Aïssaoui, R. (2013). Readiness for change: An institutional perspective. *Journal of Change Management, 13*(1), 69–95. doi:10.1080/14697017.2013.768435

Appelbaum, S., St-Pierre, N., & Glavas, W. (1998). Strategic organizational change: The role of leadership, learning, motivation and productivity. *Management Decision, 36*(5), 289–301. doi:10.1108/00251749810220496

Atwater, L., Waldman, D., Atwater, D., & Cartier, P. (2000). An upward feedback field experiment: Supervisors' cynicism, reactions, and commitment to subordinates. *Personnel Psychology, 53*(2), 275–297. doi:10.1111/j.1744-6570.2000.tb00202.x

Avolio, B., & Gardner, W. (2005). Authentic leadership development: Getting to the root of positive forms of leadership. *The Leadership Quarterly, 16*(3), 315–338. doi:10.1016/j.leaqua.2005.03.001

Avolio, B., & Reichard, R. (2008). The rise of authentic followership. In R. Riggio, I. Chaleff, & J. Lipman-Blument (Eds.), *The art of followership: How great followers create great leaders and organizations* (pp. 325–337). Jossey-Bass.

Bakari, H., Hunjra, A., & Niazi, G. (2017). How does authentic leadership influence planned organizational change? The role of employees' perceptions: Integration of Theory of Planned Behavior and Lewin's three step model. *Journal of Change Management, 17*(2), 155–187. doi:10.1080/14697017.2017.1299370

Baker, S. (2007). Followership: The theoretical foundation of a contemporary construct. *Journal of Leadership & Organizational Studies*, *14*(1), 50–60. doi:10.1177/0002831207304343

Bandura, A. (2010). Self-efficacy. In I. Weiner & W. Craighead (Eds.), *The Corsini encyclopedia of psychology* (pp. 1534–1536). John Wiley & Sons. doi:10.1002/9780470479216.corpsy0836

Bass, B., & Avolio, B. (1993). Transformational leadership and organizational culture. *Public Administration Quarterly*, *17*(1), 112–121.

Battilana, J., Gilmartin, M., Sengul, M., Pache, A., & Alexander, J. (2010). Leadership competencies for implementing planned organizational change. *The Leadership Quarterly*, *21*(3), 422–438. doi:10.1016/j.leaqua.2010.03.007

Beer, M., & Eisenstat, R. (2000). The silent killers of strategy implementation and learning. *Sloan Management Review*, *41*(4), 29–40.

Bernerth, J., Armenakis, A., Feild, H., & Walker, H. (2007). Justice, cynicism, and commitment: A study of important organizational change variables. *The Journal of Applied Behavioral Science*, *43*(3), 303–326. doi:10.1177/0021886306296602

Beyer, J. (1999). Taming and promoting charisma to change organizations. *The Leadership Quarterly*, *10*(2), 307–330. doi:10.1016/S1048-9843(99)00019-3

Bligh, M. (2011). Followership and follower-centred approaches. In A. Bryman, D. Collinson, K. Grint, B. Jackson, & M. Uhl-Bien (Eds.), *The SAGE handbook of leadership* (pp. 425–436). SAGE Publicaitons Inc.

Bloom, J., Devers, K., Wallace, N., & Wilson, N. (2000). Implementing capitation of Medicaid mental health services in Colorado: Is "readiness" a necessary condition? *The Journal of Behavioral Health Services & Research*, *27*(1), 437–445. doi:10.1007/BF02287825 PMID:11070637

Bunker, K., & Wakefield, M. (2004). In search of authenticity: Now more than ever, soft skills are needed. *Leadership in Action*, *24*(1), 17–21. doi:10.1002/lia.1055

Burkhardt, M., & Brass, D. (1990). Changing patterns or patterns of change: The effects of a change in technology on social network structure and power. *Administrative Science Quarterly*, *35*(1), 104–127. doi:10.2307/2393552

Burns, J. (1978). *Leadership*. Harper & Row.

By, R., Armenakis, A., & Burnes, B. (2015). Organizational change: A focus on ethical cultures and mindfulness. *Journal of Change Management, 15*(1), 1–7. doi:10.1080/14697017.2015.1009720

Caldwell, C., Dixon, R., Atkins, R., & Dowdell, S. (2011). Repentance and continuous improvement: Ethical implications for the modern leader. *Journal of Business Ethics, 102*(3), 473–487. doi:10.100710551-011-0825-x

Cameron, K., & Caza, A. (2004). Introduction: Contributions to the discipline of positive organizational scholarship. *The American Behavioral Scientist, 47*(6), 731–739. doi:10.1177/0002764203260207

Cameron, K., & Dutton, J. (2003). *Positive organizational scholarship: Foundations of a new discipline*. Berrett-Koehler Publishers.

Camus, A. (1942). *The myth of Sisyphus and other essays* (J. O'Brien, Trans.). Vintage International.

Carlyle, T. (1993). *On heroes, hero-worship, and the heroic in history* (Vol. 1). University of California Press. doi:10.1525/9780520911536

Carsten, M., & Uhl-Bien, M. (2013). Ethical followership: An examination of followership beliefs and crimes of obedience. *Journal of Leadership & Organizational Studies, 20*(1), 49–61. doi:10.1177/1548051812465890

Černe, M., Jaklič, M., & Škerlavaj, M. (2013). Authentic leadership, creativity, and innovation: A multilevel perspective. *Leadership, 9*(1), 63–85. doi:10.1177/1742715012455130

Collinson, D. (2006). Rethinking followership: A post-structuralist analysis of follower identities. *The Leadership Quarterly, 17*(2), 179–189. doi:10.1016/j.leaqua.2005.12.005

Cooperrider, D., & Srivastva, S. (2017). Appreciative Inquiry in Organizational Life. In A. Shani & D. Noumair (Eds.), *Research in organizational change and development* (pp. 81–142). Emerald Publishing Limited. doi:10.1108/S0897-301620170000025003

Cording, M., Harrison, J., Hoskisson, R., & Jonsen, K. (2014). Walking the talk: A multistakeholder exploration of organizational authenticity, employee productivity, and post-merger performance. *The Academy of Management Perspectives, 28*(1), 38–56. doi:10.5465/amp.2013.0002

Crawford, J., Dawkins, S., & Kelder, J.-A. (2019). *True to self, and true to others? A triadic model of authenticity, sincerity, and self.* Unpublished Manuscript.

Crawford, J., Dawkins, S., Martin, A., & Lewis, G. (2018). Conceptualising authentic followers and developing a future research agenda. In D. Cotter-Lockard (Ed.), *Authentic Leadership and Followership: International Perspectives* (pp. 271–293). Palgrave Macmillan. doi:10.1007/978-3-319-65307-5_11

Crawford, J., Dawkins, S., Martin, A., & Lewis, G. (2020). Putting the leader back into authentic leadership: Reconceptualising and rethinking leaders. *Australian Journal of Management*, *45*(1), 114–133. doi:10.1177/0312896219836460

Cunningham, C., Woodward, C., Shannon, H., MacIntosh, J., Lendrum, B., Rosenbloom, D., & Brown, J. (2002). Readiness for organizational change: A longitudinal study of workplace, psychological and behavioural correlates. *Journal of Occupational and Organizational Psychology*, *75*(4), 377–392. doi:10.1348/096317902321119637

Dawkins, S., Martin, A., Scott, J., & Sanderson, K. (2015). Advancing conceptualization and measurement of psychological capital as a collective construct. *Human Relations*, *68*(6), 925–949. doi:10.1177/0018726714549645

de Zilwa, D. (2016). The strengths and capacities of Authentic Followership. *Leadership and Organization Development Journal*, *37*(3), 310–324. doi:10.1108/LODJ-01-2014-0010

de Zilwa, D., Lapierre, L., & Carsten, M. (2014). A new conceptual framework for authentic followership. In L. Lapierre & M. Carsten (Eds.), *Followership: What is it, and why do people follow* (pp. 47–72). Emerald Group Publishing.

Dichev, C., & Dicheva, D. (2017). Gamifying education: what is known, what is believed and what remains uncertain: a critical review. *International Journal of Educational Technology in Higher Education*, *14*(1), 1–36. doi:10.118641239-017-0042-5

Doorewaard, H., & Benschop, Y. (2003). HRM and organizational change: An emotional endeavor. *Journal of Organizational Change Management*, *16*(3), 272–286. doi:10.1108/09534810310475523

Doucet, K. (2000). Let's make a deal! *CMA Management*, *74*(8), 9.

Edú-Valsania, S., Moriano, J. A., & Molero, F. (2016). Authentic leadership and employee knowledge sharing behavior: Mediation of the innovation climate and workgroup identification. *Leadership and Organization Development Journal*, *37*(4), 487–506. doi:10.1108/LODJ-08-2014-0149

El-Bawab, N. (2019). *Marriott plans to launch home-rental market platform that would compete with Airbnb, report says.* CNBC.

Eriksen, M. (2009). Authentic leadership: Practical reflexivity, self-awareness, and self-authorship. *Journal of Management Education*, *33*(6), 747–771. doi:10.1177/1052562909339307

Feldman, M. (2004). Resources in emerging structures and processes of change. *Organization Science*, *15*(3), 295–309. doi:10.1287/orsc.1040.0073

Ferris, G., Treadway, D., Kolodinsky, R., Hochwarter, W., Kacmar, C., Douglas, C., & Frink, D. (2005). Development and validation of the political skill inventory. *Journal of Management*, *31*(1), 126–152. doi:10.1177/0149206304271386

Franken, A., Edwards, C., & Lambert, R. (2009). Executing strategic change: Understanding the critical management elements that lead to success. *California Management Review*, *51*(3), 49–73. doi:10.2307/41166493

Fredrickson, B., & Joiner, T. (2002). Positive emotions trigger upward spirals toward emotional well-being. *Psychological Science*, *13*(2), 172–175. doi:10.1111/1467-9280.00431 PMID:11934003

Freud, S. (1921). *Group psychology and the analysis of the ego.* International Psychoanalytic Publishing House.

Fugate, M., Prussia, G., & Kinicki, A. (2012). Managing employee withdrawal during organizational change: The role of threat appraisal. *Journal of Management*, *38*(3), 890–914. doi:10.1177/0149206309352881

Gardner, W., Cogliser, C., Davis, K., & Dickens, M. (2011). Authentic leadership: A review of the literature and research agenda. *The Leadership Quarterly*, *22*(6), 1120–1145. doi:10.1016/j.leaqua.2011.09.007

Gerdin, J., & Greve, J. (2004). Forms of contingency fit in management accounting research—A critical review. *Accounting, Organizations and Society*, *29*(3-4), 303–326. doi:10.1016/S0361-3682(02)00096-X

Gilley, A., Dixon, P., & Gilley, J. W. (2008). Characteristics of leadership effectiveness: Implementing change and driving innovation in organizations. *Human Resource Development Quarterly*, *19*(2), 153–169. doi:10.1002/hrdq.1232

Gilley, A., McMillan, H., & Gilley, J. (2009). Organizational change and characteristics of leadership effectiveness. *Journal of Leadership & Organizational Studies*, *16*(1), 38–47. doi:10.1177/1548051809334191

Gillham, J., & Seligman, M. (1999). Footsteps on the road to a positive psychology. *Behaviour Research and Therapy*, *37*(1), 163–173. doi:10.1016/S0005-7967(99)00055-8 PMID:10402701

Gleeson, D., & Shain, F. (2003). Managing ambiguity in further education. In N. Bennett, M. Crawford, & M. Cartwright (Eds.), *Effective educational leadership* (pp. 229–246). Paul Chapman Publishing.

Goffman, E. (1959). *The presentation of self in everyday life*. Doubleday.

Grant, A. (2008). Does intrinsic motivation fuel the prosocial fire? Motivational synergy in predicting persistence, performance, and productivity. *The Journal of Applied Psychology*, *93*(1), 48–58. doi:10.1037/0021-9010.93.1.48 PMID:18211134

Grant, M., & Booth, A. (2009). A typology of reviews: An analysis of 14 review types and associated methodologies. *Health Information and Libraries Journal*, *26*(2), 91–108. doi:10.1111/j.1471-1842.2009.00848.x PMID:19490148

Grijalva, E., Harms, P., Newman, D., Gaddis, B., & Fraley, R. (2015). Narcissism and leadership: A meta-analytic review of linear and nonlinear relationships. *Personnel Psychology*, *68*(1), 1–47. doi:10.1111/peps.12072

Groves, K. (2005). Linking leader skills, follower attitudes, and contextual variables via an integrated model of charismatic leadership. *Journal of Management*, *31*(2), 255–277. doi:10.1177/0149206304271765

Guerrero, S., Lapalme, M., & Séguin, M. (2015). Board chair authentic leadership and nonexecutives' motivation and commitment. *Journal of Leadership & Organizational Studies*, *22*(1), 88–101. doi:10.1177/1548051814531825

Haffar, M., Al-Karaghouli, W., Irani, Z., Djebarni, R., & Gbadamosi, G. (2019). The influence of individual readiness for change dimensions on quality management implementation in Algerian manufacturing organisations. *International Journal of Production Economics*, *207*(1), 247–260. doi:10.1016/j.ijpe.2016.08.024

Hannah, S., & Avolio, B. (2010). Moral potency: Building the capacity for character-based leadership. *Consulting Psychology Journal*, *62*(4), 291–310. doi:10.1037/a0022283

Hansen, P. (2007). Organizational culture and organizational change: The transformation of savings banks in Denmark, 1965–1990. *Enterprise and Society*, *8*(4), 920–953. doi:10.1093/es/khm071

Harter, S. (2002). Authenticity. In C. Synder & S. Lopez (Eds.), *Handbook of positive psychology* (pp. 382–394). Oxford University Press.

Hayes, J. (2014). *The theory and practice of change management* (4th ed.). Palgrave Macmillan. doi:10.1007/978-1-137-28902-5

Heidegger, M. (1962). *Being and time* (J. Macquarrie & E. Robinson, Trans.). Harper Collins.

Herzig, S., & Jimmieson, N. (2006). Middle managers' uncertainty management during organizational change. *Leadership and Organization Development Journal, 27*(8), 628–645. doi:10.1108/01437730610709264

Holten, A., & Brenner, S. (2015). Leadership style and the process of organizational change. *Leadership and Organization Development Journal, 36*(1), 2–16. doi:10.1108/LODJ-11-2012-0155

Hughes, D. J., Lee, A., Tian, A. W., Newman, A., & Legood, A. (2018). Leadership, creativity, and innovation: A critical review and practical recommendations. *The Leadership Quarterly, 29*(5), 549–569. doi:10.1016/j.leaqua.2018.03.001

Hussain, S., Lei, S., Akram, T., Haider, M., Hussain, S., & Ali, M. (2018). Kurt Lewin's change model: A critical review of the role of leadership and employee involvement in organizational change. *Journal of Innovation & Knowledge, 3*(3), 123–127. doi:10.1016/j.jik.2016.07.002

Johansson, C., & Heide, M. (2008). Speaking of change: Three communication approaches in studies of organizational change. *Corporate Communications, 13*(3), 288–305. doi:10.1108/13563280810893661

Judge, T., & Bono, J. (2001). Relationship of core self-evaluations traits—self-esteem, generalized self-efficacy, locus of control, and emotional stability—with job satisfaction and job performance: A meta-analysis. *The Journal of Applied Psychology, 86*(1), 80–92. doi:10.1037/0021-9010.86.1.80 PMID:11302235

Kelley, R. (1988). *In praise of followers*. Harvard Business Review Case Services.

Kelley, R. (1991). Combining followership and leadership into partnership. In R. Kilmann & I. Kilmann (Eds.), *Making organizations competitive: Enhancing networks and relationships across traditional boundaries* (pp. 195–220). Jossey-Bass.

Kelley, R. (2008). Rethinking followership. In R. Riggio, I. Chaleff, & J. Lipman-Blumen (Eds.), *The art of followership: How great followers create great leaders and organizations* (pp. 5–16). John Wiley & Sons.

Kernis, M., & Goldman, B. (2006). A multicomponent conceptualization of authenticity: Theory and research. *Advances in Experimental Social Psychology, 38*, 283–357. doi:10.1016/S0065-2601(06)38006-9

Kim, K., & Huh, C. (2019). An Effects of Authentic Leadership and Transformational Leadership on Change Supportive Behavior in Small and Medium-size Business: Focused on Mediating Effect of Positive Psychological Capital. *Asia-Pacific Journal of Business Venturing and Entrepreneurship*, *14*(2), 135–149.

Kira, M., Balkin, D., & San, E. (2012). Authentic work and organizational change: Longitudinal evidence from a merger. *Journal of Change Management*, *12*(1), 31–51. doi:10.1080/14697017.2011.652374

Klarner, P., By, R., & Diefenbach, T. (2011). Employee emotions during organizational change—Towards a new research agenda. *Scandinavian Journal of Management*, *27*(3), 332–340. doi:10.1016/j.scaman.2011.06.002

Klein, K., & Kozlowski, S. (2000). From Micro to Meso: Critical Steps in Conceptualizing and Conducting Multilevel Research. *Organizational Research Methods*, *3*(3), 211–236. doi:10.1177/109442810033001

Klein, K., & Sorra, J. (1996). The challenge of innovation implementation. Academy of Management Review, 21(4), 22-42.

Kotter, J. (2007, Jan.). *Leading change: Why transformation efforts fail. Harvard Business Review.*

Lehman, W., Greener, J., & Simpson, D. (2002). Assessing organizational readiness for change. *Journal of Substance Abuse Treatment*, *22*(1), 197–209. doi:10.1016/S0740-5472(02)00233-7 PMID:12072164

Lewis, T., Marginson, S., & Snyder, I. (2005). The network university? Technology, culture and organisational complexity in contemporary higher education. *Higher Education Quarterly*, *59*(1), 56–75. doi:10.1111/j.1468-2273.2005.00281.x

Luthans, F. (2002). The need for and meaning of positive organizational behavior. *Journal of Organizational Behavior*, *23*(6), 695–706. doi:10.1002/job.165

Luthans, F., & Avolio, B. (2003). Authentic leadership development. In K. Cameron, J. Dutton, & R. Quinn (Eds.), *Positive organisational scholarship: Foundations of a New Discipline* (pp. 241–258). Berrett Koehler Publishers.

Lyu, Y., Wang, M., Le, J., & Kwan, H. (2019). Effects of authentic leadership on work–family balance in China. *Journal of Managerial Psychology*, *34*(2), 110–123. doi:10.1108/JMP-08-2018-0340

Mazutis, D., & Slawinski, N. (2008). Leading organizational learning through authentic dialogue. *Management Learning*, *39*(4), 437–456. doi:10.1177/1350507608093713

Meaney, M., & Pung, C. (2008). McKinsey global results: Creating organizational transformations. *The McKinsey Quarterly*, *7*(3), 1–7.

Mhatre, K., & Conger, J. (2011). Bridging the gap between gen x and gen y: Lessons from authentic leadership. *The Journal of Leadership Studies*, *5*(3), 72–76. doi:10.1002/jls.20235

Morgan, D., & Zeffane, R. (2003). Employee involvement, organizational change and trust in management. *International Journal of Human Resource Management*, *14*(1), 55–75. doi:10.1080/09585190210158510

Morrell, K., Loan-Clarke, J., & Wilkinson, A. (2004). Organisational change and employee turnover. *Personnel Review*, *33*(2), 161–173. doi:10.1108/00483480410518022

Morrison, E., & Milliken, F. (2000). Organizational silence: A barrier to change and development in a pluralistic world. *Academy of Management Review*, *25*(4), 706–725. doi:10.5465/amr.2000.3707697

Nwanzu, C., & Babalola, S. (2019). Examining psychological capital of optimism, self-efficacy and self-monitoring as predictors of attitude towards organizational change. *International Journal of Engineering Business Management*, *11*. Advance online publication. doi:10.1177/1847979019827149

Pardo del Val, M., & Martínez Fuentes, C. (2003). Resistance to change: A literature review and empirical study. *Management Decision*, *41*(2), 148–155. doi:10.1108/00251740310457597

Pasmore, W. A. (2011). Tipping the balance: Overcoming persistent problems in organizational change. *Research in Organizational Change and Development*, *19*, 259–292. doi:10.1108/S0897-3016(2011)0000019011

Piderit, S. (2000). Rethinking resistance and recognizing ambivalence: A multidimensional view of attitudes toward an organizational change. *Academy of Management Review*, *25*(4), 783–794. doi:10.5465/amr.2000.3707722

Popper, M., & Amit, K. (2009). Attachment and leader's development via experiences. *The Leadership Quarterly*, *20*(5), 749–763. doi:10.1016/j.leaqua.2009.06.005

Rego, A., Ribeiro, N., Cunha, M., & Jesuino, J. (2011). How happiness mediates the organizational virtuousness and affective commitment relationship. *Journal of Business Research*, *64*(5), 524–532. doi:10.1016/j.jbusres.2010.04.009

Reichers, A., Wanous, J., & Austin, J. (1997). Understanding and managing cynicism about organizational change. *The Academy of Management Perspectives*, *11*(1), 48–59. doi:10.5465/ame.1997.9707100659

Reis, G., Trullen, J., & Story, J. (2016). Perceived organizational culture and engagement: The mediating role of authenticity. *Journal of Managerial Psychology*, *31*(6), 1091–1105. doi:10.1108/JMP-05-2015-0178

Ryan, P., & Danaher, M. (2019). The role of leadership and motivation during change. In F. Sheerin & E. Curtin (Eds.), *Leadership for Intellectual Disability Service: Motivating Change and Improvement* (pp. 85–107). Routledge. doi:10.4324/9781351172400-4

Schraeder, M., Tears, R., & Jordan, M. (2005). Organizational culture in public sector organizations: Promoting change through training and leading by example. *Leadership and Organization Development Journal*, *26*(6), 492–502. doi:10.1108/01437730510617681

Sendjaya, S., Pekerti, A., Härtel, C., Hirst, G., & Butarbutar, I. (2016). Are authentic leaders always moral? The role of Machiavellianism in the relationship between authentic leadership and morality. *Journal of Business Ethics*, *133*(1), 125–139. doi:10.100710551-014-2351-0

Shakespeare, W. (1954). *Hamlet* (3rd ed.). Yale University Press.

Sheldon, K., & King, L. (2001). Why positive psychology is necessary. *The American Psychologist*, *56*(3), 216–217. doi:10.1037/0003-066X.56.3.216 PMID:11315247

Shirey, M., White-Williams, C., & Hites, L. (2019). Integration of Authentic Leadership Lens for Building High Performing Interprofessional Collaborative Practice Teams. *Nursing Administration Quarterly*, *43*(2), 101–112. doi:10.1097/NAQ.0000000000000339 PMID:30839447

Specht, J., Kuonath, A., Pachler, D., Weisweiler, S., & Frey, D. (2018). How Change Agents' Motivation Facilitates Organizational Change: Pathways Through Meaning and Organizational Identification. *Journal of Change Management*, *18*(3), 198–217. doi:10.1080/14697017.2017.1378696

Stanley, D., Meyer, J., & Topolnytsky, L. (2005). Employee cynicism and resistance to organizational change. *Journal of Business and Psychology*, *19*(4), 429–459. doi:10.100710869-005-4518-2

Sterling, J. (2003). Translating strategy into effective implementation: Dispelling the myths and highlighting what works. *Strategy and Leadership*, *31*(3), 27–34. doi:10.1108/10878570310472737

Strebel. P. (1996, May-June) Why do employees resist change? In *Harvard Business Review on Change* (pp. 139-157). Boston: Harvard Business School Publishing.

Tanno, J., & Banner, D. (2018). Servant leaders as change agents. *Journal of Social Change, 10*(1), 1–18. doi:10.5590/JOSC.2018.10.1.01

Taylor, J., Flanagin, A., Cheney, G., & Seibold, D. (2001). Organizational communication research: key moments, central concerns, and future challenges. In W. Gudykunst (Ed.), *Communication Yearbook* (pp. 99–137). SAGE Publications. doi:10.1080/23808985.2001.11678983

Trilling, L. (2009). *Sincerity and authenticity*. Harvard University Press. doi:10.2307/j.ctvjhzrdp

Turner Parish, J., Cadwallader, S., & Busch, P. (2008). Want to, need to, ought to: Employee commitment to organizational change. *Journal of Organizational Change Management, 21*(1), 32–52. doi:10.1108/09534810810847020

Van de Ven, A., & Poole, M. (1995). Explaining development and change in organizations. *Academy of Management Review, 20*(3), 510–540. doi:10.5465/amr.1995.9508080329

van den Bosch, R., & Taris, T. (2014). The authentic worker's well-being and performance: The relationship between authenticity at work, well-being, and work outcomes. *The Journal of Psychology, 148*(6), 659–681. doi:10.1080/00223980.2013.820684 PMID:25175889

Van Vugt, M. (2006). Evolutionary origins of leadership and followership. *Personality and Social Psychology Review, 10*(4), 354–371. doi:10.120715327957pspr1004_5 PMID:17201593

Velu, C., & Stiles, P. (2013). Managing decision-making and cannibalization for parallel business models. *Long Range Planning, 46*(6), 443–458. doi:10.1016/j.lrp.2013.08.003

Wanous, J., Reichers, A., & Austin, J. (2000). Cynicism about organizational change: Measurement, antecedents, and correlates. *Group & Organization Management, 25*(2), 132–153. doi:10.1177/1059601100252003

Wee, E., & Taylor, M. (2018). Attention to change: A multilevel theory on the process of emergent continuous organizational change. *The Journal of Applied Psychology, 103*(1), 1–13. doi:10.1037/apl0000261 PMID:28933908

Weiner, B. (2009). A theory of organizational readiness for change. *Implementation Science; IS, 4*(1), 67–75. doi:10.1186/1748-5908-4-67 PMID:19840381

Wright, B., Christensen, R., & Isett, K. (2013). Motivated to adapt? The role of public service motivation as employees face organizational change. *Public Administration Review*, *73*(5), 738–747. doi:10.1111/puar.12078

Youssef, C., & Luthans, F. (2007). Positive organizational behavior in the workplace: The impact of hope, optimism, and resilience. *Journal of Management*, *33*(5), 774–800. doi:10.1177/0149206307305562

Chapter 11
Four Constituents of an Entrepreneurial Culture Within Business Organizations:
A Reflective Analysis

Omar Javaid
Institute of Business Management, Karachi, Pakistan

ABSTRACT

A culture of fear, control, and meaninglessness can effectively kill the entrepreneurial spirit within an organization. This chapter will explore why such a culture typically takes root and how it is deadly for the organization's entrepreneurial orientation. The chapter is based on an interdisciplinary reflective analysis done by exploring disciplines including depth psychology, neuroscience, positive psychology, and organizational behavior. The chapter argues from the perspectives of these disciplines that it is perhaps the factor of safety, risk-taking, collaboration, and meaningfulness if present in organizational culture that will eventually cultivate the spirit of entrepreneurship in an organization. While discussing these factors, the chapter also explains how seemingly irrational forces of the unconscious mind keep the leadership from adopting a behavior which is fundamentally important in fostering a culture where entrepreneurial behavior takes root. The chapter also explains how these psychic forces can be turned around to cultivate an entrepreneurial culture in an organization.

DOI: 10.4018/978-1-7998-2807-5.ch011

INTRODUCTION

Generally speaking, employees who join a company are often enthusiastic, excited, and forward-looking, however, their zeal may die off over time. If their enthusiasm is too hard to kill, they gradually spend their energy not on bringing new ideas rather on following the old norms already prevalent within the organization. Even if they remain successful in bringing new ideas, their implementation is often hijacked by the prevalent organizational culture. No matter how resilient humans are, their energies, imaginations, and aspirations can fade away likewise. If new employees can retain their drive to take initiatives, the organizational culture and its bureaucratic system can use their drive to feed the status quo instead (Campagnolo & Vivel, 2012; Hardy & Thomas, 2014).

This chapter argues through a reflective analysis of relevant literature that it is primarily the top positions of power in an organization that can create, influence, or destroy a culture of initiative, innovation, creativity, collaboration, and entrepreneurship. The top leadership sets the precedence, which is then trickled down typically by the subsequent layers of managers and supervisors to the very bottom. The choice of the type of organizational management systems also affect the entrepreneurial orientation of employees, and this choice is perhaps also dependent on the preferences of the top leadership during organizational evolution, particularly in the earlier years (Semler, 2007).

The extant literature extensively discusses the types of leadership, their impact on organizational culture, and employee creativity, however, a deeper psychological analysis which (a) looks at the unconscious and neurological reasons behind leadership behavior toward their employees, particularly when the employees commit mistakes, and (b) analyse the neurological effect of their reaction on the employees, is seldom found in the extant literature. If the source of a behavior is unconscious for example, then many of the contemporary methods to change behavior which do not address the contents of the unconscious mind, will not be sufficient, and at best will superficially address the problem. If this is true then a more informed approach will be needed, and appropriate therapeutic interventions may be necessary to address the unconscious cause of leadership behavior unconducive to foster an entrepreneurial culture in an organization.

This article therefore uses the perspectives from depth psychology, positive psychology, and to an extent from neuroscience, to explore the unconscious causes behind unconducive leadership's behavior which kills the entrepreneurial spirit, and what can be done to address the unconscious causes. The author's personal experience of working in several organizations in the corporate, non-profit, and educational sectors, also influences the outcomes of the reflective analysis present in this chapter. Evaluation of the author's experience in the light of the perspectives from multiple domains of psychology and relevant literature on management and leadership has led the author to argue for four factors, which may be pivotal for an entrepreneurial culture within an organization. The four factors emerging from the author's analysis are:

1. Employee's sense of safety,
2. A culture of risk-taking,
3. A culture of collaboration, and
4. A sense of meaning and purpose

The next section will explain the research method. The following section on Key Findings will explain how the four factors influence entrepreneurial culture. This will be followed by Recommendation, Conclusion and Future Research.

RESEARCH METHOD

This paper is based on a reflective analysis of interdisciplinary literature (Brydges & Butler, 2012). The findings from the literature review were reflected upon in the light of questions related to the role of leadership in fostering a culture of innovation. These questions emerged from the author's personal experience of 16 years of working in the corporate, manufacturing, non-profit and educational sectors. During the course of this experience the author got a chance to work with at least 5 supervisors or managers along the business owners or their bosses running the business. These managers and the organizational leaders to whom they reported (having titles ranging from CEO, President, and Managing Director) possessed varying styles of leadership ranging from autocratic to collaborative. During these 16 years, author not just experienced the influence of these managers and business leaders on his own creative output, but also the culture they fostered under them. The reflection on the experience led the author to ask some questions regarding the source of their leadership styles and how these styles influenced employees. Following are the questions which emerged during author's experience:

- What causes the leaders to overreact and take it personally when an employee makes a mistake affecting the reputation of the organization?
- What is the psychological and neurological impact on employees if the leadership has a persistent habit of overreacting?
- What are the psychological and neurological reasons behind employee's reluctance to take risks and vice versa?

- What are the psychological and neurological reasons behind employee's reluctance to collaborate with others to work and resist change?
- What changes - a shift in leader's attitude - brings in the minds and hearts of employees?
- Why and why not the documented purpose and mission of an organization have any effect on the employee's ownership and creativity?

These questions did not emerge in such a sequence nor in the way articulated above. The articulation of these questions follow an approach of 'retrospective plausibility' as explained by Taleb (2012) which involves restructuring one's reflection on incoherent past experiences into a coherent causal sequence. The type of literature review - which was done as and when the questions arrived during reflection - is referred in the relevant literature as 'Critical Interpretive Synthesis' or CIS (Depraetere et al., 2020) which is rather "iterative, reflexive, and exploratory" (Xiao & Watson, 2017). From its definition it implies that CIS is an ongoing process, therefore, the arguments in this article may further evolve in future exploration of the subject. Since the inferences converged to four factors in response to the research questions, therefore, an attempt has been made to explain authors learning about these factors which emerged in the process.

The research paradigm known as social constructivism fully acknowledge the role of human bias in research, and even declare it impossible to separate (Guba & Lincoln, 1982; Javaid & Hyder, 2018). The best can be done is to articulate the bias of the author and cross check it with other observers or extant literature to see if they get to the conclusions same as those of author's (Lincoln & Guba, 2013). It is therefore stated that author considers the leadership's role as the primary cause behind the organizational culture, entrepreneurial or otherwise. The reverse causality in this context appears to the author to be highly unlikely unless the organization is essentially a cooperative, where the top managers are instead hired by the members of the cooperative (Diaz-Foncea & Marcuello, 2013). The literature explored and cited in this paper also appears to be in line with author's view on the subject.

It should be noted that the literature exploration in the light of the question was not deliberate. The literature from Jungian psychology, trauma psychology, and contemporary management discourse was picked for review for reasons other than to look for answers to the aforementioned questions, but coincidently the review also provided answers to the questions author had related to the role of leadership in developing an entrepreneurial culture. Reflection on the literature eventually lead to convergence toward the four factors explained in this paper in the light of the questions mentioned above. This convergence happened despite the literature was interdisciplinary. The convergence thus fulfil a key validating criteria as required in social constructivist paradigm (Javaid & Hyder, 2018).

KEY FINDINGS

1. Employee's Sense of Safety

During his professional experience author observed on numerous occasions that a culture of fear was antagonistic to the culture of creativity, and despite trying hard, employees could not bring out creative solutions to the organizational problems. This observation is analogues to findings in the discipline of neuropsychology which explains the reason behind this drop of creativity in an atmosphere of fear. The relevant literature suggests that a sense of safety is a prerequisite for the activation of creative regions of the human brain, more so for the motivation to execute a creative idea (Meier et al., 2020). So, organizational leaders who do not make their employees feel safe, or maintain an environment of uncertainty in the organizations they lead, can make it unconducive for their employees to bring out and execute creative ideas (Y. Yang et al., 2021). But why any organizational leader would not want to make employees feel safe? It is perhaps unintended, as human beings' organizational leaders may also be susceptible to overreact when they are stressed or perhaps fearful of a financial loss or disrepute of the organization. Overreactions if frequent can create a unsafe environment for the employees (Guo et al., 2018).

These overreactions can be frequent due to some aching nerves, or unhealed emotional wounds from the past, some psychological injuries referred to as trauma in the literature (Maté, 2013). These wounds are often invisible to humans themselves during ordinary circumstances (van der Kolk, 2014). They surface when retraumatized by an external stimulus and eventually cause an extra intense response (Ziveig, 1997). This is perhaps one of the key reasons why some people react more than others in ordinary situations.

However, it is perhaps their sympathetic-nervous-system in action which is the part of the nervous system designed to keep us safe when faced by a threat even if the threat is only perceived and not real (van der Kolk, 2014). Unhealed emotional wounds from the past can also keep our sympathetic-nervous-system active most of the time, keeping them typically in a fight mode. When injured, we are over-cautious, and it can be exhausting if we have a lot of work to do. If the injury happened in the distant past, which we may not consciously remember, but to keep us safe our sympathetic-nervous-system may still keep us on high-alert. Overworking, or becoming a workaholic can be an unconscious reaction to protect us from failures that may have been emotionally painful in the past. This can keep us under high stress, while overreactions in such scenarios can feel very much justified (Maté, 2013).

So, if a leader overreacts but cannot recall if he or she is carrying any psychological injuries from the past, distant past to be specific, they might want to see if they are taking a mistake of any of their employees a little too personally? Like if an employee unintentionally does something which results in bad word of mouth for the organization, how would a leader react in such a situation? If the leader is reacting as if they have taken it personally, then it may be because of an unhealed psychological injury from the past. The injury would be invisible to the employees; however, the leader's reaction will be visible and it may have a strong trickle-down effect particularly if it threatens the self-respect of the employees (Chappell et al., 2019).

Overreaction to unexpected incidents may not be the only indication. Even if the leadership appears to be calm, composed and supportive in most situations, they may have created systems where employees are put in strict control, are often micromanaged, and are manipulated through conflicting KPIs. Such systemization (or bureaucratization) may also hint towards leadership's assumptions about employees that they cannot be trusted, they may go off the track, act dishonestly and avoid work even. So, the top management needs to maintain control over them, maintain an oversight, even do this systematically so that they do not wander off, rather generate a predictable outcome. A system designed from the point of view of Theory X rather than Theory Y or Z (Lunenburg, 2011).

If yes, then the leadership perhaps does carry a sense of fear, and to keep things under control to the very micro details may make them feel safe. Of course, the leaders may also legally own the company, have their skin and stakes involved, but what will happen if all of it is lost, will that make the leader or the owner lose their sense of self-identity, an identity which was created to protect them from retraumatizing past injuries (Maté, 2003)? As a leader you may ask, 'do I see my company's image as an extension of my self-image', or I see my 'self' as a distinct entity from the business I own or run? Of course, losing what one has created can be painful, if the company is not seen as an extension of the leader's self, if the leader feels complete and safe with or without what has been put at stake in the company, then perhaps reason to maintain control is not a defense mechanism to protect from retraumatizing of past injuries. Perhaps the systems of excessive control have been put in place just because other organizations were doing the same, or perhaps that is what the organization's managers with MBA degrees decided to do (Mcdonald, 2017).

In either case, as a leader, one may consider that any system to control employees, keep them under check, and manipulate them with performance indicators, prevents them from using their wisdom to do something out of the box when needed (B. Schwartz & Sharpe, 2010). Such systems, though claiming to reward employees for their performance, primarily use fear as a motivator. Under such systems, a culture grounded in fear eventually sets in. Such a culture pushes the employees towards the survival mode, and neurologically, can reduce the activity in the creative centers of their brain (Meier et al., 2020). On top of that, if the leaders or owners are also carrying a sense of insecurity at the back of their minds, they may overreact to employees' mistakes, making things even worse (Guo et al., 2018).

If the leaders and owners are not carrying any unconscious fear, rather feel safe in their existence, they eventually take a more objective approach and see things as they are (Harris, 1969; Vos & van Rijn, 2021). A failure of an employee which brings financial loss or disrepute to the organization may not threaten suchleaders and the owners at a personal level. If their sense of identity is perhaps well-grounded in their beings, and the organization's public image is not an extension of their self-image, a loss or disrespect to the organization will not be then seen as a loss or disrespect of their being at a very personal level.

Leaders and owners who do not feel personally threatened; would not easily enter into fight or flight mode, fight mode in particular, thus will not be attacking the self-respect of their employees, (Meier et al., 2020), as they will not see a direct threat to their self-image or self-worth. They would be able to objectively assess the situation, identify the root cause and take corrective action to eradicate the root cause and not make it personal with the employees even if they have to lay off some of them if necessary (Collins, 2009). Such leaders and owners are also perhaps able to see the goodness in other people, and rather follow the Theory-Y of management (Lunenburg, 2011). Leadership with unconscious fears may rather anticipate threats everywhere, their sympathetic-nervous-system would remain on high alert, often overestimating the potential of a situation to bring some kind of a loss to the organization, thus penalize employees when they should not, and penalize a lot more than they should when needed, as a result often hurting the self-respect of the employees (Fang et al., 2019).

It will be unlikely for an organization with a culture of uncertainty and fear to develop an entrepreneurial culture, as employees would rather rely on the instructions from the top while most of them would focus on obeying instructions to play safe. Any initiatives would involve taking permissions from every layer of management above, the red-tapism and the risk of any negative consequences of thinking out of the box perhaps expels the very spirit of innovation from the organization (Campagnolo & Vivel, 2012). So, the employees who have the potential to innovate, feel unfulfilled and prefer to leave if possible; while those employees, who are comfortable with just following orders, stay behind (Dixon & Hart, 2010).

So, an entrepreneurial culture can barely develop unless the owners of the business or perhaps their next generation learn the source of their unconscious fears, identify the unhealed psychological injuries they may be carrying. For this, they may even want to consult therapists or counsellors to identify the unconscious fears within themselves, not just for the sake of organization only, but also to live a more content life on a very personal level (Hillman, 1968). Once they do, it may be expected that their transformed behavior will eventually have a trickledown effect, slowly and gradually, making the people below them feel safer and thus more open to experimenting with new ideas for the betterment of the organization. The system to micromanage employees also needs to go, but more on this in Section 3 of this chapter.

2. A Culture of Risk Taking

The author had the experience of working with bosses who appear to have an intrinsic sense of security, and those who appeared to be internally insecure. In this experience author observed the impact of leadership behavior on his own creative output, and the creative output of his coworkers. The employees working under a leader with a sense of security appeared to be experimenting more despite the risk of failure. Literature also sides with the author's inference in this context. Extent literature suggests that intrinsically secure owners may not scare their employees or may not create systems only to control everyone out of fear of uncertainty (Semler, 2007). However, they do need to encourage employees to think out of the box, be innovative, unleash their creative spark, make mistakes while trying new stuff, and learn from their mistakes. From Herzberg's view, only removing the dissatisfiers will no work, satisfiers like recognition or appreciation will also be needed (Herzberg, 2003).

One of the first employer of the author supplied parts to the local assembler of Toyota vehicles. This led author to have an exposure of the Toyota Production system. It has been documented that at Toyota factories, the workers are encouraged to suggest improvements in the processes to avoid wastage of time, resources, effort, etc. (wastage is a cost as per Toyota's philosophy) and most of these suggestions are taken seriously by the management and implemented. Toyota believes that the best person to suggest an improvement in the process is the person who is directly involved in the process on the day to day basis (Chiarini et al., 2018). It is typically encouraging for the employee if their suggestions are taken seriously and recognized irrespective of their rank in the organization. Being seen, recognized, and valued by seniors can have a powerful impact on the employee's self-worth, and can be highly motivating (Hansen et al., 2002).

It is perhaps important to note at this point that it might take a long time to develop such a culture. The effort will be undone rather quickly if there is an overreacting tendency in the top leadership. Further, if the top leadership or the owners act in a self-interested way, protecting or boosting their ego only, even taking credit to the contribution of the employees (Wisse & Rus, 2012), then it can set precedence for a perception of 'us' versus 'them' (Hardy & Thomas, 2014). Such a disempowering and unsafe culture though is difficult to create if the leaders or members of top management are intrinsically secure, as mentioned earlier. So, first thing first; the transition needs to begin with soul searching at the very top of organizational hierarchy, and if there are barriers at the top, then it is perhaps unlikely for such a culture to take root among the lower ranks of the organization.

Self-Ownership as a Prerequisite for Employee's Ownership

Semco is a Brazilian firm lead by Ricardo Semler which is highly acclaimed for its profoundly empowering and ultra-democratic culture. Semco's experience suggests that employees develop a sense of ownership when the company they work for owns them, or more specifically the people on the top owns the employees (Semler, 2007). Looking at Semco's experience through the lens of Jungian psychology would suggest that the leadership can better own the employees only when the leaders possesses a strong sense of ownership of their 'selves'. As per Jungians, one cannot own others, when one does not own one's self. Likewise, one cannot respect others with honesty, if he or she cannot respect a part of himself or herself. One cannot truly accept others with sincerity if he or she cannot accept a part of him or herself. People cannot truly own, respect, and accept themselves if they have been conditioned to feel resentment towards a part of their own. This resented part of one's self is referred to as the 'shadow' in Jungian psychology (Chappell et al., 2019; Ziveig, 1997). It's hard for a layman to see such an internal conflict going on in between the conscious and subconscious minds of the leadership. They may only appear to be reactive or aggressive to others, or distant, even look alright during normal circumstances. It requires a trained eye to see through and identify the conflict in the apparent and hidden parts of their psyche.

The cause behind a lack of self-ownership may be traced in early childhood experiences. If during the process of upbringing a person has been shamed by their elders for some unapproved behavior or habit and if such shaming has become a constant part of the childhood experience, for example, then it can leave a person to develop a strong shadow. Such shaming and resulting rejection from guardian figures can also result in an emotional wound. If the parents have ignored (inadvertently of course) a part of their children's personality, then that part of their personality often becomes invisible or deemed unworthy when they grow up (Perry & Szalavitz, 2006; R. C. Schwartz, 2013).

So, if a person has gone through such an upbringing, then he or she may unconsciously find it hard to accept some aspects of his or her personality, either because it has been shamed or ignored by their elders. If so then such a person will find it hard to fully own him or herself. Such people may also find it hard to fully acknowledge some aspects of the personalities of others which remind them of their own shamed parts. Often these parts form our vulnerable side, which we have been taught to keep hidden from others. A person who rather accept his or her vulnerable side, may not reject the vulnerable side of others as well. If the other person is one's employee then such an act would make them feel safe, as safe is what we feel when we are feel accepted and respected with all our vulnerabilities (Chappell et al., 2019; Ziveig, 1997).

Since the rejection of other's vulnerabilities that remind us of our wounds typically happens on a very unconscious level, so the person may consciously come up with incorrect explanations as to why he or she does not like or is ignoring an aspect of other's personalities. The suggested solution by Jungians (Hillman, 1968) is to explore the content of the unconscious and the shadow self and thus own and respect every aspect of one's existence, this will eventually also help us to acknowledge all aspects of other's personalities. To do this, we also need to identify the shaming voice inside of us, and learn how to neutralize it (R. C. Schwartz, 2013). If a person finds it difficult to excavate his or her unconscious and shadow on their own, then the help of a trained therapist in Jungian methods (Hillman, 1968; Jung, 2006; Woodman, 1993) or Richard Schwartz's approach referred to as Internal Family System therapy (R. C. Schwartz, 2013) may be sought.

Micromanagement and Risk Taking

Leadership having unconscious fears may want to micromanage their employees as well. This also brings us to the problem of vague boundaries (Ashforth et al., 2000). If the employees feel that seniors will not interfere in their domains of work, that they will not be micromanaged, that they will feel ownership (both in symbolic and real terms), that they will feel the urge to see their domain and the organization nurture and grow into something better, that they will be allowed to take the credit of the results of their contributions, and have a tangible share in the results a well, then the employees are likely to feel the ownership and will eventually be encouraged to take initiatives to make things better (Semler, 2007; White, 2010).

Leadership on the top may, out of their unconscious fears, often do not delegate enough authority, or try to micromanage, and thus hardly allow their employees to claim the results as well. Unconscious fears can also make it difficult for people to know where the boundaries of others begin because they have difficulty seeing where the boundary of their own 'self' ends (Levine & Frederick, 1997). Only a single supervisor who is unconsciously afraid to trust his employees can destroy feeling of ownership among his or her subordinates by getting inside their boundaries (White, 2010). The unconscious fear, or neurologically speaking a dysregulated nervous system with a sympathetic dominance, makes a person triggered by the actions of others a lot more then needed often unnecessarily, so they may also unconsciously want to control the actions of others to avoid the feeling of threat (van der Kolk, 2014).

This is perhaps also a result of confused identities of 'self' often caused by the shame they may be carrying in their subconscious, which can also make them take the consequences of other's actions very personally (Jung, 2006; Levine & Frederick, 1997). If I as an owner see the disrespect of the organization or a financial loss caused by an honest mistake of an employee as my own disrespect or loss, then I would overreact more as compared to a person who can see the difference between their 'self' and the organization. So, leadership, managers or supervisors having an inner sense of security, or at least sufficient self-awareness about the unconscious fears, will be able to respect the boundary of every employee, which may also enable the employees to own and take responsibility of their share in the organization. If they have fears lurking in their unconscious minds then they need to do the necessary shadow work (Chappell et al., 2019) to see where their boundaries end, so they can respect the boundaries of their subordinates.

3. A Culture of Collaboration

So far, the discussion has focused on what happens at an individual level. This section will now focus on how individual employees collaborate for innovation within an organization when they do not feel safe and are trying to survive, versus, when they feel safe and go beyond their job description, think out of the box, and go proactive for the betterment of the organization. Working in both types of work environment allowed author to notice the degree of collaboration between employees in respective environments.

It was noted by the author, also mentioned in the relevant literature, that when employees do not feel safe in an organization, their interactions with others are typically meant to avoid any disagreement particularly with their bosses. Their communication regarding official matters is passive and unidirectional most of the time and typically flows through the formal hierarchy. They receive instructions, execute, and report. They may chat or make jokes with their coworkers during lunchtime, however, when it comes to their formal responsibilities, they can seldom expect involuntary support from others or offer the same unless their boss instructs them to do so, or they may get or offer such support if they are on very good terms with some co-workers in a personal capacity (Diefenbach & Sillince, 2011).

Extent literature suggests that organizational problems are often interdepartmental and experienced firsthand by the lower-level management or workers involved in the execution (Liker & Convis, 2012; Semler, 2007). So, if the communication between employees only flows through the formal hierarchy, then it can eventually create bottlenecks. On top of that, in a culture of fear, where every employee is forced to prioritize his or her survival, dirty organizational politics can take root. To protect their interest, middle management, in particular, may get involved in leg-pulling others who they see as a threat to their reputation or survival (Buchanan & Badham, 1999). Neurologically when our brain is occupied in a struggle to survive, the creative centers of our brain shuts down, and our ability to collaborate is only restricted to a very selected interest (safe) group, while everyone else is perceived as either irrelevant or a threat to one's survival (Levine & Frederick, 1997; Meier et al., 2020).

A mind which is motivated more by fear prefers the familiar over the unfamiliar despite the familiar being comfortable (Perry & Szalavitz, 2006). So past practices, routine stuff, tools, and tricks from within-the-box will be preferred during an act of collaboration within a culture dominated by fear. Employees perhaps will also form groups with people with whom they feel safer, where their traditional practices are generally endorsed by everyone in the group. Such a group may also typically resist any attempts to bring change. If an organizational culture is based on fear, many such informal groups may emerge to defend the status quo. Such groups often restrict open flow of information, and communicate with other groups more in an act of self-preservation and less for the benefit of the organization. An atmosphere of fear can breed tribalism and turf wars (Diamond, 2012).

As a result of such restricted communication between different organizational departments, involuntary collaboration to fix a problem, or avoid a problem in the future may happen due to the fear of being penalized. However, the ability for collaborative acts – to take the organization ahead in terms of a new offering, or enhancing customer experience, saving costs or eliminate wastage, or the ability to do something out of the box – is thus compromised.

Institutionalizing Fear, Bureaucratic Control and Obedience

There is perhaps a structural grounding of such a culture of fear. Leaders may prefer to predict, control, and stabilize every outcome of the organizational activity and thus adopt a bureaucratic system of management. The bureaucratic system of management is grounded in Theory-X of management, therefore considers every employee as fallible to their 'irrational-unconscious-urges' until proven otherwise (Fukuyama, 2011). So inflexible rules and standard operating procedures are enforced, and a system of accountability is needed against anyone who breaks the rules (Hales, 2002; Sørensen, 2007). Some level of structure and rules are indeed required for every organization, but over-reliance on them eventually can take away the flexibility of doing anything out of the box, let alone collaborate with others for that matter (B. Schwartz & Sharpe, 2010).

Many decades before Harris (1969) explained that children tend to create rules because a structure of rules generating predictable outcomes makes them feel safe. The same is perhaps true for internally insecure adults who want to make themselves feel safe. So, the culture of obedience to authority, rules and SOPs (Standard Operating Procedures) dominate in a bureaucratic system, while mistakes leading to unexpected outcomes are highly discouraged. A culture of risk-taking and experimentation is against the very essence of a bureaucratic environment. From

Weber to Schumpeter, to Drucker, to Phelps, all have agreed that a bureaucratic culture is where the entrepreneurial spirit dies (Brouwer, 2002; Campagnolo & Vivel, 2012; Phelps, 2006; White, 2010).

The bureaucratic paradigm also sees only the rational aspect of one's personality and treats everyone as if they do not have a heart or a soul. It also presumes that people are generally motivated purely through quantitative results of their efforts, which everyone is expected to achieve without involving their emotions or value judgments. Human to human interaction is emphasized on vertical lines, with restricted possibilities of horizontal interactions. Every interaction is expected to occur purely on rational grounds (Javaid & Suri, 2016; Vogl et al., 2019).

Emotions are unpredictable, while one's conscience can take a stand against any unjustified instruction coming from the top (Jackall, 1983). The implied message from the system is thus clear to the employees: 'the system does not care about what you feel for anything or anyone, or what you believe is right, just do your job, perform as asked, take your paycheck and go home'. So, owners, do not fully see their employees, let alone empower them, but when they also bureaucratize every relationship and interaction, it creates an infertile ground for a culture of innovation or collaboration for any out-of-the-box activity which may benefit the organization.

What can be a possible antidote? Do we need to look at first why the owners want to have such a system? If you are the person in charge of an organization, you may want to ask yourself that if you have an unconscious need to feel safe and in control? Do you feel your existence threatened if you observe a mistake happening in your organization that may incur financial and reputation loss? If you are taking things personally then you must ask yourself if the organization is an extension of your existence. If you are not taking things personally, then you need to ask why you have such a system of control in place which does not allow employees to improvise on how to get things done. Do you distrust your employees? Do you believe in Theory X instead of Theory Y? If you treat people as untrustworthy and uninterested in work, then they may also tend to behave that way, a self-fulfilling prophecy (Shadnam, 2019). If it is not the top management directly, then the system in place may give the employees a message that they are being seen as untrustworthy (White, 2010).

The leaders of such an organization may ask themselves that how would they feel if they give more authority to the employees to make decisions without consulting them, or how would they feel if the lower staff is encouraged to make decisions to make things better without asking their bosses even, or how would they feel about creating systems that encourage employees to deviate from the norm for the betterment of the organization without permission. If they feel reluctance, then it's perhaps time for some soul searching. The example of Brazilian entrepreneur Ricardo Semler may be looked upon as an inspiration and food for thought (Semler, 2007).

4. A Sense of Meaning and Purpose

None of the organizations, except a non-profit, where the author was employed in the last sixteen years, actually stood by their vision or mission statement. It appeared like more of a formality. At the end of day what mattered was the bottom line. On many occasions particularly at the time of external audits, employees were literally asked to memorize the vision and mission statements. But during the routine, the priorities of the leadership showed the author exactly what the organization stood for. Such experiences made author to wonder, if actions of top leadership speak louder than words, and that employees do not need to read the vision or mission statements to know what the organization actually stands for. Leadership experts like Sinek (2014) and Collins (2009) would agree with author's inference. The literature also agree that typically the ultimate purpose of every business organization is to make money, even claims of creating some kind of social impact on the society need to reflect positively on the income statement (Besser & Jarnagin, 2010; Friedman, 2007; Kotler & Lee, 2005; J. Yang & Basile, 2019). It is generally profits which is the raison d'etre, and employees typically know it, no matter how much the top management claims otherwise (Collins & Porras, 1997).

Examples are set during difficult times in particular when the top management or the owners have to choose between a healthy income statement and the social impact (Sinek, 2014). If the top management or leadership choose the social impact over profits, but at the same time lay off employees to improve the numbers of the income statement, then the message is again loud and clear. Employees who are not laid off realize that it is either profits or market reputation which eventually translate into profits, and not really about making things better for the society because the employees who are laid off are also part of the society, and neglecting them during difficult times while doing good for the society is nothing short of hypocritical (Bakan, 2004).

In the light of above observations, one may ask, can we expect the employees to give their best to the organization when they see the top management to be caring more about the firm's reputation and profits than employee's wellbeing? Will they feel safe? Now if an organization focuses on the wellbeing of the employees and at least tries to ensure job security, will it be good enough if the organization focuses exclusively on profits? It may be argued that an organization that openly admits its purpose to be profit only, is perhaps better than an organization that lies about its purpose to be other than profits when it is all about money or higher shareholder's value.

Literature suggests that working for companies purely driven by profits may not satisfy a core psychological need of employees. This core need is ignored even by Maslow in his Hierarchy of Needs model (Maslow, 1943), but later brought to the limelight by Frankle (1997). This need is to have a meaning or purpose for our existence, and seeing every action to be a step forward or at least aligned with a higher purpose. A purposeless or meaningless life is agonizing particularly when one's basic physiological and emotional needs are met (Jung, 2006).

A very strong sense of purpose often transcends beyond one's self, as humans can even sacrifice their physiological and emotional needs to fulfill that purpose. This goes opposite to what Maslow suggests. Frankle (1997) came up with this insight during his time at Auschwitz (the Nazi Concentration Camp) where the circumstances were least favorable for the physiological and emotional needs of the inhabitants. It was Frankle's sense of purpose beyond his existence, to contribute in other's lives, which kept him going amidst the horrors of a Nazi concentration camp. Jung (2006) would also agree with Frankle.

So, as a leader you may ask, does working for your organization give meaning to the lives of employees? Is there a purpose beyond profits for which the organization stands for and do not exclude employees or leave them behind while achieving that purpose? If not then at least working for your organization does not give them a sense of purpose to their lives, a purpose which they cannot find elsewhere at least (Collins, 2009; Collins & Porras, 1997).

Now the purpose can vary from business to business, and industry to industry; however, it is perhaps more important to ask here that does the leadership or owners of a business have a meaningful purpose in their lives? And how does the organization they have created, facilitate in achieving that purpose? It is perhaps likely for the organization to have a purpose beyond making money if the owners have a purpose in their lives which is beyond making money (Javaid et al., 2020). A purpose by definition is larger than one's existence, 'something worth dying for'. It cannot be self-serving in a very material sense, or merely focusing on lower levels of Maslow's model (Frankl, 1997). Neurologically, if it is self-serving then it will keep us in a survival mode, instead of putting us on a path of spiritual growth, thus keeping us from achieving higher levels of inner satisfaction (van der Kolk, 2014).

In a very generic sense, any person or organization can focus on enhancing the wellbeing of all stakeholders by trying to bring relief or keeping them away from any form of physical, economical, and emotional harm. This may be done by acknowledging all types of needs of all stakeholders more specifically employees and smaller vendors or suppliers. The natural environment, the ecosystem, can also be an important stakeholder in this context (Javaid, 2019; Javaid et al., 2020).

The purpose may be specifically articulated according to the nature of business. However, it needs to be noted that if the organization ignore any stakeholder in the process of deciding or striving for its purpose even when it can take care of that stakeholder in some way, then it delivers a wrong message to the rest of the stakeholders. Either the leadership should have a very good explanation of ignoring the needs of a particular stakeholder or they need to show concern for the well-being of every stakeholder in every way possible. If it sounds too idealistic, then the owners can at least use this ideal to set a direction to keep striving to maximize their contribution.

Will it significantly compromise the profits of the company? This is perhaps not the right question, it may rather be asked: will such an approach allow the organization to keep growing to increase their reach and extent of contribution toward all stakeholders if growth is even necessary in the first place? Such questions are often raised by scholars studying community-based entrepreneurship, where the stakeholders are community members and often expect the business to provide them employment and offer services at a price they can afford (Javaid et al., 2018). A few years back the author interviewed the owner of a firm in Pakistan who had employed an entire village and provided them residence within the premises of the factory because of ethnic affiliation despite their limited contribution to the business. Such decisions of facilitating the stakeholders need to be taken keeping in view the capacity of the business to support, as otherwise it may lead to bankruptcy.

A lot more can be written here, but the fact is that it is difficult but possible and reciprocally beneficial for the organization to take extra care of all stakeholders. If the organization stands for it, because the owners believe in serving every stakeholder to the extent possible, the employees can be inspired to do the same. If employees see themselves as part of a transformative force (the organization) which strives to bring betterment in their lives and their community and tries to protect the local environment, it may positively impact their creative output (Cohen-Meitar et al., 2009).

RECOMMENDATIONS

In this article, the focus has been on behavior of the organizational leadership, its psychological and neurological causes and subsequent influence on organizational culture and employee's behavior. A number of suggestions to business leaders have emerged from the discussion in the preceding section. Following is a brief summary of these recommendations:

- Self-awareness and understanding of the unconscious source of one's behavior in difficult situations, and knowing how it may affect the employees, can help business leaders to be more mindful of their behaviors and adjust their response to maintain a conducive culture in the organization.
- If the source of unwanted behavior is not possible to identify nor rectify then therapeutic intervention need to be sought.

- Creating a safe environment where experimentation, and initiatives are not avoided due to fear of disrespect from the leaders, or any other kind of unjust punishment, is fundamental to foster an entrepreneurial culture within an organization.
- Voluntary collaboration for troubleshooting happen again in a safe culture, while resistance to change and organization politics to resist change emerge in a culture of fear, implying again how significant an atmosphere of safety is for creating an entrepreneurial culture.
- Preaching and not practicing takes away the trust of the employees from their leaders, particularly when the leaders verbally emphasize on neatly articulated vision and purpose of the organization, but do not practically demonstrate their commitment through their actions, or at least exclude employees from the scope of vision.
- A sense of meaning and being part of something bigger then themselves can motivate employees however the leaders need to demonstrate through their actions if they also stand for a higher purpose, and that employees are also treated as partners in pursuit of the purpose and not as expense in the income statement.

CONCLUSION

The discussion in this chapter suggests that the culture of an organization is typically shaped by the nonverbal behavior of the leadership. The non-verbal behavior of the management reporting to the top leadership is also important as it has a trickle-down effect to the very bottom. The causes of unfavorable behavior of the top management and leadership are typically in their unconscious minds, so to effectively change their behavior the toolkit offered by depth psychology may be effective to foster a culture fertile enough for an entrepreneurial mindset among employees. If the culture encouraged employees to involuntarily venture into the unfamiliar, collaborate freely to do out-of-the-box experiments for the betterment of the organization, without fear of failure or fear of being reprimanded or losing their self-respect in case they commit an honest mistake, then such a culture may develop entrepreneurial orientation. To ignite the entrepreneurial spark further, the culture may also recognize and reward their contribution, give them enough ownership of their work, encourage free collaboration and give employees a sense of purpose in their lives.

FUTURE RESEARCH

In this article four factors were articulated based on previous work of authors and scholars from diverse background. A more concrete analysis can be done in future research by creating a theoretical framework with precise constructs or variables, along with appropriate measuring instrument for each variable. This framework may also be statistically tested by collecting relevant data about leadership behaviors, and its impact on organizational culture and employee's creative outcomes in specific organizations, particularly the ones operating in sectors where being creative and entrepreneurial is essential for organizational survival. Measurement of autonomic disbalance through Heart Rate Variability (HRV) of the people in leadership positions and the employees may also be taken to quantitatively substantiate the state of mind of employees working in stressful and non-stressful work environments. Such quantitative measurements may be preferred over subjective reporting of level of stress and fear in the work environment (Chevalier & Sinatra, 2011). Also, effectiveness of depth psychology to change leadership behavior and foster an entrepreneurial culture can also be empirically tested in future research.

REFERENCES

Ashforth, B. E., Kreiner, G. E., & Fugate, M. (2000). All in a Day's Work: Boundaries and Micro Role Transitions. *Academy of Management Review*, *25*(3), 472–491. doi:10.5465/amr.2000.3363315

Bakan, J. (2004). The Corporation: The Pathological Pursuit of Profit and Power. Free Press (Simon and Schuster Inc.).

Besser, T. L., & Jarnagin, S. K. (2010). *Corporate Social Responsibility: Small businesses and small towns* (No. 5; History of Corporate Social Responsibility). Academic Press.

Brouwer, M. T. (2002). Weber, Schumpeter and Knight on entrepreneurship and economic development. *Journal of Evolutionary Economics*, *12*(1–2), 83–105. doi:10.100700191-002-0104-1

Brydges, R., & Butler, D. (2012). A reflective analysis of medical education research on self-regulation in learning and practice. *Medical Education*, *46*(1), 71–79. doi:10.1111/j.1365-2923.2011.04100.x PMID:22150198

Buchanan, D., & Badham, R. (1999). Politics and Organizational Change: The Lived Experience. *Human Relations*, *52*(5), 609–629. doi:10.1177/001872679905200503

Campagnolo, G., & Vivel, C. (2012). Before Schumpeter: Forerunners of the theory of the entrepreneur in 1900s German political economy – Werner Sombart, Friedrich von Wieser. *European Journal of the History of Economic Thought*, *19*(December), 908–943. doi:10.1080/09672567.2012.737006

Chappell, S., Cooper, E., & Trippe, G. (2019). Shadow work for leadership development. *Journal of Management Development*, *38*(5), 326–335. doi:10.1108/JMD-08-2018-0216

Chevalier, G., & Sinatra, S. T. (2011). Emotional Stress, Heart Rate Variability, Grounding, and Improved Autonomic Tone: Clinical Applications. *Integrative Medicine*, *10*(3), 16–21. https://www.proquest.com/scholarly-journals/emotional-stress-heart-rate-variability-grounding/docview/939527167/se-2?accountid=135034

Chiarini, A., Baccarani, C., & Mascherpa, V. (2018). Lean production, Toyota Production System and Kaizen philosophy. *The TQM Journal*, *30*(4), 425–438. doi:10.1108/TQM-12-2017-0178

Cohen-Meitar, R., Carmeli, A., & Waldman, D. A. (2009). Linking Meaningfulness in the Workplace to Employee Creativity: The Intervening Role of Organizational Identification and Positive Psychological Experiences. *Creativity Research Journal*, *21*(4), 361–375. doi:10.1080/10400410902969910

Collins, J. C. (2009). Good to Great (Why Some Companies Make the Leap and others Don't). *NHRD Network Journal*, *2*(7), 102–105. doi:10.1177/0974173920090719

Collins, J. C., & Porras, J. I. (1997). *Built to last: Successful habits of visionary companies*. HarperBusiness.

Depraetere, J., Vandeviver, C., Keygnaert, I., & Vander Beken, T. (2020). The critical interpretive synthesis: An assessment of reporting practices. *International Journal of Social Research Methodology*, 1–21. doi:10.1080/13645579.2020.1799637

Diamond, J. M. (2012). *The World Until Yesterday: What Can We Learn From Traditional Societies?* Viking.

Diaz-Foncea, M., & Marcuello, C. (2013). Entrepreneurs and the context of cooperative organizations: A definition of cooperative entrepreneur. *Canadian Journal of Administrative Sciences*, *30*(4), 238–251. doi:10.1002/cjas.1267

Diefenbach, T., & Sillince, J. A. A. (2011). Formal and Informal Hierarchy in Different Types of Organization. *Organization Studies*, *32*(11), 1515–1537. doi:10.1177/0170840611421254

Dixon, M. L., & Hart, L. K. (2010). The Impact of Path-Goal Leadership Styles on Work Group Effectiveness and Turnover Intention. *Journal of Managerial Issues*, *22*(1), 52–69. http://www.jstor.org/stable/25822515

Fang, Y.-C., Chen, J.-Y., Wang, M.-J., & Chen, C.-Y. (2019). The Impact of Inclusive Leadership on Employees' Innovative Behaviors: The Mediation of Psychological Capital. In *Frontiers in Psychology* (Vol. 10, p. 1803). https://www.frontiersin.org/article/10.3389/fpsyg.2019.01803

Frankl, V. (1997). *The Man's Search for Ultimate Meaning*. Insight Books.

Friedman, M. (2007). The social responsibility of business is to increase its profits. In W. C. Zimmerli, M. Holzinger, & K. Richter (Eds.), Corporate Ethics and Corporate Governance (pp. 173–178). Springer. doi:10.1007/978-3-540-70818-6_14

Fukuyama, F. (2011). *The Origins of Political Order: From Prehuman Times to the French Revolution*. Profile Books Ltd.

Guba, E. G., & Lincoln, Y. S. (1982). Epistemological and methodological bases of naturalistic inquiry. *Educational Communication and Technology*, *30*(4), 233–252. doi:10.1007/BF02765185

Guo, L., Decoster, S., Babalola, M. T., De Schutter, L., Garba, O. A., & Riisla, K. (2018). Authoritarian leadership and employee creativity: The moderating role of psychological capital and the mediating role of fear and defensive silence. *Journal of Business Research*, *92*, 219–230. doi:10.1016/j.jbusres.2018.07.034

Hales, C. (2002). 'Bureaucracy-lite' and continuities in managerial work. *British Journal of Management*, *13*(1), 51–66. doi:10.1111/1467-8551.00222

Hansen, F., Smith, M., & Hansen, R. B. (2002). Rewards and Recognition in Employee Motivation. *Compensation and Benefits Review*, *34*(5), 64–72. doi:10.1177/0886368702034005010

Hardy, C., & Thomas, R. (2014). Strategy, Discourse and Practice: The Intensification of Power. *Journal of Management Studies*, *51*(2), 320–348. doi:10.1111/joms.12005

Harris, T. A. (1969). I'm OK You're OK: A practical guide to transactional analysis. In *I'm ok you're ok: A practical guide to transactional analysis*. Harper & Row.

Herzberg, F. (2003). One More Time: How Do You Motivate Employees? *Harvard Business Review*. https://hbr.org/2003/01/one-more-time-how-do-you-motivate-employees

Hillman, J. (1968). *Insearch: Psychology and Religion*. Charles Scribner's Sons.

Jackall, R. (1983). Moral Mazes: Bureaucracy and Managerial Work. *Harvard Business Review*. https://hbr.org/1983/09/moral-mazes-bureaucracy-and-managerial-work

Javaid, O. (2019). Islamic System of Production And Consumption: A Guide For Muslim Entrepreneurs. *Journal of Business Innovation, 4*(1), 1–12.

Javaid, O., & Hyder, I. (2018). Using Eisenhardt's Method to Study Ethnic Entrepreneurial Communities. *South Asian Journal of Management Sciences, 12*(1), 25–45. doi:10.21621ajms.2018121.02

Javaid, O., Shamsi, A., & Hyder, I. (2018). *Building a Theoretical Model of Socially Sustainable Entrepreneurship Through Comparative Case Analysis of Ethnic Entrepreneurial Communities*. Institute of Business Management.

Javaid, O., Shamsi, A. F., & Hyder, I. (2020). Religious entrepreneurial communities as a solution for socioeconomic injustice. *Journal of Enterprising Communities: People and Places in the Global Economy, 14*(3), 415–446. doi:10.1108/JEC-03-2020-0023

Javaid, O., & Suri, A. W. (2016). Bureaucratic system of management in Islamic financial institutions: Implications and alternatives for social inclusion. *Journal of Islamic Business and Management, 6*(2), 89–114.

Jung, C. C. (2006). *The Undiscovered Self (reprint)*. New American Liberary.

Kotler, P., & Lee, N. (2005). *Corporate Social Responsability: Doing the Most Good for Your Comapny and your Cause*. John Wiley & Sons, Inc.

Levine, P. A., & Frederick, A. (1997). *Waking the tiger: Healing trauma: The innate capacity to transform overwhelming experiences*. North Atlantic Books.

Liker, J. K., & Convis, G. L. (2012). *Toyota Way to Lean Leadership: Achieving and Sustaining Excellence through Leadership Development*. McGraw-Hill Education. https://www.accessengineeringlibrary.com/content/book/9780071780780

Lincoln, Y. S., & Guba, E. G. (2013). *The Constructivist Credo* (Issue 1). Left Coast Press, Inc.

Lunenburg, F. C. (2011). Organizational Culture-Performance Relationships: Views of Excellence and Theory Z. *National Forum of Educational Administration and Supervision Journal, 29*(4), 1–10.

Maslow, A. H. (1943). A theory of human motivation. *Psychological Review, 50*(4), 370–396. doi:10.1037/h0054346

Maté, G. (2003). *When The Body Says No: The Cost of Hidden Stress*. A.A. Knopf Canada.

Maté, G. (2013). Addiction: Childhood Trauma, Stress and the Biology of Addiction. *Journal of Restorative Medicine*, *1*(1), 56–63. doi:10.14200/jrm.2012.1.1005

Mcdonald, D. (2017). *The Golden Passport: Harvard Business School, the Limits of Capitalism, and the Moral Failure of the MBA Elite*. HarperCollins.

Meier, M., Unternaehrer, E., Schorpp, S. M., Wenzel, M., Benz, A., Bentele, U. U., Dimitroff, S. J., Denk, B., & Prüssner, J. C. (2020). The opposite of stress: The relationship between vagal tone, creativity, and divergent thinking. In Experimental Psychology (Vol. 67, Issue 2, pp. 150–159). Hogrefe Publishing. doi:10.1027/1618-3169/a000483

Perry, B. D., & Szalavitz, M. (2006). The boy who was raised as a dog and other stories from a child psychiatrist's notebook: What traumatized children can teach us about loss, love, and healing. In *The boy who was raised as a dog and other stories from a child psychiatrist's notebook: What traumatized children can teach us about loss, love, and healing*. Basic Books.

Phelps, E. S. (2006). Dynamic capitalism. *The Wall Street Journal*. https://www.wsj.com/articles/SB116043974857287568

Schwartz, B., & Sharpe, K. (2010). *Practical wisdom: The right way to do the right thing*. Riverhead Books.

Schwartz, R. C. (2013). Moving From Acceptance Toward Transformation With Internal Family Systems Therapy (IFS). *Journal of Clinical Psychology*, *69*(8), 805–816. doi:10.1002/jclp.22016 PMID:23813465

Semler, R. (2007). Out of this world: Doing things the Semco way. *Global Business and Organizational Excellence*, *26*(5), 13–21. doi:10.1002/joe.20161

Shadnam, M. (2019). A Postpositivist Commentary on Self-Fulfilling Theories. *Academy of Management Review*, *44*(3), 684–686. doi:10.5465/amr.2017.0460

Sinek, S. (2014). *Leaders eat last: Why some teams pull together and some don't*. Portfolio - Penguine.

Sørensen, J. B. (2007). Bureaucracy and entrepreneurship: Workplace effects on entrepreneurial entry. *Administrative Science Quarterly*, *52*(3), 387–412. doi:10.2189/asqu.52.3.387

Taleb, N. N. (2012). *Antifragile: Things That Gain From Disorder*. Random House.

van der Kolk, B. A. (2014). The Body Keeps the Score: Brain, mind, and body in the healing of trauma. In *The body keeps the score: Brain, mind, and body in the healing of trauma*. Viking.

Vogl, T. M., Seidelin, C., Ganesh, B., & Bright, J. (2019). Algorithmic Bureaucracy: Managing Competence, Complexity, and Problem Solving in the Age of Artificial Intelligence. SSRN *Electronic Journal*, 148–153. doi:10.2139/ssrn.3327804

Vos, J., & van Rijn, B. (2021). The Evidence-Based Conceptual Model of Transactional Analysis: A Focused Review of the Research Literature. *Transactional Analysis Journal*, *51*(2), 1–42. doi:10.1080/03621537.2021.1904364

White, R. D. Jr. (2010). The Micromanagement Disease: Symptoms, Diagnosis, and Cure. *Public Personnel Management*, *39*(1), 71–76. doi:10.1177/009102601003900105

Wisse, B., & Rus, D. (2012). Leader self-concept and self-interested behavior: The moderating role of power. *Journal of Personnel Psychology*, *11*(1), 40–48. doi:10.1027/1866-5888/a000054

Woodman, M. (1993). Conscious Femininity: Interviews with Marion Woodman. In Studies in Jungian Psychology by Jungian Analysts. Inner City Books.

Xiao, Y., & Watson, M. (2017). Guidance on Conducting a Systematic Literature Review. *Journal of Planning Education and Research*, *39*(1), 93–112. doi:10.1177/0739456X17723971

Yang, J., & Basile, K. (2019). The impact of corporate social responsibility on brand equity. *Marketing Intelligence & Planning*, *37*(1), 2–17. doi:10.1108/MIP-02-2018-0051

Yang, Y., Li, Z., Liang, L., & Zhang, X. (2021). Why and when paradoxical leader behavior impact employee creativity: Thriving at work and psychological safety. *Current Psychology (New Brunswick, N.J.)*, *40*(4), 1911–1922. doi:10.100712144-018-0095-1

Ziveig, C. (1997). A tale of shadow-work. *Psychological Perspectives*, *36*(1), 86–91. doi:10.1080/00332929708403332

KEY TERMS AND DEFINITIONS

Dysregulated Nervous System: A state in which the sympathetic side dominates the parasympathetic side of the autonomic nervous system in humans.

Shadow: Part of our life experiences which we do not want to consciously accept, or hated parts of our own selves which we do not want to consciously admit to have. Negative reaction or attitude of parents typically against the emotional reactions of their children teaches children to suppress their emotions, or even dissociate from parts of their beings where these emotions are even felt.

Sympathetic Dominance: This is state in which a person's sympathetic-nervous-system gets stuck in a fight or flight mode in response to constantly facing a threatening situation for weeks or months. So even after the threat or a stressor is gone, a person remains in the state of anxiety, elevated heartbeat and keep experiencing other stress symptoms.

Sympathetic Nervous System: A part of our nervous system which is responsible for generating a fight or flight response in a threatening or painful situation.

Theory X and Y: Theory X assumes that employees are not interested to work, Theory Y is the opposite of X thus assumes that employees are intrinsically motivated to work.

Trauma: Trauma is generated in bodies when we are not able to complete the emotional response of an event and rather push the emotions into the shadow, the emotional charge remains in our bodies and keep affecting our responses and health.

Unconscious: Part of our mind which we are not consciously aware of, but it exists and influence our emotions, thoughts, and behaviors. The term was introduced by Sigmund Freud, however Carl Jung and his disciples developed and finetuned the techniques to understand and bring the unconscious content into the conscious awareness.

Compilation of References

Abbott, K. W., Green, J. F., & Keohane, R. O. (2016). Organizational ecology and institutional change in global governance. *International Organization, 70*(2), 247–277. doi:10.1017/S0020818315000338

Abdinnour-Helm, S., Lengnick-Hall, M., & Lengnick-Hall, C. (2003). Pre-implementation attitudes and organizational readiness for implementing an enterprise resource planning system. *European Journal of Operational Research, 146*(2), 258–273. doi:10.1016/S0377-2217(02)00548-9

Abdullah, A., Ling, Y., & Peng, C. (2017). Workplace happiness, transformational leadership and affective commitment. *Advanced Science Letters, 23*(4), 2872–2875. doi:10.1166/asl.2017.7588

About Tata Trusts. (n.d.). Retrieved April 08, 2021, from https://www.tatatrusts.org/about-tatatrusts

Adair, J. (2013). *Confucius on Leadership*. Pan Macmillan.

Agote, L., Aramburu, N., & Lines, R. (2016). Authentic leadership perception, trust in the leader, and followers' emotions in organizational change processes. *The Journal of Applied Behavioral Science, 52*(1), 35–63. doi:10.1177/0021886315617531

Agrawal, S., & Wadia, J. (2008). *Tata Nano: the 'big' wonder.* Tata Motors. https://www.tata.com/article/inside/pJI3huSRc!$$$! 0=/TLYVr3YPkMU=

Água, P. B., & Correia, A. (2020). Innovation governance in practice: A business policy approach. *Corporate Board: Role. Duties and Composition, 16*(2), 54–64. doi:10.22495/cbv16i2art5

Aiyelabola, T. (2010, June). *Trade unionism and Trade unions: An Introductory perspective.* Retrieved from http://solidarityandstruggle.blogspot.com/2010/06/trade-unionism-and-trades-unions.html

Albrecht, S. L. (2002). Perceptions of integrity, competence and trust in senior management as determinants of cynicism toward change. *Public Administration and Management: An Interactive Journal, 7*(4), 320–343.

Aldrich, H. E., & Pfeffer, J. (1976). Environments of organizations. *Annual Review of Sociology, 2*(1), 79–105. doi:10.1146/annurev.so.02.080176.000455

Aldrich, H. E., & Ruef, M. (2006). *Organizations Evolving* (2nd ed.). Sage.

Allen, D. W. (1998). How nurses become leaders: Perceptions and beliefs about leadership development. *The Journal of Nursing Administration*, *28*(9), 15–20. doi:10.1097/00005110-199809000-00005 PMID:9745657

Alvesson, M., & Einola, K. (2019). *Warning for excessive positivity: Authentic leadership and other traps in leadership studies. Leadership Quarterly.*

Amiot, C., Terry, D., Jimmieson, N., & Callan, V. (2006). A longitudinal investigation of coping processes during a merger: Implications for job satisfaction and organizational iden-tification. *Journal of Management*, *32*(4), 552–574. doi:10.1177/0149206306287542

Amis, J., & Aïssaoui, R. (2013). Readiness for change: An institutional perspective. *Journal of Change Management*, *13*(1), 69–95. doi:10.1080/14697017.2013.768435

Anderson, A. M. (2015). *The Characteristics of a True Leader*. Retrieved from https://www.forbes.com/sites/amyanderson/2015/03/01/the-characteristics-of-a-true-leader/#335df0372324

Anderson, D. (2006). Is building relationship the key to leadership? *Performance Improvement*, *51*(2), 15–22. doi:10.1002/pfi.21245

Anderson, M. H., & Sun, P. Y. T. (2017). Reviewing Leadership Styles: Overlaps and the Need for a New "Full-Range" Theory. *International Journal of Management Reviews*, *19*(1), 76–96. doi:10.1111/ijmr.12082

Andrews, M. (2013). Why our students need co-curricular, not extra-curricular, activities. *The Guardian*. http://www.the guardian.com/higher-education-network/blog/2013/jan/22/student-development-university-curriculum-design

Andriopoulos, C., & Dawson, P. (2009). *Managing Change, Creativity and Innovation*. Sage.

Antino, M., Gil-Rodríguez, F., Rodríguez-Muñoz, A., & Borzillo, S. (2014). Evaluating positive leadership: Pilot study on the psychometric properties of a reduced version of the Positive Leadership Assessment Scale. *Revista de Psicología Social*, *29*(3), 589–608. doi:10.1080/02134748.2014.972705

Antonakis, J., & Day, D. V. (2018). Leadership: Past, present, and future. In The nature of leadership (pp. 3-26). Sage Publication.

Antonakis, J., & House, R. J. (2013). The full-range leadership theory: The way forward. In Transformational and Charismatic Leadership: The Road Ahead 10th Anniversary Edition. Emerald Group Publishing Limited.

Antonakis, J., Avolio, B. J., & Sivasubramaniam, N. (2003). Context and leadership: An examination of the nine-factor full-range leadership theory using the Multifactor Leadership Questionnaire. *The Leadership Quarterly*, *14*(3), 261–295. doi:10.1016/S1048-9843(03)00030-4

Antonakis, J., Day, D. V., & Schyns, B. (2012). Leadership and individual differences: At the cusp of a renaissance. *The Leadership Quarterly*, *4*(23), 643–650. doi:10.1016/j.leaqua.2012.05.002

Appelbaum, S., St-Pierre, N., & Glavas, W. (1998). Strategic organizational change: The role of leadership, learning, motivation and productivity. *Management Decision*, *36*(5), 289–301. doi:10.1108/00251749810220496

Arafat, S. Y., Kar, S. K., Menon, V., Kaliamoorthy, C., Mukherjee, S., Alradie-Mohamed, A., Sharma, P., Marthoenis, M., & Kabir, R. (2020). Panic buying: An insight from the content analysis of media reports during COVID-19 pandemic. *Neurology, Psychiatry & Brain Research*, *37*, 100–103. doi:10.1016/j.npbr.2020.07.002 PMID:32834528

Arakawa, D., & Greenberg, M. (2007). Optimistic managers and their influence on productivity and employee engagement in a technology organisation: Implications for coaching psychologists. *International Coaching Psychology Review*, *2*(1), 78–89.

Armenakis, A. A., & Bedeian, A. G. (1999). Organizational change: A review of theory and research in the 1990s. *Journal of Management*, *25*(3), 293–315. doi:10.1177/014920639902500303

Armenakis, A. A., Harris, S. G., & Feild, H. S. (2000). Making change permanent a model for institutionalizing change interventions. *Research in Organizational Change and Development*, *12*, 97–128. doi:10.1016/S0897-3016(99)12005-6

Armstrong, M. (2006). *A Handbook of Human Resource Management Practice* (10th ed.). Kogan Page Publications.

Arora, K. (2018, Jun 6). *Tata motors may say goodbye to nano, ratan tata's pet project, in 2019*. Financial Express. Retrieved from http://ezproxy.hct.ac.ae/login?url=https://www-proquest-com.ezproxy.hct.ac.ae/newspapers/tata-motors-may-say-goodbye-nano-ratan-tatas-pet/docview/2050324206/se-2?accountid=1215

Ashford, S. J. (1988). Individual strategies for coping with stress during organizational transitions. *The Journal of Applied Behavioral Science*, *24*(1), 19–36. doi:10.1177/0021886388241005

Ashforth, B. E., Kreiner, G. E., & Fugate, M. (2000). All in a Day's Work: Boundaries and Micro Role Transitions. *Academy of Management Review*, *25*(3), 472–491. doi:10.5465/amr.2000.3363315

Ashoor, W. A. (2021). Transformational Leadership and Innovation for Competitive Advantage in Large Firms and SMEs. *International Journal of R&D Innovation Strategy*, *3*(1), 1–12. doi:10.4018/IJRDIS.20210101.oa2

Atwater, L., Waldman, D., Atwater, D., & Cartier, P. (2000). An upward feedback field experiment: Supervisors' cynicism, reactions, and commitment to subordinates. *Personnel Psychology*, *53*(2), 275–297. doi:10.1111/j.1744-6570.2000.tb00202.x

Autry, J. A. (2004). *The Servant Leader: How to Build a Creative Team, Develop Great Morale, and Improve Bottom-Line Performance*. Three Rivers Press.

Avey, J. B., Reichard, R. J., Luthans, F., & Mhatre, K. H. (2011). Meta-analysis of the impact of positive psychological capital on employee attitudes, behaviors, and performance. *Human Resource Development Quarterly*, *22*(2), 127–152. doi:10.1002/hrdq.20070

Avolio, B. (2007). Promoting more integrative strategies for leadership theory-building. *The American Psychologist, 62*(1), 25–33. doi:10.1037/0003-066X.62.1.25 PMID:17209677

Avolio, B. (2010). Pursuing authentic leadership development. In N. Nohria & R. Khurana (Eds.), *Handbook of leadership theory and practice* (pp. 739–768). Harvard Business School Publishing Corporation.

Avolio, B. J., & Gardner, W. L. (2005). Authentic leadership development: Getting to the root of positive forms of leadership. *The Leadership Quarterly, 16*(3), 315–338. doi:10.1016/j.leaqua.2005.03.001

Avolio, B., & Bass, B. (2002). *Manual for the multifactor leadership questionnaire (Form 5X).* Mindgarden.

Avolio, B., Bass, B., & Jung, D. (1999). Re-examining the components of transformational and transactional leadership using the Multifactor Leadership. *Journal of Occupational and Organizational Psychology, 72*(4), 441–462. doi:10.1348/096317999166789

Avolio, B., & Reichard, R. (2008). The rise of authentic followership. In R. Riggio, I. Chaleff, & J. Lipman-Blument (Eds.), *The art of followership: How great followers create great leaders and organizations* (pp. 325–337). Jossey-Bass.

Avolio, B., Walumbwa, F., & Weber, T. (2009). Leadership: Current theories, research, and future directions. *Annual Review of Psychology, 60*(1), 421–449. doi:10.1146/annurev.psych.60.110707.163621 PMID:18651820

Ayman, R., & Lauritsen, M. (2018). Contingencies, context, situation, and leadership. In J. Antonakis & D. V. Day (Eds.), *The nature of leadership* (pp. 138–166). Sage Publications. doi:10.4135/9781506395029.n6

Babu, S. (2017, November 22). *Ratan TATA: The visionary.* Retrieved April 08, 2021, from https://www.thehindubusinessline.com/news/variety/Ratan-Tata-The-visionary/article20545504.ece

Back, A., Werro, T. M., & Peter, L. M. (2019). Practical Implications On How Established Companies Innovate With Startups: Tools and Guidelines for Innovation Managers. *International Journal of R&D Innovation Strategy, 1*(2), 1–20. doi:10.4018/IJRDIS.2019070101

Bakan, J. (2004). The Corporation: The Pathological Pursuit of Profit and Power. Free Press (Simon and Schuster Inc.).

Bakari, H., Hunjra, A., & Niazi, G. (2017). How does authentic leadership influence planned organizational change? The role of employees' perceptions: Integration of Theory of Planned Behavior and Lewin's three step model. *Journal of Change Management, 17*(2), 155–187. doi:10.1080/14697017.2017.1299370

Baker, S. (2007). Followership: The theoretical foundation of a contemporary construct. *Journal of Leadership & Organizational Studies, 14*(1), 50–60. doi:10.1177/0002831207304343

Balthazard, P. A., Waldman, D. A., & Warren, J. E. (2009). Predictors of the emergence of transformational leadership in virtual decision teams. *The Leadership Quarterly*, *20*(5), 651–663. doi:10.1016/j.leaqua.2009.06.008

Bandura, A. (2010). Self-efficacy. In I. Weiner & W. Craighead (Eds.), *The Corsini encyclopedia of psychology* (pp. 1534–1536). John Wiley & Sons. doi:10.1002/9780470479216.corpsy0836

Banks, G. C., Mccauley, K. D., Gardner, W. L., & Guler, C. E. (2016). A meta-analytic review of authentic and transformational leadership: A test for redundancy. *The Leadership Quarterly*, *27*(4), 634–652. doi:10.1016/j.leaqua.2016.02.006

Barbuto, J. E. Jr. (2005). Motivation and transactional, charismatic, and transformational leadership: A test of antecedents. *Journal of Leadership & Organizational Studies*, *11*(4), 26–40. doi:10.1177/107179190501100403

Barbuto, J. E. Jr, & Wheeler, D. W. (2006). Scale Development and Construct Clarification of Servant Leadership. *Group & Organization Management*, *31*(3), 300326. doi:10.1177/1059601106287091

Bartsch, S., Weber, E., Büttgen, M., & Huber, A. (2021). Leadership matters in crisis-induced digital transformation: How to lead service employees effectively during the COVID-19 pandemic. *Journal of Service Management*, *32*(1), 71–85. doi:10.1108/JOSM-05-2020-0160

Bartunek, J. M., & Moch, M. K. (1987). First-order, second-order, and third-order change and organization development interventions: A cognitive approach. *The Journal of Applied Behavioral Science*, *23*(4), 483–500. doi:10.1177/002188638702300404

Barwick, J. (2007). Following the leader and leading the followers. *Leadership in place: How academic professionals can find their leadership voice,* 149-168.

Bass, B. (1997). Does the transactional–transformational leadership paradigm transcend organizational and national boundaries? *The American Psychologist*, *52*(2), 130–139. doi:10.1037/0003-066X.52.2.130

Bass, B. M. (1981). *Stogdill's Handbook of Leadership*. Free Press.

Bass, B. M. (1985). *Leadership and Performance Beyond Expectations: Free Press*. Collier Macmillan.

Bass, B. M. (1990). From transactional to transformational leadership: Learning to share the vision. *Organizational Dynamics*, *18*(3), 19–31. doi:10.1016/0090-2616(90)90061-S

Bass, B. M. (1998). *Transformational Leadership: Industry, Military and Educational Impact. Majah*. Lawrence Erlbaum.

Bass, B. M., & Avolio, B. J. (1997). *Full Range Leadership Development: Manual for the Multifactor Leadership Questionnaire*. Mind Garden.

Bass, B. M., Avolio, B. J., Jung, D. I., & Berson, Y. (2003). Predicting unit performance by assessing transformational and transactional leadership. *The Journal of Applied Psychology, 88*(2), 207–218. doi:10.1037/0021-9010.88.2.207 PMID:12731705

Bass, B. M., & Riggio, R. E. (2006). *Transformational Leadership*. Lawrence Erlbaum Associates. doi:10.4324/9781410617095

Bass, B., & Avolio, B. (1993). Transformational Leadership and Organizational Culture. *Public Administration Quarterly*, (Spring), 112–121.

Bass, B., & Avolio, B. (1993). Transformational leadership and organizational culture. *Public Administration Quarterly*, *17*(1), 112–121.

Bass, B., & Avolio, B. (1995). *MLQ Multifactor Leadership Questionnaire*. Mind Garden.

Bass, B., & Steidlmeier, P. (1999). Ethics, character, and authentic transformational leadership behavior. *The Leadership Quarterly*, *10*(2), 181–217. doi:10.1016/S1048-9843(99)00016-8

Bastardoz, N., & Van Vugt, M. (2019). The nature of followership: Evolutionary analysis and review. *The Leadership Quarterly*, *30*(1), 81–95. doi:10.1016/j.leaqua.2018.09.004

Batson, C. D. (2011). *Altruism in humans*. Oxford University Press.

Battilana, J., Gilmartin, M., Sengul, M., Pache, A., & Alexander, J. (2010). Leadership competencies for implementing planned organizational change. *The Leadership Quarterly*, *21*(3), 422–438. doi:10.1016/j.leaqua.2010.03.007

Baum, J. A. C., & McKelvey, B. (Eds.). (1999). *Variations in Organization Science: In honour of Donald T. Campbell*. Sage.

Beatty, E. R., & Page, R. (2007). Leadership as place. In J. F. Wergin (Ed.), *Leadership in Place: How academic professional can find their leadership voice* (pp. 192–223). Jossey-Bass.

Beer, M., & Eisenstat, R. (2000). The silent killers of strategy implementation and learning. *Sloan Management Review*, *41*(4), 29–40.

Behan, B. A., Kirschner, J., & Snyder, S. M. (2009). Succession in practice. *Chief Executive*, *239*(Mar/Apr), 28.

Bell, R., & Coyne, A. (2016, Jul 20). Tata funds fellowships for indian students. *The Greenville News*. Retrieved from http://ezproxy.hct.ac.ae/login?url=https://www-proquest-com.ezproxy.hct.ac.ae/newspapers/tata-funds-fellowships-indian-students/docview/1805513518/se-2?accountid=1215

Bellmann, L., & Hübler, O. (2020). *Job Satisfaction and Work-Life Balance: Differences between Homework and Work at the Workplace of the Company*. IZA Discussion Paper.

Bendixen, S. M., Campbell, M., Criswell, C., & Smith, R. (2016). *Change-Capable Leadership: The Real Power Propelling Successful Change*. White Paper. Greensboro, NC: Centre for Creative Leadership.

Bernerth, J., Armenakis, A., Feild, H., & Walker, H. (2007). Justice, cynicism, and commitment: A study of important organizational change variables. *The Journal of Applied Behavioral Science, 43*(3), 303–326. doi:10.1177/0021886306296602

Besser, T. L., & Jarnagin, S. K. (2010). *Corporate Social Responsibility: Small businesses and small towns* (No. 5; History of Corporate Social Responsibility). Academic Press.

Beyer, J. (1999). Taming and promoting charisma to change organizations. *The Leadership Quarterly, 10*(2), 307–330. doi:10.1016/S1048-9843(99)00019-3

Bickel, R. D., & Lake, P. F. (1999). *The rights and responsibilities of the modern university: Who assumes the risks of college life?* Carolina Academic Press.

Bivens, J., Engdahl, L., Gould, E., Kroeger, T., McNicholas, C., Mishel, L., Mokhiber, Z., Shierholz, H., Zipperer, B. M., & Wilson, V. (2017). *How today's unions help working people Giving workers the power to improve their jobs and unrig the economy. Report.* Economic Policy Institute.

Blanchard, K. (2018). What is Leadership. In K. Blanchard & R. Broadwell (Eds.), *Servant Leadership in Action: How you can achieve great relationships and results* (pp. 7–13). Berrett-Koehler Publishers.

Blanchard, K., & Broadwell, R. (2018). *Servant Leadership in action: How you can achieve great relationships and results.* Berrett-Koehler Publishers.

Blanch, J., Gil, F., Antino, M., & Rodríguez-Muñoz, A. (2016). Positive Leadership Models: Theoretical Framework and Research. *Psychologist Papers, 37*(3), 170–176.

Blankership, M. (2018, November 29). *A theory of Technical Followership.* Retrieved from https://medium.com/@marcusblankenship/the-diverse-and-dark-sides-of-followership-d9b9e6ad9836

Bligh, M. (2011). Followership and follower-centred approaches. In A. Bryman, D. Collinson, K. Grint, B. Jackson, & M. Uhl-Bien (Eds.), *The SAGE handbook of leadership* (pp. 425–436). SAGE Publicaitons Inc.

Bloomingdale, S. (2016, August). *Unity is the tool workers have to gain power.* Speech presented at the 29th Biennial Convention of the Wisconsin state American Federation of Labour –Congress of Industrial Organizations, Madison, WI.

Bloom, J., Devers, K., Wallace, N., & Wilson, N. (2000). Implementing capitation of Medicaid mental health services in Colorado: Is "readiness" a necessary condition? *The Journal of Behavioral Health Services & Research, 27*(1), 437–445. doi:10.1007/BF02287825 PMID:11070637

Boeddrich, H. J. (2004). Ideas in the Workplace: A New Approach Towards Organizing the Fuzzy Front End of the Innovation Process. *Creativity and Innovation Management, 13*(4), 274–285. doi:10.1111/j.0963-1690.2004.00316.x

Bogers, M., Ollila, S., & Yström, A. (2016). Designing and being designed: Organizing complex collaborative innovation in a societal challenge. *Best Paper Proceedings of the Academy of Management.*

Bolman, L. G., & Gallos, J. V. (2011). *Reframing academic leadership*. Jossey-Bass.

Bono, J., & Ilies, R. (2006). Charisma, positive emotions and mood contagion. *The Leadership Quarterly*, *17*(4), 317–334. doi:10.1016/j.leaqua.2006.04.008

Bourke, J., & Dillion, B. (2016). *The six signature traits of inclusive leadership: Thriving in a diverse new world.* Retrieved from https://www2.deloitte.com/us/en/insights /topics/talent /six-signature-traits-of-inclusive-leadership.html

Boyatzis, R. (1993). Beyond competence: The choice to be a leader. *Human Resource Management Review*, *3*(1), 1–14. doi:10.1016/1053-4822(93)90007-Q

Boyatzis, R. (2006a). An overview of intentional change from a complexity perspective. *Journal of Management Development*, *25*(7), 607–623. doi:10.1108/02621710610678445

Boyatzis, R. (2006b). Using tipping points of emotional intelligence and cognitive competencies to predict financial performance of leaders. *Psicothema*, *18*(SUPPL.1), 124–131. PMID:17295969

Boyatzis, R., & Kolb, D. (1995). From learning styles to learning skills the exec skills profile. *Journal of Managerial Psychology*, *10*(5), 3–17. doi:10.1108/02683949510085938

Brant, J., Dooley, R., & Iman, S. (2008). Leadership succession: An approach to filling the pipeline. *Strategic HR Review*, *7*(4), 17–24. doi:10.1108/14754390810880499

Braun, S., Peus, C., Weisweiler, S., & Frey, D. (2013). Transformational leadership, job satisfaction, and team performance: A multilevel mediation model of trust. *The Leadership Quarterly*, *24*(1), 270–283. doi:10.1016/j.leaqua.2012.11.006

Breuer, H., & Upadrasta, V. (2017). *Values-based product innovation – the case of tata nano.* Manchester: The International Society for Professional Innovation Management (ISPIM). Retrieved from http://ezproxy.hct.ac.ae/login?url=https://www-proquest-com.ezproxy.hct.ac.ae/conference-papers-proceedings/values-based-product-innovation-case-tata-nano/docview/1920222446/se-2?accountid=1215

Brodbeck, F. C., Frese, M., Akerblom, S., Audia, G., Bakacsi, G., Bendova, H., & Wunderer, R. (2000). Cultural variation of leadership prototypes across 22 European countries. *Journal of Occupational and Organizational Psychology*, *73*(1), 1–29. doi:10.1348/096317900166859

Brouwer, M. T. (2002). Weber, Schumpeter and Knight on entrepreneurship and economic development. *Journal of Evolutionary Economics*, *12*(1–2), 83–105. doi:10.100700191-002-0104-1

Brown, J., Kurzweil, M., & Pritchett, W. (2017). *Quality assurance in U.S. higher education: The Current landscape and principles for reform.* ITHAKA. https://sr.ithaka. org/publications/quality-assurance-in-u-s-higher-education/ doi:10.18665/sr.303620

Brown, M. E., & Mitchell, M. S. (2010). Ethical and Unethical Leadership: Exploring New Avenues for Future Research. *Business Ethics Quarterly*, *20*(4), 583–616. doi:10.5840/beq201020439

Brown, M. E., & Treviño, L. K. (2006). Ethical leadership: A review and future directions. *The Leadership Quarterly*, *17*(6), 595–616. doi:10.1016/j.leaqua.2006.10.004

Brydges, R., & Butler, D. (2012). A reflective analysis of medical education research on self-regulation in learning and practice. *Medical Education*, *46*(1), 71–79. doi:10.1111/j.1365-2923.2011.04100.x PMID:22150198

Bryman, A. (1992). *Charisma and Leadership in Organizations*. Sage Publications.

Bryson, J. M. (1989). *Strategic Planning for Public and Non Profit Organizations*. Jossey-Bass publishers.

Buchanan, D., & Badham, R. (1999). Politics and Organizational Change: The Lived Experience. *Human Relations*, *52*(5), 609–629. doi:10.1177/001872679905200503

Bucknor, C. (2016). *Black Workers, Unions and Inequality*. Center for Economic and Policy Research. Retrieved from http://cepr.net/images/stories/reports/ black-workers-unions-2016-08.pdf ?v=2

Buller, J. L. (2012). *The essential department chair: A comprehensive desk reference*. Jossey-Bass.

Bunker, K., & Wakefield, M. (2004). In search of authenticity: Now more than ever, soft skills are needed. *Leadership in Action*, *24*(1), 17–21. doi:10.1002/lia.1055

Burgelman, R. A. (1991). Interorganizational ecology of strategy making and organizational adaptation: Theory and field research. *Organization Science*, *2*(3), 239–262. doi:10.1287/orsc.2.3.239

Burke, W. W. (2008). Organization Change: Theory and Practice (2nd ed.). Los Angeles, CA: sage.

Burke, W. W. (2008). Organization Change: Theory and Practice (2nd ed.). Los Angeles, CA: Sage.

Burkhardt, M., & Brass, D. (1990). Changing patterns or patterns of change: The effects of a change in technology on social network structure and power. *Administrative Science Quarterly*, *35*(1), 104–127. doi:10.2307/2393552

Burnes, B. (2004). *Managing change: A strategic approach to organisational dynamics*. Pearson Education.

Burns, J. (1978). *Leadership*. Harper & Row.

Burns, J. M. (1978). Leadership; Harper and Row Publishers; New York, NY. *Business Review (Federal Reserve Bank of Philadelphia)*, *57*(2), 106–114.

Butler, J., & Kern, M. L. (2016). The PERMA-Profiler: A brief multidimensional measure of flourishing. *International Journal of Wellbeing*, *6*(3), 1–48. doi:10.5502/ijw.v6i3.526

By, R. T., Hughes, M., & Ford, J. (2016). Change Leadership: Oxymoron and Myths. *Journal of Change Management, 16*(1), 8–17. doi:10.1080/14697017.2016.1137425

By, R., Armenakis, A., & Burnes, B. (2015). Organizational change: A focus on ethical cultures and mindfulness. *Journal of Change Management, 15*(1), 1–7. doi:10.1080/14697017.2015.1009720

Calarco, A. (2020). *Adaptable leadership: What it takes to be a quick-change artist*. White Paper. Center for Creative Leadership.

Caldwell, C., & Dixon, R. D. (2010). Love, forgiveness, and trust: Critical values of the modern leader. *Journal of Business Ethics, 93*(1), 91–101. doi:10.100710551-009-0184-z

Caldwell, C., Dixon, R., Atkins, R., & Dowdell, S. (2011). Repentance and continuous improvement: Ethical implications for the modern leader. *Journal of Business Ethics, 102*(3), 473–487. doi:10.100710551-011-0825-x

Caldwell, C., Hayes, L. A., & Long, D. T. (2010). Leadership, trustworthiness, and ethical stewardship. *Journal of Business Ethics, 96*(4), 497–512. doi:10.100710551-010-0489-y

Calkins, P. (2021). India. *Encyclopædia Britannica*. https://www.britannica.com/place/India

Cameron, K. (2008). *Positive Leadership - Strategies for extraordinary performance* (1st ed.). Berrett-Koehler.

Cameron, K. (2010). Five keys to flourishing in trying times. *Leader to Leader, 2010*(55), 45–51. doi:10.1002/ltl.401

Cameron, K., Bright, D., & Caza, A. (2004). Exploring the Relationships between Organizational Virtuousness and Performance. *The American Behavioral Scientist, 47*(6), 766–790. doi:10.1177/0002764203260209

Cameron, K., & Caza, A. (2004). Introduction: Contributions to the discipline of positive organizational scholarship. *The American Behavioral Scientist, 47*(6), 731–739. doi:10.1177/0002764203260207

Cameron, K., & Dutton, J. (2003). *Positive organizational scholarship: Foundations of a new discipline*. Berrett-Koehler Publishers.

Cameron, K., Dutton, J., & Quinn, R. (2013). An Introduction to Positive Organizational Scholarship. In K. Cameron, J. Dutton, & R. Quinn (Eds.), *Positive Organizational Scholarship* (pp. 3–13). doi:10.1108/S2046-410X(2013)0000001004

Cameron, K., Mora, C., Leutscher, T., & Calarco, M. (2011). Effects of positive practices on organizational effectiveness. *The Journal of Applied Behavioral Science, 47*(3), 266–308. doi:10.1177/0021886310395514

Cameron, K., Quinn, R. E., & Caldwell, C. (2017). Positive leadership and adding value – a lifelong journey. *International Journal of Public Leadership, 13*(2), 59–63. doi:10.1108/IJPL-12-2016-0055

Campagnolo, G., & Vivel, C. (2012). Before Schumpeter: Forerunners of the theory of the entrepreneur in 1900s German political economy – Werner Sombart, Friedrich von Wieser. *European Journal of the History of Economic Thought, 19*(December), 908–943. doi:10.1080/09672567.2012.737006

Campbell, D. T. (1969). Variation and selective retention in socio-cultural evolution. *General Systems, 16*, 69–85.

Camus, A. (1942). *The myth of Sisyphus and other essays* (J. O'Brien, Trans.). Vintage International.

Carbery, R., & Garavan, T. N. (2005). Leadership and management development. In J. P. Wilson (Ed.), International Human Resource Development - Learning, education and training for individuals and organizations (3rd ed.). Kogan Page.

Carlyle, T. (1993). *On heroes, hero-worship, and the heroic in history* (Vol. 1). University of California Press. doi:10.1525/9780520911536

Carnevale, J. B., & Hatak, I. (2020). Employee adjustment and well-being in the era of COVID-19: Implications for human resource management. *Journal of Business Research, 116*(May), 183–187. doi:10.1016/j.jbusres.2020.05.037 PMID:32501303

Carr, D., Hard, K., & Trahant, W. (1996). *Managing the Change Process: A Field Book for Change Agents, Consultants, Team Leaders, and Reengineering Managers*. McGraw-Hill.

Carriveau, R. S. (2016). *Connecting the dots*. Stylus Publishing, LLC.

Carsten, M., & Uhl-Bien, M. (2013). Ethical followership: An examination of followership beliefs and crimes of obedience. *Journal of Leadership & Organizational Studies, 20*(1), 49–61. doi:10.1177/1548051812465890

Case, W. (2021, January 31). *Pulling apart Malaysia's pandemic politics*. East Asia Forum. https://www.eastasiaforum.org/2021/01/31/pulling-apart-malaysias-pandemic-politics/

Černe, M., Jaklič, M., & Škerlavaj, M. (2013). Authentic leadership, creativity, and innovation: A multilevel perspective. *Leadership, 9*(1), 63–85. doi:10.1177/1742715012455130

Chacko, P., Noronha, C., & Agrawal, S. (2010). *Small Wonder. The Making of the Nano*. Tata Sons Limited.

Chan, K. Y., & Drasgow, F. (2001). Toward a theory of individual differences and leadership: Understanding the motivation to lead. *The Journal of Applied Psychology, 86*(3), 481–498. doi:10.1037/0021-9010.86.3.481 PMID:11419808

Chappell, L. (2008). In U.S. tour, mr. tata gives jaguar and rover dealers a hug. *Automotive News, 82*(6314), 3-37. Retrieved from http://ezproxy.hct.ac.ae/login?url=https://www-proquest-com.ezproxy.hct.ac.ae/trade-journals/u-s-tour-mr-tata-gives-jaguar-rover-dealers-hug/docview/219504170/se-2?accountid=1215

Chappell, S., Cooper, E., & Trippe, G. (2019). Shadow work for leadership development. *Journal of Management Development, 38*(5), 326–335. doi:10.1108/JMD-08-2018-0216

Chappell, S., Pescud, M., Waterworth, P., Shilton, T., Roche, D., Ledger, M., & Rosenberg, M. (2016). Exploring the process of implementing healthy workplace initiatives: Mapping to Kotter's leading change model. *Journal of Occupational and Environmental Medicine, 58*(10), 341–348. doi:10.1097/JOM.0000000000000854 PMID:27525528

Cheltenham, E. E. (2016). Corporate Venturing: Organizing for Innovation. *Science & Public Policy, 43*(4), 576–578. doi:10.1093cipolcv066

Chemers, M. M. (1995). Contemporary leadership theory. In J. T. Wren (Ed.), *The Leader's Companion: Insights On Leadership Through the Ages* (pp. 83–99). Free Press.

Chemers, M. M. (2000). Leadership research and theory: A functional integration. *Group Dynamics, 4*(1), 27–43. doi:10.1037/1089-2699.4.1.27

Chen, J. K. C., & Sriphon, T. (2021). Perspective on COVID-19 pandemic factors impacting organizational leadership. *Sustainability, 13*(3230), 1–21.

Chevalier, G., & Sinatra, S. T. (2011). Emotional Stress, Heart Rate Variability, Grounding, and Improved Autonomic Tone: Clinical Applications. *Integrative Medicine, 10*(3), 16–21. https://www.proquest.com/scholarly-journals/emotional-stress-heart-rate-variability-grounding/docview/939527167/se-2?accountid=135034

Chew, I. K. H., & Putti, J. (1995). Relationship on work-related values of Singaporean and Japanese managers in Singapore. *Human Relations, 48*(10), 1149–1170. doi:10.1177/001872679504801003

Chiarini, A., Baccarani, C., & Mascherpa, V. (2018). Lean production, Toyota Production System and Kaizen philosophy. *The TQM Journal, 30*(4), 425–438. doi:10.1108/TQM-12-2017-0178

Child, J. (1972). Organizational structure, environment and performance: The role of strategic choice. *Sociology, 6*(1), 1–22. doi:10.1177/003803857200600101

Christensen, C. (2006). Identifying and Developing Capable Leaders. *Harvard Business Review*, 1–12.

Chu, M. (2011). *Conflict management styles of pastors and organizational servant leadership: A descriptive study* (Unpublished doctoral dissertation). Southern Baptist theological Seminary, Louisville, KY.

Cilliers, F. (2011). Positive psychology leadership coaching experiences in a financial organisation. *SA Journal of Industrial Psychology, 37*(1), 1–14. doi:10.4102ajip.v37i1.933

Çitaku, F., & Ramadani, H. (2020). Leadership Competency Model-Drenica: Generalizability of Leadership Competencies. *International Journal of Organizational Leadership, 9*(3), 152–162.

Ciulla, J. B. (2005). Integrating leadership with ethics; Is good Leadership Contrary to Human Nature? In J. P. Doh & S. A. Strumpf (Eds.), *Handbook of Responsible Leadership and Governance in Global Business* (pp. 122–138). Edward Elgar Publishing Limited. doi:10.4337/9781845425562.00017

Cohen, D. S. (2005). *The heart of change field guide: Tools and tactics for leading change in your organization*. Harvard Business Press.

Cohen-Meitar, R., Carmeli, A., & Waldman, D. A. (2009). Linking Meaningfulness in the Workplace to Employee Creativity: The Intervening Role of Organizational Identification and Positive Psychological Experiences. *Creativity Research Journal, 21*(4), 361–375. doi:10.1080/10400410902969910

Cohen, W. A. (1990). *The Art of a Leader*. Prentice Hall.

Çokpekin, Ö., & Knudsen, M. P. (2012). Does Organizing for Creativity Really Lead to Innovation? *Creativity and Innovation Management, 21*(3), 304–314. doi:10.1111/j.1467-8691.2012.00649.x

Collins, J. (2007). De bom a excelente (3a ed.). Lisboa: Casa das Letras.

Collins, D. (1998). *Organizational Change: Sociological Perspectives London*. Routledge.

Collins, J. (2001). Level 5 leadership. The triumph of humility and fierce resolve. *Harvard Business Review, 79*(1), 66–76. PMID:11189464

Collins, J. C. (2009). Good to Great (Why Some Companies Make the Leap and others Don't). *NHRD Network Journal, 2*(7), 102–105. doi:10.1177/0974173920090719

Collins, J. C., & Porras, J. I. (1997). *Built to last: Successful habits of visionary companies*. HarperBusiness.

Collinson, D. (2006). Rethinking followership: A post-structuralist analysis of follower identities. *The Leadership Quarterly, 17*(2), 179–189. doi:10.1016/j.leaqua.2005.12.005

Contreras, F., Baykal, E., & Abid, G. (2020). E-Leadership and Teleworking in Times of COVID-19 and Beyond: What We Know and Where Do We Go. *Frontiers in Psychology, 11*(December), 1–11. PMID:33362656

Conway, D. (2016). *International students issue report*. Unpublished report. Dallas, TX: Department of Education Policy and Leadership, Southern Methodist University.

Cooney, M. A., Pernick, J., Rice, K., & Monago, E. A. (2016). Utilization of Change Theory to Implement an Appreciative Advising Model. *Journal of Research, Assessment, and Practice in Higher Education, 1*(1), 21–25.

Cooperrider, D., & Srivastva, S. (2017). Appreciative Inquiry in Organizational Life. In A. Shani & D. Noumair (Eds.), *Research in organizational change and development* (pp. 81–142). Emerald Publishing Limited. doi:10.1108/S0897-301620170000025003

Cording, M., Harrison, J., Hoskisson, R., & Jonsen, K. (2014). Walking the talk: A multistakeholder exploration of organizational authenticity, employee productivity, and post-merger performance. *The Academy of Management Perspectives*, *28*(1), 38–56. doi:10.5465/amp.2013.0002

Cortina, J. M., Köhler, T., Keeler, K. R., & Pugh, S. D. (2020). Situation strength as a basis for interactions in psychological models. *Psychological Methods*. https://doi-org.ezproxy.sunway.edu.my/10.1037/met0000372

Covin, T. J., Sightler, K. W., Kolenko, T. A., & Tudor, K. R. (1996). An investigation of post-acquisition satisfaction with the merger. *The Journal of Applied Behavioral Science*, *32*(2), 125–142. doi:10.1177/0021886396322001

Cox, J. III, & Robinson, E. (2017). Applying Goldratt's thinking processes to prevent mistakes. *Human Systems Management*, *36*(4), 315–340. doi:10.3233/HSM-17116

Coyle-Shapiro, J. A., & Morrow, P. C. (2003). The role of individual differences in employee adoption of TQM orientation. *Journal of Vocational Behavior*, *62*(2), 320–340. doi:10.1016/S0001-8791(02)00041-6

Crawford, J., Dawkins, S., & Kelder, J.-A. (2019). *True to self, and true to others? A triadic model of authenticity, sincerity, and self.* Unpublished Manuscript.

Crawford, J. A., Dawkins, S., Martin, A., & Lewis, G. (2019). Putting the leader back into authentic leadership: Reconceptualising and rethinking leaders. *Australian Journal of Management*, 1–44.

Crawford, J., Dawkins, S., Martin, A., & Lewis, G. (2018). Conceptualising authentic followers and developing a future research agenda. In D. Cotter-Lockard (Ed.), *Authentic Leadership and Followership: International Perspectives* (pp. 271–293). Palgrave Macmillan. doi:10.1007/978-3-319-65307-5_11

Csikszentmihalyi, M. (2000). *Flow: The psychology of optimal experience*. Harper & Row.

Cummings, T. G., & Worley, C. G. (2009). *Organization Development and Change*. Cengage Learning.

Cummings, T. G., & Huse, E. F. (1989). *Organization Development and Change* (4th ed.). West Publishing.

Cunha, M. P., Rego, A., & Lopes, M. P. (2013). Comportamento organizacional positivo. *Análise Psicológica*, *31*(4), 313–328. doi:10.14417/ap.804

Cunningham, C., Woodward, C., Shannon, H., MacIntosh, J., Lendrum, B., Rosenbloom, D., & Brown, J. (2002). Readiness for organizational change: A longitudinal study of workplace, psychological and behavioural correlates. *Journal of Occupational and Organizational Psychology*, *75*(4), 377–392. doi:10.1348/096317902321119637

Cunningham, G. B. (2006). The relationships among commitment to change, coping with change, and turnover intentions. *European Journal of Work and Organizational Psychology*, *15*(1), 29–45. doi:10.1080/13594320500418766

Daniels, K. (2000). Measures of Five Aspects of Affective Well-Being at Work. *Human Relations*, *53*(February), 275–294. doi:10.1177/a010564

Dansereau, F. (1995). A dyadic approach to leadership: Creating and nurturing this approach under fire. *The Leadership Quarterly*, *6*(4), 479–490. doi:10.1016/1048-9843(95)90022-5

Daraba, D., Wirawan, H., Salam, R., & Faisal, M. (2021). Working from home during the corona pandemic: Investigating the role of authentic leadership, psychological capital, and gender on employee performance. *Cogent Business and Management*, *8*(1), 1–17. doi:10.1080/23311975.2021.1885573

Dawkins, S., Martin, A., Scott, J., & Sanderson, K. (2015). Advancing conceptualization and measurement of psychological capital as a collective construct. *Human Relations*, *68*(6), 925–949. doi:10.1177/0018726714549645

Dawson, P. (1994). *Organizational Change: A Processual Approach. Paul Chapman Publishing*.

Day, D. (2011). Leadership Development. In A. Bryman, D. Collinson, K. Grint, B. Jackson, & M. Uhl-Bien (Eds.), The Sage Handbook of Leadership (1st ed., pp. 37–50). Sage Publications Ltd.

Day, D. V. (2011). Leadership Development. In A. Bryman, D. Collinson, K. Grint, B. Jackson, & M. Uhl-Bien (Eds.), The Sage Handbook of Leadership (pp. 37–50). SAGE Publications Ltd.

Day, D. V. (2001). Leadership development: A review in context. *The Leadership Quarterly*, *11*(4), 581–613. doi:10.1016/S1048-9843(00)00061-8

Day, D. V. (2014). Introduction: Leadership and organizations. In D. V. David (Ed.), *The Oxford handbook of leadership and organizations* (pp. 3–12). Oxford University Press.

Day, D., Gronn, P., & Salas, E. (2004). Leadership capacity in teams. *The Leadership Quarterly*, *15*(6), 857–880. doi:10.1016/j.leaqua.2004.09.001

Day, G. S. (2007). Is it real? Can we win? Is it worth doing. *Harvard Business Review*, *85*(12), 110–120. PMID:18283921

De Hoogh, A. H., & Den Hartog, D. N. (2008). Ethical and despotic leadership, relationships with leader's social responsibility, top management team effectiveness and subordinates' optimism: A multi-method study. *The Leadership Quarterly*, *19*(3), 297–311. doi:10.1016/j.leaqua.2008.03.002

De Vries, R. E. (2012). Personality predictors of leadership styles and the self–other agreement problem. *The Leadership Quarterly*, *23*(5), 809–821. doi:10.1016/j.leaqua.2012.03.002

De Vries, R. E., Bakker-Pieper, A., & Oostenveld, W. (2010). Leadership= communication? The relations of leaders' communication styles with leadership styles, knowledge sharing and leadership outcomes. *Journal of Business and Psychology*, *25*(3), 367–380. doi:10.100710869-009-9140-2 PMID:20700375

de Zilwa, D. (2016). The strengths and capacities of Authentic Followership. *Leadership and Organization Development Journal*, *37*(3), 310–324. doi:10.1108/LODJ-01-2014-0010 de Zilwa, D., Lapierre, L., & Carsten, M. (2014). A new conceptual framework for authentic followership. In L. Lapierre & M. Carsten (Eds.), *Followership: What is it, and why do people follow* (pp. 47–72). Emerald Group Publishing.

Deal, J. J. (2014). Leadership for All Ages. *Chief Learning Officer*, (December), 66–68.

DeCelles, K. A., DeRue, D. S., Margolis, J. D., & Ceranic, T. L. (2012). Does power corrupt or enable? When and why power facilitates self-interested behavior. *The Journal of Applied Psychology*, *97*(3), 681–689. doi:10.1037/a0026811 PMID:22250668

Demers, C. (2007). *Organizational Change Theories: A Synthesis*. Sage.

DeMeuse, K. P., Dai, G., Swisher, V. V., Eichinger, R. W., & Lombardo, M. M. (2012). Leadership development: Exploring, clarifying, and expanding our understanding of learning agility. *Industrial and Organizational Psychology: Perspectives on Science and Practice*, *5*(3), 280–286. doi:10.1111/j.1754-9434.2012.01445.x

Deming, D. J. (2017). The value of soft skills in the labor market. *NBER Reporter*, *4*, 7–11.

Den Hartog, D., & Koopman, P. (2001). Leadership in organizations. In *Handbook of Industrial, Work an Organizational Psychology* (pp. 167–187). Sage Publication, Inc.

Depraetere, J., Vandeviver, C., Keygnaert, I., & Vander Beken, T. (2020). The critical interpretive synthesis: An assessment of reporting practices. *International Journal of Social Research Methodology*, 1–21. doi:10.1080/13645579.2020.1799637

Deschamps, J. P. (2008). *Innovation Leaders: How Senior Executives Stimulate, Steer and Sustain Innovation*. Jossey-Bass.

Dettmer, H. W. (2000). Constraint Management. Quality America Ed.

Dettmer, H. W. (1998). *Breaking The Constraints To World-Class Performance. Milwaukee*. ASQ Quality Press.

Dettmer, H. W. (2011). *Strategic Navigation*. ASQ Quality Press.

Devos, G., Buelens, M., & Bouckenooghe, D. (2007). Contribution of content, context, and process to understanding openness to organizational change: Two experimental simulation studies. *The Journal of Social Psychology*, *147*(6), 607–630. doi:10.3200/SOCP.147.6.607-630 PMID:18314790

Dhingra, G., Gupta, M., & Gupta, H. (2013). Study of transformational leaders in business and qualities required being a successful business leader. *Journal of Commerce and Management Thought*, *4*(3), 692–703. http://ezproxy.hct.ac.ae/login?url=https://www-proquest-com.ezproxy.hct.ac.ae/scholarly-journals/study-transformational-leaders-business-qualities/docview/1523932379/se-2?accountid=1215

Diamond, J. M. (2012). *The World Until Yesterday: What Can We Learn From Traditional Societies?* Viking.

Diaz-Foncea, M., & Marcuello, C. (2013). Entrepreneurs and the context of cooperative organizations: A definition of cooperative entrepreneur. *Canadian Journal of Administrative Sciences*, *30*(4), 238–251. doi:10.1002/cjas.1267

Diaz-Saenz, H. R. (2011). Transformational leadership. In D. C. A. Bryman, K. Grint, B. Jackson, & M. Uhl-Bien (Eds.), The Sage Handbook of Leadership (pp. 299-310). Sage.

Dichev, C., & Dicheva, D. (2017). Gamifying education: what is known, what is believed and what remains uncertain: a critical review. *International Journal of Educational Technology in Higher Education*, *14*(1), 1–36. doi:10.118641239-017-0042-5

Diefenbach, T., & Sillince, J. A. A. (2011). Formal and Informal Hierarchy in Different Types of Organization. *Organization Studies*, *32*(11), 1515–1537. doi:10.1177/0170840611421254

Diener, E. (2000). Subjective well-being: The science of happiness and a proposal for a national index. *The American Psychologist*, *55*(1), 34–43. doi:10.1037/0003-066X.55.1.34 PMID:11392863

Diener, E., Lucas, R., & Oishi, S. (2002). Subjective Well-Being The Science of Happiness and Life Satisfaction. In C. Snyder & S. Lopez (Eds.), *Handbook of Positive Psychology* (pp. 63–73). Oxford University Press.

Dimitrov, D. (2015). Leadership in a humane organization. *European Journal of Training and Development*, *39*(2), 122–142. doi:10.1108/EJTD-07-2014-0051

Dingman, W. W., & Stone, A. G. (2007). Servant Leadership's Role in the Succession Planning Process : A Case Study. *International Journal of Leadership IStudies, 2*(2), 133–147.

Dixon, M. L., & Hart, L. K. (2010). The Impact of Path-Goal Leadership Styles on Work Group Effectiveness and Turnover Intention. *Journal of Managerial Issues*, *22*(1), 52–69. http://www.jstor.org/stable/25822515

Dollard, M. F., & Neser, D. (2013). Worker health is good for the economy: Union density and psychosocial safety climate as determinants of country differences in worker health and productivity in 31 European countries. *Social Science & Medicine*, *92*(9), 114–123. doi:10.1016/j.socscimed.2013.04.028 PMID:23849285

Doorewaard, H., & Benschop, Y. (2003). HRM and organizational change: An emotional endeavor. *Journal of Organizational Change Management*, *16*(3), 272–286. doi:10.1108/09534810310475523

Doucet, K. (2000). Let's make a deal! *CMA Management*, *74*(8), 9.

Douglas, M. (2003). *Natural symbols*. Routledge. (Original work published 1970)

Drotter, S. (2010). Leadership Pipeline. *Leadership Excellence*, *27*(8), 11.

Drucker, P. (1992). *Managing for the Future: The 1990s and beyond*. Truman Talley Books/Dutton.

Drucker, P. (2002). *Managing in the Next Society*. St Martin's Press.

Drucker, P. F. (1986). *The Practice of Management*. Harper Business.

Dugan, B., & O'Shea, P. (2014). Leadership Development: Growing Talent Strategically. *Society for Human Resource Management (SHRM) and Society for Industrial and Organizational Psychology (SIOP) Science of HR White Paper Series*, 1–17.

Duignan, P. (2006). *Educational leadership: key challenges and ethical tensions*. Cambridge University Press.

Dumdum, U. R., Lowe, K. B., & Avolio, B. J. (2013). A meta-analysis of transformational and transactional leadership correlates of effectiveness and satisfaction: An update and extension. In Transformational and Charismatic Leadership: The Road Ahead 10th Anniversary Edition (pp. 39-70). Emerald Group Publishing Limited.

Dunn, E. (2003). Life Through Learning: Learning Through Life. In *The Lifelong Learning Strategy for Scotland: Summary* (p. 3). The Scottish Government. Retrieved from: http://www.scotland.gov. uk/Resource/Doc/47032/0028820.pdf

Dunphy, D. C., & Stace, D. A. (1988). Transformational and coercive strategies for planned organizational change: Beyond the OD model. *Organization Studies*, *9*(3), 317–334. doi:10.1177/017084068800900302

Dunphy, D., & Stace, D. (1993). The strategic management of corporate change. *Human Relations*, *46*(8), 905–920. doi:10.1177/001872679304600801

Dunsworth, M., & Billings, D. (2012). *Effective program evaluation*. Solution Tree Press.

Dutra, A., & Griesedieck, J. (2010). Succession Success. *Leadership Excellence*, *27*(5), 14.

Eaton, S. C. (1992, June). *Union Leadership Development in the 1990s and Beyond*. CSIA Discussion Paper 92-05, Kennedy School of Government, Harvard University.

Eby, L. T., Adams, D. M., Russell, J. E., & Gaby, S. H. (2000). Perceptions of organizational readiness for change: Factors related to employees' reactions to the implementation of team-based selling. *Human Relations*, *53*(3), 419–442. doi:10.1177/0018726700533006

Edmondson, A. (2008, July). The competitive imperative of learning. *Harvard Business Review*, 60–67.

Edmondson, A. (1999). Psychological safety and learning behavior in work teams. *Administrative Science Quarterly*, *44*(2), 350–383. doi:10.2307/2666999

Edú-Valsania, S., Moriano, J. A., & Molero, F. (2016). Authentic leadership and employee knowledge sharing behavior: Mediation of the innovation climate and workgroup identification. *Leadership and Organization Development Journal*, *37*(4), 487–506. doi:10.1108/LODJ-08-2014-0149

El-Bawab, N. (2019). *Marriott plans to launch home-rental market platform that would compete with Airbnb, report says*. CNBC.

Elengoe, A. (2020). COVID-19 outbreak in Malaysia. *Osong Public Health and Research Perspectives*, *11*(3), 93–100. doi:10.24171/j.phrp.2020.11.3.08 PMID:32494567

Elkington, R., van der Steege, M., Glick-Smith, J., & Moss Breen, J. (2017). *Visionary leadership in a turbulent world: Thriving in the new VUCA context*. Emerald Publishing Limited. doi:10.1108/9781787142428

Ende, J. V. D., Frederiksen, L., & Prencipe, A. (2015). The front end of innovation: Organizing search for Ideas. *Journal of Product Innovation Management*, *32*(4), 482–487. doi:10.1111/jpim.12213

Erickson, T. (2010). The leaders we need now. *Harvard Business Review*, (May), 1–4. PMID:20429251

Eriksen, M. (2009). Authentic leadership: Practical reflexivity, self-awareness, and self-authorship. *Journal of Management Education*, *33*(6), 747–771. doi:10.1177/1052562909339307

Etzioni. (1964). *Modern organizations*. Prentice Hall.

Eva, N., Robin, M., Sendjaya, S., Dierendonck, D. V., & Liden, R. C. (2019). Servant Leadership: A systematic review and call for future research. *The Leadership Quarterly*, *30*(1), 111–132. doi:10.1016/j.leaqua.2018.07.004

Evans, A., & Chun, E. B. (2007). *Are the walls really down? Behavioral and organizational barriers to faculty and staff diversity*. Josey-Bass.

Executive Order 13780. (2017, March 6). *Protecting the nation from foreign terrorist entry into the United States*. The White House. https://www.whitehouse.gov/the-press-office/2017/03/06/executive-order-protecting-nation-terrorist-entry-united-states

Fairhurst, G. T., & Grant, D. (2010). The social construction of leadership: A sailing guide. *Management Communication Quarterly*, *24*(2), 171–210. doi:10.1177/0893318909359697

Fairlie, P. (2011). Meaningful work, employee engagement, and other key employee outcomes: Implications for human resource development. *Advances in Developing Human Resources*, *13*(4), 508–525. doi:10.1177/1523422311431679

Fang, Y.-C., Chen, J.-Y., Wang, M.-J., & Chen, C.-Y. (2019). The Impact of Inclusive Leadership on Employees' Innovative Behaviors: The Mediation of Psychological Capital. In *Frontiers in Psychology* (Vol. 10, p. 1803). https://www.frontiersin.org/article/10.3389/fpsyg.2019.01803

Feldman, M. (2004). Resources in emerging structures and processes of change. *Organization Science*, *15*(3), 295–309. doi:10.1287/orsc.1040.0073

Ferris, G., Treadway, D., Kolodinsky, R., Hochwarter, W., Kacmar, C., Douglas, C., & Frink, D. (2005). Development and validation of the political skill inventory. *Journal of Management*, *31*(1), 126–152. doi:10.1177/0149206304271386

Fiedler, F. E. (1971). Validation and extension of the contingency model of leadership effectiveness: A review of empirical findings. *Psychological Bulletin*, *76*(2), 128–148. doi:10.1037/h0031454 PMID:4942584

Fiedler, F. E. (1981). Leadership effectiveness. *The American Behavioral Scientist, 24*(5), 619–632. doi:10.1177/000276428102400503

Field, A. (2007). When the boomers leave, will your company have the leaders it needs? *Harvard Business Review*, (April), 1–6.

Figueiredo, P. (2013). Planning and Developing Leadership within the Organization. *Organizational Cultures -. International Journal (Toronto, Ont.), 12*(3), 31–48.

Fincher, C. (2003). *Administrative leadership: In academic governance and management.* University Press of America, Inc.

Fisher, C. D. (2010). Happiness at Work. *International Journal of Management Reviews, 12*(4), 384–412. doi:10.1111/j.1468-2370.2009.00270.x

Foo, L. P., Chin, M. Y., Tan, K. L., & Phuah, K. T. (2020). The impact of COVID-19 on tourism industry in Malaysia. *Current Issues in Tourism*, 1–5. doi:10.1080/13683500.2020.1777951

Ford, J. D., Ford, L. W., & D'Amelio, A. (2008). Resistance to change: The rest of the story. *Academy of Management Review, 33*(2), 362–377. doi:10.5465/amr.2008.31193235

Ford, J., & Harding, N. (2018). Followers in leadership theory: Fiction, fantasy and illusion. *Leadership, 14*, 3–24.

Forrester, K. (2010). Labor Education. In *International Encyclopedia of Education* (3rd ed., pp. 139–143). Elsevier BV. doi:10.1016/B978-0-08-044894-7.00022-1

Franken, A., Edwards, C., & Lambert, R. (2009). Executing strategic change: Understanding the critical management elements that lead to success. *California Management Review, 51*(3), 49–73. doi:10.2307/41166493

Frankl, V. (1997). *The Man's Search for Ultimate Meaning*. Insight Books.

Fredrickson, B. (1998). What good are positive emotions? *Review of General Psychology, 2*(3), 300–319. doi:10.1037/1089-2680.2.3.300 PMID:21850154

Fredrickson, B. L. (2001). The role of positive emotions in positive psychology: The broaden-and-build theory of positive emotions. *The American Psychologist, 56*(3), 218–226. doi:10.1037/0003-066X.56.3.218 PMID:11315248

Fredrickson, B., & Joiner, T. (2002). Positive emotions trigger upward spirals toward emotional well-being. *Psychological Science, 13*(2), 172–175. doi:10.1111/1467-9280.00431 PMID:11934003

Freeman, R. B., & Medoff, J. L. (1984). *What do unions do?* Basic Book.

French, W. L., & Bell, C. (1999). Organization development: Behavioral Science Interventions for Organization Improvement. Auflage: Prentice Hall.

Freud, S. (1921). *Group psychology and the analysis of the ego*. International Psychoanalytic Publishing House.

Friedman, M. (2007). The social responsibility of business is to increase its profits. In W. C. Zimmerli, M. Holzinger, & K. Richter (Eds.), Corporate Ethics and Corporate Governance (pp. 173–178). Springer. doi:10.1007/978-3-540-70818-6_14

Fugate, M., Prussia, G., & Kinicki, A. (2012). Managing employee withdrawal during organizational change: The role of threat appraisal. *Journal of Management*, *38*(3), 890–914. doi:10.1177/0149206309352881

Fukuyama, F. (2011). *The Origins of Political Order: From Prehuman Times to the French Revolution*. Profile Books Ltd.

Fullagar, C., Gallagher, D. G., Clark, P. F., & Carroll, A. (2004). Union commitment and participation: A 10-year longitudinal study. *The Journal of Applied Psychology*, *89*(4), 730–737. doi:10.1037/0021-9010.89.4.730 PMID:15327358

Fu, W., & Deshpande, S. P. (2012). Factors impacting ethical behavior in a Chinese state-owned steel company. *Journal of Business Ethics*, *105*(2), 231–237. doi:10.100710551-011-0962-2

Gable, S. L., & Haidt, J. (2005). What (and why) is positive psychology? *Review of General Psychology*, *9*(2), 103–110. doi:10.1037/1089-2680.9.2.103

Galinsky, A. D., Magee, J. C., Rus, D., Rothman, N. B., & Todd, A. R. (2014). Acceleration with steering: The synergistic benefits of combining power and perspective-taking. *Social Psychological & Personality Science*, *5*(6), 627–635. doi:10.1177/1948550613519685

Galle, J. K., & Galle, J. (2010). Building an integrated student learning outcomes assessment for general education: Three case studies. *New Directions for Teaching and Learning*, *2010*(121), 79–87. doi:10.1002/tl.390

García-Morales, V., Jiménez-Barrionuevo, M., & Gutiérrez-Gutiérrez, L. (2012). Transformational leadership influence on organizational performance through organizational learning and innovation. *Journal of Business Research*, *65*(7), 1040–1050. doi:10.1016/j.jbusres.2011.03.005

Gardner, W., Avolio, B., Luthans, F., May, D., & Walumbwa, F. (2005). "Can you see the real me?" A self-based model of authentic leader and follower development. *The Leadership Quarterly*, *16*(3), 343–372. doi:10.1016/j.leaqua.2005.03.003

Gardner, W., Cogliser, C., Davis, K., & Dickens, M. (2011). Authentic leadership: A review of the literature and research agenda. *The Leadership Quarterly*, *22*(6), 1120–1145. doi:10.1016/j.leaqua.2011.09.007

Garman, A. N., & Glawe, J. (2004). Succession Planning. *Consulting Psychology Journal*, *56*(2), 119–128. doi:10.1037/1061-4087.56.2.119 PMID:15524307

Gavin, J. H., & Mason, R. O. (2004). The virtuous organization: The value of happiness in the workplace. *Organizational Dynamics*, *33*(4), 379–392. doi:10.1016/j.orgdyn.2004.09.005

Georg-August-University. (2017). *Call for papers, "Metamorphoses of the Political"/ Time and Money: Themes in Labour Relations International Workshop, 15 – 16 December 2017*. Centre for Modern Indian Studies: Georg-August-University.

George, B., Sims, P., McLean, A., & Mayer, D. (2007). Discovering Your Authentic Leadership. *Harvard Business Review*, (February), 1–8. PMID:17345686

George, J. M. (2000). Emotions and leadership: The role of emotional intelligence. *Human Relations*, *53*(8), 1027–1055. doi:10.1177/0018726700538001

Gerdin, J., & Greve, J. (2004). Forms of contingency fit in management accounting research—A critical review. *Accounting, Organizations and Society*, *29*(3-4), 303–326. doi:10.1016/S0361-3682(02)00096-X

Giambatista, R., Rowe, W., & Riaz, S. (2005). Nothing succeeds like succession: A critical review of leader succession literature since 1994. *The Leadership Quarterly*, *16*(6), 963–991. doi:10.1016/j.leaqua.2005.09.005

Gibson, J. L., Ivancevich, J. M., Donnelly, J. H., & Konopaske, R. (2003). *Organizations: Behaviour, structure, processes*. McGraw-Hill.

Giles, S. (2016). The Most Important Leadership Competencies, According to Leaders Around the World. *Harvard Business Review*, (March), 2–7.

Gilley, A., Dixon, P., & Gilley, J. W. (2008). Characteristics of leadership effectiveness: Implementing change and driving innovation in organizations. *Human Resource Development Quarterly*, *19*(2), 153–169. doi:10.1002/hrdq.1232

Gilley, A., McMillan, H., & Gilley, J. (2009). Organizational change and characteristics of leadership effectiveness. *Journal of Leadership & Organizational Studies*, *16*(1), 38–47. doi:10.1177/1548051809334191

Gillham, J., & Seligman, M. (1999). Footsteps on the road to a positive psychology. *Behaviour Research and Therapy*, *37*(1), 163–173. doi:10.1016/S0005-7967(99)00055-8 PMID:10402701

Giroux, H. (2011, October 6). *Got Class Warfare? Occupy Wall Street Now!* Retrieved from https://truthout.org/articles/got-class-welfare-occupy-wall-street-now

Gleeson, D., & Shain, F. (2003). Managing ambiguity in further education. In N. Bennett, M. Crawford, & M. Cartwright (Eds.), *Effective educational leadership* (pp. 229–246). Paul Chapman Publishing.

Gmelch, W. H., & Miskin, V. D. (1993). *Leadership skills for department chairs*. Anker Publishing Company, Inc.

Gmelch, W. H., & Miskin, V. D. (2011). *Department chair leadership skills*. Atwood Publishing.

Goffee, R., & Jones, G. (2005). Managing authenticity: The paradox of great leadership. *Harvard Business Review*, *83*(12), 86–94. PMID:16334584

Goffee, R., & Jones, G. (2013). Creating the best workplace on earth. *Harvard Business Review*, *91*(5). PMID:23898736

Goffman, E. (1959). *The presentation of self in everyday life*. Doubleday.

Goglio-Primard, K., & Crespin-Mazet, F. (2015). Organizing Open Innovation in Networks- the role of boundary relations. *International Management, 19,* 135-147.

Goldsmith, M. (2009). Internal Successors. *Leadership Excellence*, *26*(8), 15.

Goleman, D. (2000, Mar.). Leadership that gets results. *Harvard Business Review,* 78–90.

Goleman, D. (1998). What makes a leader? *Harvard Business Review*, 82–91. PMID:10187249

Goleman, D. (2000). Leadership that gets results. *Harvard Business Review*, *78*(2), 78–90.

Goleman, D., Boyatzis, R., & Mckee, A. (2001). Primal Leadership : The Hidden Driver of Great Performance. *Harvard Business Review*, (December), 42–51.

Gomes, A. R., & Cruz, J. (2007). Abordagem carismática e transformacional: Modelos conceptuais e contributos para o exercõcio da liderança. *Psicologia USP*, *18*(3), 143–161. doi:10.1590/S0103-65642007000300008

Goodman, F. R., Disabato, D. J., Kashdan, T. B., & Kauffman, S. B. (2018). Measuring well-being: A comparison of subjective well-being and PERMA. *The Journal of Positive Psychology*, *13*(4), 321–332. doi:10.1080/17439760.2017.1388434

Graen, G. B., & Uhl-Bien, M. (1995). Relationship-based approach to leadership: Development of leader-member exchange (LMX) theory of leadership over 25 years: Applying a multi-level multi-domain perspective. *The Leadership Quarterly*, *6*(2), 219–247. doi:10.1016/1048-9843(95)90036-5

Graetz, F., & Smith, A. C. (2010). *Managing organizational change: A philosophies of change.* Academic Press.

Grant, A. (2008). Does intrinsic motivation fuel the prosocial fire? Motivational synergy in predicting persistence, performance, and productivity. *The Journal of Applied Psychology*, *93*(1), 48–58. doi:10.1037/0021-9010.93.1.48 PMID:18211134

Grant, M., & Booth, A. (2009). A typology of reviews: An analysis of 14 review types and associated methodologies. *Health Information and Libraries Journal*, *26*(2), 91–108. doi:10.1111/j.1471-1842.2009.00848.x PMID:19490148

Greenleaf, K. (2008). The servant as leader (rev. ed.) Westfield, IN: Greenleaf Center for Servant Leadership.

Greenleaf, R. K. (2006). *Start here. What is Servant Leadership?* Retrieved from https://www.greenleaf.org/what-is-servant-leadership/

Greenleaf, R. K. (1977). *Servant Leadership A Journey into the Nature of Legitimate Power and Greatness*. Paulist Press.

Greenleaf, R. K. (1977). *Servant leadership: A journey into the nature of legitimate power and greatness*. Paulist Press.

Greenleaf, R. K. (1977). *Servant Leadership: A Journey Into the Nature of Legitimate Power and Greatness*. Paulist Press.

Greenleaf, R. K. (1998). *The power of servant-leadership*. Berrett-Koehler.

Greiner, L. E. (1972). Evolution and Revolution as Organizations Grow. *Harvard Business Review, 50*(4), 37-46. https://ssrn.com/abstract=1504482

Grijalva, E., Harms, P., Newman, D., Gaddis, B., & Fraley, R. (2015). Narcissism and leadership: A meta-analytic review of linear and nonlinear relationships. *Personnel Psychology, 68*(1), 1–47. doi:10.1111/peps.12072

Grint, K. (2005). Problems, problems, problems: The social construction of 'leadership'. *Human Relations, 58*(11), 1467–1494. doi:10.1177/0018726705061314

Grint, K. (2007). *Leadership, management, and command: Rethinking D-Day*. Springer.

Grint, K. (2008). Wicked problems and clumsy solutions: The role of leadership. *Clinical Leader, 1*(2), 11–25.

Grint, K. (2010). The cuckoo clock syndrome: Addicted to command, allergic to leadership. *European Management Journal, 28*(4), 306–313. doi:10.1016/j.emj.2010.05.002

Grint, K. (2020). Leadership, management and command in the time of the Coronavirus. *Leadership, 16*(3), 314–319. doi:10.1177/1742715020922445

Groves, K. (2005). Linking leader skills, follower attitudes, and contextual variables via an integrated model of charismatic leadership. *Journal of Management, 31*(2), 255–277. doi:10.1177/0149206304271765

Groves, K. S. (2007). Integrating leadership development and succession planning best practices. *Journal of Management Development, 26*(3), 239–260. doi:10.1108/02621710710732146

Guba, E. G., & Lincoln, Y. S. (1982). Epistemological and methodological bases of naturalistic inquiry. *Educational Communication and Technology, 30*(4), 233–252. doi:10.1007/BF02765185

Guerrero, S., Lapalme, M., & Séguin, M. (2015). Board chair authentic leadership and nonexecutives' motivation and commitment. *Journal of Leadership & Organizational Studies, 22*(1), 88–101. doi:10.1177/1548051814531825

Guo, C., & Acar, M. (2005). Understanding collaboration among non-profit organizations: Combining resource dependency, institutional, and network perspectives. *Nonprofit and Voluntary Sector Quarterly, 34*(3), 340–361. doi:10.1177/0899764005275411

Guo, L., Decoster, S., Babalola, M. T., De Schutter, L., Garba, O. A., & Riisla, K. (2018). Authoritarian leadership and employee creativity: The moderating role of psychological capital and the mediating role of fear and defensive silence. *Journal of Business Research*, *92*, 219–230. doi:10.1016/j.jbusres.2018.07.034

Haffar, M., Al-Karaghouli, W., Irani, Z., Djebarni, R., & Gbadamosi, G. (2019). The influence of individual readiness for change dimensions on quality management implementation in Algerian manufacturing organisations. *International Journal of Production Economics*, *207*(1), 247–260. doi:10.1016/j.ijpe.2016.08.024

Hales, C. (2002). 'Bureaucracy-lite' and continuities in managerial work. *British Journal of Management*, *13*(1), 51–66. doi:10.1111/1467-8551.00222

Haller, M., & Hadler, M. (2006). How social relations and structures can produce happiness and unhappiness: An international comparative analysis. *Social Indicators Research*, *75*(2), 169–216. doi:10.100711205-004-6297-y

Hamlin, R. (2004). In support of universalistic models of managerial and leadership effectiveness: Implications for HRD research and practice. *Human Resource Development Quarterly*, *15*(2), 189–215. doi:10.1002/hrdq.1098

Hamlin, R., Ellinger, A. D., & Beattie, R. S. (2008). The emergent 'coaching industry': A wake-up call for HRD professionals. *Human Resource Development International*, *11*(3), 287–305. doi:10.1080/13678860802102534

Hamlin, R., & Hatton, A. (2013). Toward a British taxonomy of perceived managerial and leadership effectiveness. *Human Resource Development Quarterly*, *24*(3), 365–406. doi:10.1002/hrdq.21163

Hammer, T. H., Bayazit, M., & Wazeter, D. L. (2009). Union leadership and member attitudes: A multi-level analysis. *The Journal of Applied Psychology*, *94*(2), 392–410. doi:10.1037/a0013613 PMID:19271797

Hannah, S., & Avolio, B. (2010). Moral potency: Building the capacity for character-based leadership. *Consulting Psychology Journal*, *62*(4), 291–310. doi:10.1037/a0022283

Hannan, M. T., & Freeman, J. (1977). The population ecology of organizations. *American Journal of Sociology*, *82*(5), 929–964. doi:10.1086/226424

Hansen, F., Smith, M., & Hansen, R. B. (2002). Rewards and Recognition in Employee Motivation. *Compensation and Benefits Review*, *34*(5), 64–72. doi:10.1177/0886368702034005010

Hansen, P. (2007). Organizational culture and organizational change: The transformation of savings banks in Denmark, 1965–1990. *Enterprise and Society*, *8*(4), 920–953. doi:10.1093/es/khm071

Hardman, G. J. (2009). *Regenerative leadership: an integral theory for transforming people and organisations for sustainability in business, education, and community*. Academic Press.

Hardy, C., & Thomas, R. (2014). Strategy, Discourse and Practice: The Intensification of Power. *Journal of Management Studies*, *51*(2), 320–348. doi:10.1111/joms.12005

Harms, P. D., & Credé, M. (2010). Emotional intelligence and transformational and transactional leadership: A meta-analysis. *Journal of Leadership & Organizational Studies, 17*(1), 5–17. doi:10.1177/1548051809350894

Harms, P. D., Wood, D., Landay, K., Lester, P. B., & Lester, G. V. (2018). Autocratic leaders and authoritarian followers revisited: A review and agenda for the future. *The Leadership Quarterly, 29*(1), 105–122. doi:10.1016/j.leaqua.2017.12.007

Harris, A. (2002). Effective leadership in schools facing challenging contexts. *School Leadership & Management, 22*(1), 15–26. doi:10.1080/13632430220143024a

Harris, A., & Deflaminis, J. (2016). Distributed leadership in practice. *Management in Education, 30*(4), 141–146. doi:10.1177/0892020616656734

Harris, T. A. (1969). I'm OK You're OK: A practical guide to transactional analysis. In *I'm ok you're ok: A practical guide to transactional analysis*. Harper & Row.

Harter, J. K., Schmidt, F. L., & Keyes, C. L. M. (2003). Well-being in the workplace and its relationship to business outcomes: A review of the Gallup studies. In C. L. M. Keyes & J. Haidt (Eds.), *Flourishing: Positive psychology and the life well-lived* (pp. 205–224). doi:10.1037/10594-009

Harter, S. (2002). Authenticity. In C. Synder & S. Lopez (Eds.), *Handbook of positive psychology* (pp. 382–394). Oxford University Press.

Hartnell, C. A., Ou, A. Y., & Kinicki, A. (2011). Organizational Culture and Organizational Effectiveness: A Meta-Analytic Investigation of the Competing Values Framework's Theoretical Suppositions. *The Journal of Applied Psychology, 96*(4), 677–694. doi:10.1037/a0021987 PMID:21244127

Harvey, P., Martinko, M., & Gardner, W. (2006). Promoting Authentic Behavior in Organizations: An Attributional Perspective. *Journal of Leadership & Organizational Studies, 12*(3), 1–11. doi:10.1177/107179190601200301

Hassan, H. (2020, March 17). *Malaysia bans travel abroad, shuts schools and businesses over coronavirus spread; lockdown till March 31*. The Straits Times. https://www.straitstimes.com/asia/se-asia/malaysia-to-impose-lockdown-from-wednesday-to-march-31

Hatcher, L., & Ross, T. L. (1991). From individual incentives to an organization-wide gainsharing plan: Effects on teamwork and product quality. *Journal of Organizational Behavior, 12*(3), 169–183. doi:10.1002/job.4030120302

Hayes, J. (2014). *The theory and practice of change management* (4th ed.). Palgrave Macmillan. doi:10.1007/978-1-137-28902-5

Heidegger, M. (1962). *Being and time* (J. Macquarrie & E. Robinson, Trans.). Harper Collins.

Henderson, G. M., & Provo, J. (2006). A New World Ahead-Are We Ready? *Human Resource Development Review, 5*(2), 274–277. doi:10.1177/1534484306287606

Hernez-Broome, G., & Hughes, R. L. (2012). Leadership Development: Past, Present, and Future. *Human Resource Planning*, 24–32.

Hersey, P., & Blanchard, K. (1988). *Management of Organizational Behavior*. Prentice Hall.

Hersey, P., Blanchard, K. H., & Johnson, D. E. (2001). *Management of Organisational Behaviour* (8th ed.). Prentice-Hall.

Herzberg, F. (2003). One More Time: How Do You Motivate Employees? *Harvard Business Review*. https://hbr.org/2003/01/one-more-time-how-do-you-motivate-employees

Herzig, S., & Jimmieson, N. (2006). Middle managers' uncertainty management during organizational change. *Leadership and Organization Development Journal*, *27*(8), 628–645. doi:10.1108/01437730610709264

Heyler, S. G., & Martin, J. A. (2018). Servant leadership theory: Opportunities for additional theoretical integration 1. *Journal of Managerial Issues*, *30*(2), 230. http://ezproxy.hct.ac.ae/login?url=https://www-proquest-com.ezproxy.hct.ac.ae/scholarly-journals/servant-leadership-theory-opportunities/docview/2186639350/se-2?accountid=1215

Hillman, J. (1968). *Insearch: Psychology and Religion*. Charles Scribner's Sons.

Hirsch, P. M., & Lounsbury, M. (1997). Putting the organization back into organization theory: Action, change, and the" new" institutionalism. *Journal of Management Inquiry*, *6*(1), 79–88. doi:10.1177/105649269761015

Hock, D. (1999). *Birth of the Chaordic Age*. Berrett-Koehler Publishers.

Hodges, J., & Gill, R. (2014). *Sustaining Change in Organizations*. Sage.

Hoffman, B. J., Woehr, D. J., Maldagen-Youngjohn, R., & Lyons, B. D. (2011). Great man or great myth? A quantitative review of the relationship between individual differences and leader effectiveness. *Journal of Occupational and Organizational Psychology*, *84*(2), 347–381. doi:10.1348/096317909X485207

Hofstede, G. (2001). *Culture's consequences: Comparing values, behaviors, institutions and organizations across nations*. Sage publications.

Hollander, E. (1995). Ethical challenges in the leader-follower relationship. In J. Ciulla (Ed.), Ethics: The Heart of Leadership (2nd ed., pp. 47–58). doi:10.2307/3857272

Hollander, E. (1992). Leadership, followership, self, and others. *The Leadership Quarterly*, *3*(1), 43–54. doi:10.1016/1048-9843(92)90005-Z

Holt, D. T., Armenakis, A. A., Feild, H. S., & Harris, S. G. (2007). Readiness for organizational change the systematic development of a scale. *The Journal of Applied Behavioral Science*, *43*(2), 232–255. doi:10.1177/0021886306295295

Holten, A., & Brenner, S. (2015). Leadership style and the process of organizational change. *Leadership and Organization Development Journal*, *36*(1), 2–16. doi:10.1108/LODJ-11-2012-0155

Hordijk, A. (1978). Trade Unionism and Ethics. In C. V. Dam & L. M. Stallaert (Eds.), *Business Ethics* (pp. 43–50). Springer.

Horner, M. (1997). Leadership theory: Past, present and future. *Team Performance Management, 3*(4), 270–287. doi:10.1108/13527599710195402

House, R. J., Hanges, P. J., Ruiz-Quintanilla, S. A., Dorfman, P. W., Javidan, M., & Dickson, M. (1999). Cultural influences on leadership and organizations: Project GLOBE. In W. F. Mobley, M. J. Gessner, & V. Arnold (Eds.), Advances in global leadership (Vol. 1, pp. 171–233). Academic Press.

House, R. J. (1971). A path goal theory of leader effectiveness. *Administrative Science Quarterly, 16*(3), 321–339. doi:10.2307/2391905

House, R. J., Hanges, P. J., Javidan, M., Dorfman, P. W., & Gupta, V. (Eds.). (2004). *Culture, leadership, and organizations: The GLOBE study of 62 societies.* Sage Publications.

House, R., & Aditya, R. (1997). The social scientific study of leadership : quo vadis? The social scientific study of leadership : quo vadis? *Journal of Management, 23*(3), 409–473. doi:10.1177/014920639702300306

Howell, J. M., & Avolio, B. J. (1993). Transformational leadership, transactional leadership, locus of control, and support for innovation: Key predictors of consolidated-business-unit performance. *The Journal of Applied Psychology, 78*(6), 891–902. doi:10.1037/0021-9010.78.6.891

Hughes, D. J., Lee, A., Tian, A. W., Newman, A., & Legood, A. (2018). Leadership, creativity, and innovation: A critical review and practical recommendations. *The Leadership Quarterly, 29*(5), 549–569. doi:10.1016/j.leaqua.2018.03.001

Humphreys, J. H., & Einstein, W. O. (2003). Nothing new under the sun: Transformational leadership from a historical perspective. *Management Decision, 41*(1), 85–95. doi:10.1108/00251740310452934

Hunter, J. C. (2008). *The Servant: A Simple Story About The True Essence of Leadership.* Currency Publishers.

Huppert, F. A. (2009). Psychological Well-being: Evidence Regarding its Causes and Consequences. *Applied Psychology. Health and Well-Being, 1*(2), 137–164. doi:10.1111/j.1758-0854.2009.01008.x

Hurwitz, M. (2017). *Exploring Distributed Leadership: A Leader–Follower Collaborative Lens.* Distributed Leadership.

Hussain, S., Lei, S., Akram, T., Haider, M., Hussain, S., & Ali, M. (2018). Kurt Lewin's change model: A critical review of the role of leadership and employee involvement in organizational change. *Journal of Innovation & Knowledge, 3*(3), 123–127. doi:10.1016/j.jik.2016.07.002

Ibarra, H., & Hansen, M. T. (2011). Are you a Collaborative Leader? *Harvard Business Review, 89*(7/8), 68–74. PMID:21800471

Iles, P. (2012). Leadership Development and Talent Management. In M. Lee (Ed.), *Human Resource Development as we know it - Speeches that Have Shaped the Field* (1st ed.). Routledge Studies.

Iles, P., & Preece, D. (2006). Developing Leaders or Developing Leadership? The Academy of Chief Executives' Programmes in the North East of England. *Leadership*, *2*(3), 317–340. doi:10.1177/1742715006066024

ILO. (2006). *Manual for Indonesian Trade Unions on Trade Unions Administration*. International Labour Office.

ILO. (2017a). *The future of work*. Retrieved from http://www.ilo.org/global/topics/future-of-work/WCMS_541627/lang--en/index.htm

ILO. (2017b). *Organization of work and production.* Retrieved from http://www.ilo.org/global/topics/ future-of-work/WCMS_541635/lang--en /index.htm

Industrial World of Workers. (2015). *Ethics and the Unions–Part 1*. Retrieved from https://iww.org/history/library/Dolgoff/newbeginning/1

Industrial-Global Union. (2019). *5 Reasons to Join a Union*. Retrieved from http://www.industriall-union.org/5-reasons-to-join-a-union

Ingraham, P. W. (2006). The Challenge and the Opportunity. *American Review of Public Administration*, *36*(4), 374–381. doi:10.1177/0275074006293630

Intagliata, J., Ulrich, D., & Smallwood, N. (2000). Leveraging leadership Competencies to produce Leadership Brand. *Human Resources Planning*, *23*(4), 12–23.

International Labour Organization & Gallup Inc. (2017). *Towards a better future for women and work: Voices of women and men.* Retrieved from https://www.ilo.org/wcmsp5 /groups/public/---dgreports/---dcomm/---publ/documents/publication/wcms_546256. pdf

Ioannidis, J. P. (2005). Why most published research findings are false. *PLoS Medicine*, *2*(8), e124. doi:10.1371/journal.pmed.0020124 PMID:16060722

Irawanto, D. W. (2009). An analysis of national culture and leadership practices in Indonesia. *Journal of Diversity Management*, *4*(2), 41–48. doi:10.19030/jdm.v4i2.4957

Irving, J. A., & Longbotham, G. J. (2007). Team effectiveness and six essential servant leadership themes: A regression model based on items in the organizational leadership assessment. *International Journal of Leadership Studies*, *2*(2), 98–113.

Jackall, R. (1983). Moral Mazes: Bureaucracy and Managerial Work. *Harvard Business Review*. https://hbr.org/1983/09/moral-mazes-bureaucracy-and-managerial-work

Jacobs, G., van Witteloostuijn, A., & Christe-Zeyse, J. (2013). A theoretical framework of organizational change. *Journal of Organizational Change Management*, *26*(5), 772–792. doi:10.1108/JOCM-09-2012-0137

Jacobs, T. O., & Jacques, E. (1990). Military executive leadership. In R. Gal & A. D. Manglesdorf (Eds.), *Handbook of Military Psychology*. John Wiley & Sons.

Javaid, O., & Suri, A. W. (2016). Bureaucratic system of management in Islamic financial institutions: Implications and alternatives for social inclusion. *Journal of Islamic Business and Management, 6*(2), 89–114.

Javaid, O. (2019). Islamic System of Production And Consumption: A Guide For Muslim Entrepreneurs. *Journal of Business Innovation, 4*(1), 1–12.

Javaid, O., & Hyder, I. (2018). Using Eisenhardt's Method to Study Ethnic Entrepreneurial Communities. *South Asian Journal of Management Sciences, 12*(1), 25–45. doi:10.21621ajms.2018121.02

Javaid, O., Shamsi, A. F., & Hyder, I. (2020). Religious entrepreneurial communities as a solution for socioeconomic injustice. *Journal of Enterprising Communities: People and Places in the Global Economy, 14*(3), 415–446. doi:10.1108/JEC-03-2020-0023

Javaid, O., Shamsi, A., & Hyder, I. (2018). *Building a Theoretical Model of Socially Sustainable Entrepreneurship Through Comparative Case Analysis of Ethnic Entrepreneurial Communities*. Institute of Business Management.

Jay, J. (2016). Sustainability-Oriented Innovation: A Bridge to Breakthroughs. In *The Sustainability Learning Forum*. CSR Academy.

Jennings, K. R., & Stahl-West, J. (2016). *The Serving Leader: Five Powerful Actions to transform your team, business and community, 10th Anniversary Edition*. San Francisco, CA: Berrett-Koehler Publishing.

Jensen, J. M., Cole, M. S., & Rubin, R. S. (2019). Predicting retail shrink from performance pressure, ethical leader behavior, and store-level incivility. *Journal of Organizational Behavior, 40*(6), 723–739. doi:10.1002/job.2366

Johansson, C., & Heide, M. (2008). Speaking of change: Three communication approaches in studies of organizational change. *Corporate Communications, 13*(3), 288–305. doi:10.1108/13563280810893661

Johns, G. (2006). The essential impact of context on organizational behaviour. *Academy of Management Review, 31*(2), 386–408. doi:10.5465/amr.2006.20208687

Johnson, R., & Cureton, A. (2017). Kant's Moral Philosophy. *The Stanford Encyclopedia of Philosophy*. Retrieved from https://plato.stanford.edu/archives/spr2017/entries/kant-moral

Jones, G. R., & George, J. M. (1998). The experience and evolution of trust: Implications for cooperation and teamwork. *Academy of Management Review, 23*(3), 531–546. doi:10.5465/amr.1998.926625

Jones, G. R., & Jones, G. R. (2013). *Organizational Theory, Design, and Change*. Pearson.

Josephson, M. (2002). *Making ethical decisions. The Basic primer on using the six pillars of Character to make better decisions, and a better life*. Josephson Institute of Ethics.

Judge, T., & Bono, J. (2001). Relationship of core self-evaluations traits—self-esteem, generalized self-efficacy, locus of control, and emotional stability—with job satisfaction and job performance: A meta-analysis. *The Journal of Applied Psychology*, *86*(1), 80–92. doi:10.1037/0021-9010.86.1.80 PMID:11302235

Judge, T., Bono, J., Ilies, R., & Gerhardt, M. (2002). Personality and leadership: A qualitative and quantitative review. *The Journal of Applied Psychology*, *87*(4), 765–780. doi:10.1037/0021-9010.87.4.765 PMID:12184579

Judge, T., & Kammeyer-Mueller, J. (2011). Happiness as a societal value. *The Academy of Management Perspectives*, *25*(1), 30–41.

Judge, T., Piccolo, R., & Kosalka, T. (2009). The bright and dark sides of leader traits: A review and theoretical extension of the leader trait paradigm. *The Leadership Quarterly*, *20*(6), 855–875. doi:10.1016/j.leaqua.2009.09.004

Jung, C. C. (2006). *The Undiscovered Self (reprint)*. New American Liberary.

Junker, N. M., & Van Dick, R. (2014). Implicit theories in organizational settings: A systematic review and research agenda of implicit leadership and followership theories. *The Leadership Quarterly*, *25*(6), 1154–1173. doi:10.1016/j.leaqua.2014.09.002

Kaplin, W. A., & Lee, B. A. (2007). *The law of higher education*. Jossey-Bass.

Karam, E., Gardner, W. L., Gillifor, D., Tribble, L., & Li, M. (2017). Authentic Leadership and High-Performance Human Resource Practices: Implications for Work Engagement. *Research in Personnel and Human Resources Management*, *35*, 103–153. doi:10.1108/S0742-730120170000035004

Keith, K. M. (2015). *The case for servant leadership* (2nd ed.). The Greenleaf Center for Servant Leadership.

Kellerman, B. (2012). *The End of Leadership*. HarperCollins.

Kelley, R. (1988). *In praise of followers*. Harvard Business Review Case Services.

Kelley, R. (1991). Combining followership and leadership into partnership. In R. Kilmann & I. Kilmann (Eds.), *Making organizations competitive: Enhancing networks and relationships across traditional boundaries* (pp. 195–220). Jossey-Bass.

Kelley, R. (2008). Rethinking followership. In R. Riggio, I. Chaleff, & J. Lipman-Blumen (Eds.), *The art of followership: How great followers create great leaders and organizations* (pp. 5–16). John Wiley & Sons.

Kelley, R. E. (2008). Rethinking Followership. In R. E. Riggio, I. Chaleff, & J. Lipman-Blumen (Eds.), *The Art of Followership: How Great Followers Create Great Leaders and Organizations* (pp. 5–16). Jossey-Bass.

Kelloway, E., Weigand, H., Mckee, M., & Das, H. (2013). Positive leadership and employee well-being. *Journal of Leadership & Organizational Studies*, *20*(1), 107–117. doi:10.1177/1548051812465892

Kelly, R. E. (1988). In praise of followers, in Managing People and Organizations. *Harvard Business Review*.

Kent, G. (2017). *On Caring*. Retrieved from https://www.transcend.org/tms/category /featured--research-paper/

Kernis, M., & Goldman, B. (2006). A multicomponent conceptualization of authenticity: Theory and research. *Advances in Experimental Social Psychology*, *38*, 283–357. doi:10.1016/S0065-2601(06)38006-9

Kesner, I., & Sebora, T. (1994). Executive succession: Past, present & future. *Journal of Management*, *20*(2), 327–372. doi:10.1177/014920639402000204

Kets de Vries, M., & Korotov, K. (2010). *Developing Leaders and Leadership Development*. Academic Press.

Kets de Vries, M., Vrignaud, P., Florent-Treacy, E., & Korotov, K. (2007). *360-degree Feedback Instruments: An overview*. doi:2007/01/EFE

Kets de Vries, M. (2001). Creating authentizotic organizations: Well-functioning individuals in vibrant companies. *Human Relations*, *54*(1), 101–111. doi:10.1177/0018726701541013

Kets de Vries, M., Vrignaud, P., & Florent-Treacy, E. (2004). The Global Leadership Life Inventory: Development and psychometric properties of a 360-degree feedback instrument. *International Journal of Human Resource Management*, *15*(3), 475–492. doi:10.1080/0958519042000181214

Kezar, A. (2001). Understanding and facilitating organizational change in the 21st century. *ASHE-ERIC Higher Education Report*, *28*(4), 147.

Kiefer, T. (2005). Feeling bad: Antecedents and consequences of negative emotions in ongoing change. *Journal of Organizational Behavior*, *26*(8), 875–897. doi:10.1002/job.339

Kim, K., & Huh, C. (2019). An Effects of Authentic Leadership and Transformational Leadership on Change Supportive Behavior in Small and Medium-size Business: Focused on Mediating Effect of Positive Psychological Capital. *Asia-Pacific Journal of Business Venturing and Entrepreneurship*, *14*(2), 135–149.

Kincaid, S. B., & Gordick, D. (2003). The return on investment of leadership development: Differentiating our discipline. *Consulting Psychology Journal*, *55*(1), 47–57. doi:10.1037/1061-4087.55.1.47

Kira, M., Balkin, D., & San, E. (2012). Authentic work and organizational change: Longitudinal evidence from a merger. *Journal of Change Management*, *12*(1), 31–51. doi:10.1080/14697017.2011.652374

Kirkpatrick, S. A., & Locke, E. A. (1991). Leadership: Do traits matter? *The Academy of Management Executive*, *5*(2), 48–60.

Klarner, P., By, R., & Diefenbach, T. (2011). Employee emotions during organizational change—Towards a new research agenda. *Scandinavian Journal of Management*, *27*(3), 332–340. doi:10.1016/j.scaman.2011.06.002

Klein, K., & Sorra, J. (1996). The challenge of innovation implementation. Academy of Management Review, 21(4), 22-42.

Klein, K. J., & House, R. J. (1995). On fire: Charismatic leadership and levels of analysis. *The Leadership Quarterly*, *6*(2), 183–198. doi:10.1016/1048-9843(95)90034-9

Klein, K., & Kozlowski, S. (2000). From Micro to Meso: Critical Steps in Conceptualizing and Conducting Multilevel Research. *Organizational Research Methods*, *3*(3), 211–236. doi:10.1177/109442810033001

Klemm, C., Das, E., & Hartmann, T. (2016). Swine flu and hype: A systematic review of media dramatization of the H1N1 influenza pandemic. *Journal of Risk Research*, *19*(1), 1–20. doi:10.1080/13669877.2014.923029

Kniffin, K. M., Narayanan, J., Anseel, F., Antonakis, J., Ashford, S. P., Bakker, A. B., ... van Vugt, M. (2021). COVID-19 and the workplace: Implications, issues, and insights for future research and action. *The American Psychologist*, *76*(1), 63–77. doi:10.1037/amp0000716 PMID:32772537

Korsgaard, M. A., Sapienza, H. J., & Schweiger, D. M. (2002). Beaten before begun: The role of procedural justice in planning change. *Journal of Management*, *28*(4), 497–516. doi:10.1177/014920630202800402

Kotler, P., & Lee, N. (2005). *Corporate Social Responsability: Doing the Most Good for Your Comapny and your Cause*. John Wiley & Sons, Inc.

Kotter, J. (2007, Jan.). *Leading change: Why transformation efforts fail. Harvard Business Review*.

Kotter, J. P. (1995). Leading change: Why transformation efforts fail. *Harvard Business Review*, *73*(2), 59–67.

Kotter, J. P. (1996). *Leading change*. Harvard Business Press.

Kotter, J. P. (2001). What leaders really do. *Harvard Business Review*, *79*(11). PMID:10104518

Kotter, J. P. (2012). *Leading Change*. Harvard Business Review Press.

Kotter, J. P., & Schlesinger, L. A. (2008). *Choosing strategies for change*. Harvard.

Kowalewski, S., Moretti, L., & McGee, D. (2011). Succession Planning: Evidence from "Best Companies in New York.". *International Journal of Management and Marketing Research*, *4*(2).

Kuipers, B. S., Higgs, M., Kickert, W., Tummers, L., Grandia, J., & Van der Voet, J. (2014). The management of change in public organizations: A literature review. *Public Administration*, *92*(1), 1–20. doi:10.1111/padm.12040

Kulkarni, V. (2017). Contingency Theory. In *The International Encyclopedia of Organizational Communication* (pp. 1–6). John Wiley & Sons, Inc. doi:10.1002/9781118955567.wbieoc041

Kurian, G. (2013). *The AMA dictionary of business and management*. Amacom Publishing Div of the American Mgmt Assn. http://proxy.libraries.smu.edu/login?url=http://search.credo reference.com/content/entry/amadictbm/employee_empowerment/0

Laal, M., & Salamati, P. (2012). Lifelong learning; why do we need it? *Procedia: Social and Behavioral Sciences*, *31*, 399–403. doi:10.1016/j.sbspro.2011.12.073

Langton, J. (1979). Darwinism and the behavioural theory of sociocultural evolution: An analysis. *American Journal of Sociology*, *85*(2), 288–309. doi:10.1086/227011

Latona, J. C., & La Van, H. (1993). Implementation of an employee involvement program in a small, emerging high-technology firm. *Journal of Organizational Change Management*, *6*(4), 17–29. doi:10.1108/09534819310042713

Laub, J. A. (1999). *Assessing the servant organization: Development of the servant organizational leadership (SOLA) instrument*. Florida Atlantic University.

Lawrence, F. L. (2009). *Views from the presidency: Leadership in higher education*. Transaction Publishers.

Leadership Team & the Tata Group. (n.d.). Retrieved April 05, 2021, from https://www.tata.com/management-team

Leaming, D. R. (1998). *Academic Leadership: A Practical Guide to Chairing the Department*. Anker Publishing Company.

Lehman, W., Greener, J., & Simpson, D. (2002). Assessing organizational readiness for change. *Journal of Substance Abuse Treatment*, *22*(1), 197–209. doi:10.1016/S0740-5472(02)00233-7 PMID:12072164

Lester, D. L., Parnell, J. A., & Carraher, S. (2003). Organizational life cycle: A five-stage empirical scale. *The International Journal of Organizational Analysis*, *11*(4), 339–354. doi:10.1108/eb028979

Levine, P. A., & Frederick, A. (1997). *Waking the tiger: Healing trauma: The innate capacity to transform overwhelming experiences*. North Atlantic Books.

Levy, A., & Merry, U. (1986). *Organizational Transformation: Approaches, Strategies, Theories*. Greenwood Publishing Group.

Lewin, K. (1947). Frontiers in group dynamics II. Channels of group life; social planning and action research. *Human Relations*, *1*(2), 143–153. doi:10.1177/001872674700100201

Lewin, K., & Lippitt, R. (1938). An experimental approach to the study of autocracy and democracy: A preliminary note. *Sociometry*, *1*(3/4), 292–300. doi:10.2307/2785585

Lewis, T., Marginson, S., & Snyder, I. (2005). The network university? Technology, culture and organisational complexity in contemporary higher education. *Higher Education Quarterly*, *59*(1), 56–75. doi:10.1111/j.1468-2273.2005.00281.x

Liao, C. (2017). Leadership in virtual teams: A multilevel perspective. *Human Resource Management Review*, *27*(4), 648–659. doi:10.1016/j.hrmr.2016.12.010

Liker, J. K., & Convis, G. L. (2012). *Toyota Way to Lean Leadership: Achieving and Sustaining Excellence through Leadership Development*. McGraw-Hill Education. https://www.accessengineeringlibrary.com/content/book/9780071780780

Lilian, S. C. (2014). Virtual Teams: Opportunities and Challenges for e-Leaders. *Procedia: Social and Behavioral Sciences*, *110*, 1251–1261. doi:10.1016/j.sbspro.2013.12.972

Lincoln, Y. S., & Guba, E. G. (2013). *The Constructivist Credo* (Issue 1). Left Coast Press, Inc.

Lindeman, L. & Rono, P. (2011) Leadership Development in Africa. *Leadership and Transformation*, *2*, 22-25.

Lintern, A., McPhillips, L., Winfrey, B., Duncan, J., & Grady, C. (2020). Best Management Practices for Diffuse Nutrient Pollution: Wicked Problems Across Urban and Agricultural Watersheds. *Environmental Science & Technology*, *54*(15), 9159–9174. doi:10.1021/acs.est.9b07511 PMID:32644784

Livermore, D. (2011). *The cultural intelligence difference: Master the one skill you can't do without in today's global economy*. AMACOM, Div of American Mgmt Assn.

Logan, M. S., & Ganster, D. C. (2007). The effects of empowerment on attitudes and performance: The role of social support and empowerment beliefs. *Journal of Management Studies*, *44*, 1523–1550.

Lok, P., Hung, R. Y., Walsh, P., Wang, P., & Crawford, J. (2005). An integrative framework for measuring the extent to which organizational variables influence the success of process improvement programmes. *Journal of Management Studies*, *42*(7), 1357–1381. doi:10.1111/j.1467-6486.2005.00547.x

Lönngren, J., & Van Poeck, K. (2020). Wicked problems: A mapping review of the literature. *International Journal of Sustainable Development and World Ecology*, 1–22.

Looy, B. V., Martens, T., & Debackere, K. (2005). Organizing for Continuous Innovation: On the Sustainability of Ambidextrous Organizations. *Creativity and Innovation Management*, *14*(3), 208–221. doi:10.1111/j.1467-8691.2005.00341.x

Lopez, S. J., & Snyder, C. R. (2012). The Oxford Handbook of Positive Psychology. In The Oxford Handbook of Positive Psychology (2nd ed.). New York: Oxford University Press.

Lord, R. G., Day, D. V., Zaccaro, S. J., Avolio, B. J., & Eagly, A. H. (2017). Leadership in applied psychology: Three waves of theory and research. *The Journal of Applied Psychology, 102*(3), 434–451. doi:10.1037/apl0000089 PMID:28125257

Losada, M., & Heaphy, E. (2004). The Role of Positivity and Connectivity in the Performance of Business Teams: A Nonlinear Dynamics Model. *The American Behavioral Scientist, 47*(6), 740–765. doi:10.1177/0002764203260208

Love, J. H., Roper, S., & Mangiarotti, G. (2007). Organizing innovation: Complementarities between cross-functional teams. *Technovation, 29*(3), 192–203. doi:10.1016/j.technovation.2008.07.008

Ludwick, P. (2007). The boomers are already gone. *Journal of Housing and Community Development, 64*(1), 22–26.

Lunenburg, F. C. (2011). Organizational Culture-Performance Relationships: Views of Excellence and Theory Z. *National Forum of Educational Administration and Supervision Journal, 29*(4), 1–10.

Lunenburg, F. C. (2010). Leader-Member Exchange Theory : Another Perspective on the Leadership Process. *International Journal of Management. Business Administration, 13*(1), 1–5.

Luthans, F. (2002). The need for and meaning of positive organizational behavior. *Journal of Organizational Behavior, 23*(6), 695–706. doi:10.1002/job.165

Luthans, F., Avey, J. B., Avolio, B. J., & Peterson, S. J. (2010). The development and resulting performance impact of positive psychological capital. *Human Resource Development Quarterly, 21*(1), 41–67. doi:10.1002/hrdq.20034

Luthans, F., & Avolio, B. (2003). Authentic leadership development. In K. S. Cameron & J. E. Dutton (Eds.), *Positive organizational scholarship*. Berrett-Koehler.

Luthans, F., & Avolio, B. (2003). Authentic leadership development. In K. Cameron, J. Dutton, & R. Quinn (Eds.), *Positive organisational scholarship: Foundations of a New Discipline* (pp. 241–258). Berrett Koehler Publishers.

Luthans, F., & Youssef, C. M. (2004). Human, social, and now positive psychological capital management: Investing in people for competitive advantage. *Organizational Dynamics, 33*(2), 143–160. doi:10.1016/j.orgdyn.2004.01.003

Lyubomirsky, S., King, L., & Diener, E. (2005). The benefits of frequent positive affect: Does happiness lead to success? *Psychological Bulletin, 131*(6), 803–855. doi:10.1037/0033-2909.131.6.803 PMID:16351326

Lyu, Y., Wang, M., Le, J., & Kwan, H. (2019). Effects of authentic leadership on work–family balance in China. *Journal of Managerial Psychology, 34*(2), 110–123. doi:10.1108/JMP-08-2018-0340

Mabin, V. (1999). Goldratt's «Theory of Constraints» Thinking Processes: A Systems Methodology linking Soft with Hard. *History (London)*.

Mabin, V., Davies, J., & Cox, J. III. (2006). Using the Theory of Constraints Thinking Processes to complement system dynamic's causal loop diagrams in developing fundamental solutions. *International Transactions in Operational Research*, *13*(1), 33–57. doi:10.1111/j.1475-3995.2006.00532.x

Madsen, S. R., Miller, D., & John, C. R. (2005). Readiness for organizational change: Do organizational commitment and social relationships in the workplace make a difference? *Human Resource Development Quarterly*, *16*(2), 213–233. doi:10.1002/hrdq.1134

Malatesta, D., & Smith, C. R. (2014). Lessons from resource dependence theory for contemporary public and non-profit management. *Public Administration Review*, *74*(1), 14–25. doi:10.1111/puar.12181

Malinga, K. S., Stander, M., & Nell, W. (2019). Positive Leadership: Moving Towards an Integrated Definition and Interventions. In L. E. Van Zyl & S. R. Sr (Eds.), *Theoretical Approaches to Multi-Cultural Positive Psychological Interventions*. doi:10.1007/978-3-030-20583-6_9

Mandal, P. C. (2020). Generating Ideas for New Product Development: Strategies and Initiatives. *International Journal of R&D Innovation Strategy*, *2*(1), 1–21. doi:10.4018/IJRDIS.2020010101

Manderscheid, S. (2008). New Leader Assimilation: An Intervention for Leaders in Transition. *Advances in Developing Human Resources*, *10*(5), 686–702. doi:10.1177/1523422308322269

Mang, P., & Reed, B. (2012). Designing from place: A regenerative framework and methodology. *Building Research and Information*, *40*(1), 23–38. doi:10.1080/09613218.2012.621341

Mann, R. D. (1959). A review of the relationships between personality and performance in small groups. *Psychological Bulletin*, *56*(4), 241–270. doi:10.1037/h0044587

Manso, G. (2017). Creating Incentives for Innovation. *California Management Review*, *60*(1), 18–32. doi:10.1177/0008125617725287

Mara, R., Bogue, B., Shen, D., & Rodgers, K. (2007). Those who leave-Assessing why students leave engineering (AC 2007-86). *Proceedings of American Society for Engineering Education*. http://search.asee.org /search/fetch

Margetts, S. (1998). *Trade Unions*. Retrieved from http://www.revisionguru.co.uk/business/unions.htm

Marie-Pier, R. (2017). *What Are the Five Contemporary Organizational Theory Models?* Bizfluent. Retrieved from https://bizfluent.com/info-8544476-five-contemporary organizational-theory models.html

Mascia, D., Magnusson, M., & Björk, J. (2015). The Role of Social Networks in Organizing Ideation, Creativity and Innovation: An Introduction. *Creativity and Innovation Management*, *24*(1), 102–108. doi:10.1111/caim.12111

Maslow, A. H. (1943). A theory of human motivation. *Psychological Review*, *50*(4), 370–396. doi:10.1037/h0054346

Mason, R., Asthana, A., & Stewart, H. (2016, July 6). Tony Blair: 'I express more sorrow, regret and apology than you can ever believe'. *The Guardian*. https://www.theguardian.com/uk-news/2016/jul/06/tony-blair-deliberately-exaggerated-threat-from-iraq-chilcot-report-war-inquiry

Maté, G. (2003). *When The Body Says No: The Cost of Hidden Stress*. A.A. Knopf Canada.

Maté, G. (2013). Addiction: Childhood Trauma, Stress and the Biology of Addiction. *Journal of Restorative Medicine*, *1*(1), 56–63. doi:10.14200/jrm.2012.1.1005

Mathis, R. L., & Jackson, J. H. (2008). *Human Resource Management* (12th ed.). South-Western Cengage Learning.

Maxwell, J. C. (2007) The 21 irrefutable laws of Leadership; Follow them and People would follow you. Nashville, TN: Thomas Nelson Publishing.

Mayer, J., DiPaolo, M., & Salovey, P. (1990). Perceiving affective content in ambiguous visual stimuli: A component of emotional intelligence. *Journal of Personality Assessment*, *54*(3&4), 772–781. doi:10.120715327752jpa5403&4_29 PMID:2348356

Mayer, J., & Salovey, P. (1997). What is Emotional Intelligence? In P. Salovey & D. Sluyter (Eds.), *Emotional Development and Emotional Intelligence* (pp. 3–31). Basic Books.

Mazur, A., & Lee, J. (1993). Sounding the global alarm: Environmental issues in the US national news. *Social Studies of Science*, *23*(4), 681–720. doi:10.1177/030631293023004003

Mazutis, D., & Slawinski, N. (2008). Leading organizational learning through authentic dialogue. *Management Learning*, *39*(4), 437–456. doi:10.1177/1350507608093713

Mccauley, C. D. (2008). *Leader Development : A Review of Research*. Center for Creative Leadership.

McCleskey, J. (2014). Situational, transformational, and transactional leadership and leadership development. *Journal of Business Studies Quarterly*, *5*(4), 117.

Mcdonald, D. (2017). *The Golden Passport: Harvard Business School, the Limits of Capitalism, and the Moral Failure of the MBA Elite*. HarperCollins.

McGuire, D. (2014). Human Resource Development (2nd ed.). SAGE Publications Ltd.

McGuire, D. (2014). *Human Resource Development*. SAGE Publications Ltd. doi:10.4135/9781473906891

McNamara, D. E. (2011). From Fayol's Mechanistic To Today's Organic Functions Of Management. *American Journal of Business Education*, *2*(1), 63–78. doi:10.19030/ajbe.v2i1.4023

Mdletye, M. A., Coetzee, J., & Ukpere, W. I. (2013). Emotional Reactions to the Experiences of Transformational Change: Evidence from the Department of Correctional Services of South Africa. *Mediterranean Journal of Social Sciences*, *4*(14), 501–518. doi:10.5901/mjss.2013.v4n14p501

Meaney, M., & Pung, C. (2008). McKinsey global results: Creating organizational transformations. *The McKinsey Quarterly*, *7*(3), 1–7.

Meier, M., Unternaehrer, E., Schorpp, S. M., Wenzel, M., Benz, A., Bentele, U. U., Dimitroff, S. J., Denk, B., & Prüssner, J. C. (2020). The opposite of stress: The relationship between vagal tone, creativity, and divergent thinking. In Experimental Psychology (Vol. 67, Issue 2, pp. 150–159). Hogrefe Publishing. doi:10.1027/1618-3169/a000483

Meindl, J. R. (1993). Reinventing leadership: A radical, social psychological approach. In J. K. Munighan (Ed.), *Social psychology in organizations: Advances in theory and research* (pp. 89–118). Prentice Hall.

Meindl, J. R. (1995). The romance of leadership as a follower-centric theory: A social constructionist approach. *The Leadership Quarterly*, *6*(3), 329–341. doi:10.1016/1048-9843(95)90012-8

Meindl, J. R., Ehrlich, S. B., & Dukerich, J. M. (1985). The romance of leadership. *Administrative Science Quarterly*, *30*(1), 78–102. doi:10.2307/2392813

Mettler, S. (2014). *Degrees of inequality: How the politics of higher education sabotaged the American dream.* Basic Books.

Meyer, J. P., Srinivas, E. S., Lal, J. B., & Topolnytsky, L. (2007). Employee commitment and support for an organizational change: Test of the three-component model in two cultures. *Journal of Occupational and Organizational Psychology*, *80*(2), 185–211. doi:10.1348/096317906X118685

Mhatre, K., & Conger, J. (2011). Bridging the gap between gen x and gen y: Lessons from authentic leadership. *The Journal of Leadership Studies*, *5*(3), 72–76. doi:10.1002/jls.20235

Miller, P., & Brankovic, A. (2010). Building a "Creative Culture" for Sustainable Innovation. IESE Business School.

Miller, D., & Friesen, P. H. (1984). A longitudinal study of the corporate life cycle. *Management Science*, *30*(10), 1161–1183. doi:10.1287/mnsc.30.10.1161

Miller, W. R., & Miller, M. F. (1997). *Handbook for college teaching*. PineCrest Publications.

Miner, E. R. (1990). *Comparative poetics: An Intercultural Essay on Theories of Literature.* Princeton University Press.

Montgomery, B. L. (n.d.). *Leadership Quote.* Retrieved from https://www.goodreads.com/quotes/713104-leadership-is-the-capacity-and-will-to-rally-men-and

Moran, J. W., & Brightman, B. K. (2001). Leading organizational change. *Career Development International*, *6*(2), 111–119.

Morgan, D., & Zeffane, R. (2003). Employee involvement, organizational change and trust in management. *International Journal of Human Resource Management*, *14*(1), 55–75. doi:10.1080/09585190210158510

Morgan, G. (1986). *Images of Organization.* Sage Publication, Inc.

Morgan, G. (1997). *Imaginization: New Mindsets for Seeing, Organizing, and Managing*. Berrett-Koehler Publishers.

Morgeson, F., DeRue, D., & Karam, E. (2010). Leadership in Teams: A Functional Approach to Understanding Leadership Structures and Processes. Journal of Management, 36. doi:10.1177/0149206309347376

Morgeson, F. P., Johnson, M. D., Campion, M. A., Medsker, G. J., & Mumford, T. V. (2006). Understanding Reactions to Job Redesign: A Quasi-Experimental Investigation of the Moderating Effects of Organizational Context On Perceptions of Performance Behaviour. *Personnel Psychology*, *59*(2), 333–363. doi:10.1111/j.1744-6570.2006.00941.x

Morrell, K., Loan-Clarke, J., & Wilkinson, A. (2004). Organisational change and employee turnover. *Personnel Review*, *33*(2), 161–173. doi:10.1108/00483480410518022

Morrison, E., & Milliken, F. (2000). Organizational silence: A barrier to change and development in a pluralistic world. *Academy of Management Review*, *25*(4), 706–725. doi:10.5465/amr.2000.3707697

Morris, R. J., & Seeman, M. (1950). The problem of Leadership: An interdisciplinary approach. *American Journal of Sociology*, *56*(9), 149–155. doi:10.1086/220696

Morris, T. L., & Laipple, J. S. (2015). How prepared are academic administrators? Leadership and job satisfaction within US research universities. *Journal of Higher Education Policy and Management*, *37*(2), 241–251. doi:10.1080/1360080X.2015.1019125

Musa, M. F., & Ahmad, Z. (2012). Higher education physical assets and facilities. *Procedia: Social and Behavioral Sciences*, *50*, 472–478. doi:10.1016/j.sbspro.2012.08.051

National Center for Education Statistics. United States. Digest of Education Statistics. (2016, February). *Office of Educational Research, Improvement*. Retrieved May 27, 2017, from https://nces.ed.gov/programs/digest/ d15/tables/dt15_105.20.asp?current=yes

Nicholson, J., & Kurucz, E. (2019). Relational Leadership for Sustainability: Building an Ethical Framework from the Moral Theory of "Ethics of Care." *Journal of Business Ethics*, *156*(1), 25–46. doi:10.100710551-017-3593-4

Nordin, N. (2011). The influence of emotional intelligence, leadership behaviour and organizational commitment on organizational readiness for change in higher learning institution. *Procedia: Social and Behavioral Sciences*, *29*(3), 129–138. doi:10.1016/j.sbspro.2011.11.217

Norman, S. M., Avolio, B. J., & Luthans, F. (2010). The impact of positivity and transparency on trust in leaders and their perceived effectiveness. *The Leadership Quarterly*, *21*(3), 350–364. doi:10.1016/j.leaqua.2010.03.002

Northouse, P. (2010). *Leadership, Theory and Practice*. Sage.

Northouse, P. G. (2001). *Leadership: Theory and Practice*. Sage Publications.

Northouse, P. G. (2021). *Leadership: Theory and practice*. Sage Publications.

Noto, G., & Bianchi, C. (2015). Dealing with multi-level governance and wicked problems in urban transportation systems: The case of Palermo municipality. *Systems*, *3*(3), 62–80. doi:10.3390ystems3030062

Nwanzu, C., & Babalola, S. (2019). Examining psychological capital of optimism, self-efficacy and self-monitoring as predictors of attitude towards organizational change. *International Journal of Engineering Business Management*, *11*. Advance online publication. doi:10.1177/1847979019827149

Nye, J. S. (2008). *The powers to lead.* Oxford University Press.

O'Leary, N. (2009). In the Shadow of the Founders. *Adweek*, *50*(27), AM4.

Offiong, L. A., & Olatuyi, A. L. (2012, March). *Situation Country Report: Nigeria as Empirical Study.* Report presented at the workshop on Trade Union training in employment relations and the informal economy, Turin, Italy.

Oishi, S., Diener, E., & Lucas, R. (2007). The Optimum Level of Well-Being: Can People Be Too Happy? *Perspective on Psychological ScienceScience*, *2*(4), 346–360. doi:10.1111/j.1745-6916.2007.00048.x PMID:26151972

Ollila, S., & Yström, A. (2016). Exploring Design Principles of Organizing for Collaborative Innovation: The case of an Open Innovation Initiative. *Design Principles for Collaborative Innovation*, *25*(3), 363–377. doi:10.1111/caim.12177

Oreg, S. (2006). Personality, context, and resistance to organizational change. *European Journal of Work and Organizational Psychology*, *15*(1), 73–101. doi:10.1080/13594320500451247

Oreg, S., Vakola, M., & Armenakis, A. (2011). Change recipients' reactions to organizational change: A 60-year review of quantitative studies. *The Journal of Applied Behavioral Science*, *47*(4), 461–524. doi:10.1177/0021886310396550

Ortiz, I., & Cummins, M. (2019, October). *Austerity the New Normal: A renewed Washington consensus.* ITUC, Initiative for Policy Dialogue, Public Services International, the Bretton Woods Project and the European Network for Debt and Developments collaboration. Retrieved from https://www.ituc-csi.org/IMG/pdf/austerity_the_new_normal_ortiz_cummins.pdf

Osborn, J. (2008). Logistic Regression. In *Best Practices in Quantitative Methods* (1st ed., pp. 568–588). Sage Publication, Inc. doi:10.4135/9781412995627

Overbeck, J. R., & Park, B. (2001). When power does not corrupt: Superior individuation processes among powerful perceivers. *Journal of Personality and Social Psychology*, *81*(4), 549–565. doi:10.1037/0022-3514.81.4.549 PMID:11642345

Owens, B. P., & Hekman, D. R. (2016). How does leader humility influence team performance? Exploring the mechanisms of contagion and collective promotion focus. *Academy of Management Journal*, *59*(3), 1088–1111. doi:10.5465/amj.2013.0660

Owens, B. P., Johnson, M. D., & Mitchell, T. R. (2013). Expressed humility in organizations: Implications for performance, teams, and leadership. *Organization Science*, *24*(5), 1517–1538. doi:10.1287/orsc.1120.0795

Owens, B., Baker, W., Sumpter, D., & Cameron, K. (2016). Relational energy at work: Implications for job engagement and job performance. *The Journal of Applied Psychology*, *101*(1), 35–49. doi:10.1037/apl0000032 PMID:26098165

Oxfam. (2017). *An Economy for the 99 percent*. Nairobi, Kenya: Oxfam International.

Paglis, L. L., & Green, S. G. (2002). Leadership self-efficacy and managers' motivation for leading change. *Journal of Organizational Behavior: The International Journal of Industrial, Occupational and Organizational Psychology and Behavior*, *23*(2), 215–235. doi:10.1002/job.137

Palma, P., Cunha, M., & Lopes, M. (2007). Comportamento organizacional positivo e empreendedorismo: Uma influência mutuamente vantajosa. *Comportamento Organizacional e Gestão*, *13*, 93–114.

Palmer, P. J. (1998). Leading from within. *Insights on leadership: Service, stewardship, spirit, and servant-leadership*, 197-208.

Palmisano, S. J., Hemp, P., & Stweart, T. A. (2005). Liderar a mudança quando o negócio corre bem. *Harvard Business Review*, *82*(12), 60–70. PMID:15605566

Palumbo, R. (2020). Let me go to the office! An investigation into the side effects of working from home on work-life balance. *International Journal of Public Sector Management*, *33*(6–7), 771–790. doi:10.1108/IJPSM-06-2020-0150

Pardo del Val, M., & Martínez Fuentes, C. (2003). Resistance to change: A literature review and empirical study. *Management Decision*, *41*(2), 148–155. doi:10.1108/00251740310457597

Parris, D. L., & Peachey, J. W. (2013). A Systematic Literature Review of Servant Leadership Theory in Organizational Contexts. *Journal of Business Ethics*, *113*(3), 377–393. doi:10.100710551-012-1322-6

Pasmore, W. A. (2011). Tipping the balance: Overcoming persistent problems in organizational change. *Research in Organizational Change and Development*, *19*, 259–292. doi:10.1108/S0897-3016(2011)0000019011

Pathak, A. A. (2016). Tata motors' successful cross-border acquisition of jaguar land rover: Key take-aways. Strategic Direction, 32(9), 15-18. doi:10.1108/SD-05-2016-0083

Peetz, D. (2015). *Are Australian trade unions part of the solution, or part of the problem?* Retrieved from http://www.australianreview.net/digest/2015/02/peetz.html

Pellet, J. (2008). What Can CEO's Do to Develop Leaders? *Chief Executive*, *234*(June), 50.

Penney, S. A., Kelloway, E. K., & O'Keefe, D. (Eds.). (2015). *Trait Theories of Leadership*. Routledge.

Perry, B. D., & Szalavitz, M. (2006). The boy who was raised as a dog and other stories from a child psychiatrist's notebook: What traumatized children can teach us about loss, love, and healing. In *The boy who was raised as a dog and other stories from a child psychiatrist's notebook: What traumatized children can teach us about loss, love, and healing*. Basic Books.

Pettigrew, A. M. (1985). *Awakening Giant: Continuity and Change in Imperial Chemical Industries*. Blackwell.

Pfeffer, J., & Salancik, G. R. (2003). *The External Control of Organizations: A Resource Dependence Perspective*. Stanford University Press.

Phelps, E. S. (2006). Dynamic capitalism. *The Wall Street Journal*. https://www.wsj.com/articles/SB116043974857287568

Pichault, F. (2007). HRM-based reforms in public organizations: Problems and perspectives. *Human Resource Management Journal, 17*(3), 265–282. doi:10.1111/j.1748-8583.2007.00041.x

Piderit, S. (2000). Rethinking resistance and recognizing ambivalence: A multidimensional view of attitudes toward an organizational change. *Academy of Management Review, 25*(4), 783–794. doi:10.5465/amr.2000.3707722

Pieterse, A., Knippenberg, D., Schippers, M., & Stam, D. (2010). Transformational and transactional leadership and innovative behavior: The moderating role of psychological empowerment. *Journal of Organizational Behavior, 31*(4), 609–623. doi:10.1002/job.650

Pina e Cunha, M., Campos e Cunha, R., & Rego, A. (2009). Exploring the Role of Leader—Subordinate Interactions in the Construction of Organizational Positivity. *Leadership, 5*(1), 81–101. doi:10.1177/1742715008098311

Plinio, A. J. (2009). Ethics and leadership. *International Journal of Disclosure and Governance, 6*(4), 277–283. https://doi-org.proxy.libraries.smu.edu/10-1057/jdg.2009.20

Popper, M. (2011). Towards a theory of Followership. *Review of General Psychology, 15*(1), 29–36. doi:10.1037/a0021989

Popper, M. (2012). *Fact and fantasy about leadership*. Edward Elgar Publishing. doi:10.4337/9780857936158

Popper, M., & Amit, K. (2009). Attachment and leader's development via experiences. *The Leadership Quarterly, 20*(5), 749–763. doi:10.1016/j.leaqua.2009.06.005

Pouramini, Z., & Fayyazi, M. (2015). The Relationship between Positive Organizational Behavior with Job Satisfaction, Organizational Citizenship Behavior, and Employee Engagement. *International Business Research, 8*(9), 57–66. doi:10.5539/ibr.v8n9p57

Poverty eradication programmes and urbanisation in India – UN India. (n.d.). Retrieved April 16, 2021, from https://in.one.un.org/poverty-and-urbanisation/

Prentice, W. (2004). *Understanding leadership.* Retrieved April 30, 2021, from https://hbr.org/2004/01/understanding-leadership

Pritchards, S. (2013, January 24). *9 Qualities of a servant leader.* Retrieved from https://www.skipprichard. com/9-qualities-of-the-servant-leader/

PTI. (n.d.). We changed our 'conservative' ways after economic reforms in 1991: Ratan Tata - Times of India. *The Times of India.* https://timesofindia.indiatimes.com/business/india-business/we-changed-our-conservative-ways-after-economic-reforms-in-1991-ratan-tata/articleshow/12135103.cms

Q&A With Ratan TATA (SSIR). (n.d.). Retrieved April 16, 2021, from https://ssir.org/articles/entry/qa_with_ratan_tata

Quinn, R. E., & Rohrbaugh, J. (1983). A spatial model of effectiveness criteria: Towards a competing values approach to organizational analysis. *Management Science, 29*(3), 363–377. doi:10.1287/mnsc.29.3.363

Rafferty, A. E., & Griffin, M. A. (2004). Dimensions of transformational leadership: Conceptual and empirical extensions. *The Leadership Quarterly, 15*(3), 329–354. doi:10.1016/j.leaqua.2004.02.009

Rafferty, A. E., & Restubog, S. L. D. (2010). The impact of change process and context on change reactions and turnover during a merger. *Journal of Management, 36*(5), 1309–1338. doi:10.1177/0149206309341480

Rao, J., & Weintraub, J. (2013). How Innovative is your company's culture? *MIT Sloan Management Review*, •••, 29–38.

Ratan N tata, chairman, tata sons, tata group statement on tata trusts COVID-19 strategy. (2020). *Express Healthcare.* Retrieved from http://ezproxy.hct.ac.ae/login?url=https://www-proquest-com.ezproxy.hct.ac.ae/trade-journals/ratan-n-tata-chairman-sons-group-statement-on/docview/2384128486/se-2?accountid=1215

Ratan Tata. (2021). In *Encyclopædia Britannica.* Retrieved from https://academic-eb-com.ezproxy.hct.ac.ae/levels/collegiate/article/Ratan-Tata/474479

Ready, D. (2002). How storytelling builds next generation leaders. *MIT Sloan Management Review*, (Summer), 63–69.

Redden, E. (2017). Nearly 4 in 10 universities report drop in international student applications. *Inside Higher Ed.* https://www.insidehighered.com/news/2017/03/13/nearly-4-10-universities-report-drops-international-student-applications

Reed, B. (2007). Forum: Shifting from "sustainability" to regeneration. *Building Research and Information, 35*(6), 674–680. doi:10.1080/09613210701475753

Rego, A. (2019). Liderança - Humildade e Soberba. Lisboa: Edições Sílabo.

Rego, A., & Cunha, M. (2008). Perceptions of authentizotic climates and employees happiness: Pathways to individual performance? *Journal of Business Research*, *61*(7), 739–752. doi:10.1016/j.jbusres.2007.08.003

Rego, A., Cunha, M. P., & Simpson, A. V. (2018). The Perceived Impact of Leaders' Humility on Team Effectiveness: An Empirical Study. *Journal of Business Ethics*, *148*(1), 205–218. doi:10.100710551-015-3008-3

Rego, A., Ribeiro, N., & Cunha, M. P. (2010). Perceptions of organisational virtuousness and happiness as prediction of organisational citizenship behaviours. *Journal of Business Ethics*, *93*(2), 215–235. doi:10.100710551-009-0197-7

Rego, A., Ribeiro, N., Cunha, M., & Jesuino, J. (2011). How happiness mediates the organizational virtuousness and affective commitment relationship. *Journal of Business Research*, *64*(5), 524–532. doi:10.1016/j.jbusres.2010.04.009

Rego, A., Sousa, F., Marques, C., & Cunha, M. P. (2012). Authentic leadership promoting employees' psychological capital and creativity. *Journal of Business Research*, *65*(3), 429–437. doi:10.1016/j.jbusres.2011.10.003

Reg, S., & van Dam, K. (2009). Organisational justice in the context of organisational change. *Netherlands Journal of Psychology*, *65*, 127–135.

Reichers, A., Wanous, J., & Austin, J. (1997). Understanding and managing cynicism about organizational change. *The Academy of Management Perspectives*, *11*(1), 48–59. doi:10.5465/ame.1997.9707100659

Reinecke, J., & Ansari, S. (2016). Taming wicked problems: The role of framing in the construction of corporate social responsibility. *Journal of Management Studies*, *53*(3), 299–329. doi:10.1111/joms.12137

Reis, G., Trullen, J., & Story, J. (2016). Perceived organizational culture and engagement: The mediating role of authenticity. *Journal of Managerial Psychology*, *31*(6), 1091–1105. doi:10.1108/JMP-05-2015-0178

Research, H. (2013). *Strategic planning in higher education–Best practices and benchmarking*. Hanover Research.

Richards, D., & Engle, S. (1986). After the vision: Suggestions to corporate visionaries and vision champions. In J. D. Adams (Ed.), *Transforming leadership* (pp. 199–214). Miles River Press.

Rihal, C. S. (2017). *The Importance of Leadership to Organizational Success*. Retrieved from https://catalyst.nejm.org/importance-leadership-skills-organizational-success/

Rittel, H. W., & Webber, M. M. (1973). Dilemmas in a general theory of planning. *Policy Sciences*, *4*(2), 155–169. doi:10.1007/BF01405730

Robbins, S. (2004). Fundamentos do Comportamento Organizacional (7a ed.). São Paulo: Prentice Hall.

Robbins, S. P. (2001). *Organisational Behaviour: Global and Southern African Perspectives*. Pearson.

Robbins, S. P., & Judge, T. A. (2012). *Essentials of organizational behavior*. Prentice Hall.

Rodriguez, K. P. (2008). Apparel brand endorsers and their effects on purchase intentions: A study of Philippine consumers. *Philippine Management Review*, *15*(1), 83–99.

Rodríguez-Modroño, P., & López-Igual, P. (2021). Job quality and work—Life balance of teleworkers. *International Journal of Environmental Research and Public Health*, *18*(6), 1–13. doi:10.3390/ijerph18063239 PMID:33800995

Rothan, H. A., & Byrareddy, S. N. (2020). The epidemiology and pathogenesis of coronavirus disease (COVID-19) outbreak. *Journal of Autoimmunity*, *109*, 102433–102438. doi:10.1016/j.jaut.2020.102433 PMID:32113704

Rush, M. C., Thomas, J. C., & Lord, R. G. (1977). Implicit leadership theory: A potential threat to the internal validity of leader behavior questionnaires. *Organizational Behavior and Human Performance*, *20*(1), 93–110. doi:10.1016/0030-5073(77)90046-0

Russell, R., & Stone, A. G. (2002). A review of servant leadership attributes:developing a practical model. *Leadership and Organization Development Journal*, *23*(3), 145–157. doi:10.1108/01437730210424

Ryan, J. C., & Tipu, S. A. (2013). Leadership effects on innovation propensity: A two-factor full range leadership model. *Journal of Business Research*, *66*(10), 2116–2129. doi:10.1016/j.jbusres.2013.02.038

Ryan, P., & Danaher, M. (2019). The role of leadership and motivation during change. In F. Sheerin & E. Curtin (Eds.), *Leadership for Intellectual Disability Service: Motivating Change and Improvement* (pp. 85–107). Routledge. doi:10.4324/9781351172400-4

Ryder, G. (2017, April) *Humanity and Social Justice, a Must for the Future of Work*. Paper presented at a Global dialogue on the future of work we want. An ILO Centenary Initiative, Geneva, Switzerland.

Safferstone, M. (2005). Organizational Leadership: Classic Works and Contemporary Perspectives. *CHOICE: Current Reviews for Academic Libraries*, *42*(6), 959–975.

Sainger, G. (2018). Leadership in digital age: A study on the role of leader in this era of digital transformation. *International Journal on Leadership*, *6*(1), 1–6.

Salazar, A. G. (2016). *The battle to unionize Starbucks in Chile*. Retrieved from https://www.counterpunch.org/2016/01/20/the-battle-to-unionize-starbucks-in-chile-an-interview-with-andres-giordano-salazar/

Sammut-Bonnici, T., & Wensley, R. (2002). Darwinism, probability and complexity: Market-based organizational transformation and change explained through the theories of evolution. *International Journal of Management Reviews*, *4*(3), 291–315.

Santos, J. P., Caetano, A., & Tavares, S. (2015). Is Training Leaders in Functional Leadership a Useful Tool for Improving the Performance of Leadership Functions and Team Effectiveness? *The Leadership Quarterly*, *26*(3), 470–484. doi:10.1016/j.leaqua.2015.02.010

Sashkin, M., & Burke, W. W. (1987). Organization development in the 1980's. *Journal of Management*, *13*(2), 393–417.

Schein, E. H. (1996). Kurt Lewin's change theory in the field and in the classroom: Notes toward a model of managed learning. *Systems Practice*, *9*(1), 27–47.

Schmid, M., Jonas, K., & Hall, J. A. (2009). Give a person power and he or she will show interpersonal sensitivity: The phenomenon and its why and when. *Journal of Personality and Social Psychology*, *97*(5), 835–850. doi:10.1037/a0016234 PMID:19857005

Schmiedel, T., Spiegel, M., & Brocke, J. V. (2017). What Makes Change Harder - or Easier. *MIT Sloan Management Review*.

Schraeder, M., Tears, R., & Jordan, M. (2005). Organizational culture in public sector organizations: Promoting change through training and leading by example. *Leadership and Organization Development Journal*, *26*(6), 492–502. doi:10.1108/01437730510617681

Schriesheim, C., Castro, S., & Cogliser, C. (1999). Leader-member exchange (LMX) research: A comprehensive review of theory, measurement, and data-analytic practices. *The Leadership Quarterly*, *10*(1), 63–113. doi:10.1016/S1048-9843(99)80009-5

Schulman, M. (2012). How to Combat a Culture of Violence and Maybe Save Lives. *Huffington Post: The Blog*. Retrieved from www.huffingtonpost.com/mark-schulman/combat-culture-of violence_b_2371661.html

Schwartz, B., & Sharpe, K. (2010). *Practical wisdom: The right way to do the right thing*. Riverhead Books.

Schwartz, R. C. (2013). Moving From Acceptance Toward Transformation With Internal Family Systems Therapy (IFS). *Journal of Clinical Psychology*, *69*(8), 805–816. doi:10.1002/jclp.22016 PMID:23813465

Schwarz, G. M. (2012). Shaking fruit out of the tree: Temporal effects and life cycle in organizational change research. *The Journal of Applied Behavioral Science*, *48*(3), 342–379.

Schyns, B., & Day, D. (2010). Critique and review of leader–member exchange theory: Issues of agreement, consensus, and excellence. *European Journal of Work and Organizational Psychology*, *19*(1), 1–29. doi:10.1080/13594320903024922

Seemiller, C., & Whitney, R. (2020). Creating a taxonomy of leadership competency development. *Journal of Leadership Education*, *19*(1).

Self, D. R., Armenakis, A. A., & Schraeder, M. (2007). Organizational change content, process, and context: A simultaneous analysis of employee reactions. *Journal of Change Management*, *7*(2), 211–229.

Seligman, M. (2002). Positive Psychology, Positive Prevention, and Positive Therapy. In C. Snyder & S. Lopez (Eds.), *Handbook of Positive Psychology* (pp. 3–12). Oxford University Press.

Seligman, M. (2018). PERMA and the building blocks of well-being. *The Journal of Positive Psychology, 13*(4), 333–335. doi:10.1080/17439760.2018.1437466

Seligman, M., & Csikszentmihalyi, M. (2000). Positive psychology. An introduction. *The American Psychologist, 55*(1), 5–14. doi:10.1037/0003-066X.55.1.5 PMID:11392865

Seligman, M., Steen, T. A., Park, N., & Peterson, C. (2005). Positive psychology progress: Empirical validation of interventions. *The American Psychologist, 60*(5), 410–421. doi:10.1037/0003-066X.60.5.410 PMID:16045394

Semler, R. (2007). Out of this world: Doing things the Semco way. *Global Business and Organizational Excellence, 26*(5), 13–21. doi:10.1002/joe.20161

Senate Bill 11. (2015). Retrieved June 15, 2021, from https://capitol.texas.gov/tlodocs/84R/billtext/pdf/SB00011F.pdf#navpanes=0

Sendjaya, S. (2015). *Personal and Organizational Excellence through Servant Leadership: Learning to Serve, Serving to Lead, Leading to Transform (Management for Professionals).* Springer. doi:10.1007/978-3-319-16196-9

Sendjaya, S., Pekerti, A., Härtel, C., Hirst, G., & Butarbutar, I. (2016). Are authentic leaders always moral? The role of Machiavellianism in the relationship between authentic leadership and morality. *Journal of Business Ethics, 133*(1), 125–139. doi:10.100710551-014-2351-0

Sergiovanni, T. J. (1990). Adding value to leadership gets extraordinary results. *Educational Leadership, 47*(8), 23–27.

Shadnam, M. (2019). A Postpositivist Commentary on Self-Fulfilling Theories. *Academy of Management Review, 44*(3), 684–686. doi:10.5465/amr.2017.0460

Shah, A. U. M., Safri, S. N. A., Thevadas, R., Noordin, N. K., Abd Rahman, A., Sekawi, Z., Ideris, A., & Sultan, M. T. H. (2020). COVID-19 Outbreak in Malaysia: Actions Taken by the Malaysian Government. *International Journal of Infectious Diseases, 97*, 108–116. doi:10.1016/j.ijid.2020.05.093 PMID:32497808

Shakespeare, W. (1954). *Hamlet* (3rd ed.). Yale University Press.

Shamir, B., & Eilam, G. (2005). "What's your story?" A life-stories approach to authentic leadership development. *The Leadership Quarterly, 16*(3), 395–417. doi:10.1016/j.leaqua.2005.03.005

Shamir, B., House, R. J., & Arthur, M. B. (1993). The motivational effects of charismatic leadership: A self-concept based theory. *Organization Science, 4*(4), 577–594. doi:10.1287/orsc.4.4.577

Shapiro, D. L., & Kirkman, B. L. (1999). Employees' reaction to the change to work teams: The influence of "anticipatory" injustice. *Journal of Organizational Change Management, 12*, 51–67.

Shapiro, P. (2005). Too many leaders? ... or do we use the term "leader" too freely? *News & Tools Leadership*, *1*(2), 1–2.

Sheldon, K. M., & King, L. (2001). Why positive psychology is necessary. *The American Psychologist*, *56*(3), 216–217. doi:10.1037/0003-066X.56.3.216 PMID:11315247

Shirey, M., White-Williams, C., & Hites, L. (2019). Integration of Authentic Leadership Lens for Building High Performing Interprofessional Collaborative Practice Teams. *Nursing Administration Quarterly*, *43*(2), 101–112. doi:10.1097/NAQ.0000000000000339 PMID:30839447

Simonet, D. V., & Tett, R. P. (2013). Five perspectives on the leadership–management relationship: A competency-based evaluation and integration. *Journal of Leadership & Organizational Studies*, *20*(2), 199–213. doi:10.1177/1548051812467205

Simons, T., Leroy, H., Collewaert, V., & Masschelein, S. (2015). How leader alignment of words and deeds affects followers: A meta-analysis of behavioural integrity research. *Journal of Business Ethics*, *132*(4), 831–844. doi:10.100710551-014-2332-3

Sinek, S. (2014). *Leaders eat last: Why some teams pull together and some don't*. Portfolio - Penguine.

Sir Ratan Tata - University of Edinburgh Scholarship. (2011, May 25). *The Hindustan Times*. Retrieved from http://ezproxy.hct.ac.ae/login?url=https://www-proquest-com.ezproxy.hct.ac.ae/newspapers/sir-ratan-tata-university-edinburgh-scholarship/docview/868433740/se-2?accountid=1215

Skarzynski, P., & Gibson, R. (2008). *Innovation to the Core: A Blueprint for Transforming the Way Your Company Innovates*. Harbard Business Press.

Smith, P. B., Peterson, M. F., & Schwartz, S. H. (2002). Cultural values, sources of guidance, and their relevance to managerial behavior: A 47-nation study. *Journal of Cross-Cultural Psychology*, *33*(2), 188–208. doi:10.1177/0022022102033002005

Sørensen, J. B. (2007). Bureaucracy and entrepreneurship: Workplace effects on entrepreneurial entry. *Administrative Science Quarterly*, *52*(3), 387–412. doi:10.2189/asqu.52.3.387

Sosik, J., & Jung, D. (2010). *Full Range Leadership Development - Pathway for people, profit and planet* (1st ed.). Routledge - Taylor and Francis Group, LLC.

Sowa, J. E. (2009). The collaboration decision in non-profit organizations: Views from the front line. *Nonprofit and Voluntary Sector Quarterly*, *38*(6), 1003–1025.

Specht, J., Kuonath, A., Pachler, D., Weisweiler, S., & Frey, D. (2018). How Change Agents' Motivation Facilitates Organizational Change: Pathways Through Meaning and Organizational Identification. *Journal of Change Management*, *18*(3), 198–217. doi:10.1080/14697017.2017.1378696

Speers, L. C. (2010). Character and Servant Leadership: Ten Characteristics of Effective, Caring Leaders. *The Journal of Virtues & Leadership*, *1*(1), 25–30.

Spillane, J. P. (2006). *Distributed leadership*. Jossey-Bass.

Stanley, D. J., Meyer, J. P., & Topolnytsky, L. (2005). Employee cynicism and resistance to organizational change. *Journal of Business and Psychology, 19*(4), 429–459.

Steelman, L. A., & Wolfeld, L. (2018). The Manager as Coach: The Role of Feedback Orientation. *Journal of Business and Psychology, 33*(1), 41–53. doi:10.100710869-016-9473-6

Sterling, J. (2003). Translating strategy into effective implementation: Dispelling the myths and highlighting what works. *Strategy and Leadership, 31*(3), 27–34. doi:10.1108/10878570310472737

Stogdill, R. M. (1974). *Handbook of Leadership: A Survey of Theory and Research*. New York Free Press.

Stone, A. G., Russell, R. F., & Patterson, K. (2004). Transformational versus servant leadership: A difference in leader focus. *Leadership and Organization Development Journal, 25*(4), 349–361. doi:10.1108/01437730410538671

Strebel. P. (1996, May-June) Why do employees resist change? In *Harvard Business Review on Change* (pp. 139-157). Boston: Harvard Business School Publishing.

Stückelberger, C., & Mugambi, J. N. K. (Eds.). (2007). *Responsible Leadership Global and contextual ethical perspectives*. WPP Publications.

Sturnick, J. A. (2004). The Art of Regenerative Leadership: Language, Spirit, and Principles. *Education and Culture, 20*(Spring), 42–47.

Sull, D., Sull, C., & Turconi, S. (2020). When it comes to culture, Does your company walk the talk? *MIT Sloan Management Review*.

Sundarasen, S., Chinna, K., Kamaludin, K., Nurunnabi, M., Baloch, G. M., Khoshaim, H. B., Hossain, S. F. A., & Sukayt, A. (2020). Psychological impact of COVID-19 and lockdown among university students in Malaysia: Implications and policy recommendations. *International Journal of Environmental Research and Public Health, 17*(17), 6206. doi:10.3390/ijerph17176206 PMID:32867024

Taleb, N. N. (2012). *Antifragile: Things That Gain From Disorder*. Random House.

Tan, V. (2021, May 11). *MCO 3.0 not as strict as first lockdown, key is to balance health and livelihoods: Ismail Sabri*. The Channel News Asia. https://www.channelnewsasia. com/ news/asia/malaysia-covid-19-mco-3-0-not-strict-balance-health-livelihoods-14786172

Tanno, J., & Banner, D. (2018). Servant leaders as change agents. *Journal of Social Change, 10*(1), 1–18. doi:10.5590/JOSC.2018.10.1.01

Tata nano relocation from bengal hit marketability: Ratan tata. (2014, Aug 8). *Oncars India*. Retrieved from http://ezproxy.hct.ac.ae/login?url=https://www-proquest-com.ezproxy.hct.ac.ae/magazines/tata-nano-relocation-bengal-hit-marketability/docview/1552129635/se-2?accountid=1215

Tata Trusts Corporate Standee - Areas of Work. (n.d.). Retrieved from https://www.tatatrusts.org/Upload/Content_Files/tata-trusts-corporate-standee-areas-of-work.pdf

Tata Trusts Corporate Standee - Guiding Principles. (n.d.). Retrieved from https://www.tatatrusts.org/upload/pdf/tata-trusts-corporate-standee-guiding-principles.pdf

Tata trusts partners with prodea systems. (2015, Dec 5). *Entertainment Close – Up*. Retrieved from http://ezproxy.hct.ac.ae/login?url=https://www-proquest-com.ezproxy.hct.ac.ae/wire-feeds/tata-trusts-partners-with-prodea-systems/docview/1739244215/se-2?accountid=1215

Taylor, J., Flanagin, A., Cheney, G., & Seibold, D. (2001). Organizational communication research: key moments, central concerns, and future challenges. In W. Gudykunst (Ed.), *Communication Yearbook* (pp. 99–137). SAGE Publications. doi:10.1080/23808985.2001.11678983

Teicher, J., & Khan, S. I. (2020). Working in 'sweatshops': Outsourcing to developing nations. In P. Holland & C. Brewster (Eds.), *Contemporary Work and the Future of Employment in Developed Countries*. Routledge.

The Barefoot Collective. (2009). *Barefoot Guide to working with organizations and Social change*. Community Development Resource Associates.

The hindu business line: Ratan tata to receive MMA amalgamations leadership award. (2014). Chatham: Newstex. Retrieved from http://ezproxy.hct.ac.ae/login?url=https://www-proquest-com.ezproxy.hct.ac.ae/blogs-podcasts-websites/hindu-business-line-ratan-tata-receive-mma/docview/1636185039/se-2?accountid=1215

The Straits Times. (2020, December 29). *Malaysia advises asymptomatic patients to self-isolate at home*. https://www.straitstimes. com/asia/se-asia/malaysia-advises-asymptomatic-patients-to-self-isolate-at-home#:~:text=KUALA%20LUMPUR%20%E2%80%A2%20Malaysia%20is,involving%20foreign%20workers%20are%20surging

Thelin, J. R. (2011). *A history of American higher education*. Johns Hopkins University Press.

Thomas, M. (2011). *How Unions' Trickle-Down Effect Trickled Away*. Retrieved from https://www.thefiscaltimes.com/Columns/2011/03/01/How-Unions-Trickle-Down-Effect-Trickled-Away

Thompson, B. (2015). Servant, leader, or both? A fresh look at Mark 10:35-45. *The Journal of Applied Christian Leadership*, *9*(2), 54–65. http://ezproxy.hct.ac.ae/login?url=https://www-proquest-com.ezproxy.hct.ac.ae/scholarly-journals/servant-leader-both-fresh-look-at-mark-10-35-45/docview/1766243034/se-2?accountid=1215

Tinuoye, T. A. (2013). Trade Union Governance and Administration. In *Proceedings of Capacity building workshop on Leadership and Administration of Trade Unions* (pp 15-40). Ilorin, Nigeria: Felicity Press.

Tirabeni, L., Soderquist, K. E., & Pisano, P. (2016). Driving Innovation by Enhancing Employee Roles: The Balancing Act of Employee-Driven Innovation. *International Scholarly and Scientific Research & Innovation*, *10*(1), 148–156.

Tiwari, R., & Herstatt, C. (2012). *Open global innovation networks as enablers of frugal innovation: propositions based on evidence from India*. Hamburg University of Technology, Technology and Innovation Management, Working Paper (72).

Tomé, E. (2011). Human resource development in the knowledge based and services driven economy: An introduction. *Journal of European Industrial Training, 35*(6), 524–539. doi:10.1108/03090591111150077

Torbert, W. (2004). *Action inquiry: The secret of timely and transforming action*. Berrett-Koehler.

Triandis, H. C. (2006). Cultural intelligence in organizations. *Group & Organization Management, 31*(1), 20–26. doi:10.1177/1059601105275253

Trilling, L. (2009). *Sincerity and authenticity*. Harvard University Press. doi:10.2307/j.ctvjhzrdp

Trottier, T., Van Wart, M., & Wang, X. (2008). Examining the nature and significance of leadership in government organizations. *Public Administration Review, 68*(2), 319–333. doi:10.1111/j.1540-6210.2007.00865.x

Truett, R. (2018). The Empire Strikes Back: In its 10 years under tata, jaguar land rover has proved all of the naysayers wrong -- so far. *Automotive News, 92*(6831), 1. Retrieved from http://ezproxy.hct.ac.ae/login?url=https://www-proquest-com.ezproxy.hct.ac.ae/trade-journals/empire-strikes-back/docview/2047407272/se-2?accountid=1215

Turner Parish, J., Cadwallader, S., & Busch, P. (2008). Want to, need to, ought to: Employee commitment to organizational change. *Journal of Organizational Change Management, 21*(1), 32–52. doi:10.1108/09534810810847020

Tushman, M. L., Lakhani, K. R., & Lifshitz-Assaf, H. (2012). Open innovation and organizational boundaries: task decomposition, knowledge distribution and the locus of innovation. *Journal of Organizational Design,* 355-382.

Tushman, M. L., & O'Reilly, C. A. (2004). The Ambidextrous Organization. *Harvard Business Review, 82*(4), 74–81. PMID:15077368

Uhl-Bien, M. (2006). Relational Leadership Theory: Exploring the social processes of leadership and organizing. *The Leadership Quarterly, 17*(6), 654–676. doi:10.1016/j.leaqua.2006.10.007

Uhl-Bien, M., Riggio, R. E., Lowe, K. B., & Carsten, M. L. (2014). Followership theory: A review and research agenda. *The Leadership Quarterly, 25*(1), 83–104. doi:10.1016/j.leaqua.2013.11.007

UNIFOR. (2014). *Policy on Human Rights, Workers' Rights*. Retrieved from http://www.unifor.org/sites/default/files/attachments/unifor_policy_paper_-_english_-humanworkers rights.pdf

United Nations Development Programme. (2015). Human Development Report 2015: Work for Human Development. New York: United Nations Development Programme.

Vakola, M., & Nikolaou, I. (2005). Attitudes towards organizational change: What is the role of employees' stress and commitment? *Employee Relations, 27*(2), 160–174.

Van de Ven, A. H., & Poole, M. S. (1995). Explaining development and change in organizations. *Academy of Management Review*, *20*(3), 510–540.

Van de Ven, A. H., & Sun, K. (2011). Breakdowns in implementing models of organization change. *The Academy of Management Perspectives*, *25*(3), 58–74.

van den Bosch, R., & Taris, T. (2014). The authentic worker's well-being and performance: The relationship between authenticity at work, well-being, and work outcomes. *The Journal of Psychology*, *148*(6), 659–681. doi:10.1080/00223980.2013.820684 PMID:25175889

van der Kolk, B. A. (2014). The Body Keeps the Score: Brain, mind, and body in the healing of trauma. In *The body keeps the score: Brain, mind, and body in the healing of trauma*. Viking.

Van der Voet, J. (2015). Change leadership and public sector organizational change: Examining the interactions of transformational leadership style and red tape. *American Review of Public Administration*, *46*, 660–682.

Van der Voet, J., Kuipers, B. S., & Groeneveld, S. (2015). Implementing change in public organizations: The relationship between leadership and affective commitment to change in a public sector context. *Public Management Review*, *18*, 842–865.

van Dierendonck, D. (2011). Servant Leadership: A Review and Synthesis. *Journal of Management*, *37*, 1228–1261.

Van Vugt, M. (2006). Evolutionary origins of leadership and followership. *Personality and Social Psychology Review*, *10*(4), 354–371. doi:10.120715327957pspr1004_5 PMID:17201593

Van Wart, M., Roman, A., Wang, X. H., & Liu, C. (2019). Operationalizing the definition of e-leadership: Identifying the elements of e-leadership. *International Review of Administrative Sciences*, *85*(1), 80–97. doi:10.1177/0020852316681446

Velu, C., & Stiles, P. (2013). Managing decision-making and cannibalization for parallel business models. *Long Range Planning*, *46*(6), 443–458. doi:10.1016/j.lrp.2013.08.003

Veríssimo, J. M., & Lacerda, T. M. (2015). Does integrity matter for CSR practice in organizations? The mediating role of transformational leadership. *Business Ethics (Oxford, England)*, *24*(1), 34–51. doi:10.1111/beer.12065

Vogl, T. M., Seidelin, C., Ganesh, B., & Bright, J. (2019). Algorithmic Bureaucracy: Managing Competence, Complexity, and Problem Solving in the Age of Artificial Intelligence. SSRN *Electronic Journal*, 148–153. doi:10.2139/ssrn.3327804

Vogt, W. P., & Johnson, R. B. (2011). *Dictionary of statistics & methodology: a nontechnical guide for the social sciences: a nontechnical guide for the social sciences*. Sage.

Vos, J., & van Rijn, B. (2021). The Evidence-Based Conceptual Model of Transactional Analysis: A Focused Review of the Research Literature. *Transactional Analysis Journal*, *51*(2), 1–42. do i:10.1080/03621537.2021.1904364

Walker, J. H., Armenakis, A. A., & Bernerth, J. B. (2007). Factors influencing organizational change efforts: An integrative investigation of change content, context, process and indi-vidual differences. *Journal of Organizational Change Management, 20*, 761–773.

Walumbwa, F. O., Avolio, B. J., Gardner, W. L., Wernsing, T. S., & Peterson, S. J. (2008). Authentic leadership: Development and validation of a theory-based measure. *Journal of Management, 34*(1), 89–126. doi:10.1177/0149206307308913

Walumbwa, F. O., & Lawler, J. J. (2003). Building effective organizations Transformational leadership, collectivist orientation, work-related attitudes, and withdrawal behaviors in three emerging economies. *International Journal of Human Resource Management, 14*, 1083–1101.

Walumbwa, F., Luthans, F., Avey, J. B., & Oke, A. (2011). Authentically leading groups: The mediating role of collective psychological capital and trust. *Journal of Organizational Behavior, 32*(1), 4–24. doi:10.1002/job.653

Wanberg, C. R., & Banas, J. T. (2000). Predictors and outcomes of openness to changes in a reorganizing workplace. *The Journal of Applied Psychology, 85*, 132–142.

Wang, D., Hu, B., Hu, C., Zhu, F., Liu, X., Zhang, J., Wang, B., Xiang, H., Cheng, Z., Xiong, Y., Zhao, Y., Li, Y., Wang, X., & Peng, Z. (2020). Clinical characteristics of 138 hospitalized patients with 2019 novel coronavirus–infected pneumonia in Wuhan, China. *Journal of the American Medical Association, 323*(11), 1061–1069. doi:10.1001/jama.2020.1585 PMID:32031570

Wang, G., Oh, I. S., Courtright, S., & Colbert, A. (2011). Transformational leadership and performance across criteria and levels: A meta-analytic review of 25 years of research. *Group & Organization Management, 36*(2), 223–270. doi:10.1177/1059601111401017

Wanous, J., Reichers, A., & Austin, J. (2000). Cynicism about organizational change: Measurement, antecedents, and correlates. *Group & Organization Management, 25*(2), 132–153. doi:10.1177/1059601100252003

Warrick, D. (2011). The urgent need for skilled transformational leaders: Integrating transformational leadership and organization development. *Journal of Leadership, Accountability and Ethics, 8*(5), 11–26.

Waters, T., & Waters, D. (Eds.). (2015). *Weber's Rationalism and Modern Society*. Palgrave MacMillan.

Wee, E., & Taylor, M. (2018). Attention to change: A multilevel theory on the process of emergent continuous organizational change. *The Journal of Applied Psychology, 103*(1), 1–13. doi:10.1037/apl0000261 PMID:28933908

Weick, K. E., & Quinn, R. E. (1999). Organizational change and development. *Annual Review of Psychology, 50*(1), 361–386.

Weiner, B. (2009). A theory of organizational readiness for change. *Implementation Science; IS, 4*(1), 67–75. doi:10.1186/1748-5908-4-67 PMID:19840381

Weiss, A., Bates, T. C., & Luciano, M. (2008). Happiness Is a Personal(ity) Thing - The Genetics of Personality and Well-Being in a Representative Sample. *Psychological Science, 19*(3), 205–210. doi:10.1111/j.1467-9280.2008.02068.x PMID:18315789

Weisstub, E., & Galili-Weisstub, E. (2004). Collective trauma and cultural complexes. In The cultural complex: Contemporary Jungian perspectives on psyche and society. Bruner-Routledge.

Wergin, J. F. (2007). *Leadership in place: How academic professionals can find their leadership voice.* Ankor Publishing.

Wetzel, R., & Van Gorp, L. (2014). Eighteen shades of grey? An explorative literature review into the theoretical flavours of organizational change research. *Journal of Organizational Change Management, 27*(1), 115–146.

White, R. D. Jr. (2010). The Micromanagement Disease: Symptoms, Diagnosis, and Cure. *Public Personnel Management, 39*(1), 71–76. doi:10.1177/009102601003900105

Wijaya, S. (2020). *How much diversity at work is needed to avoid tokenism?* SHL Blog. https://www.shl.com/en/blog/how-much-diversity-at-work-is-needed-to-avoid-tokenism/

Wilde, R. K. (2012). Steering clear of organizational icebergs. *Public Management, 94*(9), 14–18. http://ezproxy.hct.ac.ae/login?url=https://www-proquest-com.ezproxy.hct.ac.ae/trade-journals/steering-clear-organizational-icebergs/docview/1118126339/se-2?accountid=1215

Williamson, C. P. (2017). *Servant Leadership. How to put your people before yourself.* Retrieved from https://www.forbes.com/sites/forbescoachescouncil/2017/07/19/servant-leadership-how-to-put-your-people-before-yourself/#1e681cd766bc

Winkle, B., Allen, S., Devore, D., & Winston, B. (2014). The Relationship Between the Servant Leadership Behaviors of Immediate Supervisors and Followers' Perceptions of Being Empowered in the Context of Small Business. *Journal of Leadership Education*, 70–83.

Winsor, J., Paik, J., Tushman, M., & Lakhani, K. (2019). Overcoming cultural resistance to open-source innovation. *Strategy and Leadership, 47*(6), 28–33. doi:10.1108/SL-08-2019-0114

Wisse, B., & Rus, D. (2012). Leader self-concept and self-interested behavior: The moderating role of power. *Journal of Personnel Psychology, 11*(1), 40–48. doi:10.1027/1866-5888/a000054

Wong, C. W. (2020, October 22). *Malaysia govt's U-turns, confusion and double standards in Covid-19 fight.* The Straits Times. https://www.straitstimes.com/asia/se-asia/malaysia-govts-u-turns-confusion-and-double-standards-in-covid-19-fight

Wong, L. P., & Alias, H. (2021). Temporal changes in psychobehavioural responses during the early phase of the COVID-19 pandemic in Malaysia. *Journal of Behavioral Medicine, 44*(1), 18–28. doi:10.100710865-020-00172-z PMID:32757088

Wong, P. T., & Page, D. (2003). Servant leadership: An opponent-process model and the revised servant leadership profile. *Proceedings of the Servant Leadership Research Roundtable.*

Wood, M. E., & Galasso, N. (2015). *8 Ways to Reduce Global Inequality*. Retrieved from https://inequality.org/8-ways-reduce-global-inequality

Woodman, M. (1993). Conscious Femininity: Interviews with Marion Woodman. In Studies in Jungian Psychology by Jungian Analysts. Inner City Books.

Woodman, R. W. (1989). Organizational change and development: New arenas for inquiry and action. *Journal of Management*, *15*(2), 205–228.

World Bank. (2019). *Doing Business 2019 Training for reform comparing business regulation for domestic firms in 190 economies A World Bank Group Flagship Report*. World Bank.

Wren, D. A., & Bedeian, A. G. (2020). *The evolution of management thought*. John Wiley & Sons.

Wright, B., Christensen, R., & Isett, K. (2013). Motivated to adapt? The role of public service motivation as employees face organizational change. *Public Administration Review*, *73*(5), 738–747. doi:10.1111/puar.12078

Wulffers, T. (2017). *Authentic leadership effectiveness: For individuals and teams - A coaching approach*. KR Publishing.

Wu, Z., & McGoogan, J. M. (2020). Characteristics of and important lessons from the coronavirus disease 2019 (COVID-19) outbreak in China: Summary of a report of 72 314 cases from the Chinese Center for Disease Control and Prevention. *Journal of the American Medical Association*, *323*(13), 1239–1242. doi:10.1001/jama.2020.2648 PMID:32091533

Xiao, Y., Becerik-Gerber, B., Lucas, G., & Roll, S. C. (2021). Impacts of Working From Home During COVID-19 Pandemic on Physical and Mental Well-Being of Office Workstation Users. *Journal of Occupational and Environmental Medicine*, *63*(3), 181–190. doi:10.1097/JOM.0000000000002097 PMID:33234875

Xiao, Y., & Watson, M. (2017). Guidance on Conducting a Systematic Literature Review. *Journal of Planning Education and Research*, *39*(1), 93–112. doi:10.1177/0739456X17723971

Yang, C. (2014). Does Ethical Leadership Lead to Happy Workers? A Study on the Impact of Ethical Leadership, Subjective Well-Being, and Life Happiness in the Chinese Culture. *Journal of Business Ethics*, *123*(3), 513–525. doi:10.100710551-013-1852-6

Yang, J., & Basile, K. (2019). The impact of corporate social responsibility on brand equity. *Marketing Intelligence & Planning*, *37*(1), 2–17. doi:10.1108/MIP-02-2018-0051

Yang, Y., Li, Z., Liang, L., & Zhang, X. (2021). Why and when paradoxical leader behavior impact employee creativity: Thriving at work and psychological safety. *Current Psychology (New Brunswick, N.J.)*, *40*(4), 1911–1922. doi:10.100712144-018-0095-1

Yau, E. K. B., Ping, N. P. T., Shoesmith, W. D., James, S., Hadi, N. M. N., & Loo, J. L. (2020). The behaviour changes in response to COVID-19 pandemic within Malaysia. *The Malaysian Journal of Medical Sciences: MJMS*, *27*(2), 45–50. doi:10.21315/mjms2020.27.2.5 PMID:32788840

Yavuz, M. (2019). Transformational leadership and authentic leadership as practical implications of positive organizational psychology. In *Handbook of Research on Positive Organizational Behavior for Improved Workplace Performance* (pp. 122–139). IGI Global.

Yesufu, T. M. (1984). *The Dynamics of Industrial relations. The Nigerian Experience*. University Press Limited.

Yoder, B. L. (2012). Engineering by the Numbers. In *American Society for Engineering Education* (Vol. 37). Retrieved June 4, 2016, from American Society of Engineering Educators:www.asee.org/ papers-and-publications/publications/college-profiles/11EngineeringbythNumbersPart1.pdf

Youssef, C. M., & Luthans, F. (2007). Positive organizational behavior in the workplace: The impact of hope, optimism, and resilience. *Journal of Management, 33*(5), 774–800. doi:10.1177/0149206307305562

Youssef, C. M., & Luthans, F. (2012). Positive global leadership. *Journal of World Business, 47*(4), 539–547. doi:10.1016/j.jwb.2012.01.007

Youssef-Morgan, C. M., & Luthans, F. (2013). Positive leadership: Meaning and application across cultures. *Organizational Dynamics, 42*(3), 198–208. doi:10.1016/j.orgdyn.2013.06.005

Yukl, G. (2006). *Leadership in organizations* (6th ed.). Pearson-Prentice Hall.

Yukl, G. (2012). *Leadership in Organizations* (8th ed.). Prentice Hall.

Yukl, G., Gordon, A., & Taber, T. (2002). A Taxonomy of Leadership Behavior: Integrating a Half Century of Behavior Research. *Journal of Leadership & Organizational Studies, 9*(1), 15–32. doi:10.1177/107179190200900102

Yukl, G., & Van Fleet, D. (1992). *Theory and Research on Leadership in Organizations*. Consulting Psychologists Press Inc.

Zaccaro, S. J., Kemp, C., & Bader, P. (2004). Leader traits and attributes. In D. V. D. John Antonakis (Ed.), The Nature of Leadership (pp. 101–124). Academic Press.

Zaccaro, S. (2007). Trait-based perspectives of leadership. *The American Psychologist, 62*(1), 6–16, 43–47. doi:10.1037/0003-066X.62.1.6 PMID:17209675

Zaccaro, S., Rittman, A., & Marks, M. (2001). Team leadership. *The Leadership Quarterly, 12*(4), 451–483. doi:10.1016/S1048-9843(01)00093-5

Zack, J. (2021, May 10). *PM: Whole country under MCO from May 12-June 7*. The Star. https://www.thestar.com.my/news/nation/2021/05/10/pm-whole-country-under-mco-from-may-12-june-7

Zainul, E. (2021, Jan 29). *Malaysia's daily new cases hit new record.* The Edge. https://www.theedgemarkets.com/article/malaysias-daily-new-cases-hit-new-record-5725-cumulative-cases-surpass-200000mark

Zaleznik, A. (1977). Managers and leaders: Are they different. *Harvard Business Review*, 67–78. PMID:14723179

Zbierowski, P. (2016). Positive leadership and corporate entrepreneurship: Theoretical considerations and research propositions. *Entrepreneurial Business and Economics Review*, *4*(3), 73–84. doi:10.15678/EBER.2016.040306

Zbierowski, P., & Góra, K. (2014). Positive Leadership: Its Nature, Antecedents and Consequences. *Journal of Positive Management*, *5*(1), 85. doi:10.12775/JPM.2014.008

Zeuge, A., Weigel, A., Bjorn, N., Frederike, O., & Michael, S. (2020). Leading Virtual Teams -A Literature Review. *Project: ASTAR - Competence Transfer in a VR/AR-Based Environment for Work Design*, (August), 1–9.

Ziveig, C. (1997). A tale of shadow-work. *Psychological Perspectives*, *36*(1), 86–91. doi:10.1080/00332929708403332

About the Contributors

Sajjad Nawaz Khan is currently working as an Assistant Professor (HRM) at Iqra University Karachi, Pakistan. Preparing lessons, leading class lectures, content development and consulting undergraduate and postgraduate students are the areas in which he excels. Moreover, Dr Khan is involved in supervising students at Mphil and PhD levels. His research areas include Leadership, Followership, Organizational Change and Green HRM. Dr Khan received his PhD degree from University Malaysia Sarawak, Malaysia. Likewise, he has several publications in Scopus, ESCI and SSCI indexed journals.

* * *

Sylvanus Adamade holds a BSc in Accounting, MSc and PhD in Management Sciences respectively. He is a Labour Educator, Management Consultant and Industrial Relations Specialist and also Head of the Academic and Distance Learning Department of the only Tripartite National Labour Institute in Sub-Saharan West Africa.

Pedro B. Água is a Professor of General Management at the Portuguese Naval Academy. He has authored several articles and book chapters, while continuing his research in the field of cutting-edge technology, industrialization, innovation and business policy. Professor Água has over twenty-five years of experience across high technology endeavours, from defence to telecommunications and oil and gas industry, combining his extensive professional and business background with teaching. Professor Água holds an MBA from IESE Business School and a Ph.D. in Management and Engineering awarded by the University of Lisbon.

Sriya Chakravarti is pedagogical pioneer and has extensive international academic and consultancy experience. She has worked on several committees to bring innovation into education through curriculum design, program establishment and policymaking. She believes in quality education for all and retains a strong leadership and community development perspective. She is actively associated with various societies and academies. Her academic career is decorated with several reputed awards and funding. She is a Life Fellow of the Royal Asiatic Society (FRAS, UK); Fellow of Royal Society for the Encouragement of Arts, Manufacturers, and Commerce (FRSA, UK), and a Principal Fellow of Higher Education (PFHEA, UK). She holds a chartered membership status (MCIPD, UK) with The Chartered Institute of Personnel and Development and is a member of the Royal Institute of International Affairs (Chatham House, UK). Recently, she won the Dr. B.R. Ambedkar National Prize in Education. Dr. Chakravarti has worked on various educational projects for the United Nations fraternity and has researched, developed, taught, and led educational initiatives in the USA, UAE, UK, India, Germany, Malaysia, Mexico, Thailand, Vietnam, Laos and Cambodia. More work details available on www.sriyachakravarti.com.

Deirdre "DeeDee" Conway, Ed.D., is Associate Dean of Operations for the Lyle School of Engineering and a Research Assistant Professor in the Caruth Institute for Engineering Education at Southern Methodist University. Her research agenda focuses on improving institutional leadership in higher education, Ph.D. preparation for those interested in pursuing careers as faculty, and access, diversity, and inclusion for individuals interested in pursuing a STEM degree or credential, specifically looking at Engineering disciplines. Dr. Conway holds a BA in Business Administration, a M.Ed. in Educational Policy and Leadership, and an Ed.D, in Higher Education.

Anacleto Correia is an Associate Professor and lecturer of Management and Information Systems at the Portuguese Navy Academy. He holds a Ph.D. in Computer Science, an M.Sc. in Statistics and Information Management, a B.Sc. degree in Management, and also a B.Sc. at Portuguese Naval Academy. His research interests are focused on requirements engineering, software engineering, process modeling, data mining, machine learning, and business engineering. He has also more than 20 years of experience in industry-leading projects and architecting large software development projects and is the author of several scientific papers in journals and conference proceedings.

Joseph Crawford is a leadership and behavior researcher who seeks to create empirical solutions for growing unethical behavior in leaders. He has provided conceptualizations for the authentic leader and follower, and published on best practice methodology for leadership measurement.

Cristina Nogueira da Fonseca has a degree in Sociology, specializing in Community Psychology, Positive Psychology and Human Resource Management. She is the Founder and Partner of Happytown-Happiness Science Based, the first Portuguese consultant specialized in Corporate Happiness. She is a Teacher and Trainer and is considered one of the references in the area, being a guest speaker at several events.

Paula Figueiredo has a degree in Economics with a specialization in Human Resources Economics, a Master in Human Resources Management and a PhD in Management. She is currently a professor at higher education institutions, and she has also been the Director of an institution since 2019. Paula has 20 years of experience in the business area with functions of direction, coordination, and consultancy. Throughout her professional experience, she has collaborated on leadership development projects. At the research level, she has developed research on Human Resource Development, more specifically Leadership Development in organizations, with some publications in scientific journals and conferences.

Omar Javaid has a PhD in Socially Sustainable Entrepreneurship from Institute of Business Management, MS in Management Sciences from KIET, MBA-Exec from IoBM with majors in Marketing and BE in Industrial & Manufacturing Engineering from NED University. Mr. Javaid has a total of 17 years of experience of working in corporate, non-profit and education sector; this experience also includes extensive international traveling to Japan, Taiwan, Korea, Malaysia, Indonesia, Thailand, Hong Kong, Maldives, Doha for professional and research related activities. Mr. Javaid's core competence is mentoring new startups and ventures; since 2010 he has helped hundreds of students in their entrepreneurial ambitions. He has also been empowering students to setup micro businesses for poor unemployed folks, and have successfully initiated around 600 such projects during his academic career up till now. Mr. Javaid has been invited multiple times at IBA, NED University, UIT, NEST I/O and SoL to speak on topics related to entrepreneurship. He has also published various research articles and editorials in various journals, magazines and news papers; and is a reader of Entrepreneurship, Social Entrepreneurship, Islamic Economics and Finance, and Philosophy of Economics and Business Management. Apart from teaching at IoBM he is also responsible to mentor IoBM students to setup the entrepreneurial ventures and facilitate in the process of developing of an entrepreneurial ecosystem within the Institute.

Matthew Knox is a recent graduate of the University of Tasmania, and has a deep passion for understanding the way in which humans consider themselves members of groups (or otherwise). His recent work has focused on the identity of leaders in being innovative and creative.

André Nogueira researcher is a researcher at CINAV, the Portuguese Naval Academy Research Centre, and has a background in Naval Military Sciences and

Naval Administration at Master Degree level in Naval Military Sciences. André Nogueira research interest focus on fields such as Innovation, Organizing for Innovation and Leading Change within organizations.

Victor Ogharanduku is a Principal Training and Development Officer at the Micheal Imoudu National Institute for Labour Studies and a Doctoral Student at the Centre for Peace and Strategic Studies at the University of Ilorin, Ilorin, Kwara State. His research Interest cover: Peacebuilding, Conflict, Violent Extremism and Social Protection. He has contributed to several journal and books, some of which include: Violent Extremism and Grievance in Sub-Saharan Africa (Peace Review, 2017); Strategic Leadership and Action Planning For Sustaining Trade Unionism: Building a Positive Symbiosis between Society and Trade Unions (Academic Research of SSaH, 2015);Inequality and Social Exclusion: Recipe for Urban Anarchy in Africa. In Albert, O. l. & Lawanson, T. (eds). Urbanism and Crisis Management in Nigeria (2019, University of Ibadan); International Economic Relation: Scramble in and out of Africa, Implications for Human Rights. Published in Chatsworth, S. (ed.) International Economic Relations, Foreign Policy and Human Rights Vol 2. (2017, ABS Publishers).

Hafiz Mudassir Rehman is pursuing the Ph.D. in management sciences at Universiti Tunku Abdul Rahman, Kampar, Malaysia. He has received an MPhil degree in Business Management from Arid Agriculture University Rawalpindi, Pakistan. He has been working as Research Assistant at the Faculty of Business & Finance, UTAR from 2018 to date. Mr. Mudassir Rehman was the recipient of Punjab Educational Endowment Fund Scholarship during the MPhil study from 2011 to 2015. His research interests include Industry 4.0, Human Resource Management, Managing Workforce, Innovation, Knowledge Management and Leadership.

Adekunle Tinuoye is a multi skilled, results-focused and service oriented individual with varied background and interest in Industrial relations and labour-management cooperation, Human/workers and Women Rights, Gender and Women in Employment, Local Development and Entrepreneurship, Programme Management and Labour Education, Trade Unionism and Labor legislations /workplace policy analysis, Productivity and work ethics respectively. Mr. Tinuoye is also a facilitator, mediator, communicator and human resource practitioner with cognate experience campaigning for workplace best practices, building consensus, working in dynamic and complex multicultural settings, delivering on targets, mentoring individuals, advancing workplace equality and espousing diligence. His major aspirations entail working towards the actualization of organizational and individual goals in the workplace with its positive multiplier effects on national development.

Seong-Yuen Toh teaches leadership and business ethics in Sunway University for many years. Before joining the academia, he worked in retail operations for 20 years in retail operations, in publishing for 4 years, and in manufacturing for 6 years. A combination of work experience and academic interest served him well in teaching. He serves in various undergraduate and postgraduate programme committees and chair the AACSB assurance of learning committee. Dr Toh loves reading and thinks cats are smarter than dogs.

Sarah Young is a doctoral candidate at the University of Tasmania in the College of Health & Medicine. She has a research focus on understanding the nature and predictors of mental wellbeing, and what it takes to have positive mental health.

Index

H

I

K

L

M

O

P

R

S

www.ingramcontent.com/pod-product-compliance
Lightning Source LLC
LaVergne TN
LVHW081349300926
849161LV00008B/2109